Library of
Davidson College

Thomas Attwood: The Biography of a Radical

Thomas Attwood (1783–1856), a Birmingham banker, played a prominent role in many of the important controversies in England during the first half of the nineteenth century. He wrote and published extensively, appeared as a witness before three Parliamentary committees, held a seat in the House of Commons for seven years, and earned a reputation as one of the most accomplished out-door orators of the time. In 1830–2 his leadership of the middle and working classes in the provinces allowed him to negotiate directly with the government on the question of parliamentary reform. Attwood was representative and spokesman for the new industrial towns before they achieved political influence in keeping with their economic strength; the philosophy and technique he brought to bear on the major questions of the era came, almost exclusively, from this source. Although Attwood was not alone in speaking for this economic sector he became, more than anyone else, its symbol.

In addition to his political activities, Attwood laid claim to competence as an economist, based on his experience in banking and his observation of industrial practices in Birmingham. He focused most of his attention on the gold standard and its inhibitory effect on the growth of the economy. Long before the development of modern schools of economic theory, Attwood sought the regulation of business through control of the money supply. He was unsuccessful in his challenge to the Ricardian school, which promised stability through a gold-based economy, and died disillusioned. Birmingham became identified with his brand of economic theory and a succession of economists followed his lead into the national arena.

Through his study of Attwood's career and the development of his philosophy, David Moss analyses the impact of industrialism on the individual and society.

David J. Moss is a member of the Department of History, University of Alberta.

Thomas Attwood

The Biography of a Radical

DAVID J. MOSS

McGill-Queen's University Press
Montreal & Kingston · London · Buffalo

©McGill-Queen's University Press 1990
ISBN 0-7735-0708-6

Legal deposit first quarter 1990
Bibliothèque nationale du Québec

Printed in Canada on acid-free paper

This book has been published with the help of a grant from the Canadian Federation for the Humanities, using funds provided by the Social Sciences and Humanities Research Council of Canada.

Canadian Cataloguing in Publication Data

Moss, D.J. (David John), 1938–
  Thomas Attwood
  Includes index.
  Bibliography: p.
  ISBN 0-7735-0708-6
  1. Attwood, Thomas, 1783–1856. 2. Great Britain—Politics and government—1800–1837. 3. Great Britain—Politics and government—1837–1900. 4. Politicians—Great Britain —Biography. 5. Economists—Great Britain—Biography. I. Title.
  DA565.A88M68 1990   941.07   C89-090259-3

For Leslie

Contents

Acknowledgments ix

Illustrations xi

Introduction 3

1 Family Background and Commercial Apprenticeship 17

2 Public Champion 35

3 Great Expectations 51

4 A Crime against the People 71

5 Backstairs Politics 85

6 False Hopes 100

7 New Directions 126

8 The Birmingham Political Union: A Vehicle of Protest 152

9 The Birmingham Political Union: Vindication 183

10 A Stranger in the House 228

11 Failure 262

12 The Final Years 288

Notes 307

A Note on Sources 361

Index 367

Acknowledgments

A great number of people have assisted me in both the underlying research and the preparation of the manuscript for this book. I am heavily indebted to the librarians and archivists of countless county record offices and private collections. My particular thanks are extended to the staffs of the Birmingham Public Library; British Library: Public Record Office; British Library Newspaper Library; John Rylands Library, Manchester; University of London Library; Bodleian Library; National Library of Scotland; Transport House, London; Rouen Record Office; Bank of England Archives; and Lloyds Bank Archives. Above all, I owe a special debt to Mrs Priscilla Mitchell for her kindness in granting permission to use the papers of Thomas Attwood and for her gracious hospitality during my lengthy visits.

Many friends and colleagues have contributed information, advice, and labour. The D. Phil. thesis on which this biography is based could never have been completed without Professor Peter Mathias's active interest in and deep knowledge of the subject, and the inspiration of Professor Frank Fetter. In the latter stages of its preparation, Professor "Bob" Coats has been an unfailing source of encouragement. Others, too numerous to mention by name, have read and commented on various parts of the manuscript. I am grateful to them all for their invaluable help. My heaviest debt is to my wife to whom this work is dedicated.

I should never have been able to complete the research without the generosity of the Social Sciences and Humanities Research Council of Canada, which granted funds and a leave fellowship.

Portions of this book which have appeared in the *Historical Journal*, the *Canadian Journal of History*, and *History of Political Economy* are reprinted by permission of the editors.

Thomas Attwood, c. 1804. (Courtesy Mrs P. Mitchell)

Elizabeth Attwood, c. 1815. (Courtesy Mrs P. Mitchell)

Thomas Attwood, c. 1813. (Courtesy Mrs P. Mitchell)

Thomas Attwood in 1832, wearing the fur-trimmed coat in which he appeared on great public occasions. (Courtesy Mrs P. Mitchell)

Elizabeth and Thomas Attwood with their daughter Rosabel, c. 1825. (Courtesy Mrs P. Mitchell)

Thomas Attwood portrayed by August David, c. 1838. (Courtesy Mrs P. Mitchell)

Thomas Attwood, c. 1823. (Courtesy Mrs P. Mitchell)

A daguerreotype of Thomas Attwood, c. 1845. (Courtesy Mrs P. Mitchell)

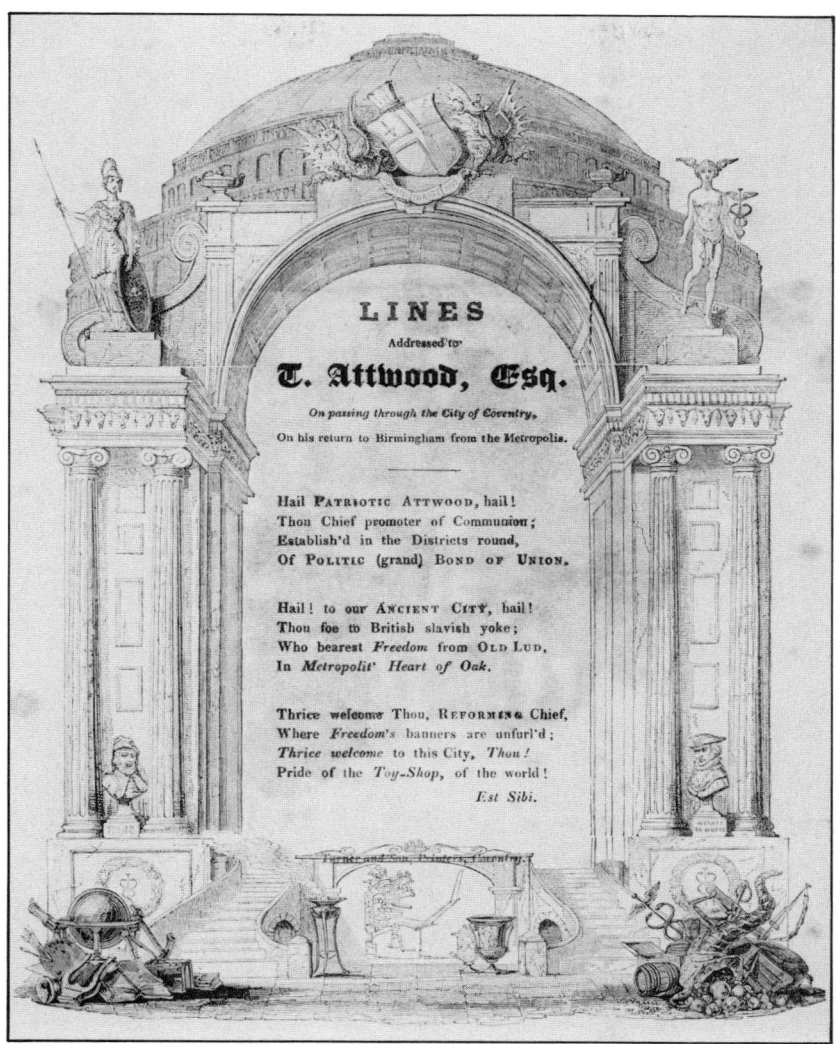

A broadsheet published in Coventry following the passage of the Reform Bill in June 1832. (Courtesy Mrs P. Mitchell)

Facing Page:
The Tory Sir Charles Wetherell presses an unwelcome draught upon a Janus-faced Britannia, while Thomas Attwood prescribes a steaming joint of roast beef; the pickpocket is Henry Goulburn, former Tory chancellor of the exchequer (*Figaro*, no. 31, 7 July 1832). (Courtesy the Trustees of the British Museum)

Benjamin Haydon's impression of a meeting of the Birmingham Political Union on Newhall Hill in 1832; the speaker is Thomas Attwood. (Courtesy the Birmingham Museum and Art Gallery)

Thomas Attwood the monetary reformer is shown leading William IV as a dancing bear (a Birmingham variation on a London print entitled *The Led Bear*) (1832). (Courtesy Mrs P. Mitchell)

Facing page:
Designed by Thomas Attwood (who wrote the accompanying verses) and drawn by George Cruikshank, this print shows country squires and huntsmen riding over men, women, and children toward the edge of a cliff, in pursuit of rooks (bankers) bearing paper money; (below) William Cobbett leads a procession of fools and radical reformers (2 June 1826). (Courtesy the Trustees of the British Museum)

A Tory view of the leading Radicals and their ally Daniel O'Connell at work: (l. to r.) O'Connell, Thomas Attwood, Joseph Hume, and Sir Francis Burdett (1 July 1832). (Courtesy the Trustees of the British Museum)

Statue of Thomas Attwood unveiled in Birmingham in 1858. (Courtesy Mrs P. Mitchell)

Below:
Medallions struck for the Birmingham Political Union in support of the Reform Bill. (Courtesy Mrs P. Mitchell)

Thomas Attwood

Introduction

Thomas Attwood, a Birmingham banker, economist, and political reformer, died in 1856 at the age of seventy-two, relatively penniless and apparently little regarded. There were a few obituaries in local and national newspapers which commented on his achievements. But the funeral was a poor affair and it took his friends several months to scratch together a small sum of money to erect a statue in his memory. The response stood in sad contrast to his "great days" during the Reform Bill crisis of a quarter of a century earlier. Then, he had been lionized with the title "King Tom," and thousands had sworn to die in his defence.

Contemporary neglect has, to some extent, been repeated in the treatment accorded to Attwood by historians. In contrast to the recognition given that other "great man" from Birmingham, Joseph Chamberlain, there has not been a major study of his career apart from a grandson's compilation of Attwood's speeches, letters, and pamphlets, which was published in 1885. Indeed, until recently, even his participation in the barrage of analysis and opinion on economic affairs, from taxation and the money supply to population growth and free trade, directed at the public in the first half of the nineteenth century has been ignored by students of economic theory. Keynes, for example, omitted Attwood from the "brave army of heretics" who challenged David Ricardo and the all-conquering "Classical Economists." Perhaps even more remarkably, political historians have been equally remiss. William Molesworth, in his pioneering description of the passage of the Reform Bill, scarcely mentions Attwood's name. Even in recent studies where Attwood has been noticed, authors have tended to concentrate on only one aspect of his activities and there has been relatively little attempt to relate one subject to another or to examine changes over time.

Events with which Attwood interacted have been allowed to overshadow the man.

A few years ago, W.L. Burn, in an attempt to widen historical perspectives, asked biographers to resist the lure of the "eccentric and exotic" and to appreciate the virtues of the "commonplace man" whose influence on society may have been significant.[1] Lately, the appearance of numerous biographies and essays dealing with minor political and literary figures illustrates that this recommendation has been heeded. Attwood, at one time or another eccentric, exotic, and commonplace, would seem to meet all of Burn's criteria, yet the neglect, in his case, has not been remedied. The reason for this contemporary and modern indifference may be a qualification of significance which Burn overlooked – the case of the self-confessed "failure." Notwithstanding that he had written and published extensively on the subject of the economy; had been an influential witness before three parliamentary committees; had held Birmingham's first seat in the Commons; and, perhaps most significantly, had become one of the most accomplished out-door orators of the day and the creator of a model extraparliamentary body, the Birmingham Political Union, Attwood took pains to broadcast his opinion that all his efforts had been useless. He believed that the objectives for which he had worked had not been achieved and that his life's work stood, at the end, in ruins.

Birmingham's citizens accepted his self-denigration; the public memory is notoriously short and a long illness prevented any public recognition for almost ten years preceding his death. Other figures commanded attention and many of the changes that Attwood had demanded had become a reality or had lost their immediate appeal. Thus, while his influence was acknowledged in the obituaries, his significance was overlooked. Historians have also taken his assessment at face value and have underplayed his contribution, preferring to see him as a minor actor with a few interesting lines. Their acceptance of a self-image of personal despair and impotence has been conveniently reinforced by a commonly held conviction, fostered by the admirers of the Classical school, that he was a monomaniac (on the subject of currency reform) who took an intemperate pleasure in predicting catastrophes or, as one critic remarked, in being the "prophet of unfulfilled doom." His advocacy of political reform and social justice is similarly dismissed as mere "breastbeating" dissonance. This study is an attempt to change that perception by exposing the superficial analysis which underpins the charges. It argues that Attwood was a pivotal figure in the development of economic, political, and social theory in the first half of the nineteenth century. In that sense, the immediate "failure" which he lamented was relatively unimportant and his unfortunate self-sentence must not be used as an excuse for undervaluation. This biography is an effort, then, to fill a notable gap in nineteenth-century historiography.

Thomas Attwood, born in Halesowen, near Birmingham, in 1783, was the son of a prosperous manufacturer and banker. His education, both in the academic and practical sense, was gained exclusively in the Midlands at a time of rapid industrialization and it was this accident of birth above all others which shaped his life. At the comparatively young age of twenty-eight he was elected to the office of high bailiff, the most important official appointment in Birmingham. He showed early qualities of leadership, for it was under his direction and patronage that the town protested the charter of the East India Company in 1812 and sent a deputation to Westminster to lobby against the Orders-in-Council. His early opinions were naive and poorly formulated, containing elements of all parties and philosophies, from High Tory to ultra-radical. Nevertheless, there were indications that he was discontented with a political system that appeared to discriminate against the urban industrial sector with which he had come to identify himself. His regard for public opinion and his condemnation of "unprincipled" time-serving foreshadowed the mixture of economic and political radicalism for which he was to become notorious.

Distress, especially acute in Birmingham, the centre of the armaments industry, following the Napoleonic Wars led Attwood to protest the government's economic policy. In 1816 he published a pamphlet, *The Remedy; or, Thoughts on the Present Distresses*, which presented a monetary explanation of the collapse. In this thirty-page polemic, the first of seven he was to publish between 1816 and 1819, he innocently proposed a remedy – an expansion of the currency supply. Attwood's argument and its subsequent modification is presented fully below. But it is essential to place it in its historical context and to suggest differences between his interpretation and those of other early nineteenth-century analysts of the economy.

The debate essentially revolved around the subjects of the gold standard, monetary theory, and the regulatory role of the Bank of England in the banking system. It was deemed fundamental by the majority of writers in the eighteenth century that the purchasing power of money (or its exchange value) be the same as the purchasing (or exchange value) of a commodity, in this case gold. The metal, therefore, had become the single most important instrument of financial regulation. Almost as significant was the Bank, established in 1694, which had gradually acquired a measure of national authority in the course of the eighteenth century. Together, the Bank, a private and profit-seeking establishment, and the standard, an internationally traded article of uncertain supply, constituted the twin pillars upon which financial order depended. This relatively simple approach to monetary stability was found wanting, however, when the "industrial revolution" began to transform the economy. Then, the flexibility of the institutions in the face of increased economic activity and larger capital requirements was severely tested. This strain was exacerbated in the last decade by a rapid rise in government expenditure and taxation in support of the war against France. Finally, unable to cope, the traditional system collapsed.

Its downfall was marked by the suspension of specie (gold) payments for the Bank's paper issues on 27 February 1797. It came in the aftermath of a panic caused by the temporary landing of French troops in Wales. But the crisis had been simmering for several years and the panic was merely the trigger. Without the underpinning of specie and Bank's notes quickly depreciated in terms of the metal (it had stood at £3 17s. 10½ d. an ounce) and on the international exchanges. The movement marked a new stage in the debate about monetary and banking theory and was to lead to the establishment of what passed for orthodoxy in the western world's financial circles before 1914.

Until 1809 the discount on gold rarely exceeded 10 per cent, but sudden shifts in direction kept the arguments alive. Explanations ranged from the simple to the complex. The Bank was a popular scapegoat; it was unrestricted by the need to redeem its notes in gold and critics claimed it overissued in a blind search for profits. The 200-year-old quantity theory of money easily explained the subsequent depreciation. Other suggestions included the inflationary effects of budget deficits, reckless expenditure, and war-related shortages. Modern analysis indicates, as is often the case, that it was a combination of these factors which was responsible.

It was not until the autumn of 1809, when the premium on gold rose to about 30 per cent and David Ricardo printed the first of his many articles castigating the Bank's irresponsibility, that the debate become urgent. Ricardo demanded a return to the gold standard as a means of stabilizing the economy.[2] Fear of the spiralling inflation was such that Parliament instructed a committee to investigate. A vigorous argument both within and outside Westminster ensued. Eventually a consensus supported a resumption of cash payments within two years, but the government, pressing a "win the war" argument (it worried about restrictions on its borrowing privileges), managed to keep the situation unchanged.³ It was agreed, however, that payments would be resumed as soon as possible after victory. In the years up to Waterloo, the "Bullionists" claimed vindication as the gold premium fluctuated between 20 per cent and 35 per cent. Commodity prices were even more volatile and in 1812–13 were close to twice their prewar level.

After 1815 the specie stocks of the Bank rose, the exchanges recovered, the premium on gold fell below 3 per cent, and commodity prices plummeted. With the affairs of the country in such apparently good order the demands for resumption became insistent. The overriding problem of the war, it was said, had been removed and few writers disagreed. Debates on the subject began to concentrate on the level of parity with gold that should be established. As has been noted in several modern commentaries, it is difficult to conclude whether the improving gold/banknote ratio resulted from a policy of contraction by the Bank of England or from its inactivity in the face of nonmonetary factors. Whatever the Bank's role, the contraction was undoubtedly compounded by a series of private bank failures and dangerously over-extended industrial and agricultural sectors. By August 1816 gold was valued at £3 19s 0d. an ounce and would have been lower if the Bank had not been buying at that price. The exchanges were above par and gold flowed into the Bank's coffers. The shift was, however, accompanied by severe economic distress.

Agricultural groups were among the first to complain. Although their primary objective was the tightening of the Corn Laws, the decline in prices was widely attributed to the contraction in the money supply. Robert Southey, writing in the *Quarterly Review,* an essentially conservative journal, chastised the government, warning against "a further subtraction of the currency (too much having already been subtracted)." He asked, "What! Is the Ghost of Bullion abroad?"⁴ The reaction in the industrial areas was more robust as riots and large-scale demonstrations reinforced the demand for a political solution to the current distress. The most distinctive protest, however, came from Birmingham. In that city, an articulate and concerted attack focused on the government's monetary policy as the primary culprit in the depression.

The fact that there was protest is, of course, not surprising. In common with that of other newly emerging urban and industrial centres Birmingham's expansion had been rapid. The war had in many ways been beneficial, since the price of iron had risen and the armaments trade had boomed, but the cessation of government demand which came with the peace had caused prices to crash.

Iron bars, whose price was often taken as a measure of Birmingham's prosperity, had sold for £15 a ton in late 1814 but fell to £11 in December 1816 and reached a low of £9 10s. in February 1817. Unemployment dramatically increased as whole factories were abandoned or sold up. The ensuing distress could have created internal strife (riots) as it did in some other towns. That it did not do so was, in part, due to a set of unique circumstances. Many of the industries which experienced the largest falls in demand were organized on a shop-by-shop or piecework system. As Asa Briggs has convincingly demonstrated, this had encouraged a greater sense of community and a fluid social structure which, in turn, led to an identification of interest.[5] Workers and employers, in consequence, were more likely to seek an external cause of their troubles and to cooperate in the expression of their grievances. There was also a conscious pride in their past achievements which, they believed, derived solely from "Brummagem" (their description) ingenuity. The town had not developed under the patronage of the nobility nor did it owe its livelihood to London. The people were proudly independent and accustomed to voicing their opinions at every level of government. Indeed, many would go further and, in an early portent of their mid-century confidence, declare that their economic destiny demanded the notice of Westminster. There were other minor contributory factors which ensured that Birmingham would deliver a loud but coherent verdict on the business of Parliament. But the single most important element in the town's response was undoubtedly the energy and personality of Thomas Attwood.

Attwood's intervention in the debate about the restoration of specie payments revealed a different perspective than that of the majority of the participants. His ideas about the economy were drawn from his experience as a banker and from his observation of industrial practice in Birmingham. Most other critics emphasized the financial marketplace as seen from a London and landed perspective. Thus their interpretation of the effects of falling prices stressed the relationship between debtors and creditors, and the relative imbalances in burdens shouldered by taxpayers as compared to owners of government debt. These criticisms did note the detrimental impact of a contracting money supply on industry and employment but, in a foretaste of modern economic policy, put such concerns in a secondary position. Deflationary activities by the Bank and the government were, in these terms, unjust, because they disturbed the economic status quo and indirectly threatened the preeminence of the landed classes. David Ricardo and William

Cobbett, men far apart on virtually every other economic and political issue, supported resumption but shared the view that it was only the distributional effect of a return to gold which required attention. Their equanimity was remarkable. Ricardo was later to claim ignorance, "I am not engaged in trade, and it [stagnation of trade] does not come much within my own knowledge." He also confessed, "I have very little practical knowledge."[6] Cobbett, who spoke for a rural England of yeoman farmers, was equally cavalier. He claimed to support resumption as a means of getting rid of country paper money, "rotten rags" which defrauded the farmer. An "equitable adjustment" of contracts was the only palliative necessary to make resumption bearable. Both writers were oblivious to the consequences of rapidly falling prices for the businessman and to the importance of confidence in the industrial sector.

Attwood's analysis had quite a different foundation. He worried about the willingness of businessmen to invest and to assume new obligations. While not neglecting the relationship between debtors and creditors, his reading of the depression emphasized the general nature of the collapse. It was the decline in the purchasing power of all sectors of society which created insurmountable obstacles to prosperity. The lack of remunerative prices for productive activity discouraged all activity. the cry for tax reduction in these circumstances was misguided, since it would lead to a decline in government expenditure and diminish aggregate demand. It is tempting to suggest that this observation was a precursor of Keynesian ideas about the stimulating benefits of deficit financing. However, although there are some hints that Attwood was aware of the connection and of the differences between high- and low-spending income groups, his primary explanation lay in the lag between the reduction in government spending and the increase in demand created by purchases made as a result of larger disposable incomes. He also disputed the Ricardian emphasis on the self-correcting mechanism of the market under all circumstances by differentiating between short- and long-run fluctuations. The former could certainly be left to the business community, *"laissez-nous faire,"* but the latter imbalance could be more speedily adjusted by government action. He abhorred the "unnecessary" distress caused by inaction when intelligent observation indicated a risk-free alternative – currency management.

Contrary to the popular interpretation given his ideas before 1819, Attwood did not propose a legal devaluation but rather an injection of demand through an issue of government paper (exchequer bills). It is equally mistaken to assume that he opposed the resumption of specie payments. His argument was quite simply that legislators should not substitute dogma for commonsense. The implementation of a restrictive monetary policy in the name of stability would be self-defeating if the result was a decline in economic activity. Specie payments for Bank of England notes was a laudable goal but, in the context of current (1816) economic conditions, it should not be undertaken lightly. The par value of the pound sterling, judiciously chosen, should conform to the real situation; it must not be slavishly returned to the 1797 level. At this time he did not specify an exact figure for the par value and his later attempts to do so floundered in the imprecision of available statistics and the fractured and uncertain nature of the market. Nevertheless, the effort was worth far more than the mindless appeals to tradition which satisfied the majority of his fellow economists.

There were two other writers of the period who argued in a similar vein. Both came from Birmingham. One was Thomas Attwood's brother, Matthias; the other was Henry James, who preceded Thomas as Cobbett's "My Lord Little Shilling of Birmingham." Their positions were more extreme at this time than that of Thomas, inasmuch as their pamphlets contained the implication that depreciation could be beneficial. It is difficult to establish the degree of cooperation between these men. Obviously the brothers might be expected to have discussed the question despite being separated (Matthias lived in London). Later, as Thomas became better known and was forced to spend more time in the capital, their views on economic questions were clearly coordinated. The relationship with James is uncertain, although the brothers knew him well. He too lived at this time in London but, apart from an occasional reference, his name is surprisingly absent from the Attwood correspondence. In any event, neither Matthias nor Henry James attained the notoriety of Thomas and it is with his name and Birmingham that contemporaries identified the notion of currency expansion as a solution for economic depression.

In 1817 Thomas Attwood published two more treatises which further developed his ideas. Although the second edition of *The Remedy* had been noticed in London, it was *Prosperity Restored* and *A Letter to the Right Honourable Nicholas Vansittart* which established his reputation. His general theory remained intact as he castigated the government for its failure to appreciate the effects of falling prices on the incentives for production. He reiterated that tax reduction could not be substituted for a sound monetary policy and advocated an expansion of the banknote issues through one form or another. There were, however, crucial additions. Profits or the expectation of profitable investment became a key point in the analysis. In a remarkably "modern" passage he wrote that the poor man cannot "flourish unless the rich man flourishes first" and that it was the duty of the government to see that opportunities for wealth creation existed. Of greater contemporary significance, however, was a series of categorical statements which emphasized the potential benefits that would accrue to the economy through devaluation. The industrial sector of the economy would suffer if the value of its inventories fell: "A country prospers under fixed prices. It prospers more under rising prices." This set Attwood apart, with James and Matthias, from other analysts. Ricardo and a host of imitators were in no doubt that inflation was a moral evil which threatened the whole fabric of society. To suggest otherwise was, in their terms, at best mistaken and at worst traitorous. Attwood's bias was now quite explicit. His proposals for economic prosperity took as their inspiration the newly emerging industrial sector and it was to its leaders that he looked for direction. The rural/commercial hierarchy which had for so long dominated society found the idea repellent.

There is one other aspect of Attwood's position in 1817 which is worthy of comment and which underlines his unique contribution to theory at this time. To keep the economy healthy he had advocated a managed money supply. The definition of "healthy" is obviously crucial if the recommendation is to have any practical value. His test of a healthy economy was a state of full employment. The fundamental disagreement with the Malthusian approach to labour is inescapable.

There is little evidence that Attwood's arguments were even considered by the government. A minor boom late in 1817 persuaded some friends that his suggestions had been heeded, but preparations for the return to gold proceeded inexorably. Progress was slower than many had expected as the Bank's directors experimented with a series of measures designed to prepare the banking system for the change; this served simply to intensify the debate. Finally, Lord Liverpool, the prime minister, bowed to public pressure and announced that inquiries by both houses of Parliament would be instituted in 1819.

Only four witnesses who appeared before the Commons committee spoke against resumption. This was not surprising. The witnesses were hand-picked to ensure relative unanimity. The House of Lords was a little more liberal and examined Matthias Attwood, among others. It made little difference. Both committees concluded in favour of an immediate resumption of cash payments.

The prewar standard of £3. 17s. 10½ d. was chosen as the logical exchange price. The complications of the inevitable reassessment of prices which must follow were conveniently forgotten. Any symptoms of distress that might appear as a short-run consequence of deflation were to be dismissed as an unfortunate side-issue. The changes in the economic structure of the country during the preceding years went apparently unnoticed.

The Resumption Act of 1819, or Peel's Act as it was to become known, was bitterly attacked by a small but vocal minority within and outside Parliament during the next two years. The general source of the complaints was the agricultural community which wanted to tie in tax and contract adjustment. The Attwoods were equally vociferous and argued that the rising level of unemployment was caused by falling prices and income transfers. They could find little support. In Parliament, Alexander Baring used Henry Thornton's widely respected 1802 publication, *Paper Credit*, to demonstrate that workers' wages responded at a different rate from that of prices.[7] The response was unequivocal: "To tamper with the public faith; to sully the honour of the country; to declare national bankruptcy! – Good God! Who in his senses could recommend it?"[8] Thomas Attwood acknowledged that the cause, as an independent crusade, could not succeed by embarking on a campaign to woo the farming interest. It, too, ultimately failed.

Improved economic conditions in 1822–3 lessened the urgency of the debate, and criticism of the gold standard virtually ended. There was a brief revival during the aftermath of the speculative craze in 1824–5 but it lacked its earlier virulence. Attwood, of course, consistently maintained that without some attention to the role of money in economic management prosperity rested on a very shaky foundation. Few interest groups agreed. There was one notable exception. Prior to 1819 Birmingham had supported the various petitions Attwood had sent to Parliament on the subject of the standard, but there had not been many independently sponsored initiatives. Following resumption this changed and, partly under the tutelage of Attwood, a school of economic theory developed. Like Attwood, its adherents used Birmingham's condition as its test of economic health. The development and influence, often regrettably negative, attained in later years by this school deserves to be as well known as that of the renowned banking and currency schools. In 1844, for example, the government's activities during the passage of the Bank Charter Act were as much an attempt to circumvent the criticisms of the Birmingham men as they were to entrench a sound central banking policy. In the 1820s, however, while the developing school provided some encouragement, Attwood became increasingly frustrated at his failure to win any concessions whatsoever from the cabinet.

In the late 1820s Attwood decided to change his approach from writing and lobbying to direct participation in politics. By doing so he joined another significant debate. A reform of the House of Commons had been advocated by a variety of interest groups for many years. The Whig party proposed reform as a means to weaken the hold of the Tories, while the radicals hoped to use it to restructure the priorities of society generally. The demand for change had become ever more insistent and its ability to capture the public imagination persuaded Attwood that participation could help his monetary crusade. The organization of the Birmingham Political Union in 1829 was the result. Over the next three years, his leadership of the Union-directed extraparliamentary agitation was superb and of critical importance in the passage of the Reform Bill in 1832. Contrary to his own sense of priorities, it was in this activity that probably his greatest contribution to British political history was made. Regrettably, in most studies the construction has been given more attention than the architect. Yet, in the years in which the Union was most effective, his conceptions of justice, economics, and the means of achieving social peace dominated. Attwood was the physical embodiment of provincial urban society and its first citizen. In that role he linked the Union with the Whigs in an irregular partnership that was unprecedented.

With the accomplishment of the Union's immediate objective, the Reform Act, the essential fragility of the organization became evident. Its success had, in part, been due to the relative simplicity of the reform issue and Attwood's brilliant leadership. The inability of reformers elsewhere to imitate the Birmingham model or to wrest the movement from him is a remarkable tribute to his skill. He was not, however, particularly disappointed by the collapse and entered the Commons as one of Birmingham's MPs with, he believed, his primary objective, economic reform, within his grasp. Sufficient "practical men of business" and radicals had been returned to win a more rational economic policy.

Sadly, his parliamentary career, like that of many of the new recruits to the House, was a disappointment. Instead of applause he met ridicule. Despite being the spokesman of the urban manufacturing interest,[9] and the undisputed leader of "the most formidable combination in the country,"[10] Attwood never overcame the handicap of being an outsider. As one nineteenth-century critic noted, "the man's life work was done before he entered the House of Commons, he made no headway there."[11] Yet a study of his experience in the Commons is instructive. The survival of the established order after 1832 had been well documented. Often that continuity is attributed to the strength of the institution itself and to the managerial ability of the ruling classes. Rarely has there been an examination of the men who were expected "to turn the scale";[12] failure is too often equated with justifiable obscurity. Their inability to make headway can, however, be given other explanations.

After a brief flurry of promises Attwood's expectations were shown to be illusory. On several occasions in 1833, a reorganization in monetary priorities seemed tantalizingly attainable, but nothing ever materialized. In the ensuing years, a futile round of agitation, cobbled coalitions, including various attempts to reactivate the Political Union, and an unflagging search for "honest men," wearied him. The reformed House of Commons was not much different from its predecessor in its appreciation of economic theory. Finally, believing that Parliament did not represent public opinion, Attwood reluctantly committed himself to the ultra-radicals who had reached a similar conclusion. It was a decision which served only to emphasize his disillusionment with the political process and his sense of alienation.

The alliance with those who became known as the Chartists was a mistake from the beginning. Although he had some sympathy for the notion of universal suffrage, Attwood did not like the rhetoric of Feargus O'Connor and other extremists who disputed his leadership. Unlike the radicals of that breed, he preferred to stress the importance of moral as opposed to physical force and the value of cooperation. Unfortunately, in 1837 he was no longer the master of the working classes and he found himself unable to impose his authority on the movement, even in Birmingham. Whereas in 1831–2 he had used the radical movement to further his vision, now he himself was being used. On 16 June 1839 he presented the Chartist petition which reputedly contained more than one million signatures. He spoke eloquently on the subject of political rights in a speech which still reads well today. Naturally, he also assured the House that the financial health of the country would be improved by a more liberal monetary system. In reply, Lord John Russell read from a Chartist broadside which condemned Attwood's currency arguments. Devastated, Attwood retired and, save for an abortive attempt to revive the Union in 1843, never reappeared in public. A losing struggle with Parkinson's disease capped a further series of misfortunes which included the deaths of his first wife and his eldest son, and the collapse of the private bank on which the family fortune was founded.

His career thus ended in anticlimax and his own assessment of his life's work – that it had been a failure – was harsh. This verdict is mistaken. A school of economic theory had been founded and not until 1857 did any of Birmingham's representatives at Westminster fail to oppose the gold standard. Letters from a variety of individuals and groups, such as the Birmingham Chamber of Commerce, kept Attwood's ideas current locally. Particularly significant was a series of letters, the *Gemini Letters,* printed in the *Midland Counties Herald* in 1843 and republished as a book in the following year. John Stuart Mill was sufficiently outraged to contribute a polemic to the *Westminster Review* designed expressly to rebut the dangerous views of the Birmingham theorists. The leader writer of the *Times,* equally disturbed, printed a violent editorial condemning all ideas remotely associated with the town. Mill's invective and the condemnation by the *Times* attributed more power to the Birmingham group than they merited. The vast majority of conservatives and radicals opposed any further tampering with the gold standard and the Birmingham school could aspire to little more than notoriety. Nevertheless, the ideas themselves became a part of the continuing debate on economic policy. Keynes is reported never to have read Attwood, but his theoretical analysis contains much which the Birmingham man would have recognized. Other modern economic theories are similarly indebted and it is a legacy which should be acknowledged.

A similar argument for recognition can be made in terms of his political career. The partnership with the ruling party in 1831–2, without which the final form of the Reform Act would have been very different, was a truly remarkable achievement. Attwood created a potent instrument for the expression of public opinion and maintained control of it through a particularly volatile period. The ground rules for future extraparliamentary action had been established and rarely in the years which followed was there a popular movement which did not use the Birmingham model as its guide. His parliamentary career was also meritorious. His compassion for and understanding of the common people demonstrated an appreciation of the complexities of urban life and was remarkable for his time.

Finally, and perhaps most significantly, during Attwood's lifetime Britain had been transformed from a rural society into "the workshop of the world." The Birmingham banker could have reasonably claimed to have been among the first to recognize that change and to have adopted a position which attempted to accommodate that reality in a coherent political and economic policy. He was not alone in his recognition of the new society, but, more than any other in the early decades of the nineteenth century, he became its symbol and its spokesman.

CHAPTER ONE

Family Background and Commercial Apprenticeship

Thomas Attwood was born on 6 October 1783, at Hawne House, in the parish of Halesowen, Shropshire. He was the third son of Matthias and Ann, née Adams, in a family of ten, seven of whom were boys.[1] The family, which could trace its lineage back to the Norman Conquest, had originally settled at Wolverly Court, Worcestershire, and had been among the first to sit in Parliament.[2] Notwithstanding their eminent origins, however, the Attwoods' future prominence in Birmingham and district was entirely due to their entrepreneurial skills as leaders in that remarkable series of events known as the industrial revolution.

George Attwood, Thomas Attwood's grandfather, moved to Halesowen in the mid-eighteenth century to mine the surface coal and iron ore deposits.[3] For many years the purchases were not profitable, but returns slowly increased as the demand for his products grew. In 1771, twenty-one years after the initial gamble, the first major purchase and the real foundation of the family's future, Corngreaves steel furnaces, was made.[4] After a short period of further consolidation George sent for his sons, Matthias and James. They had been working in Rowley Regis, Staffordshire, where the family owned a farm. A buoyant market and a willingness to take risks persuaded Matthias, using his father's money, to buy Lodge Forge Estate which at that time merely held out the promise of mineral wealth. He was not disappointed and that enterprise also flourished.

With two successful businesses in hand the family expanded their interests with astonishing vigour. A nail ironmonger partnership was set up to make use of the district's reservoir of nailers driven into the countryside by the growth of more skilled trades in the towns.[5] Shortly thereafter, about 1783, George Attwood diversified by purchasing a mill and, in a bid to become a country gentleman, 247 acres of agricultural land in the Cradley and Rowley Regis district. Sometime between 1788 and 1797 a further important step was taken with the establishment of the Adelphi Steel House at 11 Broad Street in Birmingham.[6] To complement this manufactory, a copper and rolling mill was opened in the house that had once been the home of Thomas Baskerville, the famous printer. Two estates at King's Norton which had large mineral deposits, Colmer's Hall and Middleton Hall, were next acquired to supply the raw materials.

The process of diversification was completed in 1791 when, in partnership with Isaac Spooner, the Attwoods opened a bank at Birmingham. The wealth of the Spooner family, under the private partnership provisions then in effect the co-guarantor of the bank's security, was based upon the same iron and steel foundation as the Attwoods' fortune.[7] Isaac Spooner had also been engaged in the money-lending business and he undertook to manage the enterprise as senior partner. The bulk of the working capital was, however, put up by George Attwood and there was never any doubt as to which family held the controlling interest.[8]

Thereafter the wealth and influence of both partners expanded at an ever-increasing pace. One obituarist was to attribute the rapid extension of their business profits to a monopoly of Swedish imports. It is doubtful that such a monopoly actually existed.[9] It is true that each had contacts in that country and that their bank acted as the English agents for several large Swedish companies. Even so, the most critical factor in their later success was probably the expansion of credit allowed by the ownership of two banks, a second establishment having been opened in London in 1802, and by the suspension of specie payments in 1797. Although evidence is extremely sparse, it would appear that, following the end of the need to back their currency issues with gold, the bank lent extensively to both partners. Credit was granted on the security of open mortgages on their industrial property and on simple promissory notes. The rate of interest which applied was nominal. Such practices were not uncommon in the days of the private banks. It is impossible to estimate the extent of the bank's commitment but the support given must have offered a degree of security and a means of smoothing out any business cycle imbalances for the partners' various endeavours.

During the next few years the members of the Attwood family, acting in concert and not as individuals, took advantage of every development to expand their interests. In 1800 eighteen acres of land, owned by the earl of Dudley and located in the neighbourhood of Dudley Wood and Netherton, were acquired under a twenty-one year lease. The real advantage of the lease was not its agricultural value but a clause which allowed the owner to mine the surface coal and iron ore deposits over a wide area adjacent to Netherton. Demand for iron and steel was increasing rapidly as the pace of the industrial revolution accelerated and the war with France intensified. The Attwoods, using the security of their new supply, built or leased six furnaces for the production of pig iron and erected two more refineries for the manufacture of steel over the course of the next three years.

On George Attwood's death in 1817 all the family's holdings passed to James and Matthias, and were registered in both names. George had impressed the value of cooperation on his sons and the rapid accumulation of assets since 1770 ensured that neither had any inclination to contest the legacy. Not until James died in 1818 was an equitable division between the two sides of the family achieved.[10] Of course, there was some independent activity both before and after their father's death. Matthias, for example, acquired the mineral rights to 250 acres of land across the River Stour from Hawne, and, in 1806, he bought a 175-acre estate named "The Leasowes."[11] Shortly before his death, in mineral rights alone he possessed 1,200 acres, all bought independently, valued in 1854 at £167,000.[12] Nevertheless, Matthias generally followed his father's advice and required his sons and their cousins to work in concert for family rather than personal interest.

The Attwoods were always a closely knit and dutiful family. Matthias, senior, was content with a subordinate role until his father voluntarily relinquished control, whereupon he became, in every sense, the patriarch without whom nothing could be achieved. Undoubtedly an able and forceful character, he ruled his children and kept a tight hold on the family purse up to the day he died at the age of eighty-two. C.M. Wakefield remembered that his great-grandfather had a reputation for sternness coupled with a "hard" disposition but was, on occasion, capable of being an affectionate father.[13] He was a private man and whenever possible refused public office. Duty as a magistrate in each of the counties of Salop, Stafford, Worcester, and Warwick represented the extent of his service and was more a testament to his extensive business activities than to any perceived commitment to public service. In politics he was nominally a Tory and intensely patriotic (a trait instilled in each of his sons) but his views on most issues were vague and contradictory, the only exception being an unswerving support for the Church of England. He was one of the growing number in industrialists in the Midlands and the north who resented the power of London and their own inability to influence Parliament on questions of taxation and finance. Like them, he found himself caught between a natural concern for authority (as a master he could hardly feel otherwise) and a contempt for those who legislated the laws of the land.

The influence of this rather austere figure on his children was enormous, and the similarity in the careers and opinions of each son is striking. For Thomas Attwood, memories of the lessons taught by his father were to form an integral part of his currency doctrine and political activities. On a less happy note, the success of his father in business encouraged what became for Thomas an often disastrous pursuit of personal fortune in later life. This "mania" reached its most extreme form in 1850. Attwood, then sixty-seven years old, afflicted by Parkinson's disease and barely able to sign his name, took out a patent for the production of seamless copper tubes from the worn-out rollers discarded by calico printers.[14] Needless to say, the patent was never exercised.

It was fortunate that the oppressive weight of Matthias was to some degree counterbalanced by his wife, Ann. Her family, Adams, were small farmers, yeomen would have been the term used in an earlier time. The family had lived in the village of Cakemore in the parish of Halesowen for centuries. Ann had been given a happy childhood. Comfort and hospitality and taken precedence over the acquisition of wealth. Within the district her parents had a reputation for charity and benevolence which was clearly in keeping with a strong sense of Christian duty. They had none of the ambition which marked the Attwoods. Ann, who soon won a name for piety and kindness, opened the first Sunday school in Worcestershire.[15] In marriage her gentleness and love provided the perfect match for Matthias and family relations were singularly harmonious. Thomas Attwood enjoyed an affectionate relationship with his mother and she forged bonds between each sibling which were never broken. She also imbued in her children a strong sense of responsibility, particularly with regard to those less fortunate than themselves. Only in one respect did Ann Attwood's teaching prove unhelpful. The union of religion and responsibility can, on occasion, induce unreasonable confidence in one's own conclusions; as the motive is pure, the idea is by heaven sent. Those of her sons who entered public life found it hard to accept criticism and often a rather vehement messianic tone crept into their publications and speeches which hurt rather than advanced their various causes.

Matthias and Ann had been married on 13 December 1775, in the parish church at Rowley, Staffordshire. Their house, Hawne, was one mile from the town of Halesowen, situated upon a steep hill above the river Stour. It was a picturesque mansion which had belonged to the Pechell family, whose last baronet died a debtor in Fleet prison. There was a garden and an orchard of some five acres which produced, it was said, the best cherries for miles around. A farm of approximately 150 acres adjoined the house. It proved fruitful and their table was kept well supplied with fresh produce. Matthias made only one change in the physical appearance of the building. About 1790 he added a wing to accommodate an increasing number of children.

Hawne made a beautiful home before the encroachment of the coal-pit and the smoking works' chimneys left the grime of prosperity – a feculence for which the Attwoods must bear a considerable share of the responsibility. Fortunately, during Thomas Attwood's boyhood the streams and woods were pure, bright, and teeming with life. He became a keen naturalist and kept a menagerie. All the brothers were, of course, trained to ride and shoot. All, at some time or other, possessed a licence to hunt but only George, the eldest, kept up the habit as an adult. Thomas quickly came to abhor the bloodthirsty sports practised by his contemporaries and later claimed that at school he had tried to curb the excesses of his friends.[16] In an age of callousness and cruelty such sensitivity was unusual. Country gentlemen were expected to engage in field sports and in the towns bull-baiting, dog-fighting, and similar pastimes were commonplace. To oppose these customs was regarded as antisocial and was a handicap to anyone who sought public approval. But the majority of the Attwoods made no secret of their disgust and tried to effect change by example. Drunkenness and roistering were similarly abjured and a general preference was shown for family life. In these, as in many other respects, they were among the early advocates of the more attractive prejudices and notions which have come to be identified as "middle-class," using the nineteenth-century meaning of that term.

Only the eldest son, George, was given a university education.[17] Ironically, it happened that George was the only member of the family deemed "not bright";[18] an assessment borne out by the failure of the Birmingham bank in 1865 caused in part by a series of poor investments initiated by him. The remainder of the sons trod what became a well-worn path, first to the Free School in their local village, Halesowen, followed by a few years at the rather better known institution at Wolverhampton. The best teacher, according to their father, was life itself and an apprenticeship in business far surpassed that gained elsewhere. Few records of Thomas Attwood's childhood or years at school survive. Memories jogged by the obituarist seeking colour after the death of some "famous son" must always be suspect but in this instance these are about the only source of information. Wolverhampton Grammar School, to which he was sent in 1795, had many counterparts in the educational system of the eighteenth century.[19] The curriculum conformed to the general pattern of the period. Memorization was the approved method. The classical languages, Latin and Greek, and ancient history were the preferred subjects. Attwood learned enough Latin to be able to quote a phrase or two appositely when the occasion demanded but his favourite subject was the history of Rome. He particularly admired Marcus Aurelius, naming two sons after him.[20] Grammar, composition, literature, and "some" mathematics rounded out Wolverhampton's educational core, while penmanship, the "use of globes," French, and German were also offered. In the main, it was standard fare and hardly ideal training for a career in commercial banking. Thomas does not seem to have been particularly gifted academically, except in one year when he won a prize for the best essay. Of his outside interests, there is only a cryptic reference to music and the piano. As an adult, he certainly claimed no musical talent so it is doubtful that he progressed very far, although he later became one of the most enthusiastic supporters of Birmingham's annual music festival.

The impression of Attwood's character at school, given in posthumous tributes, is clearly partial. No vices and many virtues are recalled. We are told that he was thoughtful, conscientious, and honourable; that he acted as a guide and source of inspiration to his fellow pupils. Judge, juror, and tutor in propriety and good conduct were all roles he reputedly assumed. Obviously, if these recollections are to be believed, he was an indispensable ingredient in the education of his friends. By definition exaggeration contains a measure of truth and that may be the case here.

Attwood had not entered the school unprepared. Advice in profusion had been tendered by his two elder brothers, George and Matthias. The latter, a continuing pupil, who had no wish to be embarrassed by the gaucheness of a younger brother, protected Thomas from the extremes to which the traditional bullying of younger boys were taken. For the most part, he was free to pursue his own interests and did not have to trim to meet the shifting moods of others. With respect to the posthumous claims, experience gained in balancing the contending demands of five younger brothers and sisters perhaps contributed to his ready acceptance of responsibility and the intelligent manner in which he handled the role of monitor. The opinion that he was naturally honest and conscientious, lacking the wildness of some contemporaries, can fairly be accepted, given the evidence offered elsewhere about other members of the family. All were endowed with what best can be described as common sense – a mark of the effectiveness of the teaching and the example given by their parents.

The same may be said about characteristics that many obituarists found remarkable: his empathy for the suffering of others and his championship of the underdog. Without exception the Attwoods, as a family and as individuals, were actively involved in charitable work. The youngest brother, Benjamin, for example, in later life anonymously donated the enormous sum of £400,000, in £1,000 Bank of England notes, to London charities; this generosity was discovered only after his death. Thomas Attwood was never rich enough to distribute sums of this magnitude but the hungry and neglected were never refused help, sometimes to the disadvantage of his own family. It was said that he had begun this practice at an early age and had often given away all his pocket money. If this was so, it was a singular sacrifice for a child. The character that emerges from these recollections is therefore of a relatively uncomplicated youth with a mind of his own, a strong sense of duty, and an attractive disposition; indeed, much the same assessment as was to be made of him as an adult.

From these images it may be concluded that Attwood was not unhappy at school. The respect of his peers and tolerable success at his studies meant that his four years at Wolverhampton had not been wasted. Nevertheless, when his father told him in the autumn of 1799 that he was to enter the family bank at Birmingham, he was overjoyed. At last, he was to begin his "real" education.

Attwoods & Spooner had existed for only eight years in 1799 but the range of their activities was already extensive and growing rapidly.[21] In these early years the work was not difficult to master. Deposits at 2 per cent per annum were attracted from a variety of sources. Some from the surrounding agricultural community, drawn by the fact that the Spooners were respected landowners and understood farming problems, were particularly welcome. They tended to be less volatile than those of other sectors in the local economy and afforded a degree of security not enjoyed by some of the bank's competitors. In common with that of most country bankers the business of Attwoods & Spooner was worked mostly with the capital provided in this manner.[22] If such sums had been the only source of useable assets the scope of the bank's activities would have been very limited indeed unless unacceptable risks had been taken with the reserve. Conveniently, however, this capital was supplemented by the issue of their own bank-notes; notes which rode on the security of the retained deposits (reserve) and the wealth and reputation of the partners, unlimited liability theoretically imposing its own constraints on lending. Notes from five shillings to one hundred pounds were circulated in company with the legal coin of the realm which never seemed adequate to meet the needs of an area in which economic activity was growing at an unprecedented rate. Without such local initiatives it is doubtful if the industrial revolution could have sustained its pace into the nineteenth century. Bank of England notes, mostly of higher denomination, were largely confined to London and the supply of precious metals for coin production rarely met demand. In 1800 Attwoods & Spooner was already one of the largest banks in the town with a note circulation of approximately £50,000. It was soon to grow much larger.

The practice of banking at the turn of the nineteenth century was much more of an art than a science. Thomas Attwood would quickly learn that success depended more upon a ready wit and an ability to interpret often contradictory intelligence than it did on changes in the rate of interest or the foreign exchanges as dictated by London. The largest source of profit was founded on the practice of discount, but equally important was the direct support of local business through loans, mortgages, and advances; enterprise which required considerable local knowledge if bad debts were to be avoided.[23] It is clear that Attwoods & Spooner were active in a number of what might be termed risk ventures. Mortgages on farms, apparently written up for cash to be used for agricultural improvements; mortgages on buildings and machinery; loans based on personal guarantees with some evidence of collateral in the form of deeds of property; indirect references to outstanding advances to the large ironmasters of the outlying district; and the expansion of the activities of the Attwoods and Spooners themselves in fields as diverse as glass-making and insurance, all attest to the entrepreneurial support that gave banking a key role in Birmingham's pattern of growth.[24] The remainder of the work of a bank tended to be the routine affair of tax collection and dividend payments on behalf of the government.

The study of banking necessarily involved a careful analysis of the industrial environment in which it was to be practised. For

25 Family Background and Apprenticeship

Thomas Attwood this was to mean an informed familiarity with the town of Birmingham and the remarkable revolution of which its growth was part. With little or no commitment or loyalty to the past and a family history of success under the aegis of individual enterprise, Attwood's mind proved to be singularly receptive to the "secrets" of prosperity and progress which the town had to offer. Indeed, Attwood identified in later life so completely with his "home" that Birmingham became for him almost synonymous with England itself.

The town, whose population in 1801 was 71,000, was in many ways a peculiar place. The diversification and the division of labour which reduced capital costs affected both the social structure and the environment.[25] Contemporaries claimed that Birmingham enjoyed a more equal distribution of wealth than elsewhere, to the advantage of the moral and physical condition of the inhabitants. The social structure could not help but be fluid, so that the industrious and, it must be admitted, the lucky, could aspire to the role of master as trade boomed, taking the place of the victims of an earlier down-turn in economic activity. Of course, the size of individual manufactories varied considerably. Some button-makers employed up to 250 hands, one brass foundry had a like number, and a few platers claimed up to 150 employees.[26] In most trades, however, fewer than forty workers were congregated in one place and individual talent was the key to commercial success.[27] Capital requirements in such industries were obviously low and individual returns on investment at first sight unrewarding. One estimate of 1827 put the average annual returns for each business at £4,000 per annum.[28] In aggregate the scale of investment in Birmingham was high and to the banker the returns were potentially very profitable – discount accounts were, for instance, extremely active – and secure, if only the lender could get his assessment of character right. By the end of the eighteenth century all manner of items were produced in the town: "toys," jewellery, japanned and plated goods, papier mâché, wire, pins, needles, tubes, guns, swords, sheathing for ships, hollowares of different kinds, lamps, coins and medals, glass, printed books, and steam engines, the brass and steel industry providing the raw material for most of these products.[29]

The unusual nature of Birmingham was not confined to its economy and social character. Despite the size of the population, the town's administration remained in the hands of the parish officers who worked "mediaeval" institutions. The manor court still survived with its high and low bailiffs, high and low toasters, leather searchers and constables and headborough. These rather primitive administrative devices were supplemented by a Board of Governors, set up by a local act in 1783, to provide for the poor, and street commissioners whose task was the supervision of corporate improvement. These duties were carried on with reasonable efficiency, given the complexities of the situation and the amateur status of the appointees. By tradition, for example, the high bailiff was normally of the Church of England whereas the low bailiff would be a member of one of the dissenting sects.

Undisguised mutual dependency in the economic sphere seems to have created both sympathy for the less fortunate and a sense of civic pride. Unusually, this social spirit had survived the divisions created by the reaction to the revolution in France during the previous decade. Politically, however, the situation was far less happy. Birmingham had suffered its share of "Church and King" riots, including the most famous national incident of all in 1791, when the house of the Unitarian and scientist Dr Joseph Priestley, had been destroyed because of the owner's alleged republican sympathies.[30] Liberal leaders had withdrawn from public office and several "loyal" associations had been formed for the preservation of "Liberty, Property and the Constitution of the Country." Both Isaac Spooner and Matthias Attwood, Sr, were Tories by preference; their sons were similarly disposed.[31]

Thomas Attwood entered business life in Birmingham during a period of depression. The outbreak of war with France had not helped the town's industries. Many tradesmen experienced difficulties and some failed. The number of paupers seeking relief increased alarmingly. There is even the suggestion in contemporary accounts that the population may have marginally declined.[32] In the year 1800 soup kitchens had to be set up for the unemployed; in September there were bread riots. Crowds roamed the streets and the military had to be called in. Some shops and mills were set on fire and a few rioters were killed.[33] With the example of the French Revolution and the potential for disturbance ever present in the knots of unemployed who lounged on the street corners, political questions provided the main topic of conversation in the clubs; it was a social habit which appealed to all levels of Birmingham society.

Politics was not, of course, the only subject which claimed attention. One which provoked violent debate among those with whom Attwood associated was the suspension of cash payments by the Bank of England three years before, on 6 March 1797. When that decision had been taken the townspeople had followed the example of other regions and bravely issued a declaration in support of the Bank's paper money and the local bank notes. By this means they had hoped to foster confidence and to support credit when the actions of the government seemed to argue otherwise. Circumstances had combined to thwart their intentions and the national financial system was in a chaotic state. One aspect of the change had been paradoxically to enhance the importance of London and the capital's money market. That, combined with the demands made by the prosecution of the war upon government borrowing requirements (a development that no country bank wished to leave untapped), lent greater weight to the bank's London agent and involved the individual banker in national affairs. It was for this reason that the partners contemplated opening a sister establishment in London; trust based upon family connection was safer than one which relied simply on the bond of mutual profit.

This, then, was the situation which faced the apprentice banker fresh from Wolverhampton Grammar School. It was to prove significant that Attwood learnt the art of banking under suspension conditions at a time of distress in Birmingham for this was the critical stage of his intellectual development. Although the opinions he was later to express in his economic doctrine certainly did not exist in any coherent form at this time, he did reach several decisions as to the merits of the new system; decisions which in their mature form were an integral part of his prescription for prosperity.

The family bank in New Street that was to serve as the hub of Attwood's life for over thirty years was neither grand nor imposing. The room in which all business was contracted was small; a handicap compounded by an unreasonably low ceiling and high stools at stilt-like desks. In one corner an inadequate fireplace consumed quantities of coal out of all keeping with its heating ability. Decoration was confined to some "quaint" elliptical arches and an array of blunderbusses whose efficacy if the bank had ever come under attack was fortunately never tested.[34] The building was conveniently located near the centre of Birmingham, next to the Hen and Chickens Hotel; this proximity, while good for business, was to provide many distractions for the suddenly liberated schoolboy.

Attwood's first few months at the counting house were spent in a rather leisurely introduction to the various technical aspects of his appointed trade; economic conditions dictated caution and the cash reserve had to be nurtured. It gave him an opportunity to engage in an agreeable social whirl designed to acquaint him with the town's entrepreneurs, their activities, prospects, and reliability, and, when the young man had any choice, their daughters. There were few commercial sources of amusement to be enjoyed in the brash new town if one eschewed the blood sports of cock-fighting, bear-baiting, and the like. However, Vauxhall Gardens on the eastern outskirts of the town as it then stood, a two-shilling ride by cab, made up for the lack of quantity by quality. Tree-lined walks illuminated by variegated lamps, secluded alcoves and bowers, bands, singers, and dancers offered a delightful setting in which to relax. Attwood was often to be found there with his friends in the summer evenings or on the festival days when fireworks were added to the attractions. It made for a happy, carefree time notwithstanding the social and economic distress. Occasionally, he was asked to journey to Oxford, Wolverhampton, Walsall, Nottingham, or some other midland town on errands for the bank or to make himself known to other private bankers cooperating in the use of local banknotes and the funding of complementary trades.[35] As conditions began to improve in the spring of 1801 these pleasant interludes became less frequent. Attwood had been an eager student and he learnt quickly. It was not long before he was able to assume the responsibilities of a full partner and released his brother, Matthias, for the planned extension of family interests to London.

Although the study of banking practice and town politics was time-consuming, Attwood did not neglect other pursuits. He was not shy – a reflection, perhaps, of the very good opinion he held of himself – and he enjoyed a series of amorous liaisons with several young ladies of the neighbourhood, though precisely how amorous these were is unknown. Shortly after marriage in 1806 he drew a self-portrait in caricature to amuse his young wife.[36] Included in that sketch were the qualities "wisdom," "patience," "honour," "courage," "long suffering," "forgiveness," "goodwill," and "a whole list of affections." His faults, in his own opinion, were "pride" and a penchant for "evil-speaking" – a remarkable and accurate confession because both were to be exhibited in full measure during this parliamentary career. Physically, he wrote, he had "graceful looks" and "a very pretty ear"; two attributes which suggest a further defect he had not recognized – vanity. To others his appearance appeared striking if not quite handsome. Considerably above average height, about six feet, broad-shouldered and thin, with a hint of swagger in his walk, he had many admirers.

On closer inspection his head might have been thought a trifle too large, his nose overgenerous, although not, as his grandson was at pains to point out, "Jewish," and his chin weak.[37] But most young ladies forgave these distractions and saw only the "grand, intellectual forehead," and the "far-away," dreamy look in his hazel eyes. One who particularly caught his fancy was Elizabeth Carless.

The Carless family had been connected with the town of Birmingham for at least a hundred years. Elizabeth's father had died in 1787 leaving a widow with four children. Fortunately they were comparatively well-to-do, having inherited wealth through the family's connection with the iron trade, and lived in comfort at Grove House in the village of Harborne, a few miles outside the town. Elizabeth was eighteen years old in 1802, extremely beautiful, and, by all accounts, possessed of a charming personality.[38] Thomas Attwood found her irresistible. There is no record of their first meeting, but as the Carlesses were related to the Spooners they must have known each other as children. By 1803 he was writing to her on a regular basis in the most affectionate terms; the letters were often accompanied by flowers. He himself was still only twenty and there may have been other recipients of love letters of whom nothing is known. But it was this relationship which led to marriage and gave the security and support without which his subsequent experiences as a radical and politician might have proved too demanding and have led to an early retirement.

Attwood began his courtship of Elizabeth about the time that hostilities with France recommenced. Bonaparte threatened the invasion of England and the whole nation became intensely patriotic. Only a few months before Thomas Attwood's name had been drawn, by ballot, to serve in the Warwickshire Militia.[39] The Peace of Amiens was then in effect and, in keeping with his status as a gentleman, his father had willingly hired a substitute. By midsummer, however, the renewed French threat led to the creation of three locally sponsored regiments for the defence of the realm – the Loyal Birmingham Voluntary Infantry, the Loyal Birmingham Associated Cavalry, and the Loyal Birmingham Light Horse Volunteers.

Attwoods & Spooner quickly demonstrated their commitment by contributing £315 of the £4,600 collected for the volunteers' outfits.[40] Furthermore, the senior partners encouraged Thomas Attwood to volunteer. It is likely that he did not require much persuasion as he was a romantic and the life of a soldier had its attractions when viewed from a distance. A few weeks' drilling at Warwick Castle, however, quickly blunted his enthusiasm, "this curs'd military business incapacitates a man for all rational employment."[41] A slight fever offered a welcome excuse to return home early, to recuperate. By the following spring the organization of the infantry had been completed and he was gazetted a captain in the Third Battalion.[42] At Christmas he had become engaged but this did not prevent a certain amount of philandering at the balls and dinners arranged for the entertainment of the officers when they returned to the Castle for further training. He explained to his fiancée that one or two ladies reminded him so strongly of her that he could not forbear to dance and stroll in the gardens with them.[43] Elizabeth's response is unknown.

Notwithstanding the advantages of being an officer at leisure his negative opinion of military life was soon reinforced. Although the bout of parade ground drudgery passed and the regiment was not put on active service, he decided to resign his commission.[44] One facet of this rather unhappy episode did make a lasting impression. As part of his duty, Attwood visited Warwick County jail. Prison conditions were quite horrifying and he was totally unprepared for the squalor and misery inflicted upon the hapless inmates. For the rest of his life he was to offer what help he could by providing character references, by paying for defence lawyers in various courts, and by helping convicted felons appeal by the preparation of petitions. Later, as an MP, he pleaded at the bar of the House of Commons for the commutation of sentence in cases which had come to his attention and he was a loyal supporter of all efforts to obtain general prison reform.

By the winter of 1804, Attwood was back in New Street to catch up with the bank's rapidly growing business. Only the death of his grandmother, Ann (Haden) Attwood, interrupted this one of the few relatively undisturbed periods of his life. This is not to say that his days were devoid of excitement. The courtship of Elizabeth had been born of passion and never lost its fervour. In addition, his trips on behalf of the bank to other towns continued. One was particularly important to the development of his character.

In April 1805 he was sent on an errand to London. Some East India Company business had proved difficult to complete since that body had not wished to deal directly with a small Birmingham establishment. The personal appearance of one of the partners at the Company's offices had been required and Attwood had welcomed the opportunity to make his first visit to the capital. His time there was generously extended by an injunction to become familiar with the affairs of their London office at Fish Street Hill. It had enjoyed immediate success under the energetic management of Matthias Attwood, Jr, and was rapidly becoming completely independent of the Birmingham connection. Although Attwood's original task went well, London itself proved rather overwhelming. The banking business, he confessed, appeared to be rather more complicated than it was at home and required a rather more rigorous application of rules and regulations in day-to-day transactions. This was particularly important given the type of people with whom one had to deal in the metropolis.

Attwood had encountered the pretensions of the Londoner. Speaking with a strong provincial accent and, in all likelihood, put on the defensive by disparaging remarks respecting Birmingham and "country" people in general, he was an easy mark. For a young man with more than his share of vanity this was insufferable. In consequence he concluded, "Satan seems equally to have taken up his abode in the hearts and appearances of the Londoners." While strolling in Kensington Gardens he had not been able to find a single "tolerable looking woman." He was relieved to return to Birmingham and the "beautiful Elizabeth."[45] Attwood's experiences were not unusual in these war years. Just at the time that the new industrial towns were becoming more self-conscious and sought to have greater control of their own affairs, London was finding fresh reasons to concentrate authority. Differing expectations inevitably created conflict and this, added to the Londoners' penchant for a mocking style of humour, sent many a young man home unhappy and resentful. Attwood probably never quite got over it.

After Trafalgar, 21 October 1805, fears of a French invasion dissipated though few in England were unaware that the day before that naval victory Napoleon had crushed an Austrian army at Ulm. Attwood, to the alarm of Elizabeth, concluded that Napoleon's planned conquest of the world would probably succeed.[46] News from almost every quarter was uniformly bad and he pursued each rumour with morbid interest. It was perhaps fortunate that his marriage to Elizabeth took place on 12 May 1806. Preparations for domesticity occupied his time and in the weeks before marriage he found it difficult to concentrate on anything else.

The wedding was held at Harborne parish church, the ceremony being performed by the bride's brother, the Reverend Edward Carless. They had taken a house, "The Larches," at Sparkbrook, a few miles out of town, and there Attwood settled down contentedly without any apparent ambitions. His first son, George de Bosco, was born on 15 March 1808, and a second, Thomas Aurelius, on 4 March 1810. It is clear that from the start Attwood was a devoted husband and loving father, never happier than when playing with his small sons or engaging in minor improvements to the house and gardens. On one occasion, he built a pond and canal so that the boys could sail their boats. Inevitably, he had to make numerous trips into Birmingham and to The Leasowes, the showplace estate that had become his father's preferred residence, to consult and plan for the future. It may have been these tedious journeys or a desire to be more fully employed which persuaded him to move closer to Birmingham in the spring of 1811. A row of houses, planned on the model of the famous Crescent at Bath but never finished, had been built on the outskirts of the town and the Attwoods bought No. 11. At that time the location was picturesque, being surrounded by orchards and gardens and adjoined by Love's Land, a notable trysting spot which had pleasant memories for Attwood. The change was not welcomed by his wife who preferred the open countryside and sensibly pointed out that the spot would soon be overtaken by the town's accelerating sprawl. However, it did allow more time to be spent together as a family, an advantage which had been emphasized by the severe illness experienced by their infant son, Thomas, the previous autumn.

One topic that generated considerable discussion among the larger family was the decision by Attwood's older brother, Matthias, to seek a seat in the House of Commons. Some promises of support for his candidature had been given should a recent election dispute over the borough of Malden end in the need for a new vote. Attwood was sure that his brother would become the constituents' choice and earnestly canvassed the proposal before sceptical parents. As it turned out, the committee investigating the charges of illegality disappointed them and named C.C. Western as the successful candidate.[47] Matthias had to wait a further twelve years before his ambition could be realized. However, the enthusiasm of Thomas clearly demonstrated his interest in national politics and foreshadowed an appreciation of the advantages of membership in the Commons not evident in his more public speeches at this stage of his career.

Notwithstanding such a fascinating prospect, family business naturally took precedence and both banks, as well as their diverse manufacturing interests, prospered. It is difficult to find details of this expansion, since only indirect and incomplete records have survived. But it is perhaps sufficient to note that despite the continuing war with France and, in particular, the reputedly paralysing economic blockade of Europe, the parent bank increased its own currency circulation to almost £125,000 by 1813, roughly one-quarter of all country notes issued by the town's financial establishments.[48] This evidence of expansion is supported by the bonds, deeds, and notes, dating from this period, that have been found in the firm's surviving strong box. It was also a time to attend to personal fortune. As a private banker Attwood was in an exceedingly favourable position to learn of new opportunities or old failings. Attwoods & Spooner catered to all classes and was renowned for its willingness to take small accounts from artisans and their societies as well as engage in larger undertakings. Using such contacts as well as those of his more affluent friends, Attwood wandered through the workshops and warehouses of the town taking and listening to anyone who might have an idea worth developing or needed additional capital.

He believed for a time that he had found such a man in Benjamin Cook, a gilt "toy" maker. Cook was a tinkerer who could turn his hand to almost anything but was primarily interested in metals. He had taken out his first patent in 1808, a process to make better gun barrels and ramrods. It is impossible to say when the two first met but Attwood began to visit Cook's workshop from the summer of 1810. The following year they patented their first "discovery": a method to produce brass-covered tubing for rods, cornices, and poles.[49] In 1812 a second patent to bind two metals, copper and iron or brass and iron, was granted. Whether this was the result of their own experiments, or had been pirated, is difficult to say. Certainly Sir Edward Thomason's claim that he had invented the method in 1803 but had not bothered to register the idea was later upheld.[50] In any event, there was little profit to be had. Following several more years of experiment, Cook marketed the brass over iron idea successfully but by that time his partner had gone on to other interests. Attwood never gave up his search for profitable new processes but in an increasingly desultory fashion. Only one patent was innovated – a method of fixing calico printing rollers upon a mandrill. Sadly, this project was a dismal failure.[51]

Financial rewards from Attwood's association with Cook never materialized but it did move him out into the wider community and put him into contact with the people who were to be among his most devoted followers in the adventures which were to follow. Often in public speeches he was to refer to these years as the genesis of his concern for an appreciation of the quality of the mechanics and tradesmen of Birmingham. Of the common people he was far less tolerant and had no sympathy at this time for the radical opinions they cheered. It was hardly surprising. In 1810 there were disturbances virtually on the bank's doorstep and on more than one occasion it was fortunate that the headquarters of the military was next door at the Hen and Chickens Hotel. In June 1810 he stayed in town, blunderbuss at the ready, to protect the bank against "a parcel of hungry Burdettites."[52] Such behaviour could, however, be forgiven if weighed against the general good sense of the townsfolk, particularly when they were given "wise leadership and kept employed." Attwood's notion of social harmony, upon which he was to predicate his prescription for national survival, was already half-formed.

The disturbances had been triggered by a rise in wheat prices caused by a series of bad harvests beginning in 1808–9. Initially, these had been offset by high prices in other sections of the economy. However, in the autumn of 1810 several firms trading with South America failed. Commercial problems in the following twelve months multiplied and workers were laid off or saw their wages reduced. As the price of many commodities, with the notable exception of bread, fell, new uncertainties appeared. Birmingham began to worry about the international effects of the continental blockade and feared a possible renewal of the Non-Intercourse Treaty by the United States. As confidence evaporated and distress accumulated, agitation for government action grew. It was in the midst of this rising storm, in October 1811, that Thomas Attwood was elected high bailiff.

CHAPTER TWO

Public Champion

War with France had become commonplace by 1811. Expressions of fear and hope for campaigns past, present, and to come could be heard, but now that the danger of invasion was past, cautionary tales of far-flung places and events were told more for their symbolism and romance than for any information they supplied on the progress of the war. The one exception in regard to this general insensibility concerning public affairs was the economy. Birmingham's fortunes had fluctuated wildly from slump to boom and back again in the wake of policy decisions made by a cabinet whose priority was the defeat of Napoleon and not the individual prosperity of "toy" makers. The industries which had made the greatest advances were those tied most closely to government and consequently subject to each twist in what was rapidly becoming a labyrinth of regulations. Predictably, such control of the economy, even when it implied profit, troubled men accustomed to the benign neglect of a simpler time. The town therefore searched for a means to argue its case at Westminster. The choices were few. Birmingham under the unreformed system of representation was not a separate parliamentary constituency but relied upon the ministrations of members of Parliament elected for the neighbouring counties; men whose first allegiance was to the great landowning families that often found Birmingham's frenetic business activity distasteful. The only avenue for "respectable" protest was the time-honoured rights of petition and lobby.[1] The method, on one occasion, had proved to have some merit. In 1806 Birmingham persuaded the government to abandon a projected tax of £2 a ton on pig iron – the single most important commodity in the town's economy.[2] But usually such requests went unheeded.[3]

Two questions were topics of discussion in 1811 – the Orders-in-Council of 1807 regarding trade with the continent of Europe, and the terms of the East Indian Company's charter. The first was clearly related to the economic difficulties under which the town, in company with the nation at large, was labouring. The second involved a long history of grievance and the occasion of the need for a renewal of the charter in 1813 had been eagerly anticipated. In the pursuit of change the high bailiff, the man with the authority to designate any gathering as an official town meeting, acquired additional status.

Appointment to the highest public office had not been a mark of any particular esteem but rather a matter of routine. The choice of Thomas Attwood in October was unexceptional. Arguments that he must have been working assiduously in the pursuit of some untold ambition known only to his peers is mistaken and owes more to the late Victorian view of authority than knowledge of early nineteenth-century Birmingham. As the reputation of a bank and its owners grows, the individuals intimately connected with its operation almost of necessity gravitate towards the source of power, particularly where no "ancient" hierarchy exists. Attwood was a familiar figure in a community where personal contact among the inhabitants was highly valued. His surname alone guaranteed respect in its connotations of wealth and power. A clutch of relations – one uncle, Pratchett, was an influential town commissioner, chairman of the Board of Finance notwithstanding a recent scandal, and had been high bailiff in 1804 – and family friends, not least of whom were the Spooners, assured him of support whenever it was needed. Incurably gregarious by nature, he had been an enthusiastic participant in the coffee shop and tap room debates. His position as a trusted agent in all matters financial kept him close to the daily routine of town management.

Proof of such involvement may be found in the inclusion of his name on a committee to investigate the desirability of a municipal waterworks in 1806 and, two years later, among the commissioners authorized under a new Improvement Act to build a market and to repair the roads.[4] But it is more likely that instead of seeking prominence Attwood was pitchforked into the position. The office had very little real authority yet the task of administration was time-consuming. The list of bailiffs, high and low, contains only the occasional head of family and business. By far the majority were the sons of successful men or were men unusually anxious to establish a position. Most came and went causing scarcely a ripple in Birmingham's pool of self-sufficiency. The prominence Attwood was to attain was in no small measure the result of his own response and the needs of the moment. His first "hour of adventure" added lustre to the office but its long-term significance must be seen in its effect on him rather than on local government.

Attwood dealt daily across the counter of the bank with merchants and manufacturers worried about the current decline in trade both with the continent and with America. Not content with simple cause-and-effect argument based on experience or hearsay he had been sufficiently interested to read widely. Bits and pieces of many eighteenth-century philosophers and political economists, including Adam Smith, surfaced in the speeches he was to make over the following eighteen months. Much of the material used, sometimes misused, was undigested and he had not quite arrived at the stage of thinking critically – that would come later – but his curiosity cannot be denied. He was fortunate in that the first months of tenure were comparatively uneventful, so that he could take every opportunity to discuss the issues with anyone who offered an opinion. Many hours were spent with Richard Spooner, his closest friend. On most questions their assessment of the evidence was identical and thus mutually reinforcing. More aware than their fathers of the growing pretensions of London, of the ability of politicians to distribute favours, and of their willingness to destroy provincial ambition, they determined that virtually any label or cause should be adopted if it promised to be in what they considered to be the town's best interests.[5] Spooner tended to be the more vehement, particularly when called upon to make a declaration of faith, while Attwood liked to qualify proposals with the phrase "compatible with national honour." But both took for their inspiration Birmingham itself. By the spring of 1812, believing that they represented a new and better England, they were ready to give a lead.

Since their promulgation in a somewhat hasty response to Napoleon's attempt to shut Britain out of Europe (the Berlin-Milan Decrees, 1806–7), the value of the Orders-in-Council had been disputed. The disagreement concerned their impact upon Anglo-American trade rather than that with the European continent. The United States, resenting British interference in her lucrative carrying trade, had instituted a number of non-importation controls. Birmingham's trade had suffered and attempts to substitute commercial links with South America and elsewhere had proved disastrous.[6] After three years, the Americans reestablished normal relations by passing Macon's Act in 1810. The only qualification seemed harmless enough: if either France or Britain repealed its regulations, the United States would suspend trade with the remaining offender unless it followed suit within three months. However, in August, the French, aware that Macon's Act favoured Britain, announced their intention to revoke the Berlin-Milan decrees in so far as they affected the Americans and demanded that the sanctions against their enemy be applied. When Britain procrastinated, the United States Congress concluded that it had no option and on 2 February 1811 passed a non-importation act. The effects in Britain had been felt almost immediately. Trade was already depressed; the effect of Napoleon's successes in Austria and Northern Germany had been to close the continent to British goods.

Throughout the summer and autumn of 1811 opposition to the government's refusal to meet the Americans' requests had gathered support across the country.[7] Henry Brougham, an ambitious Whig who sought to capitalize on the general discontent and antiwar sentiment to discomfit the ruling Tories, was both sponsor and coordinator. His argument, carefully promoted through the Whig newspaper, the *Morning Chronicle,* was simple: injury to the United States was no way to defeat France.[8] The government countered by calling such claims self-serving and stressed the need for sustained economic warfare.

At the counter of Attwoods & Spooner, the talk had been about war, but not with France. For some months the American correspondents of Birmingham's merchants had warned that war with their country was inevitable unless the British government moderated its policy. Opinion in the town was divided. Some were anxious to join Brougham but others, including many of the most influential, believed that in this instance the government knew best. The latter group preferred to concentrate on the chance of a withdrawal of the East India Company's charter as a means of relieving the distress. The debate in the town was duplicated in the drawing-rooms of the bank's younger partners. Richard Spooner supported both options and was for joining Brougham, but Attwood, while agreeing with his friend's analysis of the principles at stake, vacillated on the actual question of the Orders-in-Council. He admired the Americans and viewed Westminster's insistence on the right of search to be an unnecessary provocation. He accepted his friend's argument that the United States might learn to do without Birmingham's ironware as the pace of her industrialization accelerated under wartime pressure. However, the war with France continued and with no immediate prospect of victory it seemed folly to abandon a policy which utilized British economic strength even if it did involve "temporary" suffering. Therefore he somewhat reluctantly reserved his position.

Attwood's and Spooner's disagreement as to an appropriate response was a reflection of the confusion in Birmingham. As no consensus could be reached, an extraparochial organization, the Inland Commercial Committee, founded in 1783 but moribund for some years, was resurrected by the activists, one of whose leaders was Spooner, to do something about the Orders.[9] They met privately on 24 February 1812 and decided to press ahead with a petition without the official blessing of the traditional agency of such initiatives – a town meeting.[10] The document was to be carried to London by a deputation led by Richard Spooner. Attwood had been busy counselling caution. He reminded his partner of his own visits to the capital and his responsibility to the bank. But Spooner refused to be intimidated and left in high hopes of winning major concessions.

The deputies met the prime minister, Spencer Perceval, on 2 March.[11] Upon his return, Spooner gave his partner a detailed report. As was to be expected, Perceval had been courteous but unhelpful and the petition had achieved nothing. Nevertheless, Brougham had praised their efforts and urged that their activities in Birmingham be redoubled; it seemed clear from a vote in the Commons that support for the government on the issue was weakening. Would the high bailiff call a town meeting if presented with a requisition? As it happened, Attwood had already given a commitment to do exactly that. It was a promise that had not been lightly made. When Spooner brought up the subject before his departure, Attwood had not known how to respond. In some respects such agreement was automatic but the continuing opposition to the endeavour put him in a difficult position. At Liverpool, the mayor was to refuse a similar request on the somewhat suspect grounds that "the peace of the town might be disturbed."[12] Whatever Attwood's choice, there would be repercussions. Nevertheless, he had pledged to comply if the Inland Committee's approach failed. On Spooner's return he quickly honoured that promise. Two factors were responsible for the speed of his decision. Spooner's tales of government indifference to Birmingham's pleas had annoyed him. In particular, the fatuous analogy offered by George Rose, vice-president of the Board of Trade, that "we are like two men with our heads in a bucket of water and we must see who can stand the drowning the longer," suggested that all and any proposals to "educate" ministers should be supported.[13] Of greater importance, though, were the needs of his own thrust against complacency – the attack on the East India Company's charter.

Although Attwood had not become involved with the Inland Committee, he did agree that something had to be done if Birmingham was to enjoy prosperity again. While the artificial depression of the American market accounted for the decline in the metal trades, an admittedly important branch of Birmingham's industrial base, "everyone" could see that the recession was general. In debate with Spooner, Attwood had professed to take the long view. Production appeared to have surpassed the demands of the usual markets even when the dislocation caused by war had been discounted. Efforts to open new areas had met with disaster – the failure to sell ice skates to the Brazilians and the lack of eager consumers among the rocks of Heligoland in 1808 were particularly painful memories. According to the "authorities" Attwood had read, the Far East seemed a much more likely prospect for expansion. Unfortunately, the way was barred by the monopoly privileges of the East India Company; a company, it was argued, that had little interest in an export trade.[14] In contrast to the American issue there was little disagreement on this point in the town. Indeed, no one was disposed to challenge any part of Attwood's interpretation. He was considered the local expert on the subject, having attended meetings in London and read most of the pamphlets and reports of parliamentary speeches.

In fact, much of the material he quoted reveals his naiveté rather than expertise. Attwood had absorbed various blocks of information but still had not got to the stage of independent analysis. He accepted the "facts" of the major opponents of the company, including Lord Valentia and Sir George Staunton, as readily as the principles of Adam Smith.[15] Thus he repeated Staunton's claim that "Pekin alone would consume all the cutlery manufactured in Sheffield." The size of the populations of India and China beguiled Attwood, as it did many others, into believing these travellers' tales; the error would be discovered later. In the spring of 1812, however, the appearance of wisdom was sufficient. Attwood was anxious to launch a campaign of his own which could claim to represent the constituency of Birmingham. For that he needed support. Spooner and one or two others had to be persuaded to circulate a requisition to which he, as high bailiff, could respond. It was at this point that he found he could not ignore Spooner's appeal, particularly as the plan obviously contained a great deal of merit. Clearly it was essential that the North American market be reopened and, if properly conducted, the campaigns could be considered complementary. Upon this basis of agreement Spooner complied with Attwood's request for a requisition and Attwood reciprocated by agreeing to honour a similar application to debate the Orders-in-Council at a later date if it could be shown that the campaign had some hope of success. It was this commitment that was largely responsible for his decision to call a town meeting on the Orders-in-Council.

Attwood was given his chance to catch the attention of the town on 4 March 1812. Spooner hurried back from London to join him on the platform but kept silent as his partner made the most of his opportunity. Attwood's address was quiet and coherent, reflecting careful preparation. Some twenty of the principal manufacturers had been canvassed; all had reported full stocks but no orders. Upon this hard evidence of adversity he wove a superficially convincing argument which mixed current free trade principles with accusations of duplicity against the East India Company and fables of the riches of the East; all were buttressed by figures sketching the extent of American and Dutch trade with the region and the smuggling ability of the Chinese. The Orders-in-Council were not mentioned but to the displeasure of Spooner there was an exhortation to abjure economic panaceas which cast a "stain on the honour of England." The revocation of the charter was stressed as an "honourable" alternative. His speech was received rapturously.[16] To his own surprise, he had shown considerable skill with the spoken word. He was not yet an "orator" but, as he was to admit to his wife, the response had been flattering.[17]

A committee was appointed "to inquire into any measure that might be brought forward and to co-operate with other towns." Attwood drew up two petitions and wrote to other towns asking for support. The task at first did not seem difficult, since a petitioning movement had already begun in Liverpool, Bristol, Plymouth, Hull, Glasgow, and Sheffield. Unhappily, only the last-named shared Attwood's conception of the problem; the others were chiefly concerned with their commercial and shipping rivalry with London rather than the export market *per se*.[18] They wished to see the lucrative import trade with the Far East released to private merchants. Unknown to Attwood the directors of the East India Company had already accepted the inevitability of relaxation in the export trade to India; his battle was partially won before it had even begun. However, the Company assumed that the import trade would remain in the hands of London and negotiated with the government on that basis.[19]

Attwood organized a group to present the petitions and to speak for Birmingham. Before he could leave for London, however, there was the matter of the town meeting for Spooner. Attwood sat as chairman on 31 March but reserved his opinion. Spooner's speech differed from his own, given almost four weeks before, in that it was more emotional, but the substance had been discussed at some length at the bank and in each other's homes. Spooner's rhetoric of concern for the continued prosperity of Birmingham and the sentiment that the government failed to appreciate the contribution of the manufacturing industry to the wealth of the nation were common complaints which Attwood had already aired. Also, given his own plans to "attack" London, he enthusiastically applauded Spooner's demand that the voice of Birmingham must be heard "at the bar of the House of Commons."[20]

It was only when Spooner hinted at parliamentary reform that Attwood began to squirm. At this time political radicalism worried Attwood. His unease was compounded by a speech from the floor; George Villiers, a county magistrate, harangued the crowd on the subject of the "honour of the country." Villiers was shouted down and the meeting almost slipped out of control. It had been a chastening experience and Attwood later privately sympathized with an advertisement carried in the *Morning Chronicle*, signed by 167 respectable men, including Richard Spooner's father, Isaac, which deplored the whole affair.[21] His wife, a natural conservative, was pleased to learn that while willing to lend "assistance to the advocates of repeal in the form of advice in the drawing up of their petitions" and by "presiding over their deliberations," he had reserved all personal commitment.[22] It was with no small measure of relief that Attwood left for Westminster with his reputation for patriotism unsullied.

Attwood discovered on arrival that his speech in Birmingham had been reprinted in several London newspapers and copies had been sold on the Exchange. Friends assured him that it had been seen by members of the cabinet and had had "a great effect." In recognition of his prominence and the fact that he was one of the few Tories involved, he was made chairman of the committee of delegates appointed to meet with the government; an appointment which flattered him but angered Elizabeth, who felt that he should have been given overall responsibility as general chairman (that honour was awarded to the provost of Glasgow).[23] Attwood was soon at work lobbying MPs and making the rounds of the social circuit. In this he was aided by Spooner who had provided introductions to a cross-section of London society through his sister, Barbara, the wife of "little William Wilberforce," and the recently ennobled Calthorpes. The business of persuasion is seldom simple but the salons were an agreeable diversion and he thoroughly enjoyed the recognition and acceptance that his speech had won for him.

For several weeks the delegates directed a stream of propaganda at Parliament. Neither Attwood nor his friends apparently realized that in the earl of Buckinghamshire, president of the Board of Trade and the government's chief negotiator with the Company, they had a powerful ally.[24] They were aware only of the enmity and influence of the London merchants.[25] As late as 24 April Attwood confessed that he still had no idea what the prime minister intended. The only promise his committee had obtained was that the government would bring forward its resolutions "in a few days."[26] Eventually Buckinghamshire told the Company that the government would accept nothing less than the freeing of the import and export of trade of India and perhaps of China too.[27] The deputies were jubilant and Attwood spoke for them all when he boasted they had "gained everything but the China trade and I have no doubt that we shall gather that in the end."[28] Two days later the news was even better: "Ministers have, at length, determined to side with us against the India Co. and are now settling with them for the Company to possess a monopoly of *Tea* only, leaving everything else open to the country."[29] His reading was accurate; only the day before the chairman of the court of the East India Company informed the proprietors that the "negotiations had taken an ominous turn."[30] The only restrictions Perceval intended to propose hinged on the political safety of India and the "the collection of his Majesty's Revenue." On 9 May a definite promise was given that both the export and import trades in India would be thrown open to the British outports. A decision on China would be reserved until a select committee, to be appointed shortly, had reported.[31]

Attwood's contribution to what had transpired cannot be assessed as there is very little evidence to be found on the subject anywhere. He subsequently claimed a leading role but this cannot be substantiated. Huskisson, for example, whom Attwood extravagantly praised and apparently met on several occasions, makes no reference to such meetings in his private correspondence. It is true that Birmingham, under Attwood's guidance, acted before the majority of other interested towns, and his speech was quoted widely, although not always for complimentary reasons. Once in London, only his letters and his position as chairman of the negotiating committee suggest that he was at the head of affairs.

Most nonpartisan reports attribute leadership at this stage in the proceedings to Brackenbury and the outports. Incredibly, one historian of the East India Company, Phillips, even names Spooner and not Attwood as the leading representative from Birmingham.[32] This identification can be safely dismissed; Spooner was a member of the deputation and stayed in London after Attwood left but he certainly was not the town's spokesman. However, an error of this sort does suggest that whoever spoke it was not the voice of Birmingham that was dominant in the discussions over coffee. Attwood himself inadvertently adds weight to this conclusion. Whereas he had journeyed to London to seek the freedom of the East for the town's products, he quickly became converted to the outports' contention that the trade would not be viable unless all aspects of the monopoly were rescinded.[33] But the experience and his role in the affair did have a profound personal effect. He had been placed, for the first time, in contact with MPs and leaders of opinion from around the country. These meetings confirmed for him the relative merit of his own town and the validity of his own judgment grounded as it was in "honest" business practice. The obvious corollary is that what went on in London was, for the most part, dishonest. It was a conclusion that he never found reason to change.

While Attwood had been in London there had been trouble in Birmingham. Unemployed and hungry workers had assembled in the streets each evening from 20 April to listen to "agitators inciting riot."[34] The magistrates attempted to placate the people by ensuring that the town's markets were well stocked and prices were fair. Nevertheless, there had been several disturbances in the market place, particularly respecting the high price of potatoes; a concern which illustrates the straits to which the poor were reduced (the consumption of that root was a last resort) and indicates that the town's considerable Irish population had been involved. Pamphleteers and orators alike across the country blamed the Orders-in-Council for the distress. The government's initial response to the disorder, which had not been peculiar to Birmingham and had flared across the country, was provocative. It issued a proclamation that declared the Orders would be revoked only if the French first withdrew the Berlin and Milan decrees.[35] Continued disorder, however, forced a change of mind and the Commons turned itself into a committee of the whole House to hear evidence on the question. Attwood was the leading spokesman of Birmingham by right of office; he was also conveniently in

London. On 29 April he was called to give his testimony as to the economy of the town.

The high bailiff was to prove one of the least interesting witnesses from Birmingham, since, as he readily admitted, his primary concern was the East India monopoly. His replies to questions were factual or extremely circuitous.[36] They could not have advanced the repeal case materially, notwithstanding the questioning which lasted, on his own estimation, from two to three hours. A similar session before the House of Lords followed and he departed for home on 4 May. A parade of Birmingham's manufacturers and merchants, probably gathered by Spooner, followed during the rest of the week.[37] Each attested to the decline in his fortunes and to the distress of the workingman. The problem, all agreed, lay in Birmingham's dependence on the American trade.[38] The witnesses involved were naturally concerned with the immediate amelioration of their difficulties, but many further indicated that they were aware of the wider implications of their dilemma: implications which had been exemplified in Attwood's anti-charter arguments. In the years since 1807 Birmingham's productive capacity had grown while her traditional markets had remained static or had been cut away completely. The government had to recognize the existence of the new industrial sector of the economy and include its needs in any assessment of policy.

The evidence offered by Birmingham's deputies was greeted with derision by most of London's newspapers and politicians.[39] In spite of these adverse reactions, the number of delegations in London and petitions presented at Westminster multiplied. Daily meetings were held at the King's Arms Tavern, New Palace Yard, to plan strategy and to compare notes.[40] It was not until 16 June that Brougham's motion to rescind the Orders came before the House.[41] The House of Commons was not called upon to vote. Instead, Lord Liverpool declared that the government had decided to "suspend the Orders-in-Council" and to enter into discussions with America.[42] Six days later, the prince regent, acting in Council, revoked the offending regulations.[43] But the initiative was too late to stop the outbreak of war with the United States. The ships bearing the respective news crossed in mid-Atlantic. War did not, however, inhibit the resumption of trade.[44]

The return of Birmingham's deputation on 1 July became an excuse for a carnival. A crowd of some thirty thousand, led by an elected committee and the bands of two regiments of Warwickshire militia, marched down the London road to meet the deputies. In a scene which was to set a precedent the horses were removed from the carriage and the coach was carried into town. At Attwoods & Spooner the procession halted long enough to cheer Attwood who had appeared at the bank's window.[45]

Throughout the celebration no one evinced the slightest doubt regarding the identity of the instigator of the town's success. Richard Spooner received the accolades of both fellow-citizens and speakers at dinners further afield.[46] Yet, in the years which followed, the name of Thomas Attwood became attached to the campaign.[47] He came to believe it himself, and in a masterly piece of self-deception said, "I began the war against the American Orders-in-Council. I saw their abolition."[48] The confusion may be attributed to a number of related incidents that inevitably associated Attwood with every activity pursued by the town in 1812. As high bailiff it had been his responsibility to convene all meetings held on "important" questions. In addition to those respecting the charter and the Orders-in-Council, there had been meetings of the more affluent citizens to organize relief measures to alleviate distress.[49] In reports of their efforts, the name most prominent had inevitably been Attwood's. To his credit, he was certainly more willing to call such meetings than had been his predecessors. Moreover, in the majority of instances he had pursued the objectives of the requisitionists energetically.[50] With respect to the Orders-in-Council there was also a more important point. By chance Attwood had been the first witness called and his evidence received national publicity. Many newspapers quoted his testimony in full.[51] Once the novelty had gone, tales of distress were less newsworthy and only digests appeared.

Late in May a "mechanic" wrote to the *Midland Chronicle* suggesting that a meeting of artisans be held to convey their gratitude to those who had contributed to the relief of the poor and were then exerting themselves in London.[52] This had been followed by a meeting on 17 June at the Shakespear Tavern. Among the resolutions were two alluding directly to Attwood. They first offered the mechanics' "unfeigned thanks" for his valuable services to "the Cause." A second resolved that a "subscription be immediately entered into to defray the expense of a piece of silver plate, with a suitable inscription, to be presented unto him ... no person shall be allowed to give more than sixpence."[53] Considering Attwood's contribution to the well-being of the town, the award was not unjust; as a token of appreciation for services in the struggle against the Orders-in-Council, however, it should have gone to Spooner.

The high bailiff was not unaware of the injustice and accused his friend and fellow-inventor, Benjamin Cook, of promoting the business. Cook, who was later to write and publish a poem eulogizing Attwood's attack on the East India Company's charter, rejected responsibility although he did admit that he had been consulted. The thanks of the mechanics, he emphasized, were for Attwood's efforts on behalf of the poor, especially in regard to the relief measures he had initiated.[54] On this understanding, Attwood accepted the gift.[55] But commentators have refused to separate the two questions and Attwood's name became inextricably woven into the legend of the Orders-in-Council. His own conversion to the myth is less easy to excuse. It may stem from the disappointment he suffered in all his future efforts. He could look back on the piece of plate as the only mark of gratitude that he had ever received. Spooner never bothered to disagree because as he grew older he became increasingly conservative and did not care to be reminded of the "follies" of his youth.

With the battle against the government won, the towns and outports settled down to a round of self-congratulatory dinners.[56] There was also anger, for the witnesses remembered the indignities to which they had been subjected. They had been genuinely distressed by accusations of simple-mindedness made by the London press and parliamentarians.[57] The resentment was forcefully expressed at a town meeting by both Attwood and Spooner. The former abandoned his earlier caution to attack the entire policy of the cabinet and urged that peace be the primary consideration for diplomatic activity. It was a dangerous suggestion indicative of the depth of Attwood's alienation. His faith in the sagacity of the legislature had never been strong and, along with everyone else, personal contact had shattered any remaining illusions: "Such a set of feeble mortals as the members of both Houses are I never did expect to meet within this world. The best among them are scarce equal to the worst in Birmingham."[58] This disenchantment marked the genesis of Attwood's conception that an efficient House of Commons could only be achieved if it included practical men of business. It was the beginning of a tentative conversion to the ranks of the parliamentary reformers.

As might be expected, once trade began to revive, war-weariness dropped away. Wellington's success at Salamanca in July brought patriotism back into fashion.[59] Only one question remained to be settled to the satisfaction of the manufacturers – the East India Company charter. As one of his last acts as high bailiff, Attwood wrote to the prime minister, Lord Liverpool, reminding him of the agreements reached with his murdered predecessor.[60] Attwood warned that the ministers were surrounded by the enemies of the manufacturing interest, which was itself too far removed form London to advocate its cause. Using arguments which foreshadowed those adopted in his pamphlets on the currency question four years later, Attwood sought to convince by raising the spectre of enraged public opinion.[61] To his chagrin, Liverpool was too busy to reply. However, Buckinghamshire had been active, threatening the court of directors of the East India Company with legislation which would free trade and authorize the government to assume the administration of India. When the news of his ultimatum reached the provinces the forces of the previous spring began to regroup and then hurried to London to bolster the government's resolve. Attwood, with the collusion of Spooner, whose succession to the office of high bailiff underlined the new alignment in local politics, requisitioned a town meeting.

The decision to reenter the lists had not been taken lightly. Elizabeth Attwood had been annoyed by her husband's activity and was not at all pleased with his speech in August. At the time she had been in the late stages of her pregnancy and, although she did not lack for attentive relatives, preferred to see more of her husband. As it was her third child it did not promise to be a difficult birth but nothing of this nature could ever be taken for granted. Elizabeth misread his determination. Once something had been begun, he was invariably resolved to see it completed. During the Christmas holiday, he and Spooner drafted a speech. They now agreed on all points, Attwood proving as radical as his partner.

At the meeting on 8 January 1813, Attwood's argument mixed the theoretical framework of the *Wealth of Nations* with banker's gossip in a repetition of much of what he had said some twelve months before.[62] Unbounded national prosperity and moral regeneration in the Birmingham image were the rewards for the country if the government revoked the charter. To underpin such speculative predictions he drew on the residue of antipathy left from the struggles of 1812. The port of London with its "immense and corrupt" population had been joined by City interests in "outraging every principle of public justice and reason." He ended on the note with which he had concluded his letter to Liverpool, "woe unto the men that shall trifle with the people now." The audience gave him a thunderous ovation. But when Attwood went to London he travelled alone; with reviving trade most businessmen believed that politics could again be left to the politicians.[63]

Attwood remained in London for a little over three weeks. Information was as difficult to acquire as ever. MPs seemed to take a perverse delight in promising everything but doing nothing. Commitments made by those whom Attwood had canvassed had a habit of disappearing like smoke at the slightest puff of a contrary wind. Often he would wearily finish an evening at Matthias's house to vent his frustration with some new tale of duplicity. If these "representatives of the people" had behaved in such a shameful way in Birmingham they would have soon been driven from business. Members of Parliament had little regard for honour; only the possibility of public humiliation "binds public men to any principles of political integrity."[64] He was willing to exempt Wilberforce and Babbington because they had been busy promoting the case for Christian missions to India and their dedication appealed to his Anglican sense of duty. Otherwise, only the occasional dinner with Spooner's relative, the duke of Norfolk, and time spent watching Cobbett and Hunt (whom Attwood thought very clever) plead their petition against the Bristol election enlivened a tedious task.[65] Playing with Matthias's son, Wolverly, "Woovey" to his uncle, was a much more agreeable pastime. The problems experienced at Westminster stemmed exclusively from the general lack of information regarding the ministerial propositions. Negotiations were in progress and the charter was under attack; beyond this Attwood knew nothing. At the beginning of March, disgruntled, he returned home.

On 20 May Attwood finally received a noncommittal letter from Lord Liverpool acknowledging his earlier enquiries.[66] Although it did not please him, Attwood recognized that for it to be written at all hinted that the negotiations between government and Company had reached a critical stage. Thereafter events moved rapidly. From friends in London, he heard that Castlereagh had asked that the parade of witnesses cease.[67] The final outcome allowed the Company to keep the administration of India and a monopoly of the China trade; elsewhere, "all licensed merchants" were given unrestricted freedom to buy and sell.[68] It was a compromise which seemed to satisfy everyone. The directors of the Company were pleased to have retained more than they had expected.[69] The outports and manufacturing towns were disappointed to lose China but retired in good heart. Attwood subsequently claimed outright victory.

The campaigns of 1812–13 had pulled Birmingham into the mainstream of British political life and the encounter had left an indelible impression. These were the formative years in the growth of the town's sense of identity, though not as dramatic as the 1790s[70] The twin campaigns had thrown up dynamic leaders who straddled the political spectrum and causes with which the majority could sympathize. For some twenty years after, the events of these few months were used as examples of the power of organized public opinion and those who led subsequent assaults on Westminster sought to duplicate the methods then learned. Even at times of greatest polarization between Radical and Tory, for example in 1816 and again in 1819, there were those who sought in Birmingham to transcend "arbitrary" divisions as had been done in 1812–13. For Attwood, the reversal of government policy which followed the Orders-in-Council battle and the new charter reinforced his confidence in the powers of perception of businessmen and the validity of their "knowledge" of the nation's best interest. He was to evolve a coherent theory of economic behaviour from his understanding of sound business practice. Spooner took it upon himself to campaign in Warwickshire for a parliamentary seat, using the slogan "Birmingham and independence." As the years passed, Spooner enhanced his reputation as a Tory and Attwood wandered into radicalism. Between these extremes all shades of the political and social spectrum could be found in the town. But pride in Birmingham and the certainty that the town was a match for any other, especially London, overrode party and religious preferences. It was on the basis of this spirited conviction that Attwood was to build his public career.

CHAPTER THREE

Great Expectations

Thomas Attwood's quiet return in the spring of 1813 marked a temporary retirement from public duty. The unpaid stewardship he had exercised for twelve months had caused some neglect of personal fortune. The final drive to defeat Napoleon, which had the industries of war, from guns to nails, working twenty-four hours a day, offered an opportunity to redress that recklessness.¹ The affairs of the bank naturally commanded his immediate attention, but the prospects for speculation created by inflationary pressures of the period were not overlooked as he became preoccupied with the task of making money. He was not the best example of the sober businessman, ruined by the postwar deflationary policies of the Bank of England, whom he was to picture in his various works on the economy after the war.

The demand for iron and coal in 1813 encouraged him to buy an estate in partnership with Spooner; subsequently it was leased to an ironmaster named Fereday. It was bought with cash loaned by their own bank at a nominal interest rate. This was common enough practice among private bankers but it was one which contributed to an incredible expansion in the money supply and general inflation in these years. The bank must have been grossly over-extended, the assets/liabilities ratio was appalling, but there seemed little cause for concern.² Even the use of "accommodation bills," receipts for fictitious transactions, among the ironmasters in the surrounding district, produced only irritation and a self-administered injunction to be more careful. Given the behaviour of the partners themselves, caution was the last virtue likely to be observed. Attwood, in retrospect, recognized their errors but consoled himself with the thought that "honest" business had far outstripped that which could be called "speculative." His own purchase adjoined mines that belonged to his wife's family and contained proven ores; Fereday mined both.[3] This money-making scheme was relatively successful but he gained few returns from a multitude of others.

Banking in two centres and the inevitable tangles of business at the gallop forced the younger partners of Attwoods & Spooner to travel extensively during the next two years. Attwood hated the travelling, the unending round of meetings, and "ill-natured" jockeying for economic advantage. Only the chance to inspect more closely their growing London business in Gracechurch Street – the bank had moved the few hundred yards from Fish Street Hill in 1812 – made the separation from his wife even mildly bearable.

The coming of peace in 1814 presaged an end to the war-induced boom in Birmingham as it did for the rest of the country. The speed of the collapse came as a particular shock, shattering a widely held conviction of the buoyancy of the town's industries.[4] This conviction stemmed from the belief that the end of the flow of government money for the armaments industry would be more than compensated by the opening of previously closed markets. Pride in the efficiency of their division of labour techniques offset the manufacturers' expectation of difficulties that might be encountered in the transfer of productive power from one sphere to another. Enormous capital investment, it was argued, was not a prerequisite of Birmingham's entrepreneurs; skill resided in the worker, not in the machines. Special cases were made for industries with higher fixed charges and high ratios of fixed to circulating capital in the surrounding districts. Their boasts were not idle. Visitors to the town were often astonished that the creation of comparatively simple items passed through so many hands. The addition of steam power to relatively small workshops added enormously to productivity and even the most humble clerk appeared to have a knowledge of complex technology.[5] Change was a challenge, not a threat.

Trade did recover in the summer of 1815 as a speculative foreign trade was developed, not for the first or the last time, to replace those industries which had been geared to the war effort. Goods were shipped to Europe but it was soon discovered that the war-ravaged continent was unable to buy. A second and precipitous decline followed. In twelve months, the business of Attwoods & Spooner was halved and their position became so precarious as to force the sale of exchequer bills, bearing 5 per cent, at a discount and the refusal of cash advances on all mortgages.[6] Others had no such "easy" options and collapsed. Bankruptcies averaged 147 a week in 1815 and 179 in 1816.

The Tory government had anticipated that the return to a peacetime economy would be difficult, but its early attempts to endure a smooth transition were defeated in Parliament.[7] Economists and advisers to political factions preferred to focus on the twin pillars of successful politics, "Retrenchment and Reform." Vansittart's proposal, for example, to retain the property tax at a reduced 5 per cent was soundly defeated. As he had feared, the additional purchasing power left in the hands of the landed classes by the complete removal of the tax substituted inadequately for the loss of block expenditure by government. The army estimates, which proposed a plan of phased demobilization, met with the same fate. The legislation that was passed tended to deepen the difficulties, at least as the populace in general perceived them. The Corn Laws, designed to keep up the price of wheat and to succour the farmers, had been approved by parliamentarians protected by troops from their constituents. The most serious blow to the economy, however, was the decision by government and the Bank of England to honour their pledge of 1811 by returning to the gold standard.[8]

Attwood had watched the decline in the economy with astonishment. At a dinner held to celebrate the peace only a few months earlier, he had spoken optimistically about Birmingham's future. The bank's general level of lending had been continued, since both he and Richard Spooner daily expected a government initiative to alleviate the "present difficulties." Nevertheless, both knew that if the drive towards the resumption of cash (specie) payments were maintained the country banks would be forced to reduce their own note issues. This curtailment of credit would make economic recovery even more difficult to attain.

His sense of unease was strengthened when several deputations of workers sought his help on the strength of past services and promises. They wanted him to participate in the foundation of a Hampden Club in the town and in the preparation of a petition to be sent to Brougham which attacked the Corn Laws.[9] He "refused to listen to the vain delusions under which they laboured."[10] Such initiatives were useless in his opinion because they failed to address the real source of the distress. The remedy lay not in politics but in economics. Moreover, given the current unrest, a political response could be dangerous.[11] In these years his injunctions in letters and pamphlets to the government to fear an angry populace expressed his own anxiety; only in 1830, after fifteen years of frustration, were the words used as a threat.

His first step in the accomplishment of what he thought would be a simple task was a letter to Lord Liverpool advocating an immediate issue of Bank of England notes or exchequer bills as the "most immediate palliative to the country's suffering."[12] Such an issue had been made in 1793, a year, in Attwood's opinion, which bore striking similarities to 1816, and had "acted like a charm."[13] His letter was ignored. Exasperated, he concluded that "honest advice" had been countered by the same kind of ill-natured arguments which had enveloped London in a cocoon of self-interest in 1812. Angrily, he abandoned private exhortation and sought public notice by writing letters to the editors of London newspapers which occasionally aired the theories of other economists. Again he was disappointed. This left only one option, private publication. Late in 1816 a small printing house in the town produced a short pamphlet for him, *The Remedy; or, Thoughts on the Present Distress*.

A venture into the public realm with one's own view of economic theory had become common. Political economy, as it was labelled, had become a popular pastime and there seemed to be few qualifications necessary for the adoption of the title economist. Attwood was, in fact not without credentials. Practical experience as a banker and entrepreneur in one of the leading centres of industry in the country was an obvious advantage. He was also extremely well read. His interest in the academic aspects of financial policy had first been aroused by the Commons' debate on the Bullion Committee's report in 1810. The report had demanded an immediate return to the gold standard which had been abandoned in 1797. It was argued that inflation could not be contained without such a regulator. Attwood disagreed. In later life he was to claim that it had been the lack of expertise demonstrated by self-proclaimed scholars which had encouraged him to think independently and had led him to use his knowledge of country banking as a standard against which their speculations could be tested. He had been fortunate in having relatives and friends who found the subject equally fascinating. Many a weary day spent in fruitless argument with smug parliamentarians in London in 1812 and 1813 had been redeemed by energetic discussions with his brother Matthias. At home Richard Spooner had been a most welcome visitor, always ready to examine evidence of interest rate variation or the efficiency of note redemption practices. On the strength of such deliberations, Attwood had become concerned by the direction taken by debate in the Commons with its emphasis upon the so-called independence of the regulator abandoned in 1797, gold. Only the neglect of the Bullion Committee's recommendations by a cabinet anxious to win the war with Napoleon allayed those fears, but, aware of the power of "ill-natured lobbyists," he remained alert.

When Britain slipped into economic crisis in 1815 and the number of explanations was legion, he was ready with a coherent thesis of his own. The management of the economy was the responsibility of Parliament. The Bank of England was merely its handmaiden. In his first pamphlet, therefore, and in seven others published by 1819 he blamed cabinet decisions for all ills. The depression had been created by "cessation of government demand, the failure to spend most of the funds saved by those whose tax burdens had been lightened and the consequent collapse of prices." While not interested in debts and the difficulties of wealth transfer, he offered the important insight that a reduction in taxes could be and was, in 1816, deflationary in the short term. Where government expenditure had been a major contributor to total economic output a fall in tax revenue would cause a decline in business activity. The economy was not so flexible that, without help, the private sector could immediately find the resources to reemploy those dismissed from the government's war-related industries. His remedy was to maintain or even to raise the level of prices by further cabinet action, "to legislate for the benefit of the quick, and not solely for the relatively dead." By so doing the productive elements in the community might be given the incentive to use their reduced taxation burden for the benefit of the nation as a whole.[14]

This call for intervention in the market place by the creation of "money" through the sale of exchequer bills was in direct opposition to the doctrine of David Ricardo and those to whom the appellation "Classical Economists" is applied. Their desire to see gold reinstated as the bedrock of economic policy had been strengthened by their evaluation of the course taken by the economy since the Bullion Committee's report. They distrusted the Bank of England and the private banks with or without an elected master at Westminster. Both Attwood and Ricardo endorsed Adam Smith's conception of "free trade" but the Birmingham banker considered the necessary functions of government in support of that freedom overrode any "mythical" standard against which the market-place could be tried. It was an argument that few contemporaries were willing to accept and it laid Attwood as a banker, the main beneficiary of the war-induced and unregulated increase in bank note issues, open to the charge of "vested interest." Attwood was aware of the problem and his pamphlets were designed to avoid such suspicions by providing a consistent thesis and incontestable recommendations. In this he was spectacularly unsuccessful.

Attwood's argument contained two elements. His main concern was analysis and economic prescription: the practical question about which most debate on the economy revolved. But unlike Ricardo, who thought that the economic system and its interdependence had been adequately summarized by Smith, Attwood added a philosophical element. He sought to provide a vision of society in an industrial setting. He understood the advantages to be gained from increased productivity. Generalizations and principles were taken from his experience of banking and economic life in Birmingham. Attwood understood the weaknesses as well as the strengths of the fledgling structure but predicated his nostrum for national solvency on the belief that what he saw pointed the way forward. It was a noble idea that led to misunderstanding and rejection. In a community dominated by men whose position was guaranteed by the ownership of land and whose knowledge was rooted in the eighteenth century, it was folly to expect good will. For most of them, the new cities evoked fear, not admiration. The suggestion that these be encouraged because they constituted a better order sounded ridiculous. Regulation and control were the objectives of government; growth was something they did not like to think about. Yet it was this aspect of his theory which made Attwood press on for more than thirty years. A sense of truth could not on its own have sustained a campaign for action leading in directions which were often against his better judgment. Family loyalty coupled with a distaste for government could easily have provoked an early withdrawal as it had in 1813. He continued because he had a dream, an ideal for which to strive. His utopia had, he believed, flickered into life in the last years of the war, in Birmingham. Never had the people been so wedded to the nation as at that time. Science, art, and enterprise had flourished and everyone had been happily engaged in productive endeavour. It was his determination to reproduce that spirit. Attwood wrote about it in mystical terms, envisaging a collective social character in which patriotism and individual altruism were combined.

The sense of community that he had glimpsed had been broken by the depression. The problem, as he saw it, was to repair the damage and reestablish prosperity. Mass demobilization and discipline by poverty had served only to antagonize an "affectionate" people. The government had turned the natural obstacles which attended a shift from war to peace into virtually insurmountable barriers, because of the failure to understand the principles upon which an industrial nation functioned. Correction would only come if it listened to those with practical experience and stopped attempting to impose solutions distilled from academic theory. Important decisions must not be left to the whims of courtiers, "living far removed from those elements [business practices] and looking down upon them through the mists and prejudices which distance involves them."[15]

In each of his exhortations to government and public Attwood presented his optimistic evaluation of the nations' potential. His arguments usually began with a restatement of Adam Smith's maxim that labour was the foundation of all wealth.[16] The value of an article was "the aggregate of the labour and good things in life consumed in producing it." But he added a far-reaching corollary which denied the possibility of over-population – too many labourers or too much labour – in the immediate future. Using Malthusian arithmetic he accepted the geometric progression of population but held that the riches of the country multiplied at an ever higher rate, lifting the labourer and the country to ever increasing prosperity. To justify this forecast he argued that an agricultural labourer had to produce at least four times as much as he consumed: one quarter of an article's price accruing to the labourer, one quarter to the farmer, a third quarter to the landlord, and the final part used in payment of taxes and levies.[17] If agriculture was able to achieve this, then the manufacturing industry with the advantages of superior mechanical and production techniques could offer an equal return. To the classical economists' argument that new and marginal land would fail to maintain this relationship, he rejoined that the stage at which this might be true had not yet been reached in England and, in any case, the promise of the colonies was immense. Manufactured goods could be shipped in exchange for food as the resources of the nation were shifted into sectors of greater productivity.[18] Only when all limits, and he was not convinced there were any, had been reached would it be time to speak of checks and balances, celibacy and abstinence in the contemporary Malthusian fashion.[19]

Experience in Birmingham had also taught that the social classes had to act together if prosperity was to be the "natural" condition. The rich had as many responsibilities for the poor as the poor had obligations to fulfil. In an argument which owes much to the eighteenth-century philosophy of Berkeley and Butler, Attwood argued that the "Author of Nature" had ordained that men should live by the sweat of their brows; it was the clear duty of the rich to take care that the mode of livelihood was always open.[20] The mechanics of the labour market in which these obligations were to operate were relatively simple to explain. While "full employment" was enjoyed all would be happy. However, at times the demand for labour would exceed the supply. Wages would rise in "real" value, to that a greater weekly share of the good things of life would be given to the labourer. Left to itself this condition could not be prolonged. Following Malthus, he speculated that earlier marriages, more children, and a return of those who had sought work abroad would satisfy the demand. The labourer would be forced to return to his former situation of "frugality and incessant labour."[21] Attwood does not in this passage suggest that this would be at a higher level than formerly but elsewhere he preaches human betterment through improved habits derived from stable higher wages. In any event such changes were best left alone. It was the reverse situation which required attention. Unemployed labour would force wages down. The unfortunate workers would suffer. They would marry later, fewer children would be born, death would come at an earlier age, and those who were able to would emigrate. Supply would fall to the level of demand and spiral downwards. It was the correction this "unnecessary" chain reaction that Attwood sought to achieve.

Attwood argued that rival economists completely misunderstood the role of money. Too often they discussed bank notes and bullion of common exchange as "real agents," not realizing that they formed but a small (though admittedly important) proportion of the money of the country. The instruments of credit to which the bullionists had devoted so much time in 1810 were only the material objects upon which the money or "ideal exchange medium" of the country rested. These material objects had no value in themselves; they were not real in the sense of commodities to be bought and sold. His list of agents used as money is quite remarkable in that it included elements rarely appreciated by other economists of this date: "bills of exchange, transfers, book debts, bank notes, gold and silver, and indeed of everything that passes for money in any shape or way." They were creations of mind, "created by confidence, supported by confidence, and discharged by confidence."[22] The less obvious instruments contrived "twenty times the exchanges that are effected by bullion or bank notes."[23]

The crucial role to be played by bank notes rested not in their ability to make exchanges but "in giving a spirit, a confidence, to the whole."[24] Money, therefore, needed no separate existence based upon value. In his opinion, arguments for and against a particular standard, whether gold, silver, or some other object, were irrelevant. Only the nature of the continuing national debate on the resumption question persuaded Attwood to discuss it.

Gold, he warned, was a commodity in short supply and subject to market forces divorced from the realm of currency regulation.[25] Bullion had to rise in value unless there were new discoveries or increased production by existing mines.[26] Successive administrations appeared to have ignored this simple fact: he noted that the law fixed a maximum upon bullion in coins while at the same time removing any restraint whatsoever upon bullion in bars. In such a situation the circulation medium was made the subject of speculation instead of exchange.[27] Only irrational tradition "imbibed with mother's milk" gave it life as a standard.[28] Attwood firmly disputed on two grounds the bullionist claim that the adoption of a gold standard would reduce the fluctuations in money value. The price of gold (a metal whose supply England did not control) could be affected by foreign emergencies totally unrelated to English economic conditions. Second, echoing Thornton, Attwood recognized that currency responded to fluctuations in public confidence.[29] In business houses clerks industriously sorted heavy from light coins, illustrating the weakness of specie even in prosperous times. During a depression the Bank of England could not pay out new coins and expect that they would remain in circulation.[30] Irrespective of the optimistic projections of future Bank solvency and affluence, the propensity for weakness was unlikely to be remedied; "it cannot be supposed that the Bank Directors can ever be prepared to pay on *demand, in gold,* a circulation of Bank-notes for which they have not obtained gold."[31]

The above arguments were sufficient, in his view, to discourage a return to a gold standard. Similar objections could be offered to any metallic substitute. The answer was clearly to keep the system the country had stumbled into after the Bank Restriction Act – inconvertible bank notes. These, in his estimation, fulfilled the few essential requisites for an efficient circulating medium, that it be "cheap, secure and manageable."[32] A fourth criterion, that it be "the lawful coin of the realm," was easily found; Vansittart's counterproposals to the bullionist resolutions had admitted as much. Directly contradicting Ricardo's contention that an addition to the currency circulation could have no impact on economic growth, Attwood claimed that bank notes were "alive"; they could break open the "prison doors" that bound society.[33] They acted constantly upon property, creating markets by influencing both supply and demand. Simply stated, he believed that markets depended upon the natural desires and needs of the populace.[34] If the supply of objects which would satisfy those needs was facilitated, a market was consequently created and production stimulated. Unfortunately, he failed to develop a theoretical argument in support of his empirical observations and it was left to Knut Wicksell many years later to point out the relationship between bank lending and the level of real investment.

The acceptance of these ideas raised the question of control. The exact total of the note issues in the country was still difficult to establish. The stamp duty returns only very inadequately covered the monetary tokens used in Britain. Furthermore, Attwood recognized that even if this were determined, the "effective circulation" would not necessarily be indicated. Hoarding and overseas uses reduced the sum of note issue dramatically; in 1816, of an estimated £26 million then outstanding, he guessed that the effective circulation was no more than £20 million, perhaps even as low as £18 million. Moreover, the picture was further complicated by the velocity of circulation, which varied from one sector of the economy to another.[35] Despite the difficulties in assessing the existing position, he argued that certain principles could be ascertained respecting the movement of bank notes. Sounding once more remarkably like a student of Thornton, Attwood postulated two distinct actions upon currency that could reduce circulation generally. The Bank of England through its discount policies and its preeminent position in banking controlled the first of these. It could cut total circulation by reducing or rationing discounts and accommodation as it had in 1796–7, prior to restriction. Second, a diminished demand for discounts, occasioned by low property prices that decreased the number of exchange bills for which property was sold, would have a similar effect. In each case, a reduction in notes would cause a proportional fall in the number of transactions completed. For example, regarding the year 1816, he supposed £26 million supported £400 million worth of transactions. If note issues were reduced 50 per cent – that is, to £13 million – the number of exchanges completed could not be more than £200 million in value.[36] An additional note issue designed to increase circulation through an easing of discount and accommodation policies, or to keep pace with rising prosperity, would have the opposite effect.

Within the framework of his general principles, Attwood saw

few impediments to the control of note issues. There was one, however, that outweighed all others, "Caprice or alarm in the Directors of the Bank of England or erroneous or speculative views on their part, may from time to time, produce effects upon the circulation, far more injurious to the country, than the sudden invasion of the most numerous and formidable army."[37] Such alarms might precipitate changes in the total circulation that would exaggerate the original effect. Just as a loss of confidence destroyed industry and prosperity, so newly found assurances created price rises unrelated to currency issues.[38] It was essential, therefore, to maintain harmony within the banking system and continue the development of a safety net for the country banks in which the Bank of England would be the key element.

Having explained to his own satisfaction the role and nature of the medium of exchange, Attwood turned to the management of the economy. The key, he believed, was price theory. He began with a simple and generally accepted premise: "In all transactions of commerce the state of prices evidently depends equally upon two circumstances, the quality of the goods in the markets, and the quantity of currency (or money) in the markets."[39] He stated that there were two causes for a rise or fall in prices. They could be identified by the scope of their action. If prices were seen to move generally across a wide spectrum, then an "action upon currency" had occurred in the manner described. On the other hand, a rise or fall of prices in one or two sectors indicated an "action upon property." The latter was charged to the vagaries in the supply and demand circumstances, the various high and low prices of bullion and copper during the war years being an example of such an action.[40]

Changes in currency, accompanied by a general fall of prices such as that experienced on the continent in 1815–16, sprang from a combination of these factors and were largely government-inspired.[41] Regrettably, this inspiration did not imply control and almost precluded, by their nature, the rapid remedies needed to reestablish stability. If these were not forthcoming, the alteration of the whole structure of debts, obligations, and loans, together with a wholesale modification of the "modes and means by which life is supported," was inevitable.[42] Prices could not move freely in the market as Ricardian argument seemed to suggest. Society was much too complex to absorb broad shifts in demand and supply without extensive help from the authorities. Thus Attwood confronted the proponents of the classical school's position and contradicted their reliance upon the ready adaptation of the market to the altered situation provoked by changes in the supply of money. To illustrate his point he once again referred to the farmer whose income was split four ways – wages, rents, taxes, and net income. Taxes and rents, being fixed by contract and law, would be difficult to adjust, so any fall in the money supply and consequent market realignment must affect the other two. A squeeze could only cripple the labourer and the farmer.

In the individual case the output of an article that underwent a price reduction would certainly decline; in an extreme instance production would cease altogether, "because no one would give more for the production of an article than that article would redeem."[43] But when the decline came from an excess supply, Attwood held that the depressed price was often counterbalanced by the increase of real riches occasioned by that excess.[44] In his opinion, individual price falls tended to rectify themselves quite quickly and the overall economic structure suffered only slight strain. This was not true, however, of a general depression of prices caused by a withdrawal of currency. Three distinct stages might be discerned: first, the action upon currency, "second, the redundant supply of the markets by forcing out of stocks, and, third, the diminution of demand in the markets occasioned by the very impoverishment and alarm."[45] Just as an "action upon property" rectified itself without interference, an "action upon currency," given time, could be expected to lose its debasing power. But prices were unlikely to decline simultaneously. The connection between agriculture and manufacturing, to look at the question in its broadest sense, was strong but tenuous. The bottom of a slump in the latter would, he suggested, occur perhaps two years after the bottom occurred in agriculture.[46] Thus, while a gradual recovery could be anticipated, it would take place only after "a season of dreadful distress."[47] This natural remedy acted through a "diminished production of agricultural and manufacturing articles, or in other words, famine and bankruptcy." The destruction of property and "the diseased preference for money" would occupy the undivided attention of people, and the confusion of "real" and "ideal" wealth would become general.[48]

The trap of depression was extremely difficult to escape from, but relatively easy to avoid. Attwood strongly agreed with many of his contemporaries that individual interest was the best guide to national interest; governments should not interfere in the interplay of market forces. This related to the "tokens and tickets which individuals may choose to create or receive" as well as to the more commonly accepted fields. Instead of tinkering with little-understood machinery, let experience be the guide. He believed that the disasters courted by the neglect of such advice had been amply demonstrated in the past. Heretically he was even prepared to argue that rising prices, or a depreciation of currency, could be a good and not an evil. To a degree, prosperity and depreciation were, he considered, synonymous, being cause and consequence to each other. While money fell in value, property must rise, and as long as there were more men getting rich than getting poor, there would be more buyers than sellers in the markets. Furthermore, it did not matter in what proportions prices, wages, and other relationships in society nominally stood as long as they were relatively in balance.[49] Having reached this position, Attwood attempted to outline various schemes through which the economy could be controlled under an inconvertible system.

Attwood's first proposal for securing property was exceedingly simple. The government, he suggested, should borrow £20 million from the Bank of England, secured upon the Consolidated Fund. This issue was to be distributed by the Bank of England on the security of mortgages and collateral bonds to the commercial and landed interests. After a period of perhaps three years these might be redeemed with interest to free the fund for new engagements. The Bank notes, which would be the medium of issue, could be administered by commissioners as had been done in 1793 and 1812 with loans in exchequer bills.

Attwood was not the first to expound this demand-led production thesis and it must be assumed that he was not unaware of its venerable antecedents. The most famous eighteenth-century advocate of the view to which Attwood subscribed was undoubtedly John Law. Law had declared his faith in the ability of a money issue to facilitate greater and more efficient production. The increased production, Law argued, would then create full employment and add immeasurably to the nation's wealth.[50] The similarity to Attwood's argument is striking. However, one important qualification should be made. Attwood used a more sophisticated explanation of the method by which his creations might be turned into capital and used productively; Law tended to confuse money and capital.

A writer and contemporary of Attwood who had anticipated many of the Attwoodian suggestions was the Reverend T.R. Malthus. He had proposed the theory that a net increase in real wealth would follow a note issue.[51] Berkeley, Bentham, Stewart, and Lauderdale had also alluded to the possibility of an alteration in the capital holdings of the country being affected by an increased note issue.[52] Generally, however, they believed that the difficulties attendant upon such issues would be insurmountable. Attwood disagreed, believing that an efficient control system could be constructed to remove many of the features of note issue which were open to abuse. Currency depreciation should be steady and gradual, promoting "healthy activity in the different channels of commercial and agricultural interest." Temporary dislocations and injustices could be resolved by temporary solutions. Fundholders, those "keepers of dead capital," whose savings were being eroded by inflation, could be paid in kind in the manner of the corn rents of the Napoleonic Wars.[53] As for the workers, although he agreed with Copplestone that there was a danger that their wages would lag behind prices if prosperity were funded by a paper issue, a concerned government could reduce the hardship through planning.[54] It might be advisable to plan wage increases in advance of those of price. What difference did it make if workers earned "one hundred pounds a week in the course of the next century" as long as prices were in rough alignment?[55] It was an argument that critics of the war-induced inflation found insupportable.

A further objection was raised to the notion of a controlled depreciation – the threat to overseas trade. Taking their cue from the eighteenth-century economists, particularly David Hume, the critics argued that this trade would be destroyed, since British goods would be too expensive to sell abroad. Attwood rejoined that the high prices would be only notional. Bills drawn and received would be unchanged in real terms.[56] In any event foreign trade was incidental to the nation's wealth. The vision of English prosperity deriving its life force from "sucking, as it were, the blood and strength of other nations" was offensive.[57] His limited view of the role of international trade and the foreign exchanges naturally was a reflection of Birmingham's economy. It was generally believed that less than 10 per cent of its total sales went abroad. If lost, some restructuring would be needed but compensation could and would be made. The declaration was patently false; only four years earlier he had been arguing exactly the opposite. These observations must be counted among the least convincing that he ever wrote.

In addition to the open conflict among economists on the control factor, many writers discounted the ability of money to work the miracle that Berkeley and others had claimed. Law, Malthus, and Bentham generally accepted the old mercantilist contention that a country had certain minimum monetary needs. That an increase above that minimum would not be harmful and might possibly be a good was the obvious corollary. Hume, Massie, and Ricardo rejected that thesis and maintained that currency manipulation could have no effect one way or the other, save possibly in a time of war, when it could be used to pay off "foreign princes."[58] Attwood had constructed his "remedy" upon totally different principles from those of Ricardo. Consequently, it is not surprising that a Ricardian-oriented cabinet and expansionist commercial interests did not resolve their differences.

The crude outline of what was to become the Attwoodian panacea was elaborated in 1816 in the second edition of *The Remedy*. In this expanded version Attwood proposed again that a new issue of £20 million be made to meet the country's needs. An act of Parliament would authorize the Bank of England to lay out that sum in the purchase of 3 per cent Consols or other government securities. The act would remain operative at the will of Parliament and could be continued, enlarged, or confirmed in its use as the interests of the country dictated. When prices rose too high, the act would be withdrawn and the Bank compelled to sell part of its holdings; if prices fell, more securities would be bought. In this way, he envisaged a regulator through which the national fortunes would be controlled. However, the fact that the issue was intended to operate simply as a function of the market meant that it would be a very imprecise and probably valueless instrument. Rather surprisingly, Attwood seemed unaware of considerations of regional variations besides those of season, and offered no solution whatever to the multitude of technical problems raised by monetary issues. Only the danger of an all-powerful Bank of England was too widely apprehended to be ignored. Cries of "vested interest" would certainly be made if the control and issue of currency were entrusted to that institution. He recognized that the Bank already possessed greater power than any which had hitherto been vested in a national body. He therefore reiterated in the strongest terms his confidence in an independent group of commissioners appointed to oversee the project, trusting in their sense of national as opposed to private interest.[59]

The comprehensive review of depression and its remedy that Attwood attempted a year later argued for an additional issue of currency and warned more passionately of the dangers of gold. But the plan devised to provide the optimum benefit and safety from the new currency issue had changed only in detail from the 1816 design. The most radical departure from the earlier blueprint was the call for the issue to be in the form of national paper rather than Bank of England notes. Even carefully regulated participation by the Bank of England in credit management had become increasingly unattractive to the businessmen and farmers whom Attwood hoped to convince. He turned, therefore, to the obvious corollary of the control mechanism envisaged in *The Remedy*. The new instrument would be clothed with the trappings of bank notes and would work with the common currency tokens then in use. To administer the paper, lords of the treasury or, alternatively, the commissioners of the Sinking Fund were proposed. Twenty million pounds, issued in notes of all sizes from £1 to £1,000, continued to be the sum deemed adequate for the task he had in mind. An act of Parliament to authorize the purchase of an equivalent portion of National Debt would add tradition and the debt itself would provide stability. The money so created would be liberated by direct loans to merchants and manufacturers, thus transforming money into productive capital. The loans, initially tendered for three years, would be reinvested in the National Debt upon repayment. The arbiter of control for this solution was to be the price of wheat, a variable first proposed as a long-term control agent by John Locke. Attwood proposed the sum of 15 shillings a bushel as the index of prosperity. A price below that figure was to be labelled "low," and increased issues of national paper made; if the price was "high," then those issues were to be withdrawn.[60]

The establishment of this system, he believed, would free the economy from the casual and uncertain dangers inherent in discount and accommodation policies. As the Bank of England and other capitalists withdrew or expanded their contributions of money to the circulating media, the national paper would respond proportionately. Thus the power of the Bank of England would to some extent be checked while its profits and general usefulness would be secured. The problems and perversions to which the Bank was peculiarly exposed, and which rendered it suspect in the eyes of most economic critics, would be countered. Unscheduled "actions upon currency" could largely be avoided and property injured only by accidental scarcity or famine. This condition would be furthered by minor adjustments to the total issue which might even smooth the more violent fluctuations of these latter "actions."

The choice of an agricultural product as the index was not unrealistic. Subject to seasonal fluctuations and notoriously unpredictable, agriculture certainly demanded attention if the British economy was to be controlled. Like Ricardo, Attwood considered the demand for grain to be relatively inelastic; thus he proposed a judicious withdrawal of bank notes at a time of scarcity; the result, higher prices for the grain, would force out stocks. Within a relatively short period of time this should create a surplus and prices would decline. Through this controlled reduction in monetary supply he postulated that it might be possible to avoid side effects upon manufacturing, prices, wages, and stocks; a trick that would require a considerable degree of finesse because such an action could permanently force prices higher and intensify the suffering of the workers. He was also aware that the fine tuning might prove detrimental to the farming community as a whole. Agricultural wealth would decline in the face of the combination of a bad harvest and his prescription. But in his opinion agriculture was essentially an industry with long-term objectives and could withstand occasional imbalances. Therefore the effect of an "action upon currency" to rectify one of property would hurt no one permanently, yet could only enhance the nation's prosperity.

In this discussion Attwood neglected the ramifications of his recommendations. Ricardo's later criticism of the agricultural policies advocated by Attwood was founded on this omission. He pointed to the failure to explore the problems of controlling relative price movements as opposed to general ones.[61] This objection apparently threw the whole of the Attwoodian currency panacea into question and may have contributed to the complete rejection of his pleas before the Select committee which inquired into agricultural distress in 1821 – a committee on which Attwood had expected to find friends and supporters. Nevertheless, it is a mistake to apply to Attwood's efforts at this time such labels as success or failure. He may safely be counted among those theorists whose practical predilections disinclined them to offer their recommendations as universal truths in the style of James Mill or J.R. McCulloch. The banker never argued that his "remedy" was a complete reform package. His aim, always, was to cast doubts upon the contemporary preoccupation with gold and the "unbusinesslike" analysis of past experience. He was well aware that his ideas needed further elaboration; they were designed to make people think.

The general scheme to incorporate national paper in the currency medium of the country was revolutionary and Attwood was conscious of that fact. National paper sounded suspiciously like the despised French *Assignat* which had led to rampant inflation in France in the early eighteenth century, and the ideas akin to the heresies of John Law which had supported it. To forestall critical disparagement of his recommended agent he sought to make what he hoped were distinctions of pedigree and class: "Assignats ... have been generally issued, not for the purpose of circulating medium but for the sole purpose of enabling tyrannical governments to get possession of the property of their subjects, without an equivalent for the purpose of the circulating medium, and for the promotion of national interests ... They would also be sanctioned by the British Parliament, which is, in fact, the British nation, and would be issued under equivalent purchases of capital invested in the national debt."[62] The certificates would fluctuate in quantity, according to the "par" assigned to that purpose, with withdrawal as swift as issue.[63] Unfortunately, Attwood's protestations went unheeded; national paper could not so easily escape the long tradition of failure and irresponsibility to which it was heir.

Attwood anticipated such a response and therefore hedged his argument with a more moderate scheme designed to achieve his hopes for economic sanity in the short run while at the same time preparing for the full plan in the future. This stopgap scheme was simply a more elaborate version of that proposed in 1816. The Bank Restriction Act – "the grand and magnificent remedy" of 1797 – was to be extended for ten years with the intention of restoring confidence. During this respite the Bank of England was to issue new notes upon bonds, notes of hand, and other securities to individuals at 5 per cent per annum for a maximum of three years. Repayment could either be in instalments or at the convenience of the borrower. The gold guinea would be disfranchised so that notes would be given unfettered freedom. To regulate the issue of these notes a new indicator of prosperity was proposed – the rate of interest. If money was so scarce that it was not readily available at 5 per cent upon good security, then an additional issue should be made. On the other hand, a plentiful supply at 3 per cent indicated that a withdrawal of notes was necessary. He chose 5 per cent, the more important of the two intervention points, since it had been established by law and approved by universal custom and consent, thus becoming a kind of par in the value of money.[64]

The assumption that the money market could provide a viable guide to prosperity was remarkable, especially in view of Attwood's own appreciation of the inadequacy of the market in the dissemination of funds in 1817.[65] In addition it placed Attwood at odds with the generally accepted view of what exactly the rate of interest represented. The mercantilists had sought a hundred years earlier to develop a theory of the rate of interest in terms of the supply of and demand for money, but had been vigorously attacked by Hume. Hume had held that the abundance or scarcity of money could affect only prices; interest must be determined by the profits on capital. Adam Smith and later David Ricardo agreed. It was this view which gained the ascendancy in the cabinet, through Huskisson, in the 1815–19 period and the "marginal yield upon capital" doctrine became the accepted explanation of the rate of interest. Attwood's suggestion was consequently not even considered.

By the end of 1818 it was clear to Attwood that he was not being taken seriously in London. To some degree he had only himself to blame. The pamphlets of 1817 and 1818 are undisciplined and repetitive: Attwood excused himself on the ground that he had a child sitting on each knee. Ideas tend to spill over from one invention to another and the distinction between cherished panacea and temporary stopgap is difficult to discern. Furthermore, he was, above all, a businessman, pragmatic to a fault; his aim was prosperity, not personal fame. Thus, conscious of the government's commitment to gold and the growing influence of Ricardo, Attwood suggested a bewildering variety of measures to facilitate resumption, a laudable objective, but one which damaged his credibility. It confirmed the general opinion that he was only interested in obtaining an inconvertible paper currency – the one common denominator in his schemes – without caring about the means.

The inaccuracy of these impressions is best ascertained by reference to the schemes actually proposed. One, discussed at the conclusion of his pamphlet *Observations*, may serve as an illustration of Attwood's search for an acceptable solution to the nation's currency problems. In that work a compromise between his own views and that of the resumptionists was advanced. He prefaced his advice by reiterating that the Bank Restriction Act could not be repealed with any real margin of safety if further deflation was to be avoided. However, depending upon various economic indices, he was persuaded that a renewal of only two or perhaps three years might suffice. In any event, he conceded, some day the measure had to lapse. People in general were aware of this inevitable conclusion and could not embrace a system which had for its keystone a temporary expedient.[66] Therefore, during the last years of its operation the way ahead should be prepared. Coins could be reduced one quarter in value, in stages, while the government endeavoured to accustom the populace to the coming medium, national paper, by issuing exchequer bills. The new medium was to be integrated with other notes and gold; where possible it was to counteract the defects of those instruments – extreme volatility and intrinsic value.[67] Bank notes were to be made legal tender with all agents save the Bank of England; the national paper would be reducible to no other medium save itself.[68] Country notes, of which Attwood was allegedly the champion, were to disappear completely.

He alluded to the discussion in his earlier pamphlets with respect to the role of overseer for his medium of exchange, designating the Sinking Fund commissioners or a legislative commission. He fixed upon agricultural labouring wages as a par that most closely allied with national interest. Clearly, full employment was to be the norm in any representation of English prosperity. Returns were to be made every week or month to the commissioners or some other guardian of the currency, from officers in every county. Upon the basis of these reports and the price of wheat, purchases or sales of National Debt would be made.[69] So that conditions among the business community should not be neglected, he added an index, the velocity of circulation, measured by periodic assessments of the disposition among businessmen to hoard or spend – a pointer whose value seems to have been recognized by modern economists. In no sense was this or any of the other plans submitted by Attwood intended to be accepted unreservedly. They were discussion papers which offered a fresh perspective and an appeal to reconsider decisions that owed more to past complacency than current reality.

At the end, conscious of the antipathy his proposals had already engendered, Attwood abandoned his original rather extreme position on currency augmentation in favour of a simple indication of commitment to peace and prosperity. The government only had to take the "simple" step of throwing the circulation open, so as to permit free exchange by whatever means it deemed reasonable, and he would be content. He had faith in the common sense of the people to use that exchange sensibly and to the maximum benefit. On one point only was he adamant. There could be no greater error of government than "to take into its own hands the creation of a circulating medium, without taking care that those creations are always of ample amount."[70]

CHAPTER FOUR

A Crime against the People

Attwood's appeals for state intervention in the financial marketplace contain a sense of urgency which at times has a hysterical quality. Yet his everyday life at this time was, by choice, quiet and undemanding. Inconvenient excursions to neighbouring towns or London and other entanglements which might draw him away from his family were avoided. Certainly he was aware of the general discontent manifested in the periodic shouting in the streets by the sad victims of government indifference but he preferred to remain aloof. These were his contemplative years. The rhetoric of extremism to be found in his pamphlets received no other expression. It was the birth of another son, Edward Marcus, on 13 June 1816, and the reconstruction of his house on the Crescent which absorbed his attention.

It might be argued that the writing of so many pamphlets took an increasing amount of his time. There was also correspondence with a variety of "publicly spirited" men who might welcome a copy of his latest polemic and be persuaded to take up the cause. But in neither instance does the argument stand up to analysis. The style used in the tracts suggests that each was written in one highly charged outburst; there is only the barest semblance of order or planning. As for the correspondence, there is no evidence of a lengthy exchange of views, not even with Arthur Young to whom two of Attwood's publications were addressed in 1818. Some correspondents replied in the most complimentary terms but Attwood does not seem to have bothered to develop these relationships. Such quiescence can only be explained by supposing that Attwood did not, at this time, really believe his own warnings about the future; rather, his natural optimism remained intact notwithstanding government policy.

A close examination of his published opinions points to an unmistakable note of ambivalence; it is particularly noticeable in the choice and explanation of the practical examples which are designed to illustrate argument. In one pamphlet, he bolstered his theory on the question of taxation by describing the loss of a portion of his personal income caused by the bankruptcy of Fereday, the tenant of one of his mineral estates. The lament is real but the implication is one of renewal, of imminent resurrection. Attwood believed in the recuperative powers of industry through enterprise. It was a view commonly shared in Birmingham and he did not have to look far for support. Spooner, Attwood's intellectual as well as business partner, did not venture into print in these years but later maintained that his concern for the economy, while roused by events in 1810–11 and 1816–17, did not become a major anxiety until 1819. It is this mood of optimism of the immediate postwar years which marks the genesis of an identifiable school of thought in Birmingham, rather than the despair felt by many at the golden straitjacket created by the resumption of cash payments – the focal point of future campaigns.

The point of distinction between the town's entrepreneurs and those elsewhere is subtle but can be detected even in Thomas Attwood's amicable debate with his brother. At first glance, Matthias Attwood's earliest pamphlet, published in 1817, bears a striking resemblance to *Prosperity Restored;* not surprisingly, for after all he had been trained in the art of banking in the midlands. But even at this early date one can discern a darker shade of emphasis in his examination of the economy and the manufacturing sector in particular.[1] The word "speculator" is used almost exclusively in a pejorative sense, since stability is preferred to growth and country bankers are condemned for encouraging the "irresponsible." The recommendation of paper currency manipulation as a tool to correct the nation's economic ills paralleled that of Thomas but their models of the ideal society diverged. Matthias had been seduced by the London money market perspective which saw industry as a Pandora's box whose lid should be raised only by an experienced – read London – hand. Unfortunately, so little of the correspondence between the brothers survives that the points of departure are unknown beyond those which can be deduced from a simple reading of their respective public positions. These were far from being etched in stone as the many cooperative assaults on Parliament attest. Yet it is the difference in their expectations which allows the younger Attwood to restrict his anger to the printed page, not risking the perils of London or even the streets of Birmingham when the country seemed ripe for revolution.

Optimism of this sort is often rooted in self-satisfaction and it is easy to conclude that Attwood was content with the political and social status quo. Critics of his subsequent career as a radical reformer contend that his activities were born of aggravation and not principle. They point to his readiness in pamphlet after pamphlet to accept the vague promises of the Tory administration as signs of an imminent conversion to money management. Admiration expressed for William Pitt, the Younger, and tacit acquiescence in the loyalist activities of his own father and elder brother appear to add further proof to this interpretation.[2] Nonetheless, it is mistaken. Attwood's disillusionment with the political process, so marked in 1812-13, had not been miraculously translated into unthinking support. The political asides which speckle his monetary analysis were almost wholly negative. Parliament was not a forum in which ministers spoke *ex cathedra*. The institution was sacred but the members of Parliament were only men. On the subject of the best interests of business, the views of practical "Brummagems" were as authoritative as those emanating from Westminster, hence his own venture into print. Statesmen capable of recognizing commonsense (a quality he saw in Pitt) deserved support but in the present times they were difficult to identify. If any label can be attached to Attwood at this time it is that of "Independent." Events were still to determine his political affiliation; for the moment, he preferred to sit on the sidelines, restricting his participation to that of a critic, and expressing his anger at all things extreme in the written word.

Attwood's response was naturally shaped by his analysis of behaviour in Birmingham. The town's vaunted wartime community spirit had crumbled rapidly during 1816 as the price of pig iron tumbled 40 per cent. The labour-hoarding practices of the war years which had been the glue holding the small workshops together were changed by force of circumstance to those of labour-paring. A widely supported petition against the passage of the new Corn Law and a concerted campaign to keep an arms-proofing house in Birmingham did offer the illusion of common purpose. But as political radicalism became the preoccupation of the artisans and labourers a split between the various interest groups rapidly developed. Attwood, confused by their incoherence, watched the ineffectual efforts of Whig, Tory, and Radical to mold opinion without any attempt at collaboration. Inevitably, there were major disturbances. In October and November 1816 the town suffered from the extremism of both sides. There was a least one death and many injuries.[3] Nevertheless, Attwood refused to sign the petitions, advertisements, or declarations of either side.

In his early tracts there are many expressions of regret that the economy had "become a prey to anarchists and reformers," but the lament is tempered by his desire to make it clear that it was the means and not the objectives of the protesters that he condemned: "A real and beneficial reform is the last object that can ever be effected by popular excitement. Innocent, well-meaning enthusiasts begin the excitement, and when their objects are effected, they wish to go no further ... [but are] then carried away in a torrent of public passion ... [or] covered with obloquy and contempt to make room for bolder spirits."[4] Changes in the franchise qualifications might be of benefit but there was no evidence that those elected under such conditions would be any more likely to be "honourable, useful and upright" than those chosen by the rotten borough system. In any case, he added, returning to his own remedy for unrest, in a time of prosperity, no one would want to serve for all would be too busy working and enjoying themselves. The recognition of the need for political justice contained in these passages was low-key. But its presence reinforces the conclusion that if he did have Tory inclinations they were in the Pittite tradition of compromise and not the contemporary style of confrontation. The fears he expressed of a misguided populace were those that any family man with property was likely to entertain. Langford, a nineteenth-century historian of the town, remembered that the only group to grow in strength from the troubles was the "liberal."[5] There is little doubt that at this time Attwood could be counted among them.

In the following twelve months, the depression left many idle hands to wreak the havoc born of resentment and scarcely a week passed without some violent disturbance. Lack of money meant that living conditions worsened as workers found it impossible to pay their rents.[6] The predominantly workers' districts of Bordesley and Deritend became depressingly crowded; a condition made almost unbearable by the stench of over-taxed open sewers which ran beside the small houses. Improvements within the town were forgotten except where they might turn a profit (as with gas lighting) and repairs of every sort were neglected. The Court Leet's only response was to send a weak petition to Parliament urging cabinet action but without making any specific recommendations. Charitable efforts continued with soup kitchens and collections for bread, blankets, coats, relief of the sick, children, and pregnant mothers. But the scale of relief from such sources was woefully inadequate. At the Crescent a line of hungry wanderers gathered at the Attwoods' gate each evening to receive bowls of stew or whatever could be spared. At times the Attwoods went hungry themselves since so much was given away. More ambitious and systematic plans, dependent upon an increase in the poor rate, foundered on the lament of poverty from landlords and businessmen alike. The former tended to charge higher rents on unrated property and opposed all efforts to increase the rates of the rest.[7] Birmingham was fast losing its air of innocence as an ugly inner core of deprivation was created. For Attwood, the failure and consequent deterioration had a common cause – the state of the economy. Pot-holes, cesspools, and radical agitation lacked the balm of money and it was the provision of that commodity which required his full attention.

Attwood's preferred routine was broken only once. In June 1818 a law suit against the Attwood family and indirectly the bank itself for restitution of an asset confiscated for nonpayment of a debt required the attendance of a partner in London. As he had some experience in these matters, Thomas was deputed to go. The trip began as a petty annoyance to be concluded as speedily as possible but it soon proved to be one of the turning points of his life, not least because the economy had begun to rebound thanks to a more liberal monetary policy. Soon after his arrival, he attended a party given by Matthias's friend, Patrick Colquhoun, one of the champions of the agricultural interest. To his delight and surprise he was introduced to the assembly by his famous host as "the very first economist of the Age."[8]

This boost to his ego was reinforced by the unexpectedly friendly reception accorded to him when he called upon the prime minister, Lord Liverpool. The latter apparently intended to promote a treaty with France to exchange Birmingham's hardware for wine. Although not sure how much credit to take for this rather strange attempt at barter, in that it seemed to owe little to *Prosperity Restored*, Attwood did feel pleased that Birmingham had been singled out for special notice. It would seem that his efforts had actually been read and appreciated by "all public men." This revelation was all the more amazing since he had lost £150 on the publishing venture and at one point had become so discouraged by poor sales that he had halted further distribution. Colquhoun effusively assured him that there was no doubt that his pamphlets had "saved the country."[9] The banker was not so naive as to believe that these comments did not owe something to exaggeration and the occasion but they were reassuring.[10] Seventeen years later William Cobbett still spoke of Attwood's influence in the extension of paper money as one of the factors in the revival of trade in

1818. This memory of events in that year reflects what was probably a widely held conviction of the efficacy of Attwood's pamphlets, however mistaken it may have been in reality.

An election campaign in the notoriously radical Westminster constituency was also instructive: "The poor wretches who clamour for Burdett and Liberty, meaning Blood and Anarchy, are far worse in ignorance and stupidity than our Birmingham mobs. But they have got rascals among them who excite them almost to madness just like the Poissards in Paris. It is the greatest nonsense in the world to attempt to reason with them. Reason has nothing to do with their conduct. It is all a question of mere passion; and therefore such creatures ought to have nothing to do with politics."[11] This condemnation of the reforming efforts of Burdett and Hunt (the latter was categorized as "the most complete wretch that ever existed in the world") is curious, since he later equated the passion of the "Burdett gang" to that of men in love; a condition to which he was himself not immune. It would seem that they were not always without his sympathy. The problem was more one of leadership: had they not failed to endorse his own remedy for the nation's distress? Given such stubbornness they were to be despised and overcome. He had no scruples whatsoever in the manner of their ruin. Upon hearing that Maxwell, Burdett's opponent, intended to bribe electors by paying their rates and taxes, he urged that "it ought to be done."

Despite the best efforts of the Tories, and the perverseness of the Radicals in squabbling amongst themselves – Hunt stood in defiance of the Westminster junto – Burdett was victorious. Attwood, wandering the crowded streets in the Covent Garden area on the last day of polling, was pleasantly surprised by the general good-humour of the rag-taggle "Jacobins."[12] it was interesting but, he concluded, without consequence. Unlike Matthias, who was quite worried by the turn of events, Thomas Attwood expected the radical voice to remain confused, without distinction, as long as men of the Burdett type led. The cry for parliamentary reform was too vague to inspire responsible support in the country at large. His conviction was based, as ever, on instinct and not on logical analysis.

Despite the new and old friendships to be made and found in London, Attwood was unable to change the feeling of alienation that the metropolis invariably evoked in him. The women were "plugs," he moaned, no match for his wife and the ladies of the midlands.[13] Only the children, escorted by veritable dragons, compared with those at home. Modestly, he did report seeing one or two men more handsome than himself. He made the rounds of London's cultural attractions including the British Museum, where the head of Memnon had just arrived, and went to the Opera to hear *The Marriage of Figaro*. The city, however, made him feel unwell; a condition brought on, he claimed, by excessive walking rather than a surfeit of wine, which was his wife's suspicion. Consequently, as soon as the trial promised a qualified victory, he wasted no time in hurrying home to wife and children bearing gifts – an ornamental brass cannon and a green macaw.

The economic recovery in 1818 was unfortunately shortlived. While the Gas Light and Coke Company bill occupied the attention of the Court Leet, town meetings were called by others seeking relief from the distress into which both town and country were again falling. But there was no consensus. At one end of the scale the Hampden Club was revived and delegates travelled from London to Lancashire seeking the cooperation of their fellow-workers. Rumours that the arms depot was to be attacked or that the whole country was about to rise in revolution abounded. Pamphlets and handbills depicting almost every imaginable scenario, from the strangling of priests to the second coming of Christ, were passed freely or displayed in windows. The more affluent citizens were equally determined and unforgiving. On one occasion the audience at the theatre burst wildly into applause when Pope's words, "Perhaps some loyal hearts may yet be found" and "we would reign undisturbed by civil war," were declaimed.[14]

The height of excitement came in the summer of 1819 when the Hampden Club organized a meeting "on the open ground to the left of St. Paul's Square, called Newhall Hill." The gathering was to be part of a national drive to elect a people's parliament. On 19 July Birmingham chose Sir Charles Wolesley as its "Legislatorial Attorney and Representative."[15] The move was rather premature as other towns were not yet ready; the lead had, however, been given. Tension in the town became almost unbearable after a proclamation issued in London against seditious assemblies included a special reference to Newhall Hill. Worse was to follow in the form of a bill of indictment against Major Cartwright, Thomas Wooler, George Edmonds, Charles Maddox, and W.G. Lewis "for conspiracy [at the Newhall Hill meeting] to elect and return, without lawful authority Sir Charles Wolesley, Bart., as a member to represent the inhabitants of Birmingham in the Commons House of Parliament."[16] By this time, however, the focus of attention had moved to Manchester where a meeting, in part to emulate that in Birmingham, was broken up by force and the word "Peterloo" became a rallying cry for radical and reactionary alike.[17]

Until the spring of 1819 Attwood, although disturbed by the misery of the people and the threat of violence to family and bank, had wisely refrained form entering Birmingham's political debate. Somehow or other he succeeded in keeping on good terms with all sides. At Christmas 1818 the family were guests at the home of the Spooners. They were cordially received, as always, even by the patriarch of the family, Isaac, a stern Tory magistrate. Two months later, Attwood was entrusted with the transportation of two petitions to London, one from George Edmonds on behalf of Birmingham's radicals, the second from Thomas Wharton, praising existing government policy. The latter, who had long been a friend, was a member of the Court Leet and an influential Whig. Edmonds, to whom Attwood familiarly refers as Gerry, had been an acquaintance since 1813. Attwood was rather unhappy with the task, which threatened to attach political labels to his own currency crusade. "I firmly resolve never to say a civil word to a living soul again. I am sure to pay for it if I do ... It is a cruel thing to think of but the fact is true that there is a tax in England upon every civil thing that is said, upon every kind thought that is thought. Therefore, I am determined neither to say or think anything kind or civil for the future."[18] But there was one aspect of the affair which did please – the element of trust. To win monetary reform he needed the support of a wide spectrum of opinion and an unsullied personal reputation. These gestures were proof that in Birmingham his integrity was unquestioned.

Attwood packed the petitions with the depositions and contracts that he carried to London at the end of February. What had turned out to be an unsatisfactory conclusion to the trial of the previous year required another appearance at court. There was also some further work to be done on the claim for greater compensation from the canal company which crossed The Leasowes; it had gone to legal arbitration but the arguments for and against were endless. Attwood was not at all happy to be separated from his family, particularly as a fourth son, Algernon, had been born at the beginning of the month.[19] Moreover, the drafting of a new pamphlet on the currency had not been going well and he would have liked to spend a few quiet days working on it. Still, there was much to be learned in London and Attwood confessed to a measure of excitement at the prospect of again discussing the economy with those who claimed some political influence.

The visit lasted less than two weeks and, on the evidence of the trivial correspondence with his wife about the court case and another election campaign in Westminster, where one candidate, "is the high road to Hell and the other is Hell itself," one might conclude that nothing of real interest had occurred.[20] The opposite is in fact true. Attwood's anticipation of excitement on setting forth came from quite another and, apparently for his wife, a hidden source. The two Houses of Parliament had each appointed a Select Committee to inquire into the possibility of a resumption of cash payments and they were in the process of examining witnesses.

Three days before he arrived in the city, his brother Matthias had presented evidence to the Lords' committee: evidence based upon a brief sent a week earlier from Birmingham.[21] Upon arrival Thomas Attwood immediately became involved with the group Matthias had gathered to oppose the Ricardian rush to full convertibility of the currency. In 1843 Thomas still vividly recalled the frantic round of dinner engagements and coffee-house lobbying as they sought to win support.[22] Given such activities, Attwood's quick retreat to Birmingham could be construed as odd were it not for his growing reputation as a perceptive economist. Once he had become familiar with the issues and understood the problems the lobbyists faced, his time, in the opinion of his friends, would be more productively spent in finishing his pamphlet. An authoritative attack on the bullionists' proposals was needed, particularly since the verbal assault appeared to be failing. It was also time to renew the contacts made in the desultory correspondence of the last three years. Letters of exhortation were to be dispatched to anyone who had ever said a single kind word about a paper currency. Facts and figures had to be gathered and relayed to those making public speeches, particularly to his brother who was busy in London organizing the main thrust of opposition. The Attwoods and their friends were determined to defeat a measure they believed would ruin the country. Unfortunately, the government's mind would appear to have been already made up.

The imaginative theories about the relationship of money to the economy so hopefully presented in 1816 and 1817 probably had little influence on the attitudes of the Bank or the government, notwithstanding the assurances given Attwood on his various excursions to London. To follow recommendations of that nature would have involved far too radical a reconstruction of policy. The Bank's directors appeared to be uninterested in monetary policy. Indeed, the records of the meetings of the Court in 1818 and 1819 show an almost inhuman preoccupation with the problems of forgery.

The debates of the House of Commons, however, indicate that by 1818 the country was becoming restive; unless the Bank made a positive move a select committee would be appointed. In order to obtain support for the Vansittart motion, Liverpool felt obliged to report that he "entertained a confident expectation that, but for certain contemplated operations in foreign loans, our currency would have been restored."[23] Such an admission virtually guaranteed that a full-scale inquiry would be conducted by both Houses.

Committees of both Lords and Commons were instructed "to enquire into the expediency of the Bank of England resuming cash payments at the period prescribed by statute, and to take into consideration other matters connected therewith." The composition of the committee of the House of Commons was distinguished and, despite the election by secret ballot, predictable. Castlereagh as leader of the Commons and Vansittart as chancellor of the exchequer could not be excluded. The Canningites, led by George Canning himself, secured a formidable representation including Huskisson, Robinson, soon to succeed Vansittart as chancellor, Littleton, and Lamb. Other members known to be at least lukewarm advocates of resumption were Frankland Lewis, Sir James Mackintosh, and Tierney. Huskisson succeeded in persuading the young Robert Peel to be the chairman.[24] Such a committee was unlikely to surprise and Attwood's subsequent colourful comment that the country was led "like an ox to the slaughter" may well have been close to the truth.

Only four witnesses who came before them were entirely against resumption, although none suggested that it be immediate. The Bank's spokesmen emphasized the policies which they had followed for so many years, but some hesitation in their answers revealed the first signs of self-doubt.[25] Among the bullionists the exposition of the relationship between the country banks and the Bank of England was more moderate in tone. An awareness of short- and long-run fluctuations and the friction involved in these movements tempered the belief that the Bank effectively controlled the country banks' ability to expand credit. The witnesses, almost without exception, attested to the fact that total advances affected total credit and the form of credit. Amid such unanimity resumption could not fail to appear desirable, despite symptoms of distress which might appear in the short run.

The Lords committee hearings under Harrowby followed those

of the Commons, the committee faithfully examining the same witnesses. One of the few exceptions had been Matthias Attwood. He had recently contested and won an election to the Commons; he was later to be unseated by petition. Since Matthias was well known in influential London circles and was a renowned currency champion, it was the failure of the Commons committee to call him before them that was remarkable rather than the fact that he was called by the Lords. His evidence endorsed the case so ardently argued by Thomas Attwood in 1817.[26] But the predictions of Matthias Attwood had counted for nothing when opposed by those of Ricardo and the majority of witnesses. The Lords and Commons committees, after recommending that the Bank cease to pay gold for its notes while the question was under discussion, turned to more weighty measures.[27]

The major obstacle to be faced in contemplating specie payments concerned the amount of deflation necessary to effect the return to a fixed gold standard. Gold had to be bought at a lower price and commodity prices reassessed in the light of this medium and its purchasing power. The prewar price, £3. 17s. 10½d., was chosen as the most logical basis for specie payment and few in or out of Parliament disagreed with that choice. The complications that might follow from such a reduction were conveniently forgotten. Ricardo, with great optimism, suggested that a reduction of at most 5 or 6 per cent in the note issue might produce the desired result.

The date of full resumption, when all Bank of England notes were to be redeemable in gold coin, was set for 1 May 1823. The four years before that date were to be used in transitional measures that would make resumption theoretically easier to bear. Dealers and their agents, but not the general public, were to be allowed to present notes to an aggregate value not exceeding sixty ounces of gold. Between 1 February and 1 October 1820 those notes would be redeemed in gold bars at the rate of £4. 1s. an ounce. This rate was to be reduced by 1 May 1821 to the agreed and final price.[28] These and other details were derived from the Ricardian plan presented to the Commons committee. To make acceptance by the Bank's directors more certain, the government was urged to repay the advance borrowed upon securities from the Bank of England in the very near future. This recommendation had the added advantage of offering one method by which the Bank's notes could be withdrawn automatically.

Peel introduced the committees' reports in the House and clearly expressed the government's main argument for the proposed policy:

"If once hope should be held out that suspension might last for an indefinite period, that the amount of the circulating medium was to be left at the discretion of the Bank's directors, uncontrolled by any consideration but that of their own profits, it would become impossible to estimate the extent, of the mischief that might ensue."[29] The Bank's directors were, however, less convinced of the need for resumption and the alliance between the government and the Bank which had been a feature of the management of the economy since 1797 appeared in imminent danger of rupture. They declared: "It is incumbent upon them [the directors] to consider the effects of any measure to be adopted, as operating on the general issue of their notes, by which all the private banks are regulated and of which the whole currency exclusive of the notes of the private bankers, is compared. They feel obliged, by the new position in which they have been placed by the Restriction Act of 1797, to bear in mind not less their duties to the establishment over which they preside, than their duties to the community at large, whose interests in a pecuniary and commercial relation, have in a great deal been confided to their discretion."[30] The Bank obtained some support from interest groups in the House. Charles Western led a farmers' cabal that promoted over twelve hundred petitions against resumption, some of which had been sparked by letters from Birmingham. In general, however, the Bank was vigorously attacked for its dilatory behaviour. John Pearse, a former governor and an ardent defender of the Bank, was incensed by these attacks and found them quite incomprehensible: "While hon. gentlemen were deprecating the character of the Bank in Parliament, that character was the subject of ardent admiration and confidence in every part of the world."[31]

Outside Parliament a number of groups attempted to organize an effective opposition but failed to win extensive support.[32] The only major lobby that acted consistently was the one led by the Attwoods in alliance with Sir Robert Peel, the father of the chairman of the Commons committee.[33] The sole concrete result of these efforts was a petition, circulated privately, that the initiators later claimed had been signed by every banker in the city. Such a universal response was extremely unlikely, but, in any event, their efforts were unavailing.

The Birmingham reaction to the reports was limited. No town meeting was called to petition Parliament. For their part, the working classes at this time saw no merit in collaboration with the masters, and the community spirit about which so many authors have written continued to be noticeable by its absence.

Parliamentary reform remained the *sine qua non* on their agenda. Thomas Attwood had remained at home for the duration of the debate on the reports, encouraging his friends by letters. He also took the time to write an open and carefully reasoned letter to the man who had apparently heeded his views in the past, Lord Liverpool.

Attwood began his rebuttal of both committees' reports by reiterating his argument that an appeal to the conclusions of 1810 was mindless: the conditions of that year no longer applied.[34] The only sensible procedure, if the country was determined to ignore his personal choice, inconvertible paper, was the renewal of the Bank Restriction Act for five or six years, an additional three years above his recommendation in 1818 being included to allow for recovery from the deflation forced in the previous twelve months. By this method, prosperity would reestablish itself and the level at which a bullion price might be fixed could more easily be decided. He guessed that the price might be £4. 10s. 0d. However, whatever level was eventually reached by this natural method, he was convinced that it was "sure to be conformable to the national interest." In the hope that his views would be taken seriously he added a timetable of resumption which clearly represented some further reflection on the plan noted earlier and a further step towards the bullionist position.[35] There can be no doubt that Attwood damaged his credibility among both politicans and economists by these recommendations. His willingness to consider gold as a standard negated his other recommendation, and much was made of this inconsistency. Furthermore, the figure £4. 10s. 0d. encouraged those who liked to disparage him as an inflationist out to profit from speculation. They did not appreciate that Attwood had the interests of the nation at heart. His preferences had been clearly defined elsewhere; those conditions no longer applied, thanks to the passage of the act of 1819. His primary purpose was therefore to win modifications which, although second best, would allow the nation to remain solvent.

The resumptive legislation was approved in its final form on 27 July 1819, having passed unanimously.[36] Matthias Attwood, who had not yet been unseated, and his friends had been prevailed upon to be absent from the divisions on the ground that their cause was hopeless. If the country was to accept the decision at all it would be better, they were told, to show a united and determined face. Thomas was very annoyed, but knowing his brother's Tory predilections was not wholly surprised. As far as he was concerned, however, the question was not closed. Despite a sense of despair at the folly of Parliament, he wrote a second letter to Lord Liverpool.[37]

It left no doubt as to the commercial principles upon which he based his actions. The legislature was accused of enacting "unbusiness-like" measures, of regulating a "Community" which was at all times "far better qualified to take care of its own interest." The individual should be the arbiter of his own destiny, and Attwood used a French phrase that was to become famous in the years ahead to describe that philosophy, *"laissez-nous faire."*[38] These recommendations applied to a time when the currency was "equivalent to its purposes" and not, of course, to a time of depression when vigorous government action was required. Attwood assumed that "full employment" was the end of all economic policy; thus currency augmentation and "inflation" were but transitory phenomena.

The analysis Attwood offered of the causes for the postwar depression in these two letters was for the most part accurate. The restrictive monetary practices of the Bank, which were designed to secure the supposed preconditions for the efficient operation of the gold standard, coupled with an ill-conceived fiscal policy, created high unemployment and weakened the ability of the economy to adjust to the changed circumstances. Believing that the "most important" interests within the business community required an early return to the 1797 standard, the Bank of England and the cabinet had listened to the bullionists. Lamentably, businessmen themselves were largely ignored. The rate at which Britain returned to gold was unrealistic for the reasons Attwood described; the exchanges were put before any consideration of consequences for the domestic economy. The advantages gained were negligible save for a vague satisfaction that "stability" had been won and that those who had immorally profited from the war inflation had been punished. The first was to last only until the boom/recession cycle of 1825–6 and the second was never true. Conscious of the compendium of errors and misconceptions which passed for serious monetary theory, Attwood committed the remainder of his public life to bringing a measure of realism to the currency policies of Bank and government.

CHAPTER FIVE

Backstairs Politics

Attwood, stunned by the rejection of his plea for common sense, spent much of the autumn of 1819 reevaluating his position. It had become clear that argument even when incontrovertible was not enough. It was at this time that he came to an important decision. The solitary pursuit of monetary reform through pamphlets and letters had to be replaced by collective action in a broadly based movement. To attract the level of support necessary to change the mind of Westminster a sustained campaign had to be mounted to exert consistent pressure. In such a campaign effective leadership was crucial and, his friends assured him, it was his duty to take on the task. The decision to play a more prominent role would entail more time away from the comfort of the Crescent and Elizabeth resolutely opposed the change. In the end, however, she was forced to recognize that the degree of her husband's commitment left no alternative.

The new policy had three prongs. Attwood would continue to write but instead of pamphlets the main thrust would be directed to the publication of letters in various journals and newspapers. Thereby he could trade upon his reputation as an economist yet proselytize among a much wider readership. The second line was the establishment of a secure and supportive body of opinion in Birmingham. Opinion in the town had been fragmented and volatile with few areas of common purpose during the previous three years; political reform had dominated debate. Moreover, in August when the yeomanry had ridden down the crowd in St Peter's Field, Manchester, opinion had been polarized. The "Peterloo Massacre" had even split Attwood's inner circle.[1] Still, the campaigns of 1812–13 for economic justice and occasional community effort to relieve distress did demonstrate a reservoir of interest in the economy. If that could be channelled into a single drive for the repeal of the 1819 Act the monetarists would have a platform from which their appeal could be launched. Much preliminary work had already been done by Attwood, Spooner, James, and others in associating the town with their ideas. Petitions incorporating these had been dispatched to London. The intent in 1820 was to provide a focus for concern. The means were simple: at every town meeting someone was deputed to raise the question of the currency; in casual debate whether it be at the counter of the bank, the bar of the Hen and Chickens Hotel, or the open-air market in the Bull Ring, some reference to gold and paper notes was to be interjected; and, most importantly, each of them should offer to help in the formation of clubs, societies, and associations. By this means they were to be gradually "accepted as the natural leaders of Birmingham"; As such their opinions would gain added weight. The history of the following twenty years proved that, in this at least, the plan was uniquely successful.

The last thrust in the grand design was to become in 1830 the most important – direct intervention through the election of MPs to Westminster. In 1820, however, it was a project of limited scope. The idea had grown out of the ambitions of Matthias Attwood and Richard Spooner. Both liked the prospect of serving at Westminster and had been actively seeking election for some time. The advantage of having vocal support in the Commons was self-evident and Thomas Attwood went so far as to advocate in private a limited reform of the House under which "two hundred businessmen" would be brought in to balance the landed interest. But for the moment even one or two "rational" voices would be welcome.

The first tentative step in implementing these proposals was taken on 30 December 1819. Joshua Scholefield had recently become high bailiff and as a member of the inner circle was able to respond immediately to the circle's requests.[2] The requisition to the high bailiff for a town meeting was carefully phrased so as to entice as many signatures as possible. It focused on the question of distress, which no one would be bold enough to decry. At the meeting itself Attwood turned the debate from the subject of distress to that of the gold standard and the 1819 Act. Preliminary approval for a petition to Parliament was a formality, given the skilful presentation of the argument. More important, however, was the appointment of a committee of inquiry.[3] Although the claimed purpose was a simple one – the gathering of evidence of distress to support the theoretical analysis – it was a brilliant move. It gave the campaign official status and authorized Attwood and his friends to provide corps of "investigators" who would visit every business house, workshop, and warehouse in the town. At each stop their explanation of the present economic decline would be clearly outlined. Birmingham had already expressed some sympathy for the monetary theory of Attwood; now it was to become thoroughly indoctrinated.

Such an intrusion into the main stream of the town's politics was not welcomed by those who had become used to the status quo. The Chamber of Commerce and the magistrates had become accustomed to the idea that they alone represented "respectable" opinion. Dissent could be dismissed as simple-minded radicalism so long as its main source was the Hampden Club or some hand-drawn newspaper. But Attwood's group could not be so lightly categorized notwithstanding their critical analysis of the Liverpool administration. The Tory elements in the town thus moved cautiously. Their only response of note was the preparation of a petition to counteract the claims made by Attwood. The task of refutation was not easy, not simply because the manifestations of distress were too many to ignore but because those who might be called supporters of the currency school were everywhere. Some, like Spooner, were nominally Tory and sat in the Chamber of Commerce where they frustrated attempts to pass condemnatory resolutions. Clearly the initial phase of Attwood's campaign had begun well.

In January 1820, however, there was a temporary setback. Attwood became dangerously ill with pneumonia. For a time, it seemed that he would die. Three months earlier his thirty-two year-old sister, Susanna, a favourite in the family, had died and fears for Thomas may in consequence have been exaggerated. Attwood's strength returned only slowly and for some time he was confined to bed. The one advantage was that he had the leisure to spend all his time on the first task in the new plan.

Evans and Ruffey's Farmers' Journal had, since 1815, provided space for currency theorists and agricultural opinion. Sir John Sinclair,[4] one of the few men outside Birmingham who had applauded Attwood's letters to Lord Liverpool unreservedly, had submitted numerous contributions which had been printed and enjoyed the support of others through the letter columns.[5] On the 31 January 1820, Geoffrey Webb Hall, one of the most influential leaders of the agricultural interest, used the paper to attack Attwood's *Second Letter to the Earl of Liverpool*. Attwood was not slow to recognize the opportunity. In his analysis the country party had been responsible for the passage of the resumption legislation. If he could overcome their "ignorance," then that decision might be overturned. It was just the kind of task that could be accomplished during his recuperation. The plan was not as desperate as it might first appear. Attwood already had a following among the farming community, due originally to the good offices of Richard Spooner, the duke of Norfolk, Arthur Young, and Colquhoun. Moreover, among the country gentlemen there was considerable dissatisfaction with the Tory party. The distress in agriculture had not abated and there was a general clamour for action. Between 14 February and 10 July 1820, Attwood published some ten letters which won the kind of response the Birmingham circle had sought. A national debate was launched in which Attwood was taken to represent one side of the argument, a clear improvement on the Birmingham label too often attached to his ideas. Of course, many correspondents were highly critical of his approach but that did not disturb him; it was the question itself that needed to be aired.

Meanwhile both Spooner and Matthias Attwood were busy. In January the death of George III necessitated a general election. Daringly, Spooner decided to contest the constituency of Boroughbridge in the West Riding of Yorkshire for the "Liberal" interest against the duke of Newcastle's nominees. For many years it had been considered to be in the pocket of the duke. Spooner won the election only to be unseated on petition a few months later. Curiously, his experience was the reverse of Matthias's. The latter contested Callington, Cornwall, against the sitting member and lost. Two months later the seat was awarded to him, again after petition.

On 12 May the petition that had been initiated by Attwood and Spooner, with the connivance of Scholefield, complaining of the depressed state of trade in Birmingham and asking for a parliamentary inquiry, was presented by Dugdale, the member for North Warwickshire. Brougham had been primed by Attwood to speak in support but his efforts were a sad disappointment.[6] Brougham probably saw nothing in it for himself. Spooner, not yet driven out, was not nearly as hesitant and gave what was to be his first and last major speech in the Commons for many years. His remarks were Attwoodian in the sense that they paralleled Attwood's letters in the *Farmer's Journal*, but since both men had collaborated on the text anything else would have been surprising. The only difference lay in Spooner's less passionate delivery of the underconsumptionists' argument.

With Spooner, however temporarily, pressing Birmingham's plea for an inquiry in the Commons and Attwood having advanced, he hoped, his national standing, conditions were right for an all-out attack on the standard. Attwood therefore travelled to London to plan a major speech for his partner in support of a motion on the currency. To his annoyance, Spooner, anxious to make a good impression and not yet convinced that the petition to unseat him would succeed, had acceded to a request from Castlereagh that his initiative be postponed – the holidays of the House took precedence. Nevertheless, Attwood enthusiastically embarked on the task of lobbying. It was a tactic in which he had become something of an expert, although lack of success in the past meant that he was sceptical of its efficacy. The rounds were necessary because Holme Sumner was scheduled to introduce a number of resolutions for the relief of agriculture; these resolutions were widely believed to have originated with Attwood's recent antagonist, Webb Hall.

It was decided that Spooner would rise to oppose the resolutions and move an amendment calling for the appointment of a committee to inquire into the currency. Attwood boasted in a letter to his wife that Webb Hall and himself were likely to become the "great guides of Parliament." He had no doubt of ultimate victory for his opponent's troops were "fast deserting him."[7] Dinner invitations and coffee-house gatherings undoubtedly encouraged such optimism. Not for the first or last time Attwood's vanity and susceptibility to flattery were to play him false. When told of the praise for his ideas contained in a recent letter to the *Farmers' Journal* he accepted it as fact. Yet even a cursory reading reveals that the author only superficially praised Attwood's effort. Agriculture was to be protected first and only then should the currency be liberated.[8] This was the reverse order to that contained in Attwood's panacea. Another letter directed attention to foreign investment and its debilitating effect on the British economy.[9] The farming lobby was far from united and it was unlikely that many would sufficiently overcome their prejudice to follow a banker from Birmingham.

Attwood's thesis was holistic and embraced the community at large and not small sections of it. The agricultural interests, on the other hand, were concerned with particular problems and many were suspicious of the commercial and manufacturing lobby that was growing in strength at Westminster.[10] Furthermore, the Malthusian "population trap" hypothesis and Ricardo's law of diminishing returns had gripped the public's imagination and Attwood's failure to expound convincingly on these issues counted against him. His "four times consumption" argument had not included references to urban growth nor had he alluded to the effects an end of the corn-growing bounty might have. Attwood's conception of a transfer of British resources from the low (agricultural) to the high (manufacturing) productivity sectors of the economy, whereby Birmingham's ironware would pay for food grown in the colonies, was the consequence most feared by the landowners. Public interest in the subject had already begun to wane and the editor of the *Journal*, wearied perhaps by the unrelenting Attwoodian rhetoric, had reminded his correspondent several weeks earlier that the magazine was designed to accommodate discussions about agriculture, not politics. The prospect of a smashing victory in the Commons, therefore, was quite the opposite to what Attwood seemed to expect. Perhaps fortunately, he was spared the ignominy of repudiation by the loss of Spooner's seat; the projected motion disappeared with him.

Despite this inconclusive outcome, the time spent on the letters and the parliamentary campaign had not been wasted. The name Attwood had become known nationally and Thomas was acknowledged, despite occasional confusion with his brother Matthias, to be the foremost spokesman and theorist of a group of economists opposed to the Ricardians. His efforts to harness the potentially powerful agricultural community and so bridge the gap between town and country were appreciated. Men able to look beyond narrow sectional concerns began to correspond in increasing numbers and to work for common goals. In the 1840s pockets of "currency farmers," spouting Attwoodian theory, could be found; their strength was a testament to the value of an "education" provided through the letter columns of the *Farmers' Journal*.

Attwood's standing in Birmingham had also been enhanced. Although a petition to the House of Commons had been organized by the Chamber of Manufacturing and Commerce to counteract his approach in May, there was no doubt in Birmingham which was the more important and representative. Even the Tory newspaper, the *Birmingham Chronicle*, reported the speeches at the town meeting far more fully than those in the chamber.[11] The editor also carefully refrained from public criticism of the stance taken by so many prominent men at the former gathering. He was not nearly so circumspect in his reports of the radicals' tirades in support of Queen Caroline, notwithstanding the echoes they contained of the Attwood/Spooner rhetoric.[12]

Thanks to the assiduous cultivation of opinion during the summer, a town meeting called to hear the report of the committee appointed in January and to endorse a fresh resolution of action was eagerly anticipated. All aspects of the economy from the Corn Laws to the Poor Rate had been argued, often angrily, somewhere in the town and there was a mood to end the bickering. Moreover, those who had carried their request to London were likely to have new tales of cabinet and cockney "naiveté" to buttress the provincial sense of business superiority. On both counts, they were not disappointed. In both format and content the committee's report was conspicuously Attwoodian and thus, virtually by definition, both optimistic and impassioned.

The expressions of optimism were for public consumption in Birmingham. Attwood knew that any new petition had little chance of success. Lord Liverpool was not singlehandedly thwarting the town, despite what the anti-gold standard men said in their speeches. That charade was designed to enhance the standing of the monetarists by giving the populace an identifiable enemy upon whom to vent their frustration. The more pragmatic side of Attwood was reflected in the resolutions presented for approval. They were designed purely for local effect and intended to catch the mood of the town. Each resolution had been carefully drafted. Taken together, their theme is one of interdependence and the necessity of a single leadership. They present a picture of unity that resembles Asa Briggs's description of the town.[13] As a statement of the current situation the evocation was patently false. There had been no room on the platform for any of the working people's leaders. The working classes were present in the audience and cheered the speeches, but outside the hall their preference for radical reform and, occasionally, riot ensured that Attwood would maintain his distance. The idea of monetary reform enjoyed their intermittent support, but the banker and his friends were well aware of the divisions and the mutual antipathy. During their rounds as investigators in the spring, Scholefield, Spooner, and Attwood had not spent much time talking to Gerry Edmonds and the radicals. They knew that if these men and been willing to listen, the danger of identifying the currency campaign with political radicalism at this time outweighed any advantages to be gained from the backing of sheer numbers. But they also knew that this was a weakness. It was a problem of control and it was to this end that the resolutions were directed. They were a contrived view of what should be, not what was. They were an invitation to future collaboration rather than a celebration of past achievement. Attwood was intent on signalling the reemergence of the "liberal" forces in the town. Their voice had been muted in the sometimes violent struggle between conservatives and radicals in the last two years, but their resurrection held the promise of unity.

It was to be Attwood's triumph that this potent element found shelter under the currency umbrella.

The plan to assume the mantle of leadership in the town had been advanced, but all was not well with Attwood himself. It had been fortunate that Spooner had, by design, been the main proponent of the resolutions. Attwood was in an exceedingly strange mood. Up until a few days before the meeting he had been excited and confident in the knowledge that they were prepared for every eventuality. Then his wife had departed with the children to visit friends. Left alone, he brooded. In the evening, he "doctored" two sick birds, a kite and a raven, by cutting off damaged wings (somehow the raven survived). On the platform the next day he spent much of his time scowling and writing notes. If the notes contained comments similar to those included in letters to his wife it was lucky that no one else saw them. Nothing, he lamented, but error and crime could be expected from the "Aristocratic Canaille" which governed England. He did not like the "Democrats" and "as for Voltaire's favourites, the Middle Classes, they are fit for nothing but *dumb sheep* to be shorn at the will of their masters."[14] If he was their ruler, he would make them "pay dearly for the honour of being slaves." It was an intemperate letter and one wonders what was his wife's reaction. Outside the hall, Attwood uncharacteristically spent much of his time alone, wandering the river valley and beset by self-doubt. As he grew older these spells of melancholia became more frequent. The mixture of arrogance and compassion in his personality had two effects. It gave him the drive to pursue his convictions despite adversity, but it also made delay unacceptable. At this time his vision of the future was clouded and, notwithstanding the clear success of the program in Birmingham, there were few signs that the government was any more receptive to his ideas than it had been in 1819. It was entirely conceivable that he would never win his argument; thus, briefly, he turned inward in despair.

Attwood's melancholy was on this occasion a momentary aberration for a new challenge suddenly appeared. The need to gain seats in the House of Commons for the group had been asserted many times but the obstacles had been formidable. Then, at the end of August, came news of the resignation of Sir Charles Mordaunt, MP for the county of Warwickshire. Attwood quickly initiated a requisition, which was presented to Scholefield, still high bailiff, for a town meeting to secure the nomination of Richard Spooner. Spooner's chance was deemed best given his earlier experience in the House and his impeccable farming credentials – a model farm at Perry Hill near Worcester, the praise of Coke of Holkham, membership of the Bath and West of England Agricultural Society, and the support of the duke of Norfolk.

The speeches and resolutions at the meeting on 15 October offer a fair guide to Attwood's political sympathies at this time. As has been remarked elsewhere, his pamphlets and letters were polemical and hardly to be trusted as a guide to his party preference. In these months he spoke infrequently, preferring to remain in the background as a member of Spooner's committee. In that capacity he drafted the speeches of others and felt free to give expression to opinions in which the currency was not the major topic. Spooner's election address unequivocally affirmed Birmingham's belief in the right of the manufacturing and commercial interests of the country to direct political representation. While accepting that the ownership of land was an important qualification for an MP representing a county, it argued that such a background did not preclude the election of one who was "capable of justly apprehending" urban interests. The contribution of industry to the prosperity of the nation was such that "they have a fair claim to require that one of the Representatives [of the county] should be a gentleman possessing an intimate knowledge of their Trade and Manufactures."[15] These sentiments would not have satisfied the members of the Hampden Club; neither would they have gained many supporters for the Political Union in 1830. But their very innocuousness would, it was hoped, allay whatever fears the propertied electors in the county might have at this intrusion of Birmingham into "Warwickshire's affairs."

Enthusiasm in the town for the campaign was unprecedented. Each day Attwood spent some time in the campaign headquarters receiving expressions of support from people in every walk of life. It was all quite heartening. Outside Birmingham, however, the rhetoric was naturally viewed with alarm. The Tory and agricultural interest had no desire to see one of their seats usurped and their concern was heightened by an extraordinary decision. The day before the nomination formalities in Warwick, the county town, Spooner's committee organized a parade through the streets, led by Scholefield and Ryland, the bailiffs, as Birmingham's first citizens. Virtually every vehicle in Birmingham was hired to convey voters to Warwick. Blue ribbons, flags, streamers, and musicians enlivened the whole length of the road to the county town. Round every man's hat was pinned a blue paper with the inscription, "Spooner for ever." This demonstration of the degree of support enjoyed by Spooner was intended to encourage the undecided electors.[16] Presumably Attwood agreed with the decision to march and one can only attribute the miscalculation to inexperience. The demonstration itself was certain to be counterproductive even if executed flawlessly, since the county electorate were unlikely to view such a blatant identification of the candidate with Birmingham in a favourable light. For those who wielded some influence nothing was to be gained by an alliance with that provincial town, given the unreformed character of the House of Commons.

The committee should also have known, if only from the simple observation of events in the last five years, that the mobilization of large numbers of people usually ended in disorder. Yet they empanelled too few marshals and were careless in the order of march. In consequence, their ranks were swollen by the idle and footloose who contrived to make a nuisance of themselves. Lawley, the opposing candidate, had already decided that this intrusion was akin to a declaration of war and had been designed to intimidate. He instructed his supporters to answer in kind; in consequence, disturbance and disorder overshadowed the debate.

Spooner lost by 2,153 to 969 votes.[17] A petition to Parliament asking that the vote be overturned on the ground that some of the Coventry electors had been illegally prevented from voting was drawn up.[18] Only Spooner among the committee members professed any sort of confidence in this ploy.[19] He himself had been unseated by petition and he optimistically but unsuccessfully pursued his claim well into the summer of the following year, when it was dismissed as "vexatious and frivolous." Attwood had given up long before.

As treasurer for the committee Attwood remained in Warwick for several days settling bills, but he was back in Birmingham in time for the post-election dinner. It was a quiet meeting, yet there was cause for some hope. Their initial analysis of Spooner's chances had forecast an even greater defeat, so the campaign had obviously met with a positive response. The failure should be counted only as a setback. Indeed, the effort had yielded some profit. The alliance that had been forged to forward currency reform had been expanded in number and battle-hardened. The experience gained in putting together an organization to marshal support across the county was invaluable and might make a difference next time.

The sense of responsibility and the assumption of leadership by Attwood's group were strengthened in the following months. The establishment of a Society of Arts was launched with a declaration that the cultivation of the fine arts was "essential to the prosperity of the manufacturers of this town and neighbourhood."[20] On 20 March 1821 an association was formed for the "Protection of Trade against Fraudulent Bankrupts, Swindlers, etc."; parliamentary regulations were, in the members' opinion, inadequate. Birmingham needed to set its own house in order. Attwood sat on the governing committee and his bank acted as treasurer. Six weeks later, in support of a national campaign, these "liberal" citizens now under the patronage of a new high bailiff, George Muntz, another of Attwood's circle, requested a town meeting to "examine the propriety of petitioning the Legislature for a revision of the Criminal Laws." The signatures on the requisition were virtually identical to those of the previous year and, of course, included the names of Attwood, Spooner, and Scholefield. At the subsequent meeting various speakers attacked the barbarity of the laws and made the point that such a code was not consistent with the times.[21] Society had changed and with it the nature of offences. The inhabitants of Birmingham wanted the government of Britain to recognize those changes and thereby acknowledge their right to participate in the business of government.

The group's continuously growing influence in the town was enhanced by the summoning of Attwood to London. Birmingham's petition of the previous August had been joined on the table of the House of Commons by hundreds from all parts of the country. Angry landowners, farmers, workers, and merchants caught between falling prices and high fixed overheads assaulted Parliament with examples of hardship and pressed for solutions of the nation's ills. Many radical measures proved popular – the abolition of tithes, the reduction of the interest on the National debt, the redistribution of the tax burden, bimetallism, reform, and, of course, currency devaluation. Sheer weight of numbers had finally forced the Commons to appoint a select committee.[22]

Thomas Sherlock Gooch, scion of a land-owning family of Suffolk and a man who apparently favoured a change in the Resumption Act of 1819, was to be the chairman of the committee. According to Attwood, Gooch was "quite convinced that Peel's Bill was *intended* to operate a total transfer of the landed rental of the kingdom into the hands of the fundholders."[23] Attwood himself had, to date, never gone so far in his condemnation of government action. To back the chairman there was a preponderance of landowners on the committee who must surely be opposed to the "monied interest" that had the ear of Lord Liverpool. Both factors augured well for a concerted attack on the gold standard. More to the point, Attwood's attacks in the *Farmers' Journal* on Webb

Hall's solution to distress – protection – had obviously made some headway. A supporter of Webb Hall had been shouted down in Devon. At a Lewes meeting, protectionist resolutions had been rejected and an amendment for cheaper money substituted. Even Holme Sumner, who had been expected to lead the opposition as Webb Hall's champion in the Commons if Spooner's motion of the previous summer had been debated, argued that competition was no longer the cause of agricultural distress.[24] Naturally there were other factors besides Attwood's letters to explain this shift to the underconsumptionist philosophy that underpinned currency theory. But judging by the frequency with which phrases from his writings were used in debate, Attwood may be excused from believing otherwise. As Western said, the common fate of corn and iron "proved the union of the two interests."[25]

Attwood arrived in London full of confidence in his ability to sway "the sad specimens of the lords of human kind" who sat in Parliament. Several friends including the Colquhouns offered their hospitality, but he chose to stay at the Bedford Coffee House. It had the advantage of being an informal meeting-place where debate could be open and frank without the politeness essential on a formal social occasion. After two exciting days plotting strategy with his friends, he was called before the committee.

Anxious as ever to avoid the smear that he spoke for a special commercial interest, banking, Attwood immediately tried to seize the initiative by emphasizing that he appeared not simply in a private capacity but as a delegate from Birmingham. To reinforce that point he presented the evidence gathered by his working parties of the previous summer, which detailed the decline in consumption between 1818 and 1820, and their "independent" conclusions. This was hard evidence of his status which, he was certain, even "the iron heads" of the committee would find difficult to dismiss. His claim was not disputed and the early exchanges were cordial. But the opening pleasantries were deceiving. Quickly two lines of questioning developed which were unequivocally hostile. Both emanated from his known "enemies," Huskisson and Ricardo, who sat on either side of the chairman, "like Sin and Death guarding the gates of Hell."[26] Attwood had prepared with particular care when he learned of their presence on the committee, but placed his hopes for a successful engagement on the agriculturalist majority who could swamp the advocates of bullion. It did not take long to disabuse him of that expectation. The country gentlemen proved as "dull as beetles" whereas their foes were "sharp as needles and active as bees." The tactic of Huskisson was to demonstrate Attwood's ignorance on the subject of farming and farm labourers. As he was later to lament, they asked him about "fat cattle and lean and about plough-lands and frost lands, and about everything else, except the one thing needful, *viz* the cause of the low price of agricultural produce." Obviously it was to Huskisson's advantage if Attwood were revealed in his urban, banking guise so that his attraction for farmers would be thereby diminished. The banker did his best but there were too many details to cope with and he became bogged down in unproductive explanation.[27]

The second line taken by his inquisitors was led by Ricardo and sought to reveal a dogmatic provincialism based on a narrow band of experience. How was it possible for him to know the benefits which would accrue to British manufacturers if he did not understand the theory of the exchanges? He had made this admission a few answers earlier. Attwood, of course, refused to acknowledge the relevance of the theoretical implications of his remedy and, as a man of business, claimed competence to judge the practical ramifications. His reply naturally failed to satisfy his inquisitors and under pressure he was continually forced to qualify his remarks. Still, the main body of his argument was stoutly defended. His rebuttal of the most damning objection, that he did not know what he was doing and that it was unnecessary anyway, was convincing. The frequent interjections of Huskisson and Peel were proof that they feared his argument and the susceptibility of some of their fellow committee members.

Attwood's examination took two exhausting four-hour sessions to complete, but characteristically he had no doubts of his persuasiveness. He emerged from the committee rooms elated and immediately sat down to tell his wife of his triumph: "I think I have at last succeeded in making an impression. They have heard me with tolerable patience, and have had all their little difficulties removed, and some light let in on their comfortless prospects. I answered all the objections of Ricardo and Huskisson, I believe most completely and very evidently to their deep mortification."[28] For several days he congratulated himself that the committee had been firmly turned towards the question of the currency and away from a narrow preoccupation with farming distress. On all sides there was evidence to support his confidence. Sir Robert Peel told him on two occasions that "his son's opinions are *shook*, and that he thinks he repents the part he has taken."[29] He dined with Littleton and Colquhoun's son, saw the duke of Sussex who flatteringly asked for copies of his pamphlets, and heard numerous tales that members of the committee were determined to cross Huskisson by insisting on a paean to currency in their report.[30] Recognition and praise at the social round of dinners or from casual acquaintances on public occasions, including the interval at the opera, quite dazzled him. He even deemed it safe to describe that pillar of the establishment, the duke of Wellington, as a man of "not much sense or intellect."[31] The balloon was soon to be punctured.

Attwood had not counted on the managerial ability of Huskisson, who stuck rigidly to the terms of the inquiry and persisted in calling only farmers and dealers in agricultural products.[32] Other advocates of an augmentation of the currency, including two of his particular friends, Rev. R. Cruttwell and J. Rooke, who had come to London to add their voices to that of Attwood, were ignored.[33] The evidence of a few witnesses contained references to the currency issue, but their remarks were usually made with the opposite intent to Attwood's.[34] The report was unquestionably the work of Huskisson. As Ricardo admitted to a friend, it had not been easy: "I hope that you are satisfied with the Report, there are some absurdities in it, but considering how the Committee was formed, and the opposition given to sound principles by the landed gentlemen, I think it is on the whole creditable to the Committee."[35] In the end the only concession "won" by Attwood's "friends" was a restatement of the doctrine of protection for agriculture; the very point he had contested with Webb Hall had apparently been lost.[36]

The presentation of the report was, in fact, an anticlimax. The real battle for currency reform in 1821 had been fought in the House of Commons during April. While Attwood had been giving his evidence, the government had introduced a motion calling for the abandonment of Ricardo's ingot plan. Baring had seized the opportunity to move an amendment which demanded a full and exhaustive reexamination of Peel's Act. Quoting Thornton's authoritative conclusion that workers' wages adjusted at a different rate from that of prices, Baring warned Parliament that the neglect of the social implications of economic measures might encourage revolution.[37] In support, Matthias Attwood set out to encompass as broad a spectrum of opinion as possible by arguing that the distress was indeed attributable to alterations in the currency.[38] Clearly the argument was designed to complement the campaign of his brother and the supposed proponents of paper money in the committee rooms.

The gathering of forces from the country to give evidence provided a nucleus of determined lobbyists to act at social gatherings and in antechambers even if they were not called by Huskisson. The omens had been propitious but the perennial problem of accommodating a variety of conflicting expectations within a common cause bedevilled the promoters. They found it impossible to weld a cohesive pressure group together and encountered opposition from the most unexpected quarters. Edward Ellice, a professed radical and member for Coventry, had opposed the bill of 1819 and had suggested a standard far higher than anything proposed by Attwood. Yet he spoke against Baring's motion and urged that the country gentlemen "bend their attention entirely to the reduction of expenses"; an argument based almost solely on the ground that further change would be "politically disturbing."[39] This conservative attitude was to become increasingly fashionable in the months ahead.[40] Ironically, Attwood had used a similar argument prior to the passage of Peel's bill in 1819. Baring's motion was lost with a meagre twenty-seven in favour. The country gentlemen were already turning to tax relief and retrenchment. Thomas Attwood "might as well have reasoned with the winds of heaven."[41]

CHAPTER SIX

False Hopes

Attwood's sense of despair in the early summer of 1821 was profound. Letters to friends, allies, and the *Farmers' Journal* continued to be written. There was even one short pamphlet. But there is a desultory air, a lack of conviction, which is not in keeping with the Old Testament prophet-style of the past. The desire to wash the whole business of currency and the plight of the country out of his life was undoubtedly hard to resist. Temporarily the efforts to build a consensus in the town itself held little appeal if there was to be no national goal to pursue. Spooner argued valiantly and outlined a program of local initiatives which would keep their names and ideas to the fore. His friend yielded and allowed the use of his name, although he promised nothing in terms of enthusiasm. Using as pretexts the death of his sister-in-law, Sarah Carless, and the birth of a daughter, Rosabel, on 24 July, Attwood claimed that domestic ties required his presence when not at the bank.

It was at times like these that Attwood almost always turned towards the question of personal fortune. He certainly had need of cash. His family now included six children and there were various relatives, mostly on the Carless side, to support. Moreover, charity in times of economic distress beggars the giver. To invest in some new enterprise in England was unthinkable in the light of his own analysis of his country's economic prospects. He did have an opportunity to join his cousin John in developing the Dudley estate. The original lease given to his grandfather, George Attwood, by Lord Dudley had expired but the option to continue as tenants-at-will was offered. It was to prove a lucrative investment, but neither Thomas nor any of his brothers had the confidence to participate.[1]

Thomas Attwood's refusal was also determined by his belief that he had an alternative and potentially more profitable use for his available capital. Some months earlier he had solicited the help of the duke of Sussex in gaining letters of introduction for his brother James to the governor of Odessa. James was branching out into the Russian trade, particularly that of corn, and was shortly to travel through the southern part of that country. In return James had given him some interesting but selective information about conditions on the continent.[2] The rate of interest in England, he said, compared unfavourably with that in France, where profits on capital and industry were "high and secure," advantages which, "will naturally draw English capital abroad." Typically, Attwood jumped to all manner of conclusions and decided to commit the fortunes of his family in a new direction. It was of course extremely naive and inadvertent confirmation of the charges of ignorance levelled by Ricardo. He was always too willing to believe travellers' tales.

The first task was to make contact with businessmen in France who might welcome an infusion of English capital and technical knowledge. For this purpose his own bank could not help; most of its overseas business was with northern Europe and the United States. Fortunately there was another source that could be trusted. The London bank, directed by his brother Matthias, had concentrated its interests in France for some time. Throughout the remaining months of the year Attwood corresponded extensively with that bank's agents, most of whom were English, and various French bankers. For the moment the currency campaign must continue with only his tacit support. His search for a suitable location began with Paris, but the type of establishment contemplated, a cotton roller printing mill, argued for the Rouen region where the textile industry was already entrenched. The final decision depended on a personal inspection; the enthusiasm of local men often, he knew, outran their judgment. By Christmas, all the preliminary arrangements had been made for a trip to France. But the need to study the cotton factories in England more closely required a delay until May, since Attwood did not wish to venture abroad unarmed.

Distress had not abated during the autumn and winter. The respite won for the government by the Agricultural Committee's report and a little judicious retrenchment in the public economy had been shortlived. Demands for tax reduction and an alteration in the currency reemerged.[3] Attwood, watching from the sidelines and with his money-making plans nicely under way, found the clamour for some kind of monetary reform fascinating, particularly as it involved both Whigs and the country gentry in a temporary coalition against the government.[4] The chance to take advantage of the new alignments was irresistible and, almost in spite of himself, while waiting for his cotton mill plans to develop, Attwood began to dabble in politics once again.

His first impulse was to woo the Whigs. The spinelessness of the country gentlemen who had sat on the Agricultural Committee disgusted him; they had not even fought to bring their own spokesman to testify. On the other hand, Matthias, from London, warned of the disarray within the Whig party and counselled against any reliance on Henry Brougham.[5] Squabbles over the leadership and a multitude of voices in cross-hatched disagreement meant that a consensus on general policy could rarely be reached. Despite their short attention span, he was assured, the gentry would make the more reliable ally. The letters to the *Farmers' Journal* remained a talking-point and something might yet be created out of that enthusiasm. Although it was not mentioned directly, Attwood understood that his brother and his circle were Tory and likely to remain so. If the Whigs were to become Birmingham's champions it would be at the expense of their London friends. The point was further emphasized by Spooner's declaration that he, for one, had no intention of joining an approach to the Whigs. Insistence on that course risked losing much that had been won in the midland town. The advice was undoubtedly sound but, as far as Attwood was concerned, essentially negative.

Attwood's continued consideration of a link with the Whigs despite these warnings was borne of calculation rather than conviction.[6] Yet it was more serious than he led his friends to believe and could have signalled a major shift in his political position. In 1821 reform of the House of Commons had once more become the policy of one of the great parties in the House, when Lord John Russell had moved a series of resolutions; the most important of these was the establishment of a select committee to consider which new boroughs should be enfranchised. The motion had been defeated, but after some success on tax questions he had reintroduced the topic on 25 April 1822. This time the motion was even more general. It simply called for the state of representation to be seriously considered by the House. It was lost but the number voting for it, 164, had been the largest ever recorded save for Pitt's motion in 1785.[7]

Edward Davenport, a Whig who had been active at Westminster for some time in the cause of reform, wrote to Attwood in April, before Russell introduced his general resolution, outlining his own ideas and asking for comment. It could be that he was anxious to discover the extent of Attwood's commitment to reform other than in the economic sphere. If they were to work closely together, as Attwood had recently suggested, it would be necessary to have at least a tentative understanding. It is more probable, however, that he was already aware of Attwood's acceptance, in principle, of the need for a reform of both the structure and the character of the House of Commons. Attwood did not disappoint him. Two days after Lord John Russell addressed the House, he offered his qualified support.[8]

Attwood picked out three components of Davenport's proposals. Triennial parliaments, the first point, was the middle road between the existing seven-year life of the Commons and the ultra-radicals' one-year recommendation. An election every three years would increase the weight given to public opinion in drawing up policies, while allowing a new government time to get something done. The dismissal of placemen and the removal of a hundred seats from the boroughs to the great towns and counties, the second and third recommendations, would, he hoped, sufficiently reform the system so that the Tories could no longer ignore public opinion. The transfer of seats to the new industrial towns and counties was in itself a major structural alteration which would have a profound effect upon the composition of the Commons. Although there was no mention of a change in the franchise, Attwood indicated that he expected practical men of business, the class from which he sprang, to be the new administrators. They had proved their ability in trade; they used their minds and did not allow passion to rule. In such a legislature his currency panacea would be given a fair hearing. No doubt he expected Davenport to communicate his support to the Whig leaders, but as this overture was far more radical than anything then contemplated by them it is not surprising the he did not get a reply.

The lack of response and the failure of the Whigs to make headway led Attwood belatedly to follow the advice of his brother and remain silent in public on the question of parliamentary reform. In any case Lord Liverpool appeared to be reconsidering past economic decisions. Tory ministers had not been finding the country gentlemen amenable to pressure and a number of successful grumbles in the name of retrenchment had brought about some redistribution of the tax burden. On the agricultural question the early promise of poor harvests as a means of raising prices had been dashed by a spell of good weather and full storage bins.

Arbitrary price increases were out of the question, given Lord Liverpool's commitment to the legislation of 1819. The answer, a ministerial memorandum suggested, might be the extension of loans at a lower rate of interest to the commercial sector and tenants, which could trigger an upturn in the economy.

The select committee on agriculture, which had been reappointed, spent its time concocting schemes on bounties and protection in an effort to placate the country gentlemen. In the end the cabinet decided to advance £4 million in exchequer bills at 3 per cent to parishes on the security of the rates. Such advances increased the circulation and lowered interest rates. As the prime minister admitted, the general public could expect to derive some relief from an increase in the general circulation. It was a point Attwood had made unavailingly by on many occasions. However, he could claim little credit. The Bank of England's reluctance to discount despite a favourable exchange demonstrated quite clearly that the reasoning behind that conclusion owed nothing to Birmingham's contribution to economic theory. In a similar vein the reduction in the Bank's rate of interest to 4 per cent in June was dictated by outside forces and cannot be construed as a sudden conversion to the view that the economy could be managed through the manipulation of the interest rate.

The idea of an advance in the form of rate-supported loans was not received with enthusiasm. Moderate critics argued that such a paltry sum would achieve nothing, while those of more extreme views, particularly among the agriculturalists, resented the implication that their prosperity depended upon the commercial sector. Such negative reactions annoyed Attwood as much as they did Liverpool. He held no great hope that the positive effects of an issue would last unless Peel's act were to be repealed, but he saw no reason to discourage the Tories in what might be the first crack in the rationale of the legislation. The task was to exploit the situation. The exchequer bill issue indicated a certain hesitation in Peel's timetable. Attwood was further encouraged by a letter from his brother in London which suggested that "the bringing of Peel into the Ministry is only a gentle way of letting him down" and that further adjustments were likely: "The object of the Ministers, I perceive, is to *fritter away* this famous Bill so as to neutralize its operations. I am so informed from the best authority that Vansittart will shortly bring in a Bill to *legalize £1 notes* of Country Bankers. These little measures coming pretty quick one after another will I rather expect raise prices."[9] His information was correct. Vansittart and Liverpool, without warning, informed the Bank's governor of their intention to extend the life of the £1 notes until 1833. There was also a scheme afoot to relax the Bank's charter to allow for an extension in the number of partners in a private bank outside a 65-mile radius of London. In exchange the charter would be extended for a further ten years.

The apparently positive signs were reinforced by news that Western proposed to present a motion in the House of Commons on 2 May for a full reconsideration of Peel's Act. Attwood was delighted for presumably Western had some expectation of success. Matthias clearly thought so, since he had announced that he would speak in support of the motion. Heartened, Thomas Attwood began again the round of letters needed to build support.

On 24 May Vansittart introduced the predicted concessions. Only the proposal to extend the number of private partners in a private bank was omitted; the opposition of the bankers themselves had killed the idea. The reprieve given small notes was taken as a great victory by the paper enthusiasts and even the government seemed to suggest that they had bowed to public pressure. But as Boyd Hilton has pointed out, the measure originated with Huskisson as a means of restoring confidence and was not believed to be a retreat from convertibility.[10]

Attwood was not in England when the exciting news became public. Plans for a business excursion to France had finally matured and he was still of a mind to keep his personal participation in the political jungle to a minimum. He did arrange to stay a few days in London prior to departure to hear the report from the reappointed Commons committee on agricultural distress. Western had postponed his motion pending the presentation of this report and there was every expectation of a vigorous debate. Thomas Attwood was in the House to hear his brother make one of the principal speeches; although the extent of their collaboration is unknown, its tenor suggests that their unanimity of thought of some seven years' duration remained intact.

Attwood left London on 9 May and travelled south through Kent to Dover. To his not unprejudiced eye the signs of government mismanagement were unmistakable, but few of those whom he engaged in conversation seemed to be aware of the monetary cause of their distress.[11] The crossing was unpleasant for he became seasick. Once ashore in France he was overcome by excitement. Although the purpose of the journey was business, this was his first trip abroad and everything was delightfully new.[12] Almost at once he decided that France was richer than England, prices were lower, and the people happier. He was captivated by Paris, telling his wife that he could happily spend many weeks in the city "without exhausting its endless amusements."[13] Part of each day was spent walking the streets, visiting Catholic churches (he was bewitched by their decorations), and admiring Frenchwomen who were "far too good [beautiful] for the french men." Unlike many of his dour business contemporaries, Attwood loved beauty for its own sake and was easily distracted from the pursuit of profit which brought wealth to so many of his friends.

He remained in Paris for a little more than a week before travelling on to Rouen. Business went well and he began the trek through the French bureaucracy for the various permits to establish a company. Everything he had been told about prospects seemed to be true. James, his business agent, had little trouble convincing Attwood that without the benevolent interference of English entrepreneurs French industry would never become profitable. Enthusiastically Attwood signed letters of credit, applied for a licence to operate a "second class" steam engine, and negotiated to buy land.[14] Nothing seemed to stand in the way of a swift and substantial return on his investment. After visiting Rouen's outport, Le Havre, he returned triumphantly to England.

The value of this journey abroad in terms of Attwood's personal development far outran the long-run benefit to his pocketbook. Until this point his analysis of the economy and government had been blinkered, owing to his limited experience of business outside the Midlands, and he had suffered from the gibe that he represented an opinionated and self-interested minority. This was untrue, but there had been little he could do to refute the charge. Although occasionally courted by London society, he had been unable to shake off a sense of alienness; a conviction that he was regarded as an untutored provincial and thus more an object of curiosity than an accepted expert. Three weeks in France had opened a window of experience that had hitherto been the vantage-point of others. Similarly, time spent in the company of those who looked in on England – the window worked both ways – added a dimension to observation that was quite invaluable.

Upon his return to England he wasted no time in regaling his friends with his newfound expertise. European travel proved the ignorance or perfidy, one could take one's pick, of the government. Lord Liverpool had explained his "do nothing" approach to economic misfortune by contending that the difficulties were shared with France and were beyond simple remedy. Attwood admitted that his own calculations on the probable effect of a bullion drain to England and Russia as the gold standard was introduced had similarly suggested that the problem was international; a view given independent corroboration, it seemed, by the laments contained in the speeches of deputies in the French Chamber, who had made much of a decline in prices. Yet after one visit to the country, he had realized that all this evidence was unreliable. France was prosperous, land values had risen (he had been quoted a high price for the prospective site of his factory), and grain prices were roughly what one might expect, given the good harvests of 1819, 1820, and 1821.

The explanation of his own error lay not in the theory, which, he was convinced, remained essentially correct, but in a misunderstanding of French character, in particular the national propensity to hoard. The drain of gold created by a return to the gold standard elsewhere had merely skimmed the surface of a great buried treasure trove which easily supported French prices. Of course there were other factors. France had attracted capital from Britain which, to a degree, had counteracted the "suction of Bullion." Furthermore, the French had not tampered with the financial system, except for a short period during the Revolution itself, and in consequence had not suffered dramatic swings in economic fortune.

The analysis is remarkably acute, given Attwood's brief exposure to the subject. Characteristically, in what amounted to little more than a postscript he does go somewhat awry. He boldly claimed that before the war British and continental prices had been approximately equal, and if the standard had been correctly adjusted "all things would [now] have been as cheap in England as in France, at the same time we should have preserved the high nominal prices upon which our high nominal burthens were founded." This conclusion is clearly biased. Devastation caused by the wars on the continent, the improved technical efficiency in England, and changing market trends could not have maintained the status quo in real prices, as the remainder of the century was to demonstrate.[15]

Attwood's return to England coincided with the final days of Western's campaign for support on his currency motion. Debate in the House was scheduled for 11 June and the usual scurry of activity and argument disrupted Matthias Attwood's home and the bank in Gracechurch Street. Anxious to reach Birmingham, Thomas did not stay long, but there was time for him to make an astonishing suggestion. He proposed that Western include payment in bars in any bill drafted as a consequence of the motion. The objective was to win the support of David Ricardo, who was noticeably disgruntled by the abandonment of his "Ingot plan," the real keystone of his resumption policy. Attwood was confident that once this method of payment had been fixed it would be comparatively simple to shift the price of bars, first of all to the market price and thence by stages to £6. 6s. an ounce and eventually £8 an ounce. The latter figure was his latest estimate of the degree of depreciation necessary to reestablish prosperity. Both it and the mooting of an alliance with Ricardo were further indications of the mistaken despondency with which Attwood now analyzed an economy still embattled despite the government's measures. He was willing to try any avenue that offered an alternative to what he believed had become a blind alley and to consider any alliance to win his case. He also warned that others should be equally flexible because if Western's motion failed then only the sword would remain to enforce the will of the people.[16] Having made his contribution, he took the stage home.

The cabinet as a body opposed the motion. Western, for his part, did not marshal his forces skilfully or even take a leading role in the debate. That honour fell to Matthias Attwood. Although the motion had been drafted before Thomas left for France, and it was apparent from the outset that the cause was hopeless, his speeches were closely argued and brilliantly presented. The main outline, the definitions, examples, even much of the language were culled directly from Thomas Attwood's pamphlets. In the continuation of the debate a month later evidence of the collaboration was again striking. In an impassioned discussion of the worldwide fall in prices, Matthias emphasized the excessive decline in England when compared to other European economies, notably that of France.[17] He did not, however, follow his brother in the role of Cassandra. Predictions of catastrophe would have been going too far. Matthias could not forget that he sat as a Tory and a representative of the financial circles of London despite the location of his constituency.

Western's motion suffered humiliating defeat, 30–194. Many who had promised their vote in the spring had been lost to the quickening pulse of the economy as the government injected demand and the business cycle swung up. The extension granted to the issue of the country bankers' small notes had been a beginning. Bullion accumulated by the Bank of England to fill the gap created by the projected withdrawal of the notes was therefore not needed and, concerned by "excessive liquidity," the Bank encouraged borrowing. Moreover, £150,000 worth of 5 per cent stock was converted to 4 per cent, forcing capital into the markets in search of a higher return; £4 million was advanced on exchequer bills and £2 million in tax was remitted on wax and salt.[18] The emancipation of the South American colonies from Spanish control created new export potential and confidence in the recovery did the rest. Prosperity, real or imagined, ended the immediate need for a change in Peel's Act and those who had clamoured to discuss the currency now found other causes to debate in their fashionable salons.

Outside Parliament few believed in the autumn of 1822 that there was a possibility of permanent prosperity and, in Birmingham, Attwood tried to keep up the pressure. At the end of July, the *Birmingham Chronicle* printed Matthias Attwood's speech of some two days before.[19] It followed this up by publishing letters from "the celebrated French Economist, M. Say" to Henry James. Say's argument in respect of the English depression corresponded in principle and in many details to that of Attwood.[20] Of late there had been a marked slackening in the number of pieces which appeared in the midland newspapers on the subject of currency, but the Say letters were an ideal basis for renewal. It was particularly gratifying that Say concurred with Attwood's own assessment of economic conditions in France and the "exaggerations" of Tory comparisons. Quickly letters of support were sent and the local editors obligingly reprinted a selection of Attwood's own articles. The ease with which all this was accomplished tells much about the effectiveness of the earlier lobbying.

Attwood, his health undermined by the trip to France, took to his bed and began writing new letters and pamphlets. Most of them sought to deal with problems and queries raised by readers and correspondents who had been disturbed by his earlier works. But they also mark a further step in his movement towards the radical camp. The assault on Peel's Act had turned into a personal battle in which the structure of society itself stood as the enemy.[21] The legislature made mistakes because it was in the hands of "creditors of the active classes." The great landowners desired to bleed and bring down the plethora of the middle classes.[22] In 1819 they had conspired in the passage of Peel's bill which had been designed to transfer the "public property into the hands of the Jews and Brokers."[23] The press, a creditor faction, had hidden the truth from the public. There was also the question of the single most important but neglected piece of economic information – the size of private and public obligations contracted during the war. By making a series of ingenious extrapolations from very limited information, Attwood came to a figure of £2,500 million.[24] Yet the press and government chose to act as if it was of no importance. Was that decision made out of ignorance or by design?

Attwood's rhetorical questions represented the doubts of the commercial classes rather than of the farmers to whom many of the letters were addressed. The latter, while unable to fault his reconstruction of the recent past, were alienated by the denigration of a hierarchical structure in which the farmer had a considerable vested interest. Tied to the landowners for generations and bound by a social system that gave status even to the lowliest, the farmers balked at any hurdle labelled reform. Attwood, aware of the enormity of the task, softened his theoretical explanations with examples carefully chosen from an agricultural lexicon. But the essential message could not be changed and the remedy Attwood recommended was by implication too radical. Cobbett was far more appealing to the farmers with his simple call for the equitable adjustment of contract; a unilateral tax revision could be applauded even by the most orthodox Tory despite its obvious drawbacks for the economy. Attwood's miscalculation originated in the ambivalence of his own position. Within Birmingham the development of a sense of identity in keeping with its commercial roots had become clear. Attwood was perforce one of the community's spokesmen and attuned to its needs. In a simpler time it had been possible to reconcile all national economic interests beneath one umbrella, albeit with some juggling of priorities. That time had passed and, although Attwood never gave up the attempt, his appeals for unity were set against a background of discordance.

The industrial revolution forced men to choose between courses of action that were predicated on varying philosophies; within that choice of futures were some that by their nature challenged the ruling order. No matter how much Attwood protested, or how many times he appealed for common action, he stood at the cutting edge of change. His rhetoric, his solutions, even his methods bred suspicion because their starting-point stood outside the knowledge of the establishment. Attwood was aware of the taint of radicalism and his vision of an eighteenth-century society with a special, newly carved niche for industry was always carefully crafted to offer the promise of continuity.

Events overtook Thomas Attwood in 1823. The improvement in the economy rapidly assumed the proportions of a boom. Those who had forecast depression were discredited. In three years the price of bar iron, a useful if rough index of Birmingham's prosperity, more than doubled. T.C. Salt, a businessman and close friend of Attwood, admitted to the committee on manufactures in 1833 that "during the whole of 1823 and 1825 the stock went so rapidly into consumption that we could hardly keep the shopkeepers supplied fast enough."[25] The Bank of England left the capital market to itself, allowing little to interfere with its duties to its shareholders which involved the conversion of its assets to earning form. A speculative mania swept the country. Before 1824 only 150 joint stock companies with a capital of £34 million had been created; between January 1824 and December of the following year 624 with a nominal capital of £72 million circulated prospectuses – "the long-leashed hopes of the business community were ready to spring at any game that offered itself."[26] Total credit expanded constantly until the boom broke in the late summer of 1825. For the Birmingham school, the remarkable runaround in the economy was embarrassing and there were many calls for them to recant. Of course, they were not so mean-spirited as to deprecate the burgeoning economy. Sir John Sinclair was also delighted to have been proved wrong.[27] Attwood himself, however, was unrepentant. Bravely and, as it later became clear, correctly, he argued that their good fortune was the result of a change in both government and Bank of England policy founded on neglect of the implications of Peel's Act. Attwoods & Spooner, private bankers, would not, for the moment, risk their business on the chance that the economy was now properly managed.[28]

The same faithfulness to intellectual analysis was not demonstrated by his brother Matthias. As a banker in the financial capital of the world, Matthias was ideally placed to exploit the explosion of profit-making opportunities without too great a risk to himself. He had shown an interest in that type of investment a few years before when he became a member of the board of the Phoenix Assurance Company. Now, in rapid succession, he joined in promoting the General Steam Navigation Company, the Provincial Bank of Ireland, and the Imperial and Continental Gas Association. All were eminently successful.[29] Despite this lead, Thomas steadfastly restricted his business activities to the traditional services of private banking and the establishment of the mill in France. It may have been that his resources were already stretched, leaving no capital for speculation. Certainly Matthias offered to involve the Birmingham bank in his projects and was refused. But given the character of Thomas Attwood, his nonparticipation was more likely to have been motivated by a mixture of pride and principle.

The decision to be cautious had the additional advantage of allowing him the time to enjoy his first love, his family, and his second, Birmingham. In 1823 he moved his brood from the Crescent, which his wife had never liked and which was now overshadowed by Birmingham's urban sprawl, to Grove House in the village of Harborne, the home of his mother-in-law. The house stood next to the church on a hill and had a wonderful southern exposure. It was much more spacious than the Crescent and the death of Sarah had left Mrs Carless feeling rather lonely.

There were other important matters to be considered. Several close relatives, including Richard Pratchet, fell ill and required care. In the case of those who died, considerable time had to be spent putting their affairs in order. On a happier note, at fifteen Bosco, his eldest son, was at an age that required the choosing of a career. Banking was an honourable pursuit and preferable to the law or medicine; the former, according to the father, was worse than bondage and the latter was poorly paid.[30] A friend, John Price, agreed to take the boy in and Attwood had no qualms about removing Bosco from school; experience was, as his own father had said, the best teacher.

Attwood's letters in this period are unremarkable, revealing a degree of contentment and relaxation which had seemed unattainable even a few months earlier. In Birmingham, he felt free to seek companionship rather than disciples in the public houses and to gossip over the bank's counter. The visit of Frederick Robinson, the chancellor of the exchequer, to the town, and the obligatory public dinner in his honour at the Royal Hotel, provided an opportunity to congratulate the minister warmly on his recent adoption of currency principles.[31] The sense of impending disaster that had required so many fruitless journeys to London and a zealot's attention to pamphleteering departed. He might not be completely satisfied that the government knew what it was doing but the suffering caused by unnecessary unemployment had been alleviated.

With Attwood at home the development of the "liberal" party's base in Birmingham proceeded rapidly. They were not opposed but their strength was sufficient to win the return of their own candidates to the positions of high and low bailiff in 1824.[32] The administration of many of the town's charities was closely scrutinized. When any new institution such as the Eye Infirmary was contemplated, they offered their services as committee members.[33] In many instances Attwoods & Spooner were trusted with the account. Every opportunity to direct the town's energies into useful and Christian activity – petitions against slavery, poor relief, and so on – were taken. Richard Spooner was even more conscientious in these philanthropic endeavours than Attwood, but both enjoyed the gratitude of the town. At the high bailiff's dinner on 17 June Attwood's services were singled out for special mention: "Mr.

Osler again rose ... to propose the health of a Gentleman whose past services had richly entitled him to the grateful recollection of the town of Birmingham, who was not only endowed with distinguished abilities, but what was better, with a disposition which constantly encited him to devote those abilities to the service and benefit of others, and above all to the good of Birmingham."[34] As it happened, Attwood was not present and Spooner returned thanks on his friend's behalf. It is possible to read too much into these after-dinner speeches; the speakers did tend to act as a mutual admiration society. Nevertheless, the importance of Attwood's role within the group was emphasized by two unusual aspects. Apart from the obligatory toasts to the monarch and traditional public heroes, praise was rarely accorded to anyone in absentia. Secondly and perhaps of even greater significance, the panegyric issued from a self-confessed opponent of the paper money panacea.

The remainder of the year passed pleasantly enough. Harborne was at a distance of several miles from Birmingham, so Attwood took rooms near the bank. Most weekends were spent at the Grove with his family. Eventually, however, the opportunities for profit created by the boom in trade made it impossible for the ambitious to remain aloof.

In August, at a meeting in the Royal Hotel, a committee which included Attwood was appointed to make a feasibility study for a railway line connecting Liverpool and Birmingham. In company with Spooner and a number of their business friends, Attwood had already made inquiries into the procedures to be followed, had gathered lists of contacts, and had spoken to those who might object.[35] They were therefore already in possession of most of the information needed and, shortly after the meeting, were able to announce the formation of a company which would have a capital issue of £600,000 in 12,000 shares at £50 a share; their own bank would act as treasurers.[36]

The company expected opposition. Part of the problem was the route itself, which was exceedingly ambitious in that it was intended to cover most of the West Midlands with branches. The total mileage to be built was three times that of the Manchester to Liverpool project. The number of individuals and groups to be consulted was very large indeed. A further handicap was the scorn poured on the project by critics who argued that the capital of £600,000 was ridiculously inadequate for the purposes outlined and called into question the skill and knowledge of the promoters.[37]

To remedy the capital deficiency, Attwood's group proposed an increase to £800,000, largely subscribed by the principals. This suggestion almost destroyed the project. Rumours spread that the promoters were really only "profiteering speculators" to be avoided by prudent investors. Clearly they had not done a careful analysis of cost; the one-third increase in the capital was a panic measure. Attwood became sufficiently alarmed to write letters to his friends, protesting his good intentions. Still the pressure became so great that the extended issue was abandoned in favour of a new subscription. Under the new scheme, Attwood complained, he would now "have to be content with barren honour."[38]

Attwood could not have been too downcast by the turn of events because with the fever of speculation high he planned and promoted a second railway – the logical extension of the first, Birmingham to London. On 15 December the proposal that £1,000,000 in capital be raised, a figure that showed that he accepted his critics' arguments, in 20,000 shares at £50 a share, was approved. Attwoods & Spooner, with banks at both ends of the line, was the natural choice for treasurer. Although plans for the other line were well advanced, the promoters decided to solicit first funds for the London link. On the day designated for the subscription the small office of the bank was packed with eager buyers for the 2,500 shares assigned to the town.[39] Amalgamation with a London group dictated a smaller portion for Birmingham than had been expected and within a few days the shares stood at a premium of £7.[40] Other railway promotions quickly followed: the Bristol & Worcester, British Northern & Western, Grand Junction & the Northern. With the exception of the last, all asked Attwoods & Spooner to act as their Birmingham-based treasurers.

It took some months to draft the two bills to be presented to Parliament which would authorize the purchase of land and allow construction to begin. George Stephenson, the engineer in whom the Liverpool-Manchester people were to put their trust, was asked to estimate the cost of the Liverpool-Birmingham line in the hope that the cynics could be silenced. Attwood went to London to lobby support for the bills and to start them on their way through the various parliamentary committees.[41] But, as in virtually everything Attwood tried to do at Westminster, there was disappointment. By the end of February it was obvious that there were more obstacles than had been anticipated. One committee looking at the Liverpool-Birmingham project reported that the "Standing Orders" which governed a bill of this nature had not been followed and sent it to the committee of reference who could set aside the rules if they felt so inclined.[42] At every turn Birmingham was "pertinaciously and meanly opposed."[43] It soon became clear that no further purpose would be served by remaining in London. Attempts were made to improve each bill's chances during the spring and summer. The Liverpool-Birmingham steering committee added to its management as many businessmen as it could attract and made Sir Robert Peel its chairman.[44] It proved useless. Their bill was rejected by the House of Commons in June 1826. The London-Birmingham Railway Company's bill met a similar fate and *Aris' Birmingham Gazette* carried the sad news of its total failure, a victim, it was claimed, of the spectacular collapse of the economy. Fortunately not much had been spent, to that they were able to repay 15s.7d. for every £1 called.[45]

The enthusiasm for railways in the town had been given a blow but the promoters were not yet ready to let it die. The Liverpool-Birmingham Railway Company did not wind up its affairs but simply changed its name to the Birmingham & Wolverhampton – obviously a much less ambitious project. The management was not changed and Attwoods & Spooner stayed as treasurers.[46] However, the collapse of the speculative boom discouraged investment and quietly the dream faded.[47]

Railway promotions were the major but not the sole interest of Attwood and the bank in the winter of 1824–5. One of his less commendable speculations involved the formation of the Birmingham Investment Company.[48] It was designed purely as a quick profit-making operation; the profit was to be produced through the purchase and sale of estates on a rising market. It was a venture which told more about Attwood's reviving confidence in the future of the nation's economy than about the state of the family fortune. There were other schemes to which the name Attwoods & Spooner became attached, but they were sponsored at the request of George Attwood. The Worcester & Gloucester Union Canal, the Birmingham Waterworks, and the Equitable Loan Company, which grew out of the London bank's business, were successful.[49] Many more were not, but all enhanced the bank's activity and raised, for the moment, the general level of profitability.

The variety of and potential profit from these many ventures inevitably invited criticism. For the moment the grounds for dissension were not stated, but five years later they were dragged into the open to denigrate Attwood's character: "I know few men of his [Attwood's] station who have rendered less of their attendance and personal service ... except, indeed, in *getting up* public companies, the ultimate object of which requires no double sight to determine."⁵⁰ Such carping was unfair. In the midst of company promotion both Attwood and Spooner were named to the onerous posts of street commissioners and helped to organize the Mechanics Institute.⁵¹ George Attwood, with the encouragement of his brother, became high bailiff. The female members of their respective families were equally engaged in volunteer work. Elizabeth Attwood became a prominent member of the Society for the Promotion of Christian Knowledge.⁵² In local politics, both partners remained continuously active in marshalling opinion in Birmingham behind their currency campaigns. Each took positions and often spoke on public issues: against the Corn Laws, for the repeal of the duties on East Indian sugar, and for the abolition of slavery.⁵³ In addition Spooner added to his own list the question of Catholic emancipation.

The drawback to sharing in the excitement of business and everyday Birmingham life was for Attwood the enforced absence form his family. Now that Bosco was older he could spend some time with his father in Birmingham, although the apprenticeship in a friend's bank had not yet come to pass, but the other children were becoming strangers and he complained that he learned of their talents only by hearsay. Protestations of love undoubtedly pleased his wife and there is no doubt that they were entirely genuine, but Attwood, essentially gregarious, thoroughly enjoyed the dinners, late night discussions over drinks, and the limelight of public meetings.

The spring and summer of 1825 were good seasons for the Attwoods and the bank. Nevertheless, he urged caution on his friends: "Let the government drop this *stimulating system* or let the current of the Spanish minerals be turned into other directions, in either of these cases, universal depression would immediately succeed to universal confidence, affluence and prosperity."⁵⁴ He continued to limit the bank's private note issue, keeping their asset/liability ratio within a comparatively conservative range. Attwood's pessimism was not shared. Even his brother George, the senior partner, and Richard Spooner fought him on the question. They were particularly incensed by his refusal to allow the bank to acquire a major share in any of the joint stock promotions, even in those in which they had a private interest. The other banking houses in the town were not nearly so circumspect and participated fully in the expansion of credit.⁵⁵ Apart from a few distractions in labour relations created by the repeal of the Combination Acts, Attwood's friends in the banking profession challenged him to find an area of concern. An editorial in the *Birmingham Chronicle* which praised Robert Peel and expressed "general satisfaction" with "Peel's Act of 1819" passed without comment.[56] Two years earlier the paper would have been inundated with angry letters. The citizens of the town had indicated their opinion by offering a premium on the railway shares and the country at large had reinforced their view by nicknaming the chancellor of the exchequer "Prosperity" Robinson, following his glowing account in the House off Commons of the financial condition of the country. The *Annual Register* joined of other journals in paeans to the government's wisdom and called on the country gentlemen to confess their error.[57] The euphoria was not to last.

The foreign exchanges had begun to turn against Britain as early as the winter of 1824. The bullion reserves had consequently begun to fall.[58] By late spring, virtually on the heels of Robinson's speech, a number of Ricardo's disciples started to warn of potential disaster. They blamed the speculative boom for many of the nation's problems and Lord Liverpool went so far as to warn business that in the event of a depression no help could be expected from the government in the form of an issue of exchequer bills.[59] The Bank of England, as usual, had been slow to react to the changed circumstances and continued its laissez-faire policy. The drain of bullion continued through the summer and the Bank hesitantly began to contract. It was faced with "the dilemma of either continuing to discount, at the hazard of stopping itself; or of refusing to discount, and stopping the whole country."[60] Within a few weeks the markets were "in a very feverish state."[61] By mid-July, the scarcity of money induced bankers in many districts, including London, to refuse to discount merchants' bills. Two weeks later the Bank of England belatedly decided to stop lending on stock; a decision that should have been made weeks before.[62] In a further move to choke off speculation the market rate of interest, which had stood at $3\frac{1}{2}$ per cent for more than a year, was raised to 4 per cent. The cabinet tried to do its part by issuing warnings, but few speculators chose to listen.

The first major crisis occurred when the Liverpool cotton trade failed. Uncharacteristically prompt action by the Bank of England in securing credit limited the damage, but the situation was precarious.[63] Many country banks were actually insolvent and others were in a dangerously illiquid position. The Bank's reserves were very low and the directors, obliged to ignore the commercial distress, contracted its issues further. The market rate was now above the Bank rate and the Bank was forced to reject even "good" bills, those about which there was no doubt as to credit-worthiness.⁶⁴ On 10 December a run on the country banks began. Cobbett crowed his exhortation "Get Gold" to add to the confusion and one week later the run extended to the London banks.⁶⁵ Almost seventy banks failed and it became virtually impossible to discount bills. "Credit like the honour of a female," declared the *Morning Chronicle*, "is too delicate a matter to be treated with laxity – the slightest hint may inflict an injury which no subsequent effort can repair."⁶⁶

Birmingham had been one of the last towns to feel the sharp reduction in the volume of Bank of England discounts. Industrial production through 1825 lagged behind the order books; when the crisis did finally overtake the town the consequent depression was to be exceptionally severe and recovery slow. In early December the conservative *Birmingham Journal* was still praising the prime minister as "the soundest financier of the age."⁶⁷ On the eve of the run on the country banks the editor optimistically called on his readers to place their trust in the Bank of England and Lord Liverpool.⁶⁸ The *Birmingham Chronicle* was a little more critical of the Bank but expressed no concern over local conditions. It was not until the failure of Gibbons, Smith & Goode on 17 December that Birmingham was shocked into consideration of its own plight.

Attwood had been much more alive to the approaching crisis and had resumed his agitation for public pressure on the government and the Bank of England in September. Ironically, this recognition came shortly after his partners succeeded in persuading him that it was safe to invest some of the bank's assets in longer-term mortgages and to lend on stock. His resistance had been weakened by the apparent stability of Birmingham's markets and the promise that such loans would not be funded by an expansion of their private note issue. George had immediately acted, despite the evident financial clouds gathering over London. Previous storms had been weathered without any widespread disruption in trade. He reasoned that the frailty of the system elsewhere was irrelevant; their extension of credit was to be on "real" business transactions.

Thomas Attwood's initial concern grew into outright alarm in November. He knew that the state of the exchanges and the operation of Peel's Act would force the Bank at some point to contract. As a well-informed country banker he recognized the potentially dangerous consequences of credit restriction upon a banking system whose position was dangerously illiquid. Further contraction had to be avoided lest the external drain be exacerbated by an internal one as confidence declined. On 22 November Attwood wrote to Lord Liverpool directly, urging a new issue of £1 notes.⁶⁹ In a panic bankers would be faced with demands for gold and they would withdraw their own small notes leaving none for ordinary business, the payment of wages, or the buying of provisions. The subsequent distress would have to be relieved by the Bank of England. Had the Bank prepared for such an eventuality? If not it should do so at once: "It will require two hundred Bank clerks for *six weeks* merely to sign the necessary quantity ... Ought not the Bank of England to take the precaution of providing itself with ten or twelve millions of one pound notes to be issued *instanter* at such a crisis, in exchange for larger notes."⁷⁰ Naturally, if such an issue were to be made it must be accompanied by a Restriction Act so that the paper would be accepted. At a stroke public confidence would return and private strain would be eased. The prime minister did not bother to reply for he continued to believe that the circulating medium was "overcrammed" and that contraction was needed.⁷¹

Attwood had in the meantime moved on to a less direct appeal for expansion. A number of resolutions were sent to Matthias in London. He was to obtain the signatures of "Merchants and Bankers" who as Thomas had learned had been agitating for a greater liberality in the Bank's discount policies. Their intention, apparently, was to gear the circulation to the business cycle rather than the exchanges – a design with which he had obviously some sympathy.⁷²

By the first week of December it was clear to him that Britain was about to experience a severe financial crash. Desperately, Attwood appealed to his old friend and supporter Sir Robert Peel for a letter of introduction to the home secretary, Peel's son. Attwood knew that without such an entrée past antagonisms would destroy any hope of a hearing. The old man complied and wrote an enthusiastic letter in which he detailed Attwood's trusty remedy: loans in the form of exchequer bills, a liberal discounting policy on promissory notes and bills of exchange, finally an issue of £1 notes.⁷³ Letter in hand, Attwood hurried to London but apparently he entertained small expectation of a personal audience because he also carried a letter of his own, giving a full analysis of the panic and a list of his proposals.

Attwood's letter may be assumed to have contained the basic ingredients of the plan he was later to present to the court of directors of the Bank of England. The run on the country banks had hardly begun, but he forecast that the London banks would not be immune; a demand had been created which the banking community alone could not meet. He estimated that each London house had about sixty country banks drawing upon it. To avert catastrophe he advocated the appointment of a commission whose sole function would be to lend money to the country banks. It was an old oft-rejected suggestion, but it was now presented in a much more radical form. The Bank of England should be directed to "lend money to the Country Bankers instantly upon the deposit of Title Deeds, Local Bills, or Notes, or personal guarantees of their Debtors and connexions." This recommendation, if accepted, would be tantamount to a government takeover of the Bank. Unlike Huskisson and Liverpool, who could never quite make up their minds about its role, Attwood had no doubt as to the function of this privileged joint-stock company. He accepted that the directors of the Bank had a responsibility to their shareholders, but suggested that if the country banks deposited a double amount of securities that interest would be safeguarded.[74]

Two days later Pole & Thornton of London closed and brought down forty-three allied country banks. Panic-stricken, the Bank's governor and deputy governor and the cabinet held angry and recriminatory discussions. Cornelius Buller of the Bank, anxious about his reserves, demanded a promise of suspension if the pressure became too great. The ministers refused.[75] On 16 December Attwood arrived in London and, upon presenting his letters, was taken by Peel to see the prime minister. Remarkably, Attwood's views, with the exception of the argument in favour of restriction, corresponded exactly with those of the government, which needed every supporting voice it could find in the assault on the Bank. Peel was particularly pleased to obtain Attwood's view of the danger of collapse in the midlands, a subject to which his father had alluded in his letter. After a briefing session with Lord Liverpool, Attwood was quickly taken to meet the chancellor of the exchequer and then to meet with a committee of directors from the Bank of England itself.[76] At each stop Attwood outlined the measures he considered necessary for the relief of Birmingham and district and, to the directors, pressed for loans to the country bankers. As might be expected, the latter tossed out that idea without a moment's hesitation, "alleging that it is too great a variation from their usual rules."[77] But they did agree to pass these remarks on to the full court of directors on 17 December and allow him to argue his case – a remarkable concession which reflected the extent of their panic.

Attwood had been only one of many advocates shuttled around the various committee rooms on this day. The cabinet almost conceded suspension during a five-hour evening meeting; Peel had troops ready to defend Threadneedle Street from the riots that might occur if such a step was taken.[78] Without Attwood's knowledge, the Bank had, at considerable risk, accepted his and the cabinet's more moderate proposal. It agreed to buy exchequer bills, to issue £5 million in small notes, and to extend its discounts.[79] On the night of 16 December, Rothschilds secured £300,000 gold for the Bank and, seventy-two hours later, £400,000 was sent from Paris. The crisis as far as the Bank was concerned – the threat to its reserves – then faded away.

Attwood had not been taken into the confidence of his interrogators. Sadly, he decided to refuse the offer of a second meeting with the Bank's directors: they were "evidently too timid and indecisive to meet the occasion." In any case he "did not wish to put himself forward in a public cause which may be liable to misrepresentation."[80] It was a strange decision for a man who could seldom resist the limelight and prior to the crisis had had a reputation in government circles that few would have believed could sink any lower. Peel had offered some information about the Bank's plans, but had carefully and misleadingly stressed that it "is very difficult for the Government to offer any suggestions to a Commercial Body like the Bank of England which has its own particular interests to attend to with respect to the species of security on which it should advance its funds." Notwithstanding such delicacy the cabinet had communicated its opinions. Under the circumstances the directors accepted the tendered advice and favoured the liberal provision of accommodation on good security even if that meant a radical departure from the established practices of the Bank. Peel urged Attwood to accept the invitation to meet the governors a second time.[81] For a moment the banker wavered but in the end stood by his decision.

The single interview with the directors and the short session with Lord Liverpool and Peel had given Attwood his closest view to date of the machinery of government. Although his participation had been only one small interlude in the round of government/Bank negotiations, he was left with a feeling of importance not experienced since 1813. Although not yet a "minister," he felt like "a privy councillor" without whose advice the cabinet could not function. The king's ministers were in a "terrible state" and needed all the advice they could get.[82] His opinion of the cabinet had never been high, but now he was positively contemptuous. Nevertheless, he was not sure what role he had played in the crisis: "All I can say is that I did thoroughly urge upon him [Peel] the necessity of immediately *compelling* the Bank of England to increase the circulating medium by purchases of Exchequer Bills, and that such purchases were accordingly made. Whether they were made in consequence of my representations or not, I cannot say."[83] Such uncharacteristic modesty did not last. As one of the highlights of his career it naturally became a subject for boasting: "I was the means of occasioning an additional supply of £1 Bank of England notes to be prepared, and I was instrumental in promoting an issue of 1,000,000 £ notes in the buying up of Exchequer Bills; and these two measures it was, and nothing else, which then prevented universal anarchy which I had foretold and of which, Mr. Huskisson himself had assured us, we were actually 'brought within 48 hours'."[84]

Attwood may have had some influence on the course of events in December but it is unlikely that either his advice or his presence was crucial. The Bank had begun to relax its policy several days before he arrived in London.[85] Others besides Attwood had pressed the government and Bank to make these changes. In addition to the City men led by Rothschild, Thomas Joplin and Vincent Stuckey had written to advise the Bank to extend its credit facilities. There were undoubtedly many who could claim as much influence as the Birmingham man.[86]

Irrespective of the origin of this enlightened policy, Attwood, among others, believed that the government had at last been brought to some semblance of sanity on the question of currency. It had not gone as far as he would have liked, but there was more than a glimmer of hope. As Hilton has pointed out, however, this conclusion was very wide of the mark. Lord Liverpool, Huskisson, and Peel continued to regard the exchanges as the best guide for action.[87] In December the external drain had been halted, in part thanks to the September measures, and conditions became favourable for renewed expansion of the economy. Thus their pressure for the relaxation of some of the Bank's rules had nothing to do with Attwood's notion of making the circulation equivalent to the nation's needs. Nor was there any concession to the view that the Bank should operate as a lender of last resort. The only noticeable change in attitude, if indeed it can be so called, must be attributed to that least laudable of motives, self-interest. The government needed to sell some exchequer bills to relieve pressure on the Treasury.

Peel's blunt rejection of the principles behind the practical recommendations by Attwood raises an interesting question. Why did Peel offer the banker so many opportunities to believe that he was a "privy councillor"? The answer most probably lies in the nature of the office Peel filled in the cabinet – that of home secretary. When not guiding Attwood through government departments and committee rooms, he was busily corresponding with magistrates and military commanders in the country districts. The cabinet believed that rioting if not revolution might break out at any time. On 16 December Peel wrote to Sir Herbert Taylor asking for a summary of military needs to ensure control of Birmingham.[88] Two days later, two "respectable" citizens of the town, Isaac Spooner (Richard's father) and Theodore Price, were asked, in their capacity as magistrates, for information on the possibility of disruptions in "the public peace."[89] Peel had cause to worry. Birmingham and its hinterland were in a sad state. Employers did not have "sufficiency of cash to pay their men and wait for repayments on their articles."[90] One magistrate feared a union of the artisans in Birmingham with the iron and coal workers in the districts; such a union could bring terrible disturbances and injuries to the midlands.[91] In the interest of peace, Peel may well have believed that the pacification of one of Birmingham's best-known and most respected leaders would be a useful exercise. Attwood had a reputation as a troublemaker who spiced his rhetoric with violent denunciations of government policy. From all accounts he had a sizeable following among the working classes. Keeping him in London prevented him from being involved in agitation elsewhere. Of course, it is possible that Peel did think that Attwood could contribute something to the debate. However, on the evidence of Peel's published opinions in 1819 and 1821, repeated regularly in the years after 1825, on the subject of Attwood's ability, such an explanation must be deemed extremely unlikely.

Attwood's failure to exploit the opportunity presented by Peel might seem puzzling were it not for those very same dangers that the home secretary was anxious to avert. Birmingham had been caught up in the speculative craze and the subsequent panic had left the guarantors of those schemes in a perilously illiquid position. Moillet & Smith had ben under strain for some weeks.[92] When Gibbons, Smith & Goode closed, the credit of the others had been called into question.[93] The most suspect had been Taylors & Lloyds and only the arrival of a coach and four from London with fresh supplies of gold had saved that bank.[94] The reserves at Attwoods & Spooner were at a very low level and all the houses had desperately called in loans, dumped securities (in most cases at a loss), and made general appeals for help to sister establishments.

When Thomas Attwood left for London, the partners were extremely worried, and for this reason his mission was more then a simple philanthropic excursion to save the nation. Attwood carried not two but three letters to Peel on 16 December. The third came from the bank's partners, collectively, and was to be placed in the hands of the governor of the Bank of England.[95] While it is impossible to be certain, the letter may well have contained an appeal for special banking privileges to prevent collapse. If such were the case, then Attwood's refusal to press for expansion before the court of directors made sense. His excuse, "I hardly feel justified in putting myself too forward in a public cause, which may be liable to misrepresentation," was totally out of character unless one allows that he had been put in a very difficult situation.[96] A country banker whose own house was in danger was hardly in a position to lecture the institution from which he wished to borrow on the question of sound practice. There was an additional deterrent. Attwood knew that frequent meetings with the Bank of England, no matter how private, could be interpreted as a sign of weakness. Under prevailing conditions such rumours would have destroyed Attwoods & Spooner. Therefore he trod cautiously and acted with uncharacteristic delicacy. He was never to get another chance.

The Bank of England refused any special help and Attwoods & Spooner was saved from bankruptcy by John Attwood, Thomas's cousin. John had sold his iron and coal possessions, including the Corngreaves estate in south Staffordshire, to the British Iron Company for £550,000 a few months earlier. Although the purchase price was to be paid over three years, the initial payment gave him a reserve of ready cash. He lent the bank £60,000 by buying up a stock of bills, drawn on London merchants, which were at the time virtually worthless; exchange bills between even the most respectable establishments were at the time almost impossible to discount.[97] John had an ulterior motive in that he was in the process of selling some land to the bank and had no wish to see the transaction collapse. Still, his help is a singular reminder of the strength of family ties in support of the private partnership system of banking.

The Bank of England's relaxation of credit in mid-December did not solve the nation's ills overnight but allowed the beleaguered bankers to hope that there would be a secure future after all. Birmingham, nevertheless, continued to suffer. Gibbons, Smith & Goode had been the most liberal bank in the town. The bill of exchange was the most common instrument of business practice and the failed bank had held a central position in this credit system.[98] The remaining five banks were naturally reluctant to fill the gap and many tradesmen complained that even their best bills, those signed with unimpeachable Birmingham names, were not accepted. John's intervention had helped to relieve the immediate pressure, but Attwoods & Spooner was in no position to service any other than its regular customers and Matthias's London house was equally hard pressed. Attwood also now recognized that there had been no fundamental change in policy either by the Bank of England or by the cabinet. It would therefore be unwise to expand the level of discounts of the assumption that the present level of Bank support would be continued. Attwoods & Spooner did add to its stock of notes by a little over 20 per cent, £42,931 to £51,721, in late December.[99] But from the general level of the bank's activity it must be doubted that much of this addition was actually put into circulation. Even in their straitened circumstances most merchants were unwilling to take private notes when discounting their bills of exchange. To safeguard their own customer's interest, as well as those of the partners, the only feasible action for Attwoods & Spooner was to wait for recovery. In the meantime it seemed sensible to keep a larger proportion of assets in a liquid (gold) form.

CHAPTER SEVEN

New Directions

Once the shock of crisis had worn off, the theoretical debate about the gold standard and paper currencies revived. Remedies for the nation's ills that had been in vogue five years earlier reappeared suitably embellished to reflect the newly gained experience. Bimetallism engaged the attention of many including Huskisson as an answer to problems created by short-run international adjustments – correctly identified as a primary cause of the previous year's gold drain. Some, worried by the failure of so many country banks and the latent instability of a fractional reserve system, denounced the deflationary tendencies of Peel's Act. Others, beginning from exactly the same principle, reached an opposite conclusion and recommended the abolition of private banking and its replacement by joint-stock establishments on the seemingly crash-proof Scottish model.

In the House of Commons factions fought for their particular theories with single-minded fervour.[1] The government in the meantime had made up its own mind. For Lord Liverpool the crisis confirmed his suspicion that the country banks were habitually and incorrigibly insolvent. Among his friends the twin demons "speculation" and the "one pound note" became linked in a mephistophelian conspiracy.[2] Consequently, in consultation with the Bank of England, the government devised a three-pronged system of correction through currency and banking reform. The design was clear – the punishment of the private banks whose irresponsibility had come close to destroying national prosperity.[3]

Attwood's part in these deliberations was minimal. In the first few months of 1826 he had tried to regain entry to the government/Bank discussions but had been consistently rebuffed.

Peel was invariably courteous but made it quite clear that Attwood's views rendered it unlikely that he would be consulted.[4]

Lack of success in London was mirrored, temporarily at least, by a reduction in popularity in Birmingham. As a banker he could not avoid the opprobrium with which that trade now had to contend as the result of failure and a general cut-back in the volume of discount generally. The newspapers and tradesmen had rallied around the bankers of the town to maintain stability after the shock of Gibbons, Smith & Goode's collapse, the *Chronicle* observing that "We are indeed fortunate in the high respectability and the great wealth of all our local banks."[5] But concern for the solvency of their own affairs forced the banks to adopt policies which the tradespeople did not understand and before long the public mood changed.

As the year drew to a close the lack of discount facilities, upon which most of the businesses of the town depended, forced many to close for want of ready cash. Up until 22 December only one letter appeared in the newspapers voicing complaints; seven days later the correspondence columns were dominated by letters from angry businessmen.[6] The editor of the *Birmingham Chronicle* reinforced the criticism by printing a strongly worded editorial praising the joint-stock banking system of Scotland. The capital base provided by hundreds of shareholders was contrasted starkly with the fortunes of two or three men in a private establishment. The point was driven home by allusions to the success of the Scottish banks in avoiding bankruptcy during the recent crisis. This time there was no reassuring absolution from the general indictment of the English model for the local banks. The barrage even included some personal condemnation of their erstwhile champions, not directly by name, but no one could have been in doubt as to the identity of the writer whose "noisy pretensions" must now be dismissed.[7] The *Chronicle* was a Tory paper and a strong supporter of the government, but until this point concern for its circulation figures had muted its scorn for Birmingham's paper currency theorists. Between January and May 1826 not an issue of any of the district's newspapers failed to carry either an editorial or letters on the subject of the economy, ranging from the submission of wild plans for currency regulation to abstruse discussions of the exchanges. Not once did the name Attwood appear.

Attwood was well aware of the low level of his popularity and wisely retreated into the bank leaving the public forum to others. Conditions in the town were very bad: "the positive misery among the lower classes is becoming frightful."[8] All that he had prophesied for the previous ten years seemed to be coming true: "I wish I had got him [Lord Liverpool] on my books, and he had nothing but land to pay one with, and no privilege of Parliament. If I did not make a Radical of him in 20 minutes, I would lose my head."[9]

For some weeks Attwoods & Spooner tottered on the edge of bankruptcy despite the cash from John Attwood. In many respects it was the esteem in which the partners were generally held in the town that saved them. At no time was there a concerted run by depositors nor one by those who held their bank notes. Still the unpleasant business of calling in personal loan notes and mortgages, questioning business practice, and refusing any increase in discount activity had Attwood muttering, "so much for politics," with renewed venom.[10]

In April a deputation appointed by the Chamber of Manufacturing and Commerce waited upon the Bank of England's directors in London to solicit an extension of accommodation facilities for the town. The deputies had been appointed without reference to Attwood or his friends and the episode undoubtedly constituted the nadir of his influence over this body. The idea had been broached much earlier in the year when the banks had restricted their activities, but it was the news of the government's plans which had translated the grumbling into action. The deputies returned with a promise of £300,000 and, although no public confirmation could be obtained, an understanding that one of the new branches of the Bank of England would be opened in the town. Birmingham would be among the first to receive the benefits of "secure" banking under the benign influence of the politicians and their personal crutch, the "Old Lady of Threadneedle Street."[11] Ironically, Attwood may have borne a measure of responsibility for this swift decision. His importunities for aid at the same time as he had tendered advice must have strengthened the idea that Birmingham needed to be put on the "right" path. The appearance of the deputies had simply confirmed that need.

Attwood found his self-imposed withdrawal extremely annoying and vented his frustration in private, among his friends, where he could work out the details of his analysis of the current crisis and plan future campaigns. Fireside chats at Harborne, in public houses, and in the back-rooms of shops and manufactories went on long into the night and ranged as far as a proposal for the construction of a national lobby outside Westminster which could act as the rallying-point for dissidents of many persuasions. The idea was not new. Attwood had been toying with the possibility since 1819 and his group's cultivation of support in the town had given an inkling of what might be achieved. However, its development would require a major step towards radicalism that the majority of the group did not wish to take. Again the idea was shelved as they decided to wait upon events; in any case they were not sufficiently sure of their support in Birmingham at this time to feel comfortable. Their participation in the creation of the Mechanics Institute had reaffirmed their interest in the artisans, but the ties were much too fragile to exploit. On the question of the economy there was far less disagreement. Much of what was agreed upon was subsequently communicated to supporters elsewhere and, fortunately, in the case of letters exchanged with Sir John Sinclair, they were subsequently published.[12]

This correspondence has to be read carefully, since it was always intended for publication and hence written with one eye on public opinion. In contrast to that of many of his contemporaries, Attwood's examination of boom and recession is a model of sobriety and good sense. The hysterical attacks on the country banks, small notes, speculation, and over-trading that marked the outbursts of writers from Cobbett to "Prosperity" Robinson, were ridiculously overdone. Even the measures introduced by the government were so largely predicated on broad assumptions of dubious validity that they appear to be apologies designed to hide theoretical inadequacy. Attwood's letters, on the other hand, shun chauvinistic emotionalism even when discussing his favourite *bête noire*, Peel's Act. Argument is marshalled unusually skilfully; his defence of country banking is clear, consistent, and crisp. Of course, his major theme had not changed: "the danger of the Paper Currency consists solely in its convertibility into Gold." Unless mechanisms could be devised to underpin the gold standard in the face of an external drain of gold, there could be no permanent prosperity.

While Attwood was writing the mood of the town was again changing. The failure of the government's measures to reverse the tide of depression soon obscured the relative deficiency of their own bankers. A discussion of national issues superseded the narrow parochial introspection of January and February. Attwood and his friends began to appear on public occasions again, but they were not allowed to do so unchallenged. The preeminence of the liberal/currency faction since 1821 had been resented by other established interest groups in the town. With the collapse of confidence and the reduction in trade which many laid at the door of the bankers, others had sought to take the initiative. The Whigs, "the cabal of seven stars," had been among the boldest. Their target had to be what had hitherto been one of the liberals' strengths –

the currency panacea which held the component parts of the alliance together. The plan was to win general support for an alternative strategy, free trade, and thereby undercut the resurgent currency school.

In March a requisition for a town meeting promoted the repeal of the Corn Laws and touted support for a motion to that effect presently coming before the House of Commons. Initially Attwood and Spooner did not see the design as inimical to their interests, but as the document circulated and the tone of the resolutions to be proposed became known they changed their minds. Both signed the request for the meeting, largely to make sure that they would not be denied a prominent role in the proceedings. On the appointed day the speeches were for the most part deliberately vague, stressing the close ties between agriculture and industry, one of Attwood's own themes. The Whigs were clearly only out for tactical victory. Attwood made a short speech and it was left to Spooner to harangue the meeting on the evils of the metallic standard.[13] The lack of a free trade in corn was only another nail, it was far from being the coffin to which the economy had been consigned.

At the conclusion the applause for Spooner's position and the acceptance of his condemnation of the ministers, tacked on to the resolutions by amendment, appeared to offer evidence that they had gained the day. On this occasion, however, the *Chronicle,* the *Journal,* and *Aris' Birmingham Gazette* contained editorials deploring the "political" tone of the speech on what should have been a bipartisan petition. The *Chronicle* placed its emphasis on exactly the opposite conclusion to that apparently approved. It was the absence of free trade that was central to the state of the economy; the metallic standard was an incidental.

The battle was now joined. Attwood's liberals took to the newspaper columns with letters advocating a paper currency. Friends, relatives, and business acquaintances were urged to contribute. Although less than enthusiastic, the newspapers published and refrained from editorial comment. However, the depression and the discount restrictions continued to give their opponents from both ends of the political spectrum the opportunity to counter-attack. The Changer of Commerce's deputation to London to solicit immediate financial relief had returned triumphantly with the news that the cabinet was genuinely concerned by the plight of the manufacturing districts. The Tories, on this occasion in a somewhat uneasy alliance with the Whigs, used this evidence of the "government's benevolence" to suggest that Attwood's group misrepresented Westminster's knowledge of the needs of the economy. It was a clever ploy and needed to be answered smartly if the general populace were not to conclude that the chamber's interpretation was correct. The attacks on the currency school were unrelenting, but Attwood now demonstrated what was to become an increasingly sure grasp of the art of public relations by determining to work by proxy.

In July a "Committee of 102" was formed. Ostensibly the objective was to petition the House of Commons for relief and to give details of the town's distress. Only manufacturers were requested to sign; the Chamber of Commerce was not asked to help publicly: "... because the Chairman and Deputy Chairman and many of the most influential members are Bankers, who are injured or irritated by the measures of Government, and whose interest might by some be supposed to be much compromised by these measures to allow their disinterested interference."[14] Obviously the object was to forestall criticism and to give at least the illusion of freshness. The sponsors of the initiative, Charles Jones, Benjamin Hadley, and Thomas Clutton Salt, were noted paper money enthusiasts and, more to the point, friends of Attwood and less prominent members of his circle.[15] The three were delegated to carry the memorial to London and on 28 July saw the prime minister, the chancellor of the exchequer, the president of the board of trade, and the home secretary. They returned with quite a different message from that of the chamber's men. Of course, the ministers had been courteous, but they had nothing to offer: Birmingham's distress, they had declared, had been caused by speculation and over-trading which the recession would cure in its own good time. The town must look to its own resources, including its economists, and not rely on the goodwill of others.

Upon their return the delegates were sharply criticized for exceeding their authority and for pledging the memorialists to opinions on the currency which there was no evidence the majority shared. *Aris' Birmingham Gazette* condemned their presentations outright and the *Journal* believed it had discovered an "under plot" led by Attwood and Spooner.[16] Salt, anxious to continue the currency school's control of the agenda for debate wrote on behalf of the others to deny any such conspiracy. It had been time for Birmingham to resume its accustomed role in the movement for relief. He had intended to rouse the town, "which, bye the bye, I appear to have tolerably well succeeded."[17]

In October the question of free trade in corn was again raised. The anti-currency elements in the town were not yet convinced of Attwood's strength and the government's vacillation on the issue invited advice. This time, there was to be no intimidating town meeting. The Chamber of Commerce had been effective in the quest for financial relief, so a special general meeting of that relatively closed body was called. The very first resolution put the direction of the proposed petitions beyond doubt with a panegyric to the ministers for their advocacy of free trade; a tribute some of those praised would not have welcomed. In argument and subsequent resolution the tenets of the Classical school were adopted with regard to prices and wages.[18] Attwood was furious but found it difficult to couch his objections in an acceptable form. He could hardly place himself in opposition to the notion of cheaper food nor to arguments that trade restrictions were harmful. It was upon similar premises that he had built his own case for greater freedom in the financial market. No saving amendments, not even a qualifying clause, were won despite intensive lobbying. It was without doubt one of the severest public setbacks his group had suffered in the last seven years.

With this success, his opponents moved to break his long-maintained understanding with the artisans. The most visible connection at the time was the currency men's honoured positions in the year-old Mechanics Institute. A campaign smeared Spooner and Attwood, the president and treasurer respectively, with the charge that they lacked interest in the welfare of the workers and sought merely to use the positions for their own purposes.[19] The attack was not without some justification and was taken up by many of the more radical workers themselves. At the annual general meeting, Spooner admitted that he had not attended many of the weekly meetings.[20] But he tried to turn the complaint by arguing that the positions were designed to honour both of them for their past and continuing promotion of the interests of the mechanics. The day-to-day control of the institute's affairs was better left to the members themselves. The vote to change the executive would have been close had it not been for the intervention of Gerry Edmonds. His prestige as a radical was unrivalled and when he offered a spirited defence of their conduct the issue was quickly placed beyond doubt. Both were confirmed in office but, more importantly, their position among the politically aware artisans led by Edmonds was reaffirmed.

Nevertheless, at the end of 1826 the currency men's hold on Birmingham was far from secure, despite indefatigable efforts to reach into every facet of town life. When Spooner announced his intention to seek election to the Commons for the borough of

Stafford, few "Brummagems" evinced interest. There was no repetition of the marches that had accompanied his struggle to win in Warwickshire a few years earlier. Spooner's candidature quietly faded into oblivion.

Throughout much of the latter stages in the battle for leadership in the town, Attwood had been strangely silent. His failure to win the Chamber of Commerce debate had been depressing. Moreover, in retrospect he was not even sure that the effort had been worthwhile. Pessimistically, he foresaw little prospect of government action designed to alleviate the distress or to allow the commercial community the freedom necessary to reestablish "real" prosperity. In any event there were other affairs which demanded his attention. Progress on the establishment of the cotton roller printing mill at Rouen had been very slow. Delays caused by his agent's inability to obtain a variety of permits threatened the whole project. The only solution seemed to be to take charge himself. This offered a challenge that he might succeed in meeting. Eagerly he made the necessary arrangements and, with wife and younger children in tow, since it was to be an extended holiday as well as a business trip, set off for France.

After a rough Channel crossing which prostrated the travellers with seasickness, Elizabeth and the children decided to remain in their port of entry, Boulogne. Thomas travelled on and sought a house in Rouen.[21] France, he discovered afresh, was a delight. The country had apparently become even more prosperous in the three years since his last visit. French affluence stood in stark contrast to the gloomy streets left behind in Birmingham; the contrast tinged everything for him with a touch of sadness.[22] Over and over again he asked the people he met for some explanation of the discrepancy. Always an English chauvinist, he found it difficult to believe that the attraction had anything to do with the French themselves; they were an "ugly people" who could never have conquered England. Yet if one looked carefully, there was a decidedly English appearance to the region. Richard Coeur de Lion was after all buried in the cathedral at Rouen. Was this then England with enlightened government?[23] That too seemed unlikely, given the maze of bureaucratic procedure in which he had become involved in his search for a mill. Eventually, by the use of some rather convoluted logic Attwood turned full circle and arrived at the conclusion he had brought with him from England. It was not what the French had done; the secret lay in what they had not done. But for the obstinacy of Lord Liverpool these scenes of economic prosperity could have been found in England. Of course, being English it would have been so much better. The whole linear process of thinking reveals Attwood at his intellectual worst, building supposition upon assumption loosely drawn from observation. Admittedly, he sought to confirm his impressions by rather more careful inquiry, but his selection from the data subsequently gathered served only to reinforce preconceived notions.

Attwood's idyll in Rouen lasted less than two weeks for news that his father was ill reached him. Immediately he set out for England, leaving the impression that he would be back.[24] His family stayed on in Boulogne and subsequently took a house in the expectation of his imminent return. As he reported to his wife, if his father did not die in a few days he would live for years. The impression left behind, however, may have been deceptive. He had been wrong about the need for his direct involvement, the legal tangle in Rouen being quite beyond personal resolution. The agents were working as fast as they could and gradually most of it was being unravelled. He was assured that the mill would be operating before the end of the year. If he had remained he could only have acted as a goad, spurring his agents to greater efforts. Attwood was never a patient man and the probability that he was likely to become more of a hindrance than a help could not have escaped him. Short visits designed as inspection tours were far more sensible.[25] In any case, his analysis of the causes of prosperity in France had revived his flagging spirits and reaffirmed his confidence in his prescription for England. As so often happens with those of a mercurial temperament, he was ready to renew his tilting at governmental obstructionism.

Immediately upon his return, Attwood fired off letters in every direction to acquaint his correspondents with conditions in France. Robert Peel was even sent a French promissory note as evidence of the source of that country's prosperity. In contrast, Attwood claimed that his bank alone had been forced to withdraw £200,000 from the "uses of industry" since Christmas.[26] The bank's level of activity as illustrated by its cash book indicates that this was an outright lie.[27] Peel was polite and as "naive" as ever; in other words he was intransigent. The "lavish issue of paper" recommended had been the cause of the very distress of which Attwood complained. Peel also questioned Attwood's figures. If the other banks had made similar reductions there should be no trading at all. Yet information from other sources indicated that Birmingham's economy was recovering. He was correct. The town's natural resilience had effected a prosperity of sorts, but it was to prove difficult to sustain. A letter to Lord Liverpool elicited an identical response, despite Attwood's blood-curdling but routine warnings of future revolution.²⁸ More encouraging was the renewal of correspondence with old friends who accepted his reports uncritically and promised to proselytize with increased vigour.

On 1 March 1827 Canning had introduced the long-awaited resolutions on the question of the "food tax." No one doubted that the subsequent debate would be long, bloody, and ripe for exploitation by determined interest groups. The issue itself was guaranteed to arouse emotion. For the past twelve months, the commercial and manufacturing districts had sent petitions flooding into Westminster. When William Whitmore, the MP for Bridgnorth, had moved for a committee to consider revision of the Corn Laws in April 1826, the government delayed by pleading for restraint until after the next election. Distress had, however, forced its hand and, as a temporary expedient, bonded corn had been allowed in on the payment of a duty of 10s. a quarter. The agriculturalist lobby had modified the concession by obtaining a guarantee that no more than 500,000 quarters could be imported over two months. This left no one satisfied and the tangle of proposal and counter-proposal of town and country required immediate attention. The task of reconciliation between those who objected to any tampering with the 80s. a quarter duty and the free traders had not been made any easier by the presence of another divisive question of principle, Catholic emancipation. The combination guaranteed division and the prospect of strange alliances between factions within the House. It was not the first time that the Tories had been weakened by internal strife, but this time there was an added factor that made Attwood rush to London – Lord Liverpool was dying. Without his authority there was a chance that the Tory party might crack wide open.²⁹

Before leaving Birmingham, Attwood laid the groundwork for a petition. The débâcle of the Corn Law enterprise rankled and he had no wish to be undone in his lobbying by an untimely expression of anti-currency rhetoric from his own backyard. The accepted wisdom of the town remained that petitions were the most expressive means of venting public grievances and would be difficult to ignore if the appeals were numerously supported. Charles Jones, Thomas Salt, and Gerry Edmonds were entrusted with the task of organization. They called a meeting of all "the trades of Birmingham" to consult on the state of the nation and the question of wages.³⁰ The terms of the call had been discussed thoroughly and the appeal was a calculated risk. They knew that the enlistment of the support of the operatives would not be welcomed by the merchants and manufacturers. Although small manufactories and shops abounded, industrial relations were not always harmonious. There was also a large reservoir of unskilled and often unemployed labour, as in any nineteenth-century city, that created a sense of unease in most "respectable" inhabitants.

After several days of street discussion most of the major trades, including the button-makers, bone-turners, brass-founders, lamp-makers, japanners, and wire-drawers, agreed to send deputies. They met at the Crown Tavern in John Street and were treated to a round of exhortation in support of prepared resolutions which had only one object, a change in the currency laws. The plan failed. One unnamed deputy challenged the organizers in a well-prepared speech which used Attwood's own arguments to point out the danger to the workers in the currency theory, particularly his admission that depreciation did not always operate to the labourer's advantage. This appeal carried the day and no decision on the petition was made. This unexpected conclusion was welcomed by the leading members of the Whig faction as proof of the tendency to arrogation of the currency school generally.[31] There was some merit in this allegation. Salt and Jones, with Edmonds's assistance, had "got out" a crowd in this latest effort yet lacked the authority to carry it with them. On a political question Edmonds would have experienced few such problems. But on the currency many of the deputies present would have agreed with the *Journal*'s editors: the sponsors simply aimed to use them. The attack on Attwood and Spooner at the Mechanics Institute some months before had been more effective than they realized.

Attwood, impatiently waiting in London for the "spontaneous expression of the people's demands," was appalled by the outcome. Other towns were soliciting support in the Commons for all manner of legislative changes yet Birmingham was silent. It was particularly aggravating because it was the general opinion that some movement on the currency, perhaps a reprieve for the £1 note, was possible.[32] Unfortunately, the politicians were unlikely to get things right on their own. The "band of conceited drivellers" who ruled England were as venal as ever and secure in their ignorance unless one could pay their price. Fortunately, it became clear that any motion on the subject of currency would be delayed, giving Attwood a chance to rush home to correct his lieutenants' failure.

Within the week a second meeting of the deputies of all the trades was called. This time there were to be no embarrassing speeches from the floor. Working closely with Edmonds, Attwood hand-picked a few deputies to put the various resolutions. Short, sharp speeches were ordered and the whole affair passed with scarcely a murmur of dissension.[33] Even the *Journal*'s editor merely noted the petition and offered no comment. It was a brilliant exercise in the manipulation of public opinion and a lesson which Attwood would later show he had learned well.

In the event, the effort was largely wasted. The motion for the appointment of a select committee "to inquire into the causes of the severe Distress which has affected the Commercial and Industrious Classes of the Community during the last and present years" did not reach the floor of the House until 14 June.[34] By that date, the furore over Catholic emancipation and the imminent prorogation of Parliament unfortunately precluded any chance that it would get a fair hearing. Davenport, who had been plied with material, arguments, and occasionally harsh criticism,[35] and Matthias Attwood made major speeches. The former quoted extensively from *The Late Prosperity* and both men used Thomas Attwood's theoretical approach as a reference point.[36] It said much for the latter's reputation that not even Huskisson, in replying for the government, made any effort to impugn his right to be quoted as an expert. Both the sponsors and the friends of the question outside the House were aware that their cause was hopeless.[37] The petition from Birmingham which had been so carefully crafted was not even mentioned and the debate ended tamely with the withdrawal of the motion. Nevertheless, Attwood had found the volatility of the political situation at Westminster illuminating.

While the political debate had been Attwood's primary concern in London, a family matter offered what at times was a welcome distraction. During the previous winter a court case against his cousin, John Attwood, had been in progress. Gratitude for John's expression of faith in the bank at its moment of crisis and a sense of family loyalty induced Thomas Attwood to become involved in the affair over the next eight years. The case, Small v. Attwood, was tried first in the autumn of 1826. It was concluded in March 1838 before the law lords at Westminster, made the reputation of several celebrated lawyers, cost a fortune in fees and required a procession of fifteen hackney coaches to carry all the documents to the House of Lords. It had begun with an agreement dated 10 June 1825, when John Attwood sold Corngreaves estate plus numerous other ironworks and collieries to John Taylor, Henry Shears, and Robert Small of the British Iron Company. After the plaintiffs had taken possession, iron prices fell quite dramatically and they found that they had made a very bad bargain. They therefore refused to pay the due instalments on the purchase price and accused John Attwood and their own surveyor of collusion in an attempt to defraud by misrepresentation of the works' profitability. An initial skirmish to avoid payment had been resolved in Attwood's favour at the Staffordshire Assizes. The decision was, however, appealed and during March 1826 Thomas Attwood spent much of his time in the organization of John's defence at the new trial.[38] Despite the dilatoriness of the court system it proved to be a great deal more satisfying than lobbying at Westminster.

On his return to Birmingham Attwood set about reinforcing the currency school's fragile ascendancy. The near débâcle of the petition had highlighted the circle's vulnerability. Hence he redoubled his community work and joined in every conceivable activity, including some, such as the creation of a new Savings Bank and Friendly Institution, to which he had some theoretical objections. If he did not speak himself, Richard Spooner, Joshua Scholefield, or some other member of the inner circle would air their common views.

The first major opportunity "to set the town alight" came at the high bailiff's dinner on 7 June. Timothy Smith, a Whig, was put up to propose the health of Thomas Attwood, "an individual to whom the town was greatly indebted for his activity in forwarding whatever could promote the public good." The word "whatever" had been carefully chosen to allow Attwood the greatest possible latitude in his reply. Naturally, he spoke on the currency question; in itself, a remarkable and, by some, lamented departure from normal procedure for such formal occasions. It was not, however, his only unusual contribution. His concluding toast, "Our invincible army, and may their swords never be stained with the blood of the people," produced uproar. Even more remarkably, Spooner followed in a similar vein.

Over the next few weeks the town talked about nothing else since no one was quite sure what the Attwood group had intended. The local newspaper editors were appalled. The *Journal*'s writer hinted darkly at ultra-radical extremism; the health of "his Majesty's Ministers," had been, he reported, less than enthusiastically toasted and some present were even seen "to stop their ears."[39] The others were a little more rational in their assessment but all agreed that Attwood and Spooner were courting the working classes and they feared the outcome. As for Attwood he retreated to the Grove. The task had been to capture the attention of the town and in this he had succeeded handsomely. Less than three weeks later an even better opportunity occurred.

For some years the opposition party in the House of Commons had sought to attack the government on the issue of representation for the large towns such as Birmingham and Manchester at Westminster. Although most Whigs drew the line at wholesale reform in the manner advocated by the radicals, it was thought that the piecemeal reallocation of recognized "rotten" seats to these towns would win their party popularity. The Tories might also be persuaded to accept such a change, particularly as the new cabinet under the new prime minister, George Canning, included some Whigs in coalition. Charges of corruption against two boroughs, East Retford and Penryn, had led to a proposal for the disfranchisement of both. Lord John Russell had moved on 28 May to remove the Penryn seat to Manchester. Although Canning opposed the transfer many Tories were absent and the Whig supporters of the government voted for the motion.[40] Charles Tennyson had then proposed to enfranchise Birmingham at the expense of East Retford. In the case of Penryn, Lord Stanley had written to the borough-reeve of Manchester recommending that a meeting be called for publicity purposes and this had reputedly "made a great impression." Not to be outdone, Birmingham planned a similar all-party affair. On the organizing committee were the leading Tory, Charles Shaw, the Bank of England's agent in Birmingham, George Nicholls, the Quaker, Richard Cadbury, two Whig Unitarians, Joseph Parkes and Daniel Ledsam, and, of course, the currency men, Attwood, Spooner, and Jones. Only the working-class radicals, men of the old Hampden Club, chose to stand aside, unlike their Manchester counterparts who had moved an amendment to secure representation on their local committee.[41]

The public meeting on 22 June was crowded. It had been originally scheduled for the Public Office, but the crush of people required an adjournment to Beardsworth's Repository, the largest building in the town and a horse auction centre. Attwood proposed the second and third resolutions in a fiery speech in which he endorsed the ultra-radical demand that "the whole population [be] permitted to vote."[42] Others were less forthright. A petition, drawn up by Attwood and Spooner with some help from Joseph Parkes in a move which heralded a temporary liberal/Whig alliance, was agreed.[43] The principles of representation in Parliament for the commercial and manufacturing classes were endorsed. Questions of the franchise, boundaries, and other technicalities were left to the Commons for fear that "higgling and haggling" might jeopardize the transfer. This was to be a statement of constitutional right in which the morality of the case transcended any argument.[44] In the course of the next day, Saturday, 4,000 signatures were added as people queued to sign.

Nothing was to come of the initiative because Canning died

and the Whigs withdrew from the coalition. It was, however, to be renewed in each of the next two years and enthusiasm in the town remained high. On each occasion Attwood and his friends deliberately straddled the political spectrum. Radical speeches captured the headlines while quiet cooperation with their middle-class business friends dictated policy. It marked the further gestation of an idea that was to lead to the birth of the Birmingham Political Union.

The campaign to transfer the parliamentary seat of East Retford to Birmingham did not end with the petition. Attwood wisely accepted a place on the standing committee to watch events and to keep the town informed. But he was unable to give his full attention to the subject for there were distractions. Confidence in the business sector had stubbornly refused to revive. Attwoods & Spooner had increased their level of activity but their profit margins were being squeezed and this threatened the viability of the bank. The reason was the activities of the recently established branch of the Bank of England, an institution that for Attwood offered a challenge on the theoretical as well as the practical level.

Prior to the opening of the branch on 1 January 1827, the local bankers had held a series of meetings to discuss their response.[45] The choices were three: to cooperate, to hold the branch at arm's length, or to boycott it completely. The latter course had already been adopted in Exeter. The advantages of cooperation were hard to ignore. To the surprise of his colleagues Attwood played a conciliatory role and urged the first option. He was of the opinion that their customers would remain loyal so long as they would not be the worse for their loyalty. The others were persuaded and as a mark of his bank's collective good faith Attwood offered fifteen thousand sovereigns to the branch in return for a similar payment to their agents in London.[46] Such a deposit would save the Bank of England the cost and danger of sending a portion of the coin needed to support the branch and would facilitate one of the advertised services of the new office. Nicholls, warned that Attwood was likely to be his most vociferous and determined critic, was suspicious. Actually, the approach, indeed his behaviour from start to finish, foreshadowed a pattern which was to become characteristic of Attwood's conduct in the years ahead. At public forums and in theoretical debate his voice could often be heard in condemnation of both government policy and the stated goals of the Bank of England. In private, business necessities meant that some sort of working relationship with all parties needed to be effected. Despite the occasional slip into dogma, he was, above all, a businessman. The offer was imply designed to be a signal to Nicholls of good will.

Unfortunately for the spirit of compromise, within a few months the branch bank had begun to inconvenience its competitors. The agent aggressively pursued business in the most lucrative sector of the market, among the wealthiest and more substantial concerns in the district, whose owners were attracted by the prestige attached to having Threadneedle Street as their banker's address. Combined with the assumption of much of the safest side of banking business, the payment of government dividends and so on, this competition exerted pressure on the town's bankers. The situation was made intolerable by the discovery that the promised advantages of cooperation with the branch were hedged by restrictions designed by the Bank's directors to force changes in country banking practices. In October, in concert with their fellows in the surrounding district and led by Addison's of Wednesbury, the local bankers reversed their earlier decision, closed their drawing accounts and decided to pursue a determined campaign against all provincial activity by the Bank under the present terms.

The closures had followed several months of careful debate among the private bankers of whom Attwood had been one of the most vocal. For some time he had voiced the opinion that the bankers' failure to affect Parliament in 1826 could be traced to their own jealousies. Without a central, unified organization their voice would be muted and their complaints ignored. Hence their only hope was influence through collaboration. Few listened; most suspected Attwood of ulterior motives. Then Henry Burgess, a comparatively unknown writer on the subject of currency and a staunch supporter of the principle of private banking, appeared in Birmingham. Independently he had reached similar conclusions and had decided to do something about it.[47] He had been travelling widely, using London as his base, and slowly began to pull together a loose coalition of those with similar interests.

In Birmingham, Burgess was received warmly and made several return visits. He naturally gravitated to the two most articulate bankers, Attwood and Spooner. The former had been planning a new article on banking for some time and was anxious to repeat his refutation, contained in *The Late Prosperity*, of the charge that his fellow bankers indulged in over-speculation and were incompetent. With the encouragement of Burgess, Attwood published his views in the *Globe* newspaper and the articles attracted a wide readership.[48] The admiration was mutual and when Burgess's position as the representative of country bankers was made official at £1,000 per annum, Attwoods & Spooner were among the hundred private banks which guaranteed that sum at £10 each.[49] It may well have been due to his persuasiveness that, in the second half of the year, Birmingham's sense of grievance against the branch bank had become more sharply focused.

To complement the closures a memorial was sent to Westminster. It endorsed the converse side of Attwood's opinion: that the Bank of England and its branches had been given an unfair trading advantage as a monopoly with exclusive privileges. In particular the memorialists complained that the branch bank was able to compound stamps for the purpose of duty, a practice which lowered the rate charged on inland bills of exchange.[50] It was upon such technical points that the drawing accounts had been closed and upon which Attwood's objections were based. Clearly the memorial was a compromise but that it was achieved at all was a victory for him in that the notion of a central bank was not challenged. It did not embrace any of his currency notions but the gist of this analysis was unmistakable. The point was pursued at a meeting of country bankers in London. W.J. Taylor (Taylors & Lloyds) and Richard Spooner took prominent parts in the proceedings and the latter gave a major speech, the tone of which could have emanated from any one of half-a-dozen Birmingham-based economists.[51] Attwood was conspicuous by his absence. His "lack of restraint" was well known and in such conservative company his partner made an ideal substitute.

In February Attwood travelled to London to represent Birmingham in the town's efforts to gain the East Retford seat and to work a little more on John Attwood's court case. To his astonishment (one wonders what Spooner had been doing) he was approached by the standing committee and asked to represent them in a series of meetings with the governor of the Bank of England.[52] He was not an altogether unexpected choice as a mediator. As a friend of the old system of banking his credentials were impeccable. Yet his acknowledgment of the need of some kind of central bank was unquestioned.[53] Tantalizingly, there is no official record of Attwood's mediation. Only a few cryptic references in letters to his wife remain. There can be no doubt, however, that his endeavour failed for the general negotiations dragged on for several more weeks.[54] Eventually a compromise was reached; country bankers were permitted to compound and the rules governing the country note issue/gold exchange were relaxed to facilitate the demise of the £1 note. However, the mutual distrust of the private bankers and the central bank was unabated.

Attwood had much greater success at his cousin's trial, which was his third engagement in London. The British Iron Company had indicted John Attwood for perjury in an answer given twelve months before as to the state of his affairs when his holdings were purchased. The trial was held on 21 and 22 February before Lord Tenterden and a special jury. On both days the court was crowded for most of the leading legal figures were engaged on one side or the other, including Scarlett and Brougham for the defence and Gurney and Campbell for the prosecution. After the reading of the charges the judge suggested that the case proceed no further and instructed the jury to return a verdict of "Not Guilty."[55]

Following a further round of dinner engagements during which he felt, incorrectly, that he had won new converts to the currency school, including the potentially useful Whig, Lord Althorp, Attwood returned to Birmingham.[56] There he proceeded to write three further articles for the *Globe*.[57] The arguments, analyses, and recommendations remained unaltered, but his examination of the determining factors in the rate of interest does show that he was still capable of adding to his general theory.[58]

For some time Elizabeth Attwood had been urging her husband to reduce his various commitments. The younger children missed the "steadying," ever-visible hand of a father. Yet, despite Attwood's continuing protestations of family love and an almost neurotic concern for the health of his brood, he had become progressively busier. There was scarcely an aspect of community or national business in which he was not in some way interested. Even days at home were spent cloistered in his study, engaged in a never-ending round of correspondence. At forty-five he was more ready to take on new challenges and to embrace radical causes then he had been at twenty-five.

There was no shortage of subjects which needed attention. Even without the currency issue there were few questions which, he considered, could not be settled by intelligent men of the business world. Catholic emancipation and the slave trade were still earnestly debated. There was little disagreement about the inequity of the latter, but the Catholic issue was another matter. Richard Spooner, who took the lead in arguing for the change, was hardly on speaking terms with his father, Isaac. From fears of Russian dreams of empire to mundane matters of rate levies, the town was alive with debate. But it was the possibility of the transfer of the East Retford and Penryn seats that continued to occasion the greatest excitement.

The respective bills had been postponed several times. It was not because they appeared particularly radical even to the suspicious eyes of a Parliament dominated by land owners. Under the bill applying to Birmingham, the potential number of electors would be less than four thousand; a smaller figure than existed already in some other boroughs.[59] The difficulty lay more in the realm of principle and in its future application. It was this aspect which attracted Attwood and he spoke warmly in favour of the transfer, urging that nothing be done which might jeopardize Birmingham's case. Despite this plea for support without agitation, Attwood's position on the question of reform was unquestionably radical.

The temper and bearing of the townsmen of Birmingham had been impressive, in his opinion, during the great distress of 1826. The establishment of the Mechanics Institute indicated that the higher classes of operatives, at least, were bent on an improvement of the mind. Tentatively, he proposed that instead of relying upon the interpretation of opinion by enlightened businessmen, as he had recommended in 1822, it might be more sensible to relax the franchise qualification. Elections with as many as 20,000 voters in Birmingham would not be unreasonable.[60] It would be difficult to conduct a political competition without some tumult under these conditions, but there was every hope that the sober men of Birmingham would "afford an example to the other places in the Kingdom." Although he had not changed his attitude with respect to the importance of the exercise of reason over passion, he now conceded that the ordinary people could tell one from the other. The bill to transfer the seat obviously did not promise much, but "something is better than nothing."[61] Further reform might follow once the wall of privilege had been breached.[62]

Although Attwood's support for the transfer bill was unequivocal, he had not given his support without some qualms. He had as usual been following the shifts in balance between the factions in the House with interest and, once again, he was convinced that a measure to change the currency laws might now pass. New alliances and marriages of convenience were being arranged at Westminster. For a man with a program of economic reform, a network off influential friends, and the ability to organize widely supported petitions, it was obviously a time during which the legislature should not be "offended" or become too preoccupied with parliamentary reform.[63] The currency remained the priority and virtually any cabinet combination of Tory, Whig, or Radical would have been acceptable to Attwood so long as they acted "intelligently."[64]

Hence, throughout the summer of 1828, a variety of groups under his tutelage, Staffordshire ironmasters, coal mine-owners, and others, petitioned the Commons. This two-pronged approach kept Attwood and his friends very busy and very much at the head of affairs both inside and outside Birmingham.

The harvest of 1827 had been good and although bad weather in 1828 had produced a poor crop, the winter had been mild so that the Commons sat undisturbed by demands for better government. By the early spring of 1829, however, the strains placed on the social fabric as food bins were depleted began to crack the façade of unthinking optimism. Riots occurred in the Midlands and the north, from Manchester to Macclesfield, and the militia struggled to keep the peace. During the winter political tumult and party bickering at Westminster had increased and few observers of the parliamentary tangle would have disagreed with Wynn's remark that "the pack of cards has been ... completely reshuffled."[65] The deal had not yet been completed and it was difficult to gauge opinion in the House. The reluctance of Grey and Russell to take up the question of reform was particularly confusing.

Anxiously Attwood watched and did his best to warn of the danger to the economy but he lacked information. At his behest, friends made inquiries at Westminster to discover the cabinet's intentions. Davenport was provided with two or three "refreshing" questions to put to the House if all other sources failed. There had been conflicting rumours emanating from London. One portended the distribution of six million £1 notes, already signed and lying in the Bank of England's vaults, through the methods tested in 1825.[66] Conversely, another tale had the duke of Wellington, who had formed a government in January 1828, following tradition by allowing events to take their course. There was a sense of urgency for Attwood's own peculiarly Birmingham reading of the economy forecast that time had almost run out. Three thousand pigs had recently arrived in the town and had been sold at low prices. Past experience of such sales indicated that their origin lay in a calling in of accommodation loans by liquidity-conscious banks in Ireland. That, together with the planned demise in April 1829 of the £1 note, threatened public confidence and promised a financial collapse. As the weeks passed without any clear answer from any of his correspondents, he decided to act. The instrument to be employed was public opinion and the vehicle of expression was to be the town meeting.

Attwood, Spooner, and Scholefield personally carried the requisition for the meeting from door to door and few of their "respectable" friends refused such illustrious solicitors.[67] To Attwood's great regret, however, only five out of the twenty-seven bankers in the town signed. If the planned debate had been simply designed as a plea for action to relieve distress, the quality of the signatures could have given no cause for anxiety. But because their speeches, already drafted, were to be largely about currency reform, the absence of other "economists" was certain to be remarked and the whole exercise blighted. There was a second setback, one that was virtually unprecedented given the eminence of the requisitioners. The high bailiff, Joseph Walker, insisted that Attwood guarantee the cost of the meeting before he would consent to authorize it.[68] The question of responsibility for the expenditures on the East Retford campaign had not been settled and Walker claimed to be protecting the ratepayers from "unnecessary expense." The bailiff's hidden motive was to make quite sure that those to whom the petition was to be addressed were aware of its author.

On 8 May excitement mounted as the hour of the meeting drew closer. Gossip in the taverns and market-places led many to anticipate some kind of major declaration of intent that would go beyond the simple and oft-repeated pro-currency speeches. These rumours had been planted by Attwood and his fellow-conspirators in part to offset the negative aspects of Walker's ploy. But they also marked a change of emphasis. Snubs at Westminster had demonstrated the futility of the traditional round of petition and lobby, particularly in what was seen as a tired cause. They had finally recognized that more dramatic gestures were needed. Long before the principal speakers were to appear the public offices were crowded and many more stood outside demanding to be admitted. At once the high bailiff decided to adjourn to the more spacious quarters of Beardsworth's Repository and the crowd streamed down the street, hurrying to find the best spaces in the galleries.[69]

Attwood spoke for about three hours. The presence of a live audience as usual suited Attwood's emotional and colourful style. The applause, cheers, and stamping of feet lifted him to flights of imagination and rhetoric which gave his theories a persuasiveness that his more prosaic pamphlets were never able to do. The speech skilfully popularized his argument. Each member of the audience, over half of whom were artisans, was appealed to directly: There was only "one pound in your pockets, instead of two pounds." They were entitled to their bread and beer, "the just and proper beverage of the people of England." By cleverly manipulating the emotions of the meeting he succeeded in discrediting every opponent of currency reform while at the same time painting his panacea in the most attractive hues. But he did not end there. To the delight of the crowd he proclaimed what the rumours had promised and what they had really come to hear. Instead of giving the people their economic and social rights the government had acted with "supercilious contempt." Temporizing policies had been adopted, "the tedious agencies of prolonged disease." He was still willing to give the duke of Wellington further time "to break out of the straitjacket that killed Castlereagh, Canning and Liverpool." But the "people's patience" was limited and they would not wait long. Attwood's preference remained first to make the country prosperous by an alteration in the monetary standard and only secondly to win parliamentary reform, a conjunction of ideas that had been made before in his pamphlets. The difference on this occasion was that they were now given equal weight in terms of value. Proudly he reaffirmed his adherence to the ranks of "Reformers," the "Radical Reformers."[70]

Spooner followed and warmly endorsed his partner's arguments. The resolutions, twenty-five of which appertained to the general distress, were unequivocally currency reformist in form. If not all actually drafted by Attwood they bear the stamp of his thinking in content and turn of phrase.[71] The most frequent proposers and seconders of these resolutions apart from the partners were Scholefield, Jones, Hadley, and Salt. There could be no doubt where loyalties lay.

Attwood had once again caught the imagination of the town. It had not been won without careful planning. The mixture of radical sentiments and currency propositions had been concocted in numerous debates which had lasted long into the night. Spooner, as he was later to prove publicly, had some reservations about parliamentary reform but did not object to the slogan as long as monetary augmentation remained the primary objective. He had not been able to dispute Attwood's argument that the bulk of their expected support at the meeting would emanate from the artisans and mechanics, or that their cause needed a spark. He also knew that Attwood himself was not wholly convinced of the validity of the reform argument and might abandon the position later. For the moment expediency dictated silence.

The extent of their success was quickly reflected in the manner in which their critics in the town were overcome. William Redfern, a Whig closely identified with the East Retford campaign, circulated the opposition's refutation of the currency prescription and suggested that Attwood was slightly mad, the result of "too long a meditation of one subject."[72] For his pains, Redfern was laughed out of town. The *Birmingham Journal*, at this time not overly sympathetic to Attwood, but aware of his growing popularity, flatteringly printed his hitherto unpublished treatise of 1821, *An Exposition of the Causes and Remedies of Agricultural Distress*.[73]

On the other side of the political battle lines, one unexpected and not totally welcome outcome was a letter from William Cobbett praising both the timing of the petition and Attwood's speech.[74] Just twelve months earlier Attwood had found little to recommend in the notorious radical. For twenty years Cobbett had denounced the paper currency system and in 1827 had contemptuously dismissed Attwood as a crank who sought a peerage. Never one to miss an opportunity to denigrate opponents, Attwood had countered in the *Scotch Banker* and in his speech of 8 May had described the journalist as both "grossly ignorant or wilfully wrong."[75] It is true that he had added that Peter Porcupine, one of Cobbett's *noms de plume*, was a man of "various talents who had served his country well" but he would not go much further. Cobbett's olive branch was in fact a remarkable gesture, demonstrating a willingness to accept allies from any quarter despite fundamental disagreements on actual policy. The letter was useful for its propaganda value, as had been the favourable report in the *Political Register* a month earlier; both drew the attention of radicals outside Birmingham to Attwood and gave a welcome aura of authenticity to his claim to be a radical reformer.[76] There were all too many voices which suggested, with more truth than they knew, that his claim derived less from conviction than from convenience. The one danger of Cobbett's embrace from the Birmingham men's perspective lay in their fear that the "respectable" inhabitants would tar them with Cobbett's brush and currency would be forgotten.

The petition was quickly signed by 40,000 citizens and sent to Westminster. There were several new "friends" in the House. Sir Francis Burdett would unfortunately be absent as a result of a painful attack of gout, but Sir John Graham, who had presented a motion a year earlier requesting a select committee inquiry into the state of the circulation of notes under £5, could be counted on. Davenport was expected to lead and Attwood exhorted him to obtain a complete review of the monetary system. Concerned about Davenport's diffidence, Attwood sent a polished speech, replete with "lessons from antiquity" which he believed would appeal to the classicists in the Commons.[77] It was all for nought. The consensus among MPs was that Birmingham had exaggerated the degree of distress. Many, including Attwood's own brother, Matthias, disliked the political overtones and had not worked as hard as usual in getting sympathizers to the House. Others revived the well-rehearsed objections to small notes, the "rags" of Cobbett's lexicon. Many more were influenced by the hostility of the London press which went out of its way to disparage the whole enterprise.

For the last-named stumbling-block Attwood bears a measure of the blame. His calculation of the chances of mobilizing public opinion had included the constant of provincial alienation. He had long been convinced that the proprietors and editors of the national journals were biased against Birmingham and all the "new" towns. Past speeches had often been deliberately pitched to catch the echoes of provincial displeasure with London's condescension. After the meeting of 8 May these allusions had been repaid with interest. The *Morning Chronicle* had chosen to attack the "respectability" of those who had attended. Another writer reported that his speech had not been well received. Others charged that he spoke for a vested interest and dismissed the petition outright. In contrast, newspaper editors in "Edinburgh, Carlisle, Leeds, Liverpool and others" praised the meeting's objectives in their leader columns. A week earlier these papers had printed enthusiastic reviews of *The Scotch Banker.* These seemed to indicate that they understood his economic ideas as well as his political arguments and were therefore to be cherished.[78]

Attwood had welcomed the divided response. It gave him the opportunity to place Birmingham at the head of provincial opinion in opposition to London and he naively expected that this would give the campaign added weight. Letters cunningly placed in sympathetic newspapers pinpointed the differences in treatment. The currency theorists had only the interests of the nation at heart. They did not ask for unequivocal support but a fair hearing. Careful and reasoned criticism, such as that which appeared in one of Bristol's papers, was to be applauded as loudly as the numerous articles expressing agreement.[79] Only the London press had been, in Attwood's phrase, "stock-jobbing."[80] In this case, however, the cultivation of the provinces had proved to be counter-productive. When the petition came before Parliament two weeks later there was scarcely a public voice in the metropolis to defend it or its sponsors. When defeat followed, Attwood was forced to recognize the reality of London's domination of the political debate at Westminster and he became determined not to challenge it again.

While Parliament and London affected a lack of interest, Birmingham was in turmoil. The studied qualifications and injunctions regarding a reform movement in the wake of prosperity were ignored and the novelty of a member of the middle class, a banker and reputedly an intimate of those in power at Westminster, speaking so vehemently on reform and putting those sentiments in a petition stimulated argument. It was a direct challenge to all the coalitions contending for dominance in Birmingham and represented a break in the alliance of "respectable" opinion formed by the East Retford campaign. Self-proclaimed radical missionaries paraded the countryside. Charles Jones went on what one critic felt was a "proselytising crusade" of "mono-maniac" proportions.[81] The response for the radicals was gratifying, only the Tory-dominated farming community proving obdurate.[82]

Attwood was pleased but, to a degree, also sobered by the sudden enthusiasm. Many of the compliments were exclusively expressions of hope for parliamentary reform. One of the more flamboyant toasted a "champion" with the "Fire of freedom in his eye"; a "god" who trumpeted the rights of the people and shook the monarch's throne.[83] These were sentiments that hardly fitted the plea for a new monetary system. Despite deteriorating trading conditions, price falls, and wage reductions, the economy clearly continued to take second place to politics. The conversion to "radical reform" had become for his supporters the focal point of his campaign.

After some months of further reflection and a careful analysis of his options, Attwood came to a remarkable conclusion. The excitement had been contagious. Instead of holding back the more radical elements, he would encourage them. Indeed, he would go further. In the past his endeavours had been reactive; he had been content to respond to decisions he believed to be wrong. In the future he would place himself in the vanguard and actively seek political leadership. By this means political reform would follow a direction compatible with "national honour" and the restructuring of the monetary system would not be forgotten. The goals were laudable but it is impossible to escape the conclusion that the argument was a rationalization designed to hide a sense of desperation. He had tried to use the spark of parliamentary reform to enhance his economic crusade. The spark had, however, become the flame which threatened to consume the work of fourteen years.

His options were simple: to return to the pattern which had led to twelve years of frustration, or to gamble on a radical extension of his demands. The fact that he chose the latter course was typical of the man.

CHAPTER EIGHT

The Birmingham Political Union: A Vehicle of Protest

The winter of 1829–30 was harsh: "the frost has now continued a month and the canal actually stopped three weeks, with every prospect of the present interruption continuing."[1] Trade was so bad that barbers were said to charge by the dozen.[2] Subscription lists were opened in many towns to buy bread, beans, and blankets for the unemployed. But the poor harvest of 1829 had ensured that food was scarce and expensive, and in Birmingham the contributions were inadequate to feed all of the hungry. The neighbouring rural areas were in an equally bad state and the farming community viewed the future with gloom. From all quarters of the nation petitions and addresses poured into Parliament complaining of hardship.

On a cold night in December, Thomas Attwood took advantage of the discontent and followed up his pledges of May by publicly claiming the leadership of Birmingham's political reform movement.[3] He, Scholefield, and fourteen others quietly filed into the Royal Hotel late on a Monday evening after a frantic weekend of pledge-gathering. A circular, signed "Six Tradesmen," had announced the meeting and Attwood, who had been its sponsor, had canvassed support. He had hoped for an earlier date but last-minute and ultimately fruitless efforts to convince Spooner of the proposal's merits caused delays. Although there was some relief that their decision was at last being implemented it was a sombre occasion. The course on which they were about to embark was dangerous and might mean ruin not only for their ultimate aspirations but for their private lives. The agenda was short and the debate brief. An organization, entitled rather grandly a "Political Union for the Protection of Public Rights," was established and its chairman, Attwood, was delegated together with two friends,

Salt and Jones, to draw up the constitution. A week later, Attwood outlined the proposed rules and regulations. To ensure that these were legally sound and to encourage the faint-hearted, Attwood announced that he had submitted them to and won the approval of Sir Charles Wetherall and Daniel O'Connell.[4] The former had the technical knowledge while the latter had the practical experience. After an hour or two of nervous debate the group resolved to present their "Union" to the people of Birmingham at a public meeting early in the new year.[5]

Over Christmas, Attwood spent most of his days considering what might prove to be the most important speech of his life and the remainder in the preparation of a defence for the attacks which would inevitably follow. He knew that his announcement would be greeted with cries of disbelief and, in certain quarters, anger. He needed an answer should his claim that he had always been an "advocate of reform" be challenged. It would not be enough to say that he had toyed with the idea of a political union of the working and middle classes as early as 1819. Nor that friends had dissuaded him from this course on the ground that the time was not yet ripe for such an alliance.[6] Nor that he had agreed with their analyses until very recently. Such evidence could be accepted only by those whom his critics thought of as a charmed but not charming circle. And he had to admit, only to himself of course, that his memory might be a trifle selective. Still it was a task that could not be shirked and by early January a rough if not wholly convincing rationale had been constructed. How far he really believed his version is open to question, since in old age he disavowed many of the principles for which he had stood when leader. But it would be too simple to join those who question his sincerity. On one level – Attwood's desire to persuade the nation to accept his point of view and his willingness to use any tool for that purpose – the criticism may be justified. However, it should never be forgotten that his prescription for economic prosperity was based on a vision of a just and integrated society. The House of Commons was far from representative of such a state and his desire to see a government that matched the changed and changing face of the country produced a loyalty to the *idea* of political reform that went far beyond mere expediency.

In his opinion, the Commons had lost its way. It appeared to be preoccupied with the aristocrat and the "upper classes of tradesmen." The "inferior classes of tradesmen" and the workers were ignored. Trespass laws, game laws, vagrant laws, and many of the criminal laws attested to this neglect. By laws such as these the ordinary man had lost many of his hereditary rights, a *"poor man can scarcely set his foot upon the earth without trenching upon a law."*[7] Even the middle classes were threatened. Their preferred means of appeal, petition and select committee, had been subverted by those who "had the ear of the government." Witnesses, and he spoke from bitter experience, were silenced by misleading questions that sought to place the "foolish provincial" in the worst possible light. The end result would be, in his opinion, the creation of a nation of slaves. It was therefore necessary for the Commons to be reformed so that a harmonious society in which every part was given due notice could be reflected in its political system. When Attwood later gave his support to the call for a reform of the House of Lords, it was entirely in keeping with his general political philosophy. The Lords had gathered too much power and blocked the efficient interplay of contesting social forces. To redress the balance the House of Lords needed structural alterations. The difficulty of such a philosophy lies in assessing the claims of the competing pressure groups. Attwood was to come to rely on public opinion, arguably the worst source of all. His preference, of course, had been to achieve prosperity and then to alter the body politic. Circumstances reversed the order.

The composition of the self-elected Political Council in January 1830 was predictable. T.C. Salt, Charles Jones, and Benjamin Hadley had pursued the currency question at every level. George Edmonds had to be included in recognition of his influence with the working classes and his ability to bring in their other leaders as well as his friendship with Attwood. William Pare ("Snuffy Pare" to his opponents, thanks to his ownership of tobacco shops), was an Owenite and advocate of the Cooperative movement. Both he and Joseph Russell, a printer and bookbinder, spoke for the most radical body of opinion in Birmingham. Russell was without much personal following but had worked assiduously in favour of currency reform, was secretary of the Mechanics Institute, and had the added attraction of newspaper support.[8] Betts, Scholefield, and several others were close personal friends of Attwood. They had supported his business ventures and were undoubtedly willing to offer their help in his political aspirations. Two possible sources of surprise were the omission of Richard Spooner and the inclusion of George Frederick Muntz.

Spooner had supported the speech of June 1829 in which Attwood had outlined his plan for the Birmingham Political Union. But whereas Attwood had used that speech as a stepping-stone to radicalism, Spooner had stopped short. This sudden divergence was never satisfactorily explained. A few months later he appeared on a platform with Attwood and Sir Francis Burdett. He then claimed to favour a reform of Parliament not dissimilar to their own plan and a "perfect, unbought, unshackled, unrestrained representation of the people."[9] Apparently he had not joined the Union because he believed he could work more effectively as a private individual. To prove the point he was again a Tory candidate for the constituency of Stafford.

Spooner's absence was not critical. He was far less popular in Birmingham than Attwood, despite their similar credentials in the service of reform and the economy. An opponent of both damned Spooner as a man "without discretion and not to be trusted," whereas Attwood's "great kindness and the popularity of his manner gives him great influence."[10] Moreover, the two men remained friends. Only when Spooner reemerged as a candidate for one of the town's parliamentary seats a few years later did acrimony develop. Even then he played the injured party and maintained that he had never worked against his partner. One can only speculate that in 1829–30 he felt the pull of duty to his father and family friends as well as to the Tory party. Thus while not opposed to political change in an abstract way Richard Spooner could not become actively involved in a general thrust that smacked of Whiggism.

The appearance of Muntz on the council was unexpected. He was not a particular friend of Attwood, although they had known each other since 1820. His fortune was to come from the invention (or pirating) and manufacture of a special alloy for sheathing ships' bottoms. Muntz had neither spoken at the East Retford transfer meetings of 1827–8 nor been prominent in Attwood's currency campaign in 1829. On the personal level he was not the most agreeable of men; certainly not one with whom Attwood could have been very comfortable. His appearance was striking. With the exception of a small triangular spot on his lower lip, the whole of his lower face was covered by a dense mass of long black hair. One observer remarked that it "bore a striking resemblance to the beard of nimble quadruped."[11] He was reputedly domineering and arbitrary; although he affected simplicity, he was vain and could not abide any contradiction of his opinion. On the latter score he conducted a personal vendetta with the *Birmingham Journal*, the newspaper which came to offer the greatest support for the Union, because the editor questioned Muntz's infallibility. A few years later, in 1837, he was prosecuted for a physical attack on a church warden.[12] With these blemishes in his character the high position in the council's hierarchy enjoyed by Muntz requires explanation.

The council contained few men of real stature other than Attwood himself. Salt, a brass lamp-maker, and Jones, whose endeavours ranged the spectrum of Birmingham's industry, were not considered to be particularly influential in the town; many, indeed, believed they were simply Attwood's acolytes, although most admitted that Jones possessed a wildness that his leader did not share. Scholefield and Betts, a metal refiner, were of greater wealth and local respectability but rather ineffectual speakers. Pare, who later became wealthy by conventional capitalist means, remained loyal to Owen and the Cooperative movement; he was regarded as sincere but dull. Edmonds was the liaison officer with the working classes and, in consequence, the second most important member from Attwood's point of view. However, the source of his power and his record ensured that he could never command the broad spectrum of support that would be needed for success if he were ever to stand against the chairman or even to act in his name. In these circumstances, Attwood knew that the Political Council needed a strong personality in addition to his own to act in his absence and to pursue an argument boldly. His friends agreed. Moreover, they feared Attwood's mercurial temperament with its moments of self-doubt and bouts of melancholia. Muntz's more unpleasant idiosyncrasies were less obvious in 1830. He had been high bailiff in 1820–1, was a churchman, and, as a successful businessman, was a well-known representative of the middle classes. Attwood had probably met Muntz through the business of the bank and found many of his opinions similar to his own. In 1830, possibly at Attwood's prompting, Muntz brought out a pamphlet in the form of three letters to the duke of Wellington which were a declaration of Birmingham orthodoxy.[13] It contained the familiar mixture of Toryism and currency analysis in the Attwoodian style for which Spooner had been known, combined with a manifest willingness to pursue the consequences of these recommendations to the bitter end. These letters established Muntz's currency credentials and presented reasons for supporting a reform of the House of Commons. In the last paragraph of his final letter he added a few indirect comments upon his political commitment: "... nothing would give me more regret than to find, that by a continued adherence to your present plan, you should give your opponents the means to force you from your ministry, and fill your place by some one not half so much interested in the welfare of his country *as I am sure you are.*"¹⁴ It was this statement which established him as the natural successor to Spooner and, in Attwood's opinion, worthy of a high place in the Union's hierarchy.

During the following two years Attwood's confidence in the ability of Muntz to act as a counterweight to the many radicals in the council was seen to be misplaced. The subsequent wild talk of armies, secret arms' dumps, and marches upon London may be directly attributable to the want of a strong voice for moderation in the council. Attwood, as leader, was forced to make concessions to a vocal minority for the sake of unity.¹⁵ The Union was to prove a difficult instrument to control and it was solely to Attwood's credit that despite all vicissitudes and setbacks it survived to become the premier extraparliamentary instrument of political reform in 1831–2.

Amid a cacophony of predictions of revolution, riot, and disaster the Birmingham Political Union made its bid for the nation's attention in January 1830. Paid advertisements in the Birmingham newspapers announced the formal decision to call a town meeting on the subject of parliamentary reform:

We, the undersigned, being of opinion that the GENERAL DISTRESS which NOW AFFLICTS THE COUNTRY and which has been so severely felt at several periods during the last fifteen years, is entirely to be ascribed to the GROSS MISMANAGEMENT OF PUBLIC AFFAIRS, and that such mismanagement can only be effectually and permanently remedied by an EFFECTUAL REFORM IN THE COMMONS' HOUSE OF PARLIAMENT; and being also of opinion that, for the legal accomplishment of this GREAT OBJECT, and for the further REDRESS OF PUBLIC WRONGS AND GRIEVANCES, it is expedient to form a GENERAL POLITICAL UNION between the LOWER AND MIDDLE CLASSES OF THE PEOPLE.¹⁶

Prior to the announcement eight members had been added to the council. For the most part they were friends of Attwood. James W. Evans, a japanner, later to be nicknamed "Goose" Evans by his opponents after he had fainted at a union meeting, and Thomas Parsons Jr, a metal dealer, were typical of the small businessmen upon whom Attwood had relied in the past. The additions to the radical faction were the Luckcock brothers, Felix and Urban, lime and brickdealers, and Josiah "Pigmy" Ernes, sixty-two years old and the owner of a button shop. Attwood had spent some time with Edmonds debating these invitations, since he knew that an enlarged membership would dilute his personal hold and could lead to greater divisions within the council. Both Pare and Russell had already made violent speeches, yet only by their inclusion could the appearance of a united front be maintained. Certainly their antagonisms would be better controlled in private. For the radicals the issue was much more straightforward. To fight the Union would have been to risk all, to cooperate offered a chance to win power. Although they never gave up their arguments for universal suffrage, annual parliaments, and the ballot, they usually followed Attwood's directions. Diametrically opposed to their point of view were men like Joseph Allday, the editor of the *Monthly Argus* and an Ultra-Tory.[17] Rabidly anti-Catholic, he had been so incensed by the duke of Wellington's acceptance of Catholic emancipation that he had accused the duke of bungling Waterloo and of needing the assistance of Blücher to win the day. Although the council's activities were later to force his withdrawal, for the moment he fulsomely praised Attwood as a "bold, independent, talented, and truly patriotic individual."[18] Such additions nicely emphasized the all-party nature of the Union even if they were mavericks whom many in their respective parties would denounce.

The request for the town meeting had been carefully drafted. All reference to the question of currency was omitted. The object of the projected meeting was solely the formation of "a GENERAL POLITICAL UNION between the LOWER AND MIDDLE CLASSES OF THE PEOPLE." The reply by the high bailiff, William Chance, to the requisition was short and to the point. As the meeting was designed to assist in the formation of a political union it was not "any part of my duty, to call a meeting of the inhabitants of the town for a purpose of this kind."[19] This refusal was expected. At once the requisitioners announced their decision to go ahead without his sanction and advertised the first assembly for 25 January.

The tone of the comment in newspapers which carried the advertisement for the Union was cautious and basically noncommittal. The *Birmingham Journal*'s editor encouraged potential supporters with the observation that the progenitor of the effort, Thomas Attwood, was a "tower of strength."[20] The *Gazette*, on the other hand, reserved comment but did reiterate its personal distrust of currency zealots and hinted that the purpose was other than that stated.[21] It could not be said that public excitement was evident, apart from the usual gossip in the inns. Only one person chose to write to the newspapers and his complaint was purely technical. Assistant overseers had solicited signatures for the requisition, an obvious breach of etiquette and a misuse of their time.

On 7 January, two days after the requisition had begun to be circulated, the Mechanics Institute held its annual general meeting. Spooner, the chairman, by accident or design, was absent. Attwood was called to the chair. In the past he had lent his name but hardly his presence to the operation of the institute. Now he intended to turn it to his own use. Attwood forced the general business of the meeting through quickly. Speeches were ruthlessly cut short and potential areas of disagreement were assigned to future committees. The meeting seemed over in record time, when Attwood rose to reply to the customary vote of thanks given the chairman for his impartiality. The speech which followed broke every rule, written and unwritten, in the institute's constitution as well as his own earlier strictures with respect to brevity.

The need to ensure a large, sympathetic audience for the projected Union meeting was his first concern. Consequently, he chose to begin his oration with a few words of praise for the Irish Catholics, always a potential source of trouble or noisy support. Reverend Thomas McDonnell, their priest and spokesman, had prefaced his remarks with an attack on the English aristocracy and "the gee-gaw orders of the Garter and Thistle." The ritual of criticism ended, few expected Attwood, an Anglican, to comment. However, he declared that he was most impressed: "if ever I want a religion, the Church who breathes forth such just and patriotic sentiments would be my Church."[22] Such unqualified approval was unprecedented but it was not insincere. Attwood was to vote years later to reduce the possessions of the Church of Ireland and he consistently supported measures for the economic relief of that country.[23] But he was taking a risk. Just as he hoped to enlist representatives of all parties in the town, so did he want the Union to cross religious lines. Edmonds, Russell, and one or two others were the leaders of working-class dissent but most of their ministers remained aloof; they remained so until the height of the reform crisis in 1832. There was little hope of getting the Anglican clergy to join in large numbers but neither did he wish to alienate them. Attwood then declared that when he had organized the May meeting of 1829, there had been some hope of success for the objects then stated. He now believed that those hopes had been illusory; "My opinion is, that the origin of the evil is the want of a proper and efficient representation in Parliament of the lower or middle classes."

The introduction of a political subject in the proceedings of a nonpolitical club was immediately greeted by a protest from the Unitarians who formed the nucleus of the Whig faction. Just when it seemed that the meeting would end in confusion, Attwood's earlier praise of the Catholics earned a quick dividend. McDonnell's strong and authoritative voice was heard above the uproar demanding that Attwood be allowed to continue. In the ensuing semi-quiet Attwood, unabashed by the criticism, pursued his theme. He was about to describe the requisition for a town meeting to organize the Union when Parkes, the Whigs' spokesman, appealed to "the Chairman's good-sense" to stop.[24] Attwood was aware that he had achieved his maximum effect and he capitulated, simply remarking that he had only intended to advertise the forthcoming meeting. He urged that all attend and resumed his seat amid sustained applause.

The speech had undoubtedly achieved its objectives. Many artisans resented the emasculating rules which prevented "serious" discussion. The Whigs had been made to look ridiculous and not genuinely interested in a reform movement in which the lower classes could participate. Joseph Parkes lost many potential friends when he remarked that he would discuss reform only outside the Mechanics Institute. On the other hand, Attwood had not actually made a direct challenge to the principle of "no-politics." He had merely stated that a meeting was to be held at which his views on the necessity of reform would be outlined. As for his remarks on Catholicism, there was no appreciable reaction from the other sects. Many who came to his meetings in the future were from church and chapel and the antagonism demonstrated at the higher levels of society was mercifully absent. When battles were fought, for example over the church rate, the acrimony was restricted to the respective leaderships and did not materially affect the solidarity of the rank and file.

There were, of course, other gains. Attwood's concentration on backstairs politics at Westminster and currency reform had damaged his reputation among the workers of Birmingham notwithstanding recent efforts to win their approval. With these few remarks at one of their own meetings he emphasized his direct interest in their welfare. The first gathering of the Political Union was going to be important if the organization was to become viable. By openly appealing for the support of the mechanics Attwood was declaring his belief in the value of their support. He was holding out vision of a Birmingham organization which was not one-sided, middle-class oriented, or replete with concepts and terms the workers could not understand. At the same time he had alienated a powerful faction within the middle classes. There is not much doubt that he did so knowingly. Parkes and his circle might be more dangerous as allies than as enemies for they would never be content with a subordinate role.

In such cold weather the only possible site for the Union meeting was Beardsworth's Repository. To keep warm, five large coke fires were lit and all the entrances but one were sealed off. On the appointed day, a Monday, which was an idle day for most workers particularly during harsh times, the Repository was, according to one observer, filled by "an immense mob and scarcely a respectable person."[25] The description attested to the success of Attwood's appeal at the Mechanics Institute and to the management of George Edmonds. It was not strictly accurate, however. Some members of the Whig cabal, true to an earlier pledge and jealous of their rights on reform questions, were present to cast aspersions on the integrity of the speakers.

Attwood's speech followed the general outline of the previous May. Redfern, who had attempted to damn Attwood's arguments in a pamphlet the week before, had used that May harangue to prejudge the 1830 proceedings. But his statement that the Political Union presented an ominous alliance between the "High Tories and the Liberal currency men" missed the point. Attwood's intentions were given in the prospectus – to unite all parties. His introductory remarks established this objective both directly and indirectly. The old Tory definitions of good government and prerogative were married to the Whig concept of the constitution and all were imbedded in the peculiarly radical Attwoodian notions of the just society:

> Fortunately for us and for our country the constitution has yet preserved for us some conservatory principles, to which we may have recourse, and by means of which we may hope that this great and vital object may be accomplished in a just, legal and peaceful way ... these *Councils* [Political Councils] dependent upon the breath of the PEOPLE, and representing the true interests of the PEOPLE, we may yet hope to have the RIGHTS, LIBERTIES, and INTERESTS OF ALL peacefully and legally restored and secured. We shall, at any rate, succeed in collecting and organizing the public opinion, and in bringing the public wrongs and grievances to the knowledge of the legislative bodies, and more particularly the Crown itself, the natural refuge of the people under all complaints against the House of Commons. Our gracious King still possesses high and extensive prerogatives regarding the election of members of Parliament, and those prerogatives we cannot doubt that he will but enforce for the protection of his faithful people,

wherein their wants and interests shall have been fully and efficiently ascertained.[26]

The radical aspects of his plan were Wilkesite in their concentration upon the efficient organization of opinion. The Union was to *"Meet, consult, resolve* and *petition."* Each phase was to be orderly, within the law. He himself would "go with you [the people] as far as the law will allow ... I will not go further one inch." The phrase was of course essential if the speaker was to avoid arrest. O'Connell in Ireland and Edmonds in his attempted Union of 1819 had made similar declarations.

The keystone of Attwood's conception of the Union, the powers to be given to the council, was even less radical. The council was given virtually unlimited power to speak for the Union between annual general meetings. Moreover, the provision that its members be "re-chosen" each July included no machinery for a competitive election. The individual members of the Union were to pay their dues, one shilling a quarter minimum, and to "obey strictly all the just and legal directions of the Political Council." Attwood had no intention of allowing a rank-and-file revolution. Having chosen to gamble, he preferred to keep the stakes relatively modest.

Although Attwood's opinion of the skilled tradesmen in the town had risen since 1826, his private views on the common people had changed very little since 1819. A weakness which he abhorred above all others was the subjection of mind to passion. The revolutionary excesses of the French were used again and again in his early pamphlets to remind the government of the dangerous state of passion into which the people were being driven by unimaginative economic policies. While anxious to improve the condition of the people by the provision of "beer and bread" through a paper currency, Attwood never attempted to disguise his disdain for the lower orders' mental powers; they were easily led by demagogues, quickly excited, and delighted in the pursuit of "wild chimeras." Although he had been only a child at the time, he could remember the famous Birmingham riots of 1791. He had witnessed the march of the Blanketeers and had noted the hopeless campaign that culminated on Peterloo field. Moreover, although the social structure of the town held out the promise of cooperation between the orders, it was not without its darker side. Birmingham had grown monstrously since 1800, doubling its population to approximately 130,000. There was an ugly inner core of deprivation and vice whose inhabitants posed a constant threat to law and order. Outside the town lived large numbers of coal and ironworkers as well as impoverished nail-makers. They represented a danger to the peace which the magistrates were not alone in taking very seriously.

Against this had to be set the real grievances of the people. Society was unbalanced and needed reform, yet the people were too unpredictable and too dangerous an instrument of correction.[27] The problem was to find a method that could be used to achieve the justifiable changes demanded. Hence the organization was to be kept in his own hands as far as possible. To justify his decision he offered the rationale that without order, discipline, and unity the expression of public opinion would be diluted by competing voices. Moreover, without the leadership of men of long public prominence and respectability the movement would lapse into the impotence of the political associations which had held out such high hopes in 1819. It was the lack of such a combination of public support and council power which had contributed to the failure of the London Political Union a year later.[28] During the winter he had not changed his mind with respect to the necessity of using a small body of like-minded men to represent public opinion. The culmination of this policy, he privately disclosed, would be the establishment of electoral colleges, elected by universal suffrage, which would "throw" two hundred tradesmen into the Commons; a number decided many years before.[29] It was an objective consistent with the extent of his radicalism at this time – the establishment of a House of Commons aware of the "economic realities" of the nineteenth century.

Such a profession of faith would not have captured the imagination of the majority of his audience and certainly would not have won the praise of Cobbett. Fortunately for the viability of the Birmingham Political Union as an instrument of public opinion and for Attwood's reform image, his propensity for rhetoric and overstatement led him to express his principles in the inflammatory language of the ultra-radical. The Commons, he declared, was the seat of "ignorance, imbecility and indifference." It was a House elected by "four hundred rich," whose specialty was the pursuit of "power, influence and perhaps corruption" and not the "interest of the people." To justify these judgments he drew freely upon his fifteen years of frustration and regaled the meeting with a catalogue of governmental economic errors. His theme – prosperity was the natural result of good government – emphasized the need for change and was a conservative conception of reform wrapped in a fiery speech few reformers could condemn as lacking in zeal.

Strangely the major item of business, the actual petition, was not introduced until late in the meeting. Presumably it was left until the end and virtual darkness to avoid close scrutiny, for it was a copy of a petition for the repeal of beer and malt duties, read but not adopted at a small gathering of Cambridgeshire freeholders three days earlier. It had been published in the *Morning Chronicle* on 23 January.[30] Someone had noticed it and hastily pushed it forward to cover the lack of unanimity in the council. During the proceedings this ineffectual instrument was forgotten and a more specific demand for reform substituted. Attwood as ever responded to the mood of the meeting. Arguably, it was this ability to "read" his constituency that was his greatest asset.

Two voices were raised against the tumult of approval which followed. The Whigs' suspicions of Attwood's true commitment to reform had been increased rather then diminished by his concentration upon prosperity. Consequently, their spokesmen, Joseph Parkes and William Redfern, rose to criticize.[31] They made the valid point that the inconclusive currency debate of the past ten years had been remarkable for the lack of unity it had inspired in its proponents. A variety of remedies for the nation's ills had ensured petty bickering. If the Political Union was to be a success, surely such contentious questions should be avoided; otherwise the level of debate would fall so low as to destroy the very unity that Attwood was anxious to promote. Parkes followed with an obvious effort to regain the leadership of the reform movement in Birmingham. He proposed that the old methods of public petition and public education should be pursued – activities in which he would be happy to take part.[32]

A resolution to this effect was rejected overwhelmingly.[33] Nevertheless, the opposition provoked responses from Attwood and Edmonds. Attwood, contrary to his previous emphasis on unity, chose to attack Parkes and Redfern on the basis of their political affiliation, declaring that despite his disillusionment with the duke of Wellington, Peel, and other ministers of the crown, he "was always a Tory." The Whigs had never done anything for public liberty and he doubted that they ever would. Edmonds immediately supported this stand by briefly noting "the manly conduct" of the Tories as compared with the "insincere dirty conduct of the Whigs."[34] The Whigs were "patriotic tea-table politicians" who only acted behind closed doors: an indirect allusion to the opposition of Parkes and his friends to the concept of a Union expressed both at the Mechanics Institute and at the meeting itself. Edmonds added that the duke of Wellington had at least responded to the Catholic Association: "might they not expect similar effects to be produced by similiar means?"

These attacks on the Whig party indicated the direction in which Attwood and his friends looked for action despite the Union's all-party approach. The Wellington government had survived the crisis of 1829 but appeared to be in an equally precarious position in January 1830. It was widely expected that some concessions to, and alliances with, the disaffected Tories or the Ultra-Whigs would have to be made. Fortunately for the Tories, the Whigs had "spread over a whole spectrum of opinion" and were unable to present more than a token opposition in the early days of the new session. The Whig drive for reform had, for the moment, petered out and the only issue upon which they were able to achieve a measure of unity, retrenchment, offered little hope for office.[35] Edward Davenport had been a frequent visitor to Birmingham during the autumn of 1829. His opinions respecting the reforming predilections of his fellow-Whigs had been well aired.[36] Consequently, in January 1830 it must have appeared to Attwood that the most likely candidates for the leadership, or at least sponsorship, of a reform movement at Westminster were the Ultra-Tories.

One of the few debates to enliven the last days of the 1829 session had been the marquis of Blandford's resolutions on reform.[37] These had been defeated easily. Nevertheless, these resolutions reflected the general dismay of the Ultra-Tories at the concession made to Catholics and Dissenters by Wellington. In their opinion the Commons had passed measures with which the nation as a whole disagreed. In addition, rotten and nomination boroughs provided an avenue for undesirable Catholic influence on the House as well as putting a premium on monetary wealth instead of land.[38] The unrepresentative and dangerous aspects of the Commons should therefore be reformed. There were many who agreed; even the *Quarterly Review* added its voice to the general demand.[39] Attwood, while neither anti-Catholic nor anti-Dissenter, had chosen to endorse this reasoning in his speech when remarking that the nation did not want "religion and priests" but "bread, beer and meat."[40] With these words and a general platform of moderate radicalism he intended to capitalize upon political chaos and future realignment. His plan was not unreasonable. Wellington might well have followed the "sensible" course, consolidated the Tory government by wooing the disaffected with concessions, and "kept the Whigs out of office for some years, if he had brought forward a moderate measure of reform."[41]

Attwood was, at best, taking a calculated risk. During his excursions to London on the various currency reform campaigns he had rarely encountered the type of aristocrat who could be classed as an Ultra-Tory, although his brother, Matthias, hovered on the fringes of the group. He did not meet the marquis of Blandford, upon whom he was to pin his hopes, until June 1830, when he had little choice but to find him "a very handsome, manly and gentlemanly man."[42] He most certainly exaggerated the size of their following, their value to the Tory party, and, ultimately, their commitment to reform. However, for a few weeks his hopes (they could not be called anything else) appeared justified.

In February 1830 the Ultras almost succeeded in defeating Wellington's administration. Knatchbull moved an amendment to the Address during the debate on the king's speech. He claimed the distress needed a general rather than a partial approach. The Ultras thus seemed to be a very potent force and the government, saved by Whig support, very weak. In addition, during the debate the discussion touched upon the currency question and many of the Ultras indicated their support for a number of very Attwoodian principles.[43] Matthias Attwood had played a prominent role. The brothers continued to act together and Thomas's Birmingham speech was paraphrased in the Commons: the government's failure to remove the artificial constraints on the economy forced the conclusion "that the House was totally inefficient for the great functions and duties it was constituted to perform."[44] A few days before, on 29 January, Blandford had impulsively enrolled in the Union and announced his intention "to introduce a Bill into the House – falsely called the Commons House – which is so constructed as to meet every single point you dwell on in the report of your speech."[45] However, Ultra-Tory strength was more apparent then real. Knatchbull himself blamed his defeat on the unreliability of the country gentlemen. There was no sure method of anticipating the future behaviour of such a group because the alliance was born out of protest and not ideological commitment.

Temporizing was not Blandford's style and, apparently anxious to demonstrate his energy and commitment to the objectives of the Union, he took an early opportunity in the life of the new House to move an amendment of his own to the address from the throne. Couched in the language of a convinced currency theorist, it was launched with little or no preparation and seemed designed merely to irritate rather than influence his fellow MPs. Only eleven votes were mustered; votes were cast by many of Attwood's correspondents, including such known currency "maniacs" as Davenport and Western, and the incorrigibles O'Connell and Burdett. It is hard to see what else could have been expected, but both Blandford and Attwood preferred to maintain the fiction that "unimportant technicalities" had caused the defeat and that matters would be very different when the former rose to introduce "the plan."[46]

Blandford submitted his detailed reforms to the Commons on 18 February. His preamble carefully established his high Tory credentials. It was time to revive "the fundamental principles of Representations, as they had been established in the days of Henry III, and the three Edwards." A review of all enfranchised boroughs by a Commons committee was to be the first step in the purification process. Boroughs found in a "state of decay" were to be deprived of their political privileges. The vacancies thus created could then be filled by the unrepresented towns. The electoral qualification that best suited these new industrial towns was, in Blandford's opinion, the payment of scot and lot.[47] The franchise was also to be extended to all copyholders and freeholders; a proposal which would have ensured a much wider electorate than that eventually produced by the Reform Act of 1832.[48] Wages were to be paid to those elected, but the qualifications for candidature were apparently to remain unchanged. Scotland was to be placed on the same representative footing as England. Finally, if the House so desired, compensation might be paid the borough proprietors for their expropriated "property."

The plan was not without merit. Reforms of the scale proposed by Blandford would have thoroughly altered the composition of the House. Attwood, "quite well pleased,"[49] insisted, almost immediately, that the council of the Political Union adopt it despite an argument from some of the radicals who wanted to press on with a more far-reaching plan of their own.[50] Their reservations reflected much of what had been said in the parliamentary debate. Blandford's reputation was such that he had only been able to attract qualified support, even from the known advocates of reform. Joseph Hume, who had seconded the motion, had made an uncharacteristically brief speech.[51] Those who had previously promised support concentrated on expressing their "pleasure" respecting the noble marquis's efforts and were content to reaffirm their conviction of the necessity of reform in principle. Others felt obliged to record their reservations concerning both the presentation of the plan and one or two of its more unusual provisions.[52]

The implication that Blandford was a strange bedfellow for the reformers did not escape his critics. That impression was inevitably strengthened by the provision that knights of the shire would be paid twice as much as borough MPs for attendance at Westminster. Maberly, the member for Abingdon, declared that notwithstanding his sympathy for the question of reform he "could not support such a bill as this."[53] Nevertheless, the motion did attract fifty-seven votes from those whose commitment to the reform principle outweighed their reservations. One hundred and sixty others disagreed.

The decision by the Political Union's council to accept Attwood's recommendation and to adopt Blandford's plan, therefore, on the surface seems curious. Even a cursory analysis of the voting patterns on the motion and the tone of the speeches indicated that the Ultra-Tories as reformers roused little passion and found few friends. Attwood's insistence, however, was not based on such a simplistic reading. He took a longer view and two aspects of the affair were in his opinion significant. The question of parliamentary reform was very much alive and promised to remain so for the coming session. More critically, the Union had become identified with a recognizable program.

Sir Francis Burdett, in the course of a rambling speech, had struck the desired note: "he trusted that this motion would unite the whole country with the people of Birmingham in demanding that fair and full reform ... [be granted]."[54] In doing so he was putting into words the thoughts which must have been in the minds of many of those present as a result of the enormous publicity the Union had received when it was launched in January. Scarcely a newspaper in the country had ignored the prospect of an organization representing an alliance of the middle and working classes, if only for the fact that the example of the Catholic Association had not been forgotten. Consequently, the mere idea of such an instrument to channel opinion was sufficient to rouse fears of revolution or hopes of social change: "The hurricane has begun to blow that will sweep the imperious Minister and all his subservient tools from the high places of power, trust, patronage and official influence. And we defy him or them to restrain its fury. Look at Birmingham ... and see what public spirit can do when driven to extremities."[55] The *Morning Advertiser* had opened its editorial by observing that "In another part of our paper will be found a report of one of the most extraordinary and remarkable meetings which has ever been held in the kingdom."[56] The *Morning Herald* referred to the proposed Union as "one of the important signs of the times,"[57] and an editor in the *Manchester Courier* cautioned: "If they [political unions] were to become general, and were to obtain their influence over the proceedings of the legislature which their promoters seem to anticipate, the independence of Parliament would be lost."[58] Only the *Times* among the major newspapers tried to limit the impact of the Union. The editor,

Barnes, hoped the "whole nonsense" would quickly "die away quietly."[59] He adopted the Redfern/Parkes argument that the scheme was simply a stalking-horse for the one-pound note lobby and had little to do with reform. Conversely, the most important radical journal, *Cobbett's Political Register,* had commented favourably and professed "unfeigned respect for Mr. Attwood, not only on account of his great talents, but on account of the bold and honest manner in which he had expressed his indignation against the long history of foolish men who have plunged the country into such difficulties of danger."[60]

Burdett's suggestion that the House ally itself with popular opinion as manifested by the existence of the Birmingham Political Union was therefore useful. Although Blandford's actual plan might be silly, it did give substance to what had been until then merely publicity. The design of reform would undoubtedly change, but given such an excellent beginning few expected the Wellington government to withstand the barrage of debate caused by an effective propaganda campaign; a campaign which had succeeded in identifying its cause with the public good. Even Huskisson had nervously recommended that the East Retford/Birmingham transfer be approved since it would now be safer to have Attwood in the House than out – a clear acknowledgement of the banker's new status.[61] The adoption of Blandford's proposal was, therefore, remarkably sensible and at a stroke enhanced the Union's claim to be a major factor in the national push for political reform.

The ease with which the Birmingham Political Union had won and consolidated its position persuaded Attwood that success was tantalizingly close: "the present session cannot pass over without some kind of reform."[62] Elsewhere similar convictions induced those whom Attwood termed "the élite of the kingdom" to contemplate the formation of sister political unions. The movement that Attwood and his friends had sponsored appeared to be gathering momentum. If public interest and concomitant agitation could be maintained, they believed all else would ultimately follow. There was only one small blot. The Redfern/Parkes faction managed to persuade many of Birmingham's more affluent inhabitants to reserve judgment for the moment. This was to be a sore point with Attwood that would lead him to keep Parkes at arm's length, despite the latter's subsequent efforts to ingratiate himself when the Union achieved national influence. For all of Parkes's subsequent self-puffery – he later told Edward Ellice that he kept "a chain and collar round Attwood and the Birmingham Political Union" – their philosophies were too far apart for the two men ever to cooperate closely.⁶³ Nevertheless, the intervention was an annoyance and in the summer of 1830 it was to lead to further attempts to puncture the balloon.

The council was well aware that they needed the support of the people of Birmingham to maintain national attention. The Catholic Association had demonstrated the method (known and approved by Attwood) and the Birmingham leaders already had an excellent base upon which to build as a result of their efforts for currency reform. Cobbett was not the only champion of the people who had noted with dismay the extent to which the local artisans had been seduced by the small-notes arguments.⁶⁴ To broaden their appeal still further the councillors, in an extension of the strategy first outlined by Attwood in 1820, advertised: "The union would ... prevent and redress as far as practicable all the LOCAL PUBLIC WRONGS AND OPPRESSION and all LOCAL ENCROACHMENTS upon the rights, interests and privileges of the community."⁶⁵ The *Journal*, sceptical of the Unions' prospects on the national level, was impressed and forecast "a most salutary effect when brought into operation on our parish affairs."⁶⁶

The local campaign opened on 2 March with a calculated challenge to their most conspicuous rivals in the town. The "Cabal" led by Timothy Smith, Redfern, Knight, Bielby, Osler, and other prominent Whigs had announced a proposal for a new Burial Act which would cost the parish rates some £9,000 to implement.⁶⁷ Between fifteen hundred and two thousand people came to the parish meeting called to debate the issue; it was an enormous assembly compared with most such affairs. Muntz, Jones, Edmonds, and Hadley led the Union's forces and they registered a noisy protest which successfully derailed the proposition. At every opportunity thereafter, members of the council vigorously interfered in the smooth management of parish affairs and attacked every initiative unless they had given prior approval. Although such victories had little impact beyond the immediate vicinity of the town, they were satisfying. In addition to the weight added to every policy statement, the local campaign gave the council and its followers a sense of tangible achievement. For many a reform of Parliament was an abstract principle; the benefits of such a change were difficult to grasp. A vote won at vestry meeting, however, was a talking-point for weeks. As the campaign for reform dragged on, such "unimportant" skirmishes became even more critical in holding the rank and file of the Union in their place.

There was also one "minor" matter to be settled. Attwood, as an economist, was fully aware of the need for a sound financial base for an organization's many activities. Neither he nor the more affluent councillors intended to be solely responsible. So, to fund their work and to encourage greater local participation and commitment, thirteen members of the council agreed to open their shops or offices in various parts of the town to collect the penny-a-week dues from members. A Union office was also opened at No. 1 Paradise Street. But since times were hard and money short, this particular innovation was to fail. Collectors eventually had to be appointed to canvass for dues and even then not much money was gathered.

The first annual general meeting, as called for in the Union's constitution, was advertised to take place on 17 May. The council met six days earlier, in the Globe Tavern, to make the preparatory arrangements. The talks lasted well into the night, since a few of the more radical councilmen again challenged the adoption of Blandford's plan and questioned Attwood's direction. One, perhaps Pare, had written to Henry Hunt in London asking him to condemn the declaration of 16 March.[68] Hunt had done so, but Attwood tightened his grip on the council and determinedly fought to have his way. The Union was his creation and until he was shown to be wrong there was sufficient support in the council to force his opinion through. After agreement to his satisfaction had been reached, the councillors turned to the question of the meeting itself.[69]

While all accepted the necessity of some public excitement and personal involvement, some feared that the populace might forget the Union's commitment to "Peace, Law, Order." It was on this point that Edmonds's presence was most welcome. His experience of such affairs was invaluable and he gave his personal guarantee of peace. Edmonds impressed upon the council the need for careful preparation. One minor point concerned the desirability of having a musical band lead the procession through the streets, thereby creating a focal point of attention and adding a sense of occasion to the march. Attwood liked the idea and threw his weight in support of such a display.[70] It was to become one of the most popular elements in all their parades. During the next few days, the councillors continued to meet and to discuss nervously the forthcoming demonstration. It would be the first real test of the idea's viability and the outcome could not be predicted. The inaugural assembly of 25 January had relied heavily upon the long-standing acceptance of the need for currency augmentation and had met at a time of economic hardship. This annual general meeting, on the other hand, was called to debate a particular measure of parliamentary reform and more contentiously to endorse the council's announced satisfaction with Blandford's bill.

They need not have worried. At 9 A.M. well before the time advertised for the start of the parade, crowds began to assemble outside the Union's temporary headquarters in Temple Street. By 10:30 A.M. the adjoining streets were choked. The route to be taken by the procession to Beardsworth's Repository had been carefully circulated, so that windows and pavements were lined with "gaily dressed spectators." To amuse the crowd the band played "God Save the King" and "other national airs." Eventually the Unionists lined up two abreast in St Phillip's churchyard, and headed by Attwood, Muntz, and Scholefield, slowly marched to the accompaniment of "martial airs." Edmonds arranged for marshals to hold the route open and for a bodyguard to protect the council. Virtually the whole of Birmingham, the *Journal*'s report later claimed, had turned out to see the spectacle.[71] Union enrolment had increased and the official medal, the badge of membership which demonstrated Attwood's intelligent understanding of the need for a sense of identity, was to be seen everywhere.[72]

At the meeting itself only one voice, that of a mechanic named Bibb, tried to challenge the council's recommendation. Here too the council had prepared carefully. Bibb was denied the right to speak at length and Edmonds, whose qualifications as a radical were impeccable, offered a vigorous defence of their position. Speaking despite the handicap of a hoarse throat, Edmonds confessed that his earlier advocacy of "ultra-reform" had been mistaken and that the gradualist approach was the true path. The speech was an undisguised attempt to convince sceptical artisans that the household vote was as valuable a goal as universal suffrage. The meeting broke up amicably and unanimity appeared to have been maintained. However, the Ultra-Tory alliance placed a number of strains upon the Union; they could still prove unbearable. As for Bibb, his boldness drew a quick response; he was made à member of the Political Council where he could be safely squelched.

The tactic used to control Bibb was one of which Attwood became increasingly fond because it served two purposes. There had been many warnings against accepting members too readily and thereby risking *agent provocateur* infiltration. The simplest method of combating this was an open meeting to which newspaper reporters and critics had easy access. Then, increasing the size of the council allowed Attwood to argue that not much could be accomplished in such a public forum. The real business of the council must therefore be conducted through private consultations among the leaders, an arrangement that suited Attwood perfectly because it offered him complete control. Council meetings became forums for the ratification rather than for the making of policy.[73] Some argument was unavoidable but previously arranged pacts prevented open splits. Later some members tried to curb this "secret trinity" approach by raising the quorum for a meeting from five to nine and demanding a two-thirds vote for approval.[74] Attwood did not welcome the change but cut its impact by adding an amendment to the effect that the rules of order of the House of Commons be followed; thus he kept greater power for himself as chairman.

As a result of the eminently successful demonstration and the endorsement of the council's proposals on 17 May, Attwood became more confident. In particular he was impressed by the drawing power of pageantry and determined that it must be an integral part of every subsequent meeting with the membership at large. If it was to become a viable tactic, however, emphasis in planning must be on the factor of control. There were plenty of examples, including that of Peterloo, where mass demonstrations had proved unmanageable.[75] Those out of earshot or easily distracted might create a disturbance and give opponents an opportunity to discredit the cause and its leadership. To avoid that problem the council, under the guidance of Attwood and Edmonds, learned to stage-manage all aspects of the proceedings. At every level, visual and spoken, the primary focus was on legality and orderliness within the context of extravagant display.

On the platform, a controlled agenda was meticulously observed. Each motion was the occasion for a lengthy oration by one of the leaders, Attwood, Edmonds, or Muntz. The opposition might complain that this simply gave an opportunity to "a breed of ignorant, self-sufficient speechifiers," but the membership thought differently.[76] The orators became part of the show. Each adopted a different style. Attwood possessed great poise, had a clear voice, a "truly theatrical whisper," and a quickness of mind that made him a formidable platform figure.[77] Even his opponents were impressed: "he possesses great shrewdness and penetration, and powers of language and illustration which frequently enable him to make the worse appear the better reason."[78] Edmonds's down-to-earth style and power over the mob persuaded his friends to call him their local "Demosthenes"; enemies named him "Munchausen."[79] Muntz favoured a coarse, even crude style: he was often vulgar and profane but his striking appearance caught the eye.[80] There were others, some tedious, some exciting, but all sought to add to the sense of occasion. Later, as their confidence increased, two other devices were employed. One, the sentimental pledge, had long been a favourite with the working man: "In unbroken faith, through every peril and trial and privation, we devote ourselves and our children to our country's cause." Often it was followed by a prayer of gratitude. Heads were bared, eyes uplifted during the pledge; for the prayer the bare heads were bowed and the eyes downcast. The second method to avoid distraction and boredom was the use of community singing. Occasional songs between speeches broke the monotony. The "Union hymn" composed by Attwood's son Bosco, and the "Gathering of the Union" had lyrics which were somewhat overwhelming. The first began: "Hail! peace and harmony, all hail our Union, Hail! sacred liberty, bow to her shrine."[81] The second verse was equally grandiloquent. This trend was to reach its peak on 7 May 1832, when the Birmingham Union organized the "Gathering of the Unions," reputedly the largest peaceful political demonstration ever held in Britain to that date.

The addition of the "masses" to the nucleus of reform supporters, even if they were only attracted by the excitement of the occasion, was of critical importance to the Union's general reputation. Naturally, the council wanted to be quite sure that this drawing power was not overlooked. Consequently, not only were their public meetings carefully recorded and reports dispatched to both local and national newspapers but, at Attwood's insistence, the *Journal*'s editor was permitted to attend the planning sessions as the "assistance of the Press was highly desirable."[82] At the height of the Reform Bill crisis in 1832, the Union paid for a special coach to convey the reports to London so that they might be published the following day.[83] To hold the interest of the newspaper proprietors and, ultimately, the readers, the event had to be newsworthy. After the initial euphoria created by the concept of a middle and working class alliance had dissipated, the council was often forced to create "news." The ability of Birmingham to generate crowds of reformers was of service in this regard. Inevitably, such a practice was open to abuse: "A favourite, and it has proved a successful tactic with the leaders of the Union has been to propagate most exaggerated notions of the importance and power of the body; no man better than Mr. Attwood knows how to array weakness in the garb of strength."[84] Eventually the claims became too extravagant and lost all semblance of credibility. The *Annual Register* among others categorically denied the validity of the

Union's own tallies.⁸⁵ Nevertheless, even the most biased critic was forced to admit that Birmingham's reformers commanded the allegiance of a good number of the town's citizens. As a result the nation was obliged to take notice of their deliberations. The descriptions of the "grand" meetings caught the imagination of the country. Many would-be reformers in the years that followed held the image of Birmingham's effort before their supporters for inspiration.⁸⁶

Many tricks were employed to trade upon this illusion of unity and harmony. After 17 May 1830, for example, the council never called a "Birmingham Political Union Meeting" save for the annual general meetings specified in the Union's constitution. The "grand" demonstrations masqueraded under the label "town meeting." This title had an old and honourable lineage and had been used to designate the activities of a united town. Obviously there were hopes that it would be still so regarded. Their simple subterfuge worked despite the protests in letter and editorial of the "respectable" inhabitants. In the Commons a meeting called and controlled by the council was invariably taken as representative of the whole of Birmingham.⁸⁷

To emphasize the national character of the Union, Thomas Attwood insisted from the outset that the names and letters of prominent men who offered support be published. On 27 February the names of Sir Francis Burdett and Sinclair Cullen appeared in the *Birmingham Journal* together with their expressions of support for the Union. The former had been personally invited to join by Attwood after his speech in the Commons praising the first public meeting: "I am glad that you have made up your mind to join our Union, but think it doubtful if you are right in postponing it until our Petition is presented. The best proof you could give the House of your approving it would probably be to say you had felt it your duty to join it. When you write to me to say you joined us, it will be well if you would give your *reasons* and *opinions* in order that I may publish them, and produce effect upon the Country."⁸⁸ The effectiveness of this policy was amply demonstrated in October 1831. Letters received from Lord John Russell, Lord Althorp, and Sir Gray Skipworth were immediately published.⁸⁹ Reaction from Parliament was gratifying. In the Commons such open ministerial association with "Political Unions" became the subject of an acrimonious debate.⁹⁰ Russell, forced to defend his action, ended, almost to his own surprise, with a far-reaching endorsement of all the activities of these organizations and spoke of the right of the people to a role in politics: "He saw no reason why he should say to the thousands who had been awaiting with interest the result of this bill, 'You are unfit to be consulted by the king's government, and I therefore repudiate your praise.' On the contrary, he thought that he might notice the loyalty and good sense of the people of Birmingham."[91] Attwood's tactic had been extraordinarily successful.

The council understood that to be rid of the charge that its members, and Attwood in particular, were indifferent reformers they needed to curry the favour of the national leaders of the lower classes. Caution, however, was needed. A close identification with "wild-eyed" radicals would frighten potential middle-class allies and might lead to a challenge to Attwood's leadership in Birmingham. Cobbett, who, despite his opposition to paper money, may well have been the first choice as any ally, had cooled his initial enthusiasm: "The Political Union founded by Mr. Attwood, is very laudable in itself; but it will produce, I am convinced, no effect whatever. It is encumbered with regulations which prove its timidity; it exposes men to the displeasures of the powerful; and if it were more likely, which it is not, to become really formidable to that, the destruction of which it aims, it would be crushed, while all but its mere members, would look on in silence. Oh no! from *combinations* of this sort, or of any sort, no great good can come, however worthy and able the leaders may be."[92] In the space of three weeks, Cobbett had become convinced that the only way to achieve reform was to work within and through the Commons as it was then constituted. The reason for this abrupt change probably lay in the scheme which he had recently inaugurated to raise £10,000. With this money he could then buy a rotten borough and gain a seat.[93] His reforming zeal was therefore directed to this end and left no time for the slower Union strategy. With Cobbett unenthusiastic, the council turned to Sir Francis Burdett. Attwood undertook to persuade him to preside at the next Union meeting.

He went to London in the middle of June 1830. The fame of the Political Union was such that many prominent figures competed for his attention and he was flattered to find himself "a sort of lion" with more social commitments than he desired.[94] The Reform movement, whose strength in the country had been growing, claimed to take Birmingham's structure as its model, but as yet only the latter looked formidable.[95] Much of the protest was simply a poor reflection of the 1819 agitation, exhibiting tumult without organization. (It did not matter, for in this case, as so often in politics, perception was more important than reality.) Many of Attwood's social engagements were inconsequential, though there were a few exceptions. At a dinner given by Joseph Hume and Daniel O'Connell, he engaged in an interesting discussion about tactics. Unfortunately, an alliance of Ultra-Tories and Catholics in 1830 was inconceivable and for the moment it was difficult to find common ground for coordinated activity between those two gentlemen and Blandford.[96] Nevertheless, in case the Blandford liaison collapsed, several alternatives were explored.

The subject was taken up the following evening when Attwood dined with Lord Radnor, an influential Whig who was an advocate of social as well as political reform. Radnor was a friend of William Cobbett, although there is no indication that Attwood owed his introduction to that source. The talks between the two could not have been entirely amicable for Radnor was convinced that Ricardo and Malthus were the best economists of the age.[97] It was an opinion from which Attwood felt obliged to differ. Lord Blandford, who was also present (this was the first time the two had met), joined the argument on Attwood's side and the question of political reform was pushed into the background. The atmosphere was not lightened when an unnamed guest mentioned, presumably in jest, the recent running of the Derby, in which Beardsworth's horse, Birmingham, had been badly beaten. Most of the midland town had backed it and London society had joked that "The *Birmmagems* [sic] lose so much that a new copper coinage would scarcely put them right in court." The association of Attwood's cherished currency ideas with gambling even at a social occasion was something he did not appreciate.

On 22 June Attwood finally had a chance to speak with Burdett.[98] The latter agreed at once to preside at the next Union gathering, although it would have to be postponed "for a week or two for his [Burdett's] convenience."[99] At the same table when Attwood made his request were three Whigs, Hobhouse, Davenport, and Lord John Russell. He was pleased to discover that they approved his choice and, in principle, the idea of a Union. In turn, he anxiously impressed upon them that neither he nor the membership he led were potential revolutionaries: "The whole people of England [are] essentially aristocratic and inbred with respect for their superiors."[100] Both he and the Whigs took care to emphasize their open minds on the subject of reform. Attwood's caution was in response to what he had learned in the last few days about the state of the parties at Westminster. He had discovered that the Whigs were considering plans for a measure of reform. Moreover, Grey appeared to be slowly resuming the leadership of the party and Davenport's forebodings of the Whigs' unreliability might no longer be valid. In such a situation the good opinion of Lord John Russell, who had been a leading advocate of reform in the House recently, was particularly important.[101]

Although Attwood was in some ways a supplicant at this dinner, both Russell and Davenport had been at pains to flatter him. Even at this early stage some Whigs recognized the potential of the Union and wished to impress upon Attwood that their party was not unsympathetic. They added that within their circle the currency question had not been forgotten. During March a group of them had met regularly in Althorp's rooms in the Albany to discuss "important issues."[102] On several occasions, said Davenport, he had urged a policy of monetary expansion on the lines favoured by Attwood. Admittedly not all of those present had accepted his view; nevertheless, Russell assured Attwood that he supported some form of currency manipulation and had pressed for "an honest currency" in a letter to Brougham in January. These reassurances were similar to others Attwood had received in the past week. Lord Dillon, for example, had, to Attwood's surprise, allowed that Grey might be "influenced," although the form that influence might take and the results expected were unspecified.[103]

Attwood left London a few days later to consider what he had learned. Promises and verbal guarantees obtained from politicians were not always the best guide to action. The Whigs claimed to be more receptive to his ideas, economic and political, but it was as yet difficult to gauge how much their response to the currency question was simply born of a desire to gain Birmingham's allegiance to the Whig version of political reform. Whatever the motivation, their overtures did confirm the value of the current program and made the continuation of pressure from a mass movement imperative. While keeping his options open, Attwood decided to leave matters as they were. Davenport, away from his fellow Whigs, continued to express reservations on the subject of their reliability and to warn that challenging the unreformed system still looked extremely difficult.[104] Few of his colleagues, Davenport revealed, expected sweeping changes. Moreover, the Whigs themselves were reportedly convinced that they needed Ultra-Tory support to topple the government. This admission, coupled with the fact that Blandford's measure remained the only positive reform proposal before the House, demonstrated that the time was not right for a change in the direction already plotted for the Union. If nothing else it was a useful weapon to prick the hide of the Wellington administration.

The stimulating if hectic renewal of political contacts in London had been interrupted occasionally by his primary errand – the Union's opposition to the Free Grammar School bill. The issue had, in the last two weeks of May, surpassed the question of reform. Attwood had been forced to take a leading role in the name of the Union as part of the attempt to control local affairs. The bill gave permission to pull down the old school so that a larger building might be erected nearby. The council had joined in a broad coalition of condemnation on the ground that the bill failed to deal with long-standing administrative abuses which should be corrected before the governors of the school were given further privileges.[105] Attwood had undertaken to guide the opposition in London as the bill passed through its various committee stages. He was persuasive and in early July the House of Lords agreed to postpone the bill. It was a small gain that could not be expected to focus attention in Birmingham on the Union for long: nevertheless any demonstration of effectiveness was valuable at this stage. The task of building a national movement required very careful attention to detail. The focal point, for the sake of his long-term objective, currency reform, had to be the midland town and not London.

The political situation was changed by the death of George IV on 26 June. While George had remained alive, only Wellington had any degree of influence; the Whigs were regarded with royal disfavour. Now a general election would be called automatically. The proposed meeting at which Burdett was to appear had to be postponed. Originally scheduled for 5 July it was moved to 2 August, then brought forward to 26 July so as to avoid too close proximity to the election. Meanwhile, to keep Birmingham's collective attention, the Union held a procession to celebrate the king's proclamation and the council debated the "National Distress" at a special meeting. At the latter, five resolutions were unanimously approved and subsequently published. Their core was again the demand for reform.[106]

Yet all was not well with the Union. Outwardly, there were expressions of confidence but the leaders were concerned. Since Attwood's return in June, Cobbett had launched an attack: "… a pretty sight to see; a man like THOMAS ATTWOOD sending for an empty-gaping, shilly-shallying, shuffling fellow like this, to give weight to his 'UNION'."[107] A week earlier, he had, with Hunt, issued a manifesto warning the workers against all such Unions: "… listen not to those who may tell you that … half a loaf is better than no bread. In this case half a loaf is no bread … Never …

present a petition which shall not distinctly pray for annual parliaments, universal suffrage, and vote by ballot."[108] The effectiveness of this two-pronged assault was dramatized on 26 July. The Union paraded through the streets, led by the Union band wearing new uniforms, union jack caps and armbands, and headed by Attwood and Burdett arm in arm. It offered a splendid spectacle but the crowds in the streets were thinner and the attendance at the subsequent meeting was lighter then usual.[109] The visible lack of numbers was somewhat offset by the council's good news that paid-up memberships had doubled since 17 May; nevertheless, it was obvious that the workingmen's support for reform was split.[110]

The appearance of division within Birmingham was not solely the fault of the rank and file. Council meetings had not been particularly harmonious recently as priorities were challenged and Attwood's authority was once more called into question; a situation exacerbated by the failure of Blandford's proposal to make much headway in the Commons. The reason for its adoption by the council had been sound, but viewed as a practical measure its idiosyncrasies invited ridicule. It was not the focus for agitation that Attwood had envisaged. The first public sign of disagreement within the inner circle came from Scholefield. Rumours circulated that he seriously considered resigning. Later the rumours were confirmed when it was learned that his announced decision to refuse an invitation from Edward Ellice to stand in the Coventry election for the Whig party derived not from a sense of commitment to the Union but from the ill-health of his wife. Her illness would force him to curtail all his public activities.[111]

Attwood's own faltering commitment did not become known until the meeting itself. Even before he spoke watchers may have guessed that a change of direction was in the offing, for Richard Spooner sat with him on the platform, his first appearance since the inception of the Union. The reason for Spooner's presence quickly became obvious, because the emphasis in Attwood's speech was on the currency rather than parliamentary reform. The latter, he argued, continued to be an important objective but it might take some years to achieve. The point was followed up in his remarks at the evening's banquet for Burdett: "The people were asleep, lulled by *clamming* of the bells for victories bought with *borrowed money,* for which their labour, and the bread of their children in the cradle, were now mortgaged to *repay 40s. in the pound* ... where are the just and rightful profits of our honourable industry? Where are the just and necessary wages of our honest workmen?"[112] The theme that if government could "not secure honest bread for honest labour [it] must retire and give place to better men" was reiterated but with less vehemence. The state of the nation and the relation of that state to the question of currency were at the heart of his speech.

It was a reversion to an older tune but the distinction, at least for Attwood, was more of order than content. During the first six months of 1830 Attwood had put a great deal of energy into the Union idea. However, he had never neglected his basic interest as the conversations in London with Russell and Davenport testified. From the outset he had tried to press political and currency reform in tandem. Only a few weeks before the Union had been launched in 1829 he had promoted the Birmingham Currency Association.[113] In the Commons Matthias Attwood had raised the subject several times. His efforts had attracted attention, particularly after 11 February when he had proposed the adoption of bimetallism and had won the support of Baring.[114] Davenport had pursued the same ends through the introduction of a number of resolutions relating to the level of distress. Both men had been plied with facts as well as exhortations by Thomas Attwood. As for himself no speech to the Unionists was complete without a reference to the economy. For his followers political reform was always the centrepiece notwithstanding their support for a change in the currency. Now, in a somewhat arrogant fashion, he was suggesting that he alone appreciated the duality of England's problems and that the order of priorities must be readjusted.

Attwood's interpretation was reiterated in August, when the council interfered in the election of the county members for Warwickshire. On 6 August four heavily laden boats travelled by canal from Camp Hill near Birmingham to Warwick. They carried four hundred Unionists, the Union band, and a deputation from the council to attend the nomination meeting. Given a place on the platform, Attwood made the first speech. He made a number of accusations against the candidates past performances and concluded with a list of questions which he demanded that each candidate answer; the central issue was the currency.[115] Of the five questions asked, two dealt exclusively with economic matters, one dealt with corruption, another requested a statement of past endeavour, and the fifth required a pledge on reform. The emphasis paralleled Attwood's conception of the problem exactly.

In terms of immediate effect, the Union's intervention did little. The candidates, Lawley and Dugdale, easily won the nomination without having to commit themselves to anything. But from Attwood's point of view the enterprise had not been in vain. He had reasserted his aims in the clearest possible terms and they had been publicly endorsed outside Birmingham. In regard to publicity the council was delighted to discover, a few days later, that Robert Peel had described their appearance as one of the worst incidents of the election campaign.[116] But the agricultural troubles in the southern counties and the growing menace of the cholera epidemic competed for headlines.[117] What interest could be aroused during an election was likely to be fleeting and, irrespective of emphasis, the Union's struggle for recognition and unity was floundering. Moreover, the division between the radical and moderate wings of the movement was widening.

There was little improvement in its fortunes in the next two weeks. Not even Attwood's brilliantly executed capture of a Whig-inspired meeting, held to celebrate the recent French revolution, did much to relieve the sense of futility. Moreover, the Union was under siege as a number of other organizations, trying to take advantage of Attwood's recent emphasis on the currency, competed for attention. The National Association for the Protection of Labour, promoted in the town by Doherty of Manchester, Macgowan of Glasgow, and Marshall of Bolton, sought to steal the support of the working classes.[118] The bloom of the preceding spring had faded with disconcerting suddenness.

The futility of the council's piecemeal endeavours and all of Attwood's manoeuvring may be measured by an event that occurred one week later. Beardsworth's horse, Birmingham, won the St Leger at Doncaster at 40–1, odds forced up by knowledge of bribes taken by his jockey to lose. Civic pride was immediately stimulated. Flags appeared "everywhere."[119] Champagne suppers were arranged by the wealthy and the poor took a holiday. Until provincial pride in other spheres of endeavour could be stimulated Attwood's labours were unlikely to meet with success whatever direction they might take. Fortunately, events were conspiring in his favour.

CHAPTER NINE

The Birmingham Political Union: Vindication

The general election had produced a House more independent than any since 1818, yet Wellington continued to act upon the assumption of Tory strength and to persist in a policy of non-cooperation.[1] The Whigs, who had moved into more or less regular opposition during the summer, were convinced that the government was doomed despite their own losses at the polls.[2] There was general recognition that they had lost popular support by appearing too reticent in their endorsement of reform. It was clear that many people of property and education were against the present system. As their numbers grew many MPs began to understand that Parliament's current form menaced rather than served the ruling classes. In consequence, there was some shuffling among the splinter groups as some Canningites and a few Ultra-Tories moved into the opposition camp. The way was smoothed by the untimely death of William Huskisson, the Canningite leader whom both Whigs and Ultra-Tories had distrusted.[3] Within this new coalition the question of political reform was the central issue and by opening of the first session of the new Parliament on 2 November the allies had agreed to make it the subject of the first division against the government.[4]

The fashioning of an effective opposition was accompanied by debate, sometimes feverish, about a number of other issues. The agricultural workers of the south had been in a depressed condition and ignored for many years. In 1830 the prospect of another severe winter of unemployment had driven them to acts of desperation. Disorders began in Kent at the end of August and continued through September, October, and November in a number of counties. The movement was generally directed against the farmers and magistrates of the local regions. However, there were overtones of a national character which persuaded the government to reinforce garrisons and to urge upon the local justices of the peace the use of the military.[5] In urban areas, trade had generally recovered from the low point of the previous year but the Bank of England was still concerned by the depletion of its reserves and therefore continued to follow a policy of caution by rationing discount. Credit bills which would normally have been acceptable at the Bank were refused. The governor warned that if demand did not diminish interest rates would have to be increased.

The most critical factor in the emerging storm of national opposition, the Tory cabinet believed, was the slowly maturing excitement created by the revolutions on the continent. In London, Cobbett delivered a series of lectures between 9 September and 7 October on "The French and Belgian Revolutions and English Boroughmongering." Other orators provided similar diatribes and excited crowds displayed tricolour cockades to indicate their sympathies. Reports of impending insurrections, many imaginary, flooded into the Home Office from country magistrates. The government, nervously taking these tales at face value, sent troops north to prepare to resist urban agitation and to defend arms depots.[6]

Birmingham, after some initial hesitation, joined the general rejoicing. The Political Union, which had only belatedly recognized the opportunity, planned a "Dinner to celebrate the French Revolution"; it was a provocative title guaranteed to call forth opposition. In a deliberate attempt to arouse popular feeling, the council devised a gigantic public relations exercise. It marked the end of Attwood's forlorn attempt to make the currency the major feature of the Union's activities. In view of the mood at Westminster and in the country, not even he could doubt which cause in the current unrest had the greatest following. The trick, therefore, if the Union was to lead, and not simply imitate initiatives taken elsewhere as it was now doing, was to crush all rivals and resistance by making the loudest noise and by adopting the most eye-catching symbols, just as it had promised to do in January. Whether Attwood could acquire the streak of ruthlessness and sense of commitment which would be necessary to live up to that radical promise, thereby sustaining his position as the undisputed leader, remained to be seen.

Three thousand seven hundred people sat down to a sumptuous meal at Beardsworth's Repository on 11 October: "not less than 3500 lbs of butcher's meat was placed upon the table, consisting of rounds and loins of beef, fillets of veal, hams, legs of pork, legs of mutton, &c &c. Each man was allowed a pint of beer to dinner and a quart of ale afterwards." For the cynical the well-publicized announcement that such largesse would be available may have been the major reason for the enthusiastic turn-out. The evening was carefully orchestrated, indeed, there was an air of cold calculation in the whole affair. Attwood arrived to take the chair amid a fanfare of trumpets. Toasts, songs, prayers, and the "Marseillaise" led by fifty glee and chorus singers followed each other rapidly. Attwood's speech, which echoed the views expressed by the majority of newspapers and the middle class since August, was solidly unexceptionable. The French had shown courage, patriotism, humanity, generosity, and an admirable sense of liberty.[7] They had been justified in resorting to physical force. But "nothing could be more erroneous than supposing that the English people would also be justified in having recourse to force."[8] Attwood argued that Britain had gained her liberty through a series of actions which had culminated in the "Glorious Revolution" of 1688. The present problems related to a "twisting away" of those rights, a situation which could be remedied by "due course of law." He reiterated the motto embossed on the Union medal, "The Constitution, nothing less and nothing more." These remarks were most reassuring to the apprehensive members of Birmingham's respectable classes.

Attwood's unique contribution to the proceedings occurred not in his set speech but when he rose to reply to a toast. In his most impressive demagogic style, he daringly evoked the other, darker side of his Political Union. The "reasonableness" and "respectability" of middle-class morality were set aside as he played upon the emotions of the diners to obtain an ultra-radical effect: "Where is the man among you who would not follow me to the death in a righteous cause (The cheering was immense on the delivery of this passage, which lasted for some minutes, accompanied by cries, 'All, All'). I see gentlemen your hearts are mine, and mine is yours."[9]

The day undoubtedly marked one of the highpoints in his ascendancy over and sense of identification with the common people of Birmingham. Their passionate response was more than he had expected and affirmed his decision to pursue an ultra-radical policy if it proved necessary. In its wider context, this occasion may have been equally important. He had publicly and skillfully raised the spectre of civil war, with himself as one of the leaders. At the same time, he had placed in juxtaposition to this "call to arms" the "due course of law" argument. Both participants in his planned alliance were thus told exactly what they wished to hear. The middle classes learnt that the ultra-radicals could be trusted if properly led, despite their apparent predilection for revolution. The working classes, on the other hand, were offered sympathetic leadership and a recognizable program in the style to which they had long been accustomed. Peel was sufficiently worried by the prospect of a successful Union that he asked the law officers for a new assessment of its legality. He was told that there was little that could be done.

At this dinner Attwood became the focal point of the aspirations of both factions; he was, temporarily at least, the physical embodiment of the Union.[10] Factional pressures would continue to create internal dissension, but his leadership of the Union could no longer be seriously questioned, even by those like Joseph Parkes who would have preferred to supplant him. "Three men in my lifetime," Parkes declared, "have held in their hand the omnipotent means of levelling the oligarchy – Cobbett ... Brougham ... lastly Thomas Attwood, if the legitimate ends of his public efforts were consistent with the powerful means of agitation he has organized."[11] Several years after the passage of the Reform Act there were attempts to revive the Political Union. On each occasion, the organizers sought to place Attwood at their head.[12] When he at least consented, the movement achieved an animation it previously lacked. The success was fleeting in character but it testified to the continuing identification of the man with the form of agitation and his ability to reconcile what to many were contrary poles.

There was a further dimension to this remarkable pageant. Attwood, for the first time, clearly spoke in the wider context of universal principle and global struggle.[13] There had been earlier intimations of awareness of European political developments in his currency pamphlets.[14] Now the French revolution forced him to acknowledge links between nations other than those of trade. Attwood was to stick to a conception of justifiable rebellion for the remainder of his life, although it is doubtful that he ever seriously contemplated the possibility in an English context. It was, however, a useful ploy to gain attention. In November 1830 he followed up the speech by writing to Lord Melbourne a letter which threatened the creation of a new association to lead a tax revolt if Britain interfered in Belgium. Melbourne took the threat very seriously.[15]

The speech from the throne which opened the new session of Parliament on 2 November congratulated the nation on its attainment of "social happiness" and "commercial prosperity." The use of such phrases announced the government's intention to oppose any real change in the structure of society.[16] Wellington reinforced that message by making his well-known declaration against parliamentary reform of any kind: "the legislature and the system of representation possessed the full and entire confidence of the country."[17] Wellington was well aware of the strength of the forces arrayed against his administration but preferred to hold to his principles and trust that firm government would rally support as it had in 1819. He had miscalculated; the government's stance united all others against it.[18] The Whigs opened their campaign as they had planned. Lord Grey urged redress of grievance before it was too late while, in the Commons, Brougham gave notice of a reform motion for a fortnight hence. Althorp, in support, strongly criticized the Tories and made a personal commitment to the principle of reform.[19] The battle-lines had been drawn; the political world nervously awaited the debate on Brougham's motion upon which, it seemed, the government would stand or fall.

The situation outside Parliament had worsened. The activities of "Captain Swing" in the rural districts were reaching new peaks of destructiveness.[20] London witnessed a rapid deterioration in the maintenance of public order. On the evening of 2 November there were sixty-six cases of assault on the newly organized police force. Fears of a revolution on the French model grew daily. Mobs roamed the streets clashing bloodily with the police. The Home Office was besieged with reports of plots and threats to property. Both Peel and Wellington received assassination threats. There was a warning that Wellington's house at Hyde Park Gate would be burnt down. From Birmingham came reports that societies were being formed with the "express intention of intimidating the Government." The Political Union, another correspondent reported, "appears likely to become, indeed, I may say are, a most dangerous body."[21] Both the cabinet and the City of London council decided, in some panic, that 9 November might well be the day fixed for revolution. On that date, Lord Mayor's Day, the king and his ministers were to dine at the Guildhall. Normally a procession would wind its way through streets protected by the police. But with London apparently ready to explode such a concentration would leave the mobs free elsewhere. On 7 November, therefore, Wellington and Peel persuaded the king to abandon the parade.

The cancellation was an admission of failure and weakness which served to strengthen the opposition's resolve to bring down the government. Petitions from all parts of the country descended on Westminster, emphasizing the respectable support that parliamentary reform now commanded. The Political Council of Birmingham denounced the king's speech on 9 November and angrily petitioned the king "to dismiss his Ministers from his councils and presence for ever."[22] Attwood, somewhat spuriously, later attributed responsibility for the defeat of the government on 15 November to the petition.[23] The question which toppled the Wellington administration, however, was not the much-debated reform, but the more mundane Civil List. Parnell, the Whig's financial expert, tabled a motion requesting that the latter be referred to a select committee. The motion was carried with the help of the Ultra-Tories and the country gentleman by 233 votes to 204. Following the division Wellington and Peel deemed it advisable to resign rather than risk defeat on Brougham's motion. On 16 November Wellington tendered his resignation and Lord Grey was subsequently asked to form a new government.[24]

Birmingham did not celebrate the fall of Wellington. The Political Union had begun to prepare its members for a reversal in policy, but Attwood, unconvinced that the Whigs' intentions were entirely honourable, dithered.[25] To the chagrin of some in the council, he reverted to an old pattern and waited upon events. He was not confident enough of his national influence to seize command of the situation and bend it to his own purposes. When, on 13 December, the Union did discuss the change in government at a meeting called solely on the authority of the chairman and without any prior discussion in council,[26] Attwood contributed only a number of oblique and unenthusiastic references to the new ministers. He supported Grey's recent declaration that the "Aristocracy" had certain "rights" upon which other "orders" should not encroach,[27] but pointed out that these were rights which complemented those of the people. Attwood added, without much conviction, that he thought that Lord Grey was not the man "to injure either." It was an unimpressive performance. Still, he did catch the mood of his audience at one point. Grey had appealed for assistance from the country at large in the months ahead. If the prime minister received that support, Attwood told the gathering, in his only contentious remark, that he was certain "Grey would do his duty." The unspoken promise was that the Birmingham Political Union would see that he did.

Thomas Attwood was the only speaker who struck an uncompromising attitude regarding the Whig ministry. Most of the opprobrium was reserved for the Tories; Salt even called for their impeachment and execution.[28] Yet it was Attwood's caution that prevailed in the concluding motions. There was one other curious development. A series of resolutions were reportedly approved after the main business had been settled. These proposed a far greater commitment to radical reform than anything hitherto espoused by the Union. It was extremely unlikely that these emanated in any way from Thomas Attwood.[29] There was no discussion of the resolutions which appear to have been added to the original report of the proceedings. They were probably the product of a small faction within the Union, possibly led by George Edmonds. The ideas they contained were close to those supported by him in 1819. A complex taxpayer franchise was mentioned in the course of Edmonds's speech and was an obvious compromise between the universal suffrage concept he had been forced to abandon at an earlier meeting and the householder clause favoured by his middle-class friends. The inclusion of a vote by ballot resolution suggests that Edmonds was aided and abetted by Parkes, although the latter makes no such claim in his voluminous correspondence with Place.[30]

The connection between these resolutions and the ostensible purpose of the meeting, an "Address to the King," was at best tenuous. The incident does, however, confirm the existence of a body of opinion within the Union which continued to advocate a more radical approach to reform and was annoyed by Attwood's refusal to give a stronger lead. The public airing of private disagreement was, on the other hand, a further testament to Attwood's ascendancy. The method used to promote the proposals was designed by the radicals to circumvent their leader by appealing to the rank and file. The attempt failed. Attwood was furious and he reproached Edmonds vigorously. There is no evidence that a petition based upon the resolutions was ever presented in Parliament or even formally distributed for signature in Birmingham. The challenge, however, forced Attwood to realize that he could not vacillate much longer.

Expressions of radical defiance from outside Birmingham were not so easy to quash and in Atwood's opinion were all too common. The visit of Henry Hunt, the newly elected MP for Preston and head of the Metropolitan Political Union, in early January was a case in point. On the surface the consultation was amicable. Hunt had a number of private conversations with Attwood and attended a council meeting. The *Journal* guessed that the primary topic of conversation was cooperation between the London and Birmingham Political Unions, a link which Attwood did not wish to encourage. Their public discourse was full of mutual praise and the two leaders agreed to send a joint "Address to Judges" requesting commutation of the death penalties imposed on "incendiaries and machine-breakers."[31] Upon this subject it was easy to agree.[32] But the meeting, sponsored by the ultra-radicals led by Russell, had placed Attwood in a difficult position.[33] He had no desire to alienate his working-class supporters yet Hunt's public image as one who preferred confrontation to compromise posed a threat to the concept of a general Union. Moreover, the man liked the limelight and too close an identification would diminish Attwood's own standing. His only option was to flatter Hunt with theatrical gestures, while holding him at arm's length in matters of policy. This would not please Hunt but he would find it difficult to protest too openly. A month later, Attwood heard with relief that currency reform had been denounced by the London radicals. At least, on that issue, he no longer had to pretend kinship with Hunt, who "speaks out of ignorance."[34]

The council, in December, expressed its willingness to await the first acts of Grey's new government. In the meantime, its primary goal was to shore up general support in the town. Luckily there was an issue which if handled properly was perfect for its purposes. Feelings were running very high against the Church of England and some clergymen had even received threatening letters.[35] Their organization in the town was in a peculiar position, for although it was divided into many ecclesiastical parishes and districts there was only one civil parish with one poor rate. The annual church rate for so many churches had to be voted in a huge vestry meeting in St Martin's Church. The law was uncertain and the churchmen were not sure of their powers. In consequence the meeting provided an ideal forum for Political Union activity. There had been grumbles against the system before. A placard in 1828 called on the people to "come forward then, and prevent your purses being opened too wide." Edmonds had used the issue as a focal point for a protest at the time of Peterloo.[36] In 1830 Muntz, an Anglican, took the lead. Attwood had no direct part but indicated elsewhere that despite his own religious affiliation he disliked Anglican pretensions and believed the present incumbents illiberal. The interference was an unqualified success.

By July the Union had penetrated almost every branch of parish government:

Messrs Churchwardens [the *Journal* demanded], have you not found that you are responsible for your acts, and that you must yearly give a faithful account of your stewardship? (Cheers) Messrs Constables, have you discovered that you cannot commit wrong without being brought to the bar of public opinion? (Cheers) Messrs Governors of the Free Grammar School, who have obtained office for no earthly purpose, God knows, but for the obstruction of charity, have we not made you strike your flag, and submit to the influence of popular opinion? (Cheers) Messrs Guardians of the Poor, has not the Political Union purged your body by the introduction of some of its members, and enforced a principle of purity in your proceedings?[37]

In local politics only the Street Commission still escaped. Edmonds trusted that its submission would not be far off.

Events outside the town moved more slowly and the council continued to avoid what Attwood termed "premature commitments" and his opponents, "timidity." A petition, circulated at the New Year, called for leniency in respect of those "unhappy individuals" who had engaged in "Captain Swing" activities. Charles Attwood, who had founded the Northern Political Union at Newcastle upon Tyne, had submitted a petition on this subject a few weeks earlier.[38] No sooner had his appeal been presented than a number of death sentences were commuted to transportation. The publicity value of such apparent influence was enormous and Birmingham desired to duplicate that success. Moreover, Thomas Attwood wished to warn his followers that men might commit perjury or initiate criminal acts simply to inform later on their dupes. Under such circumstances, Attwood nervously cautioned, "no man's life can be secure." Attwood was well aware of the vulnerability of his own position.

The Union claimed, by the end of January 1831, some nine thousand paid-up members.[39] They were, according to Attwood, the "very essence" of Birmingham and district, commanding the moral suasion of some four hundred thousand others. This grandiloquence provoked some Whigs to circulate a petition of their own. Presented in the House by Lord Radnor, it claimed that Birmingham favoured the secret ballot above all else.[40] Their boldness was encouraged by the strong possibility that Grey's cabinet was soon to present a measure of reform to the Commons and by the hesitancy of the Union's leaders in making any national statements.

The Whigs had been further encouraged by signs of dissension in the council itself. These could have led to the disintegration of the Union notwithstanding its successful local campaign. A number of violent arguments had led to the resignation of the ultra-radicals Thomas Perkins and Joseph Russell. The latter had always been a difficult colleague. The ballads and parodies he published often exceeded good sense and occasionally the bounds of the law.⁴¹ Only his identification with the Union, even after leaving the council, kept him from prosecution.⁴² Although without a large following, such men added credibility to the Union's claim to speak for Birmingham, although, more to the point, their activities after leaving the council might reflect badly on that body.

Attwood was unusually silent. Although not particularly fond of Russell, he regretted his departure because it signalled a shift in the loose coalition the Union had created. Moreover, there were a number of personal pressures which blurred his vision of the future. His son, Marcus, was in ill health and the over-protective father worried that his own chairmanship duties might be a contributory factor. Elizabeth was also unhappy. The character of many of his supporters was not to her taste; their leaders were never invited to her home. Furthermore, the financial burden of keeping the Union afloat continued to fall disproportionately on the few. The small sums collected from the membership were totally inadequate to cover the costs of printing, meetings, meals, and the various eye-catching "gimmicks" – medals, uniforms, and so on. Attwood's later claim to have spent around £1,500 in the first twelve months of the Union's existence was likely an exaggeration, yet the total was probably not inconsiderable and he was never a rich man.⁴³ On these grounds, Elizabeth exerted some pressure to reduce his involvement.

He was reluctant to do so for there had been the occasional snippet of heartening news. Five Yorkshire Unions had published declarations which were very Attwoodian in content and the *Quarterly Review* even accused the Union of trying to "bully the authorities."⁴⁴ Both reinforced the notion that they were making progress. The most debilitating factor, however, was the secretive behaviour of the Whig government. No one knew what was being prepared, so that Attwood was at a loss to decide whether he should continue his support of Blandford or make a tactical shift. The decision had not been made any easier by events in Parliament. To his dismay, some of the Ultra-Tories had begun to return sheepishly to Wellington's fold.⁴⁵ Chandos, egged on by Peel, had proposed what amounted to little more than tinkering with the electoral system. A few seats would be transferred from "corrupt" boroughs to the "new" towns; Birmingham would receive Evesham's place in the Commons. Such cosmetic laundering was regarded as grossly inadequate, both in terms of what Attwood really intended and as a rallying cry for the Political Union.

The Whigs in Birmingham, however, had been correct in their

assessment and Attwood was, in one sense, to be saved from his indecisiveness by events at Westminster. Grey's cabinet, while aristocratic in character, was determined to introduce a sweeping measure of reform. Their object was to win "social peace and security for property" and to head off future trouble stemming from what they took to be genuine and almost universal disgust with the existing system.[46] Naturally they were also intent on strengthening their own position, for as Parkes forecast: "If they do not propose *real* Reform the Whigs will be an utterly undone party, the *last* party that can pretend to govern the country."[47] After weeks of intense speculation it was announced that their plan would be introduced in the Commons on 1 March. In preparation, and in order to strengthen their case, the previous Saturday was set aside to receive petitions favouring reform. About one hundred were presented. As promised, on the following Tuesday before a packed House, Lord John Russell rose and proceeded to astonish the House of Commons by the scope of the bill. As constituency after constituency was named to be either wholly or partially disenfranchised, gasps of incredulity were heard from all sides. Russell, who was normally rather a poor speaker, began to revel in the occasion and added a few oratorical embellishments to heighten the drama. The proposal went much beyond that of Blandford in its redistribution of seats to the more populous towns and counties.[48]

Although Attwood's immediate response is unknown, it is probable that he was as surprised as anyone. At the council meeting a few days later, he had still not quite understood all the ramifications (neither for that matter had Grey) and intimated that with regard to the £10 franchise the bill did not go as far as he would have liked. He may, of course, have been attempting to hold the radicals (who favoured universal suffrage and had been urging greater contact with radicals elsewhere) in line but it would have been unlike him to sacrifice principle to expediency on such an issue. It is more likely that he expressed reservations so that if future events made dissociation from the bill necessary, he would not be locked in an untenable position. Moreover, in his earlier speeches he had been most critical of the Whigs and, while he had begun to modify his position at the meeting in December, it would have been difficult for him to admit that he had been wholly wrong. Privately, however, he knew that in the long run he had no option but to embrace Grey's and Russell's bill. If he did not others would and in so doing would dislodge him from his position. He therefore told the council members that, notwithstanding his dissatisfaction with parts of the bill, they must concentrate the energies of the Union on behalf of "the whole bill and nothing but the bill."[49] The slogan had been chosen with care and echoed a note already sounded in the *Spectator*. The bill was something tangible whose progress could be closely monitored in its passage through Parliament. The Union would therefore have an active role both as a ginger group, to keep things moving, and as a watchdog with one eye on the Whigs.[50] In this way the rank and file would retain a sense of purpose and Birmingham would compete with Westminster for attention. Attwood soon discovered that he had, at last, made the right choice.

The first task was to send a petition to Parliament expressing the Union's approval and emphasizing its commitment to working within the constitution. Speed was essential, since the Whigs in the town had given notice of their intention to do likewise. The Union met in Beardsworth's Repository on 7 March; the Whigs' "official" town meeting followed four days later. The addresses and petitions adopted were identical. This was not surprising for the Political Council was represented at the later meeting in strength and most of the resolutions emanated from its spokesman.[51] Only Attwood and Muntz were missing from the second occasion, having been dispatched to London to deliver the Union's documents to Grey.

After completing his part in the assignment – Grey presented the "Address to the King" on the 9th and the petition to the Lords on the 10th – Attwood stayed on to listen to the debates and to try to get some feeling for the mood of the country. On this subject his brother, Matthias, and Spooner's brother-in-law, Wetherall, were of little help, being staunch Tories. Indeed, the bill was to mark the first major disagreement between the two Attwoods. Matthias believed it went much too far and he became a vehement opponent. He was later to call the Whigs "tyrannical" and the Reform Bill itself "repugnant to the first principle of justice, to the known maxims of the constitution and to everything that favoured the security of property."[52] Thomas was naturally distressed, but had little room for manoeuvre. The brothers could still agree on the currency but their alliance was temporarily broken.

Grey's government, however, did not appear to be firmly in control and Attwood discovered that there was considerable speculation as to the fate of the bill on second reading. There was nothing to be done, however, but wait. At three minutes to three in the morning of 23 March, the House divided. As customary the Noes departed and then the tellers sidled along the benches counting those who remained. The number in favour was 302. Outside, the counts of the Noes was confused but the final tally was only 301. Cheers, cries, and groans greeted the result and the chamber rapidly emptied as the members hurried to relay the news.

Attwood had made plans with the council before leaving as to the town's response if the bill passed. There was to be an illumination. Sadly, a few who feared disorder if all did not illuminate, gained the ear of the magistrates. Special constables patrolled the streets and celebrations were kept firmly under control. Lights were extinguished promptly at 11 P.M.[53] Such pusillanimity could not dampen the enthusiasm and few went to bed that night.

Talk centred on the choice of candidates for the two new parliamentary seats Birmingham was to receive under the bill. Generally, Attwood and Tennyson were the most popular candidates.[54] Attwood knew such speculation was premature. There would be time enough for such decisions once the bill was on the statute books. A claim for the seat now would only divide the Union. So he told his friends that he did not want the nomination. Family responsibilities would not allow long absences in London. Marcus remained ill. Elizabeth and the four younger children were spending much of their time in Ramsgate and London's foul air would do them no good at all. His goal was simply to see the bill passed. Events after that could take care of themselves. These expressions of disinterest failed to persuade those who were aware of his ambition. Reform was a stepping-stone on the path to economic prosperity. Until that condition was achieved all knew that he would demand a leading role.

In Parliament, the committee stage of the bill was proving difficult. The Whigs knew their vulnerability and showed that they were amenable to some minor tinkering, such as the shifting of boroughs from one schedule to another and the reprieve of a few from total disenfranchisement.[55] Wellington's leadership of the Tories was hesitant and seemed to hinge on nothing more than the Fabian tactic of delay in the expectation that passions would cool. The crisis came to a head on 20 April. An amendment put by Gascoyne required that the number of members for England and Wales would not be reduced. Given the intention of the bill to add members from Scotland and Ireland, the amendment would increase the size of the House, a change the ministers had fought. The opposition seized the opportunity and voted solidly with Gascoyne. They won 299 to 291. After some hesitation because they feared the resulting excitement as much as the Tories, the Whigs called upon the king to prorogue the House. The opposition railed in vain and it was done on 22 April.

The council went to work immediately on the election campaign. At last it had something tangible to promote and it set about basing its appeal upon the weakness of the Whigs. An address was published exhorting electors to return only friends of reform and invoking the name of the king – a patriot king – as the source of authority.[56] It was a pattern copied in almost all constituencies as the election campaign got under way. Attwood appeared at gatherings of all sizes including the nomination meeting at Warwick; at each, he fulsomely praised the king and the Whigs.[57] The reservations of the last few months were forgotten as he confidently grasped the opportunity to lead a popular movement; a movement that had the support of a major party at Westminster and exhibited many of the qualities that had won the repeal of the Orders-in-Council in 1812.

When the votes were tallied, it became clear that their local efforts had been crowned with electoral success and their preferred candidates returned. This time no one would be allowed to interfere with the people's celebration of victory. The church bells rang and the town blazed with light. A suggestion from the chairman of the Union to illuminate now had the overtones of an order. To resist was to court disaster as the Reverend Thomas Moseley of St Martin's discovered. He had refused entry to the ringers so they had climbed through a belfry window. In the excitement Moseley was manhandled and later made a great to-do about assault.[58] It was exactly the type of incident that Attwood sought to avoid. If the town was to remain in his hands, no cause must be given for legal proceedings against the Union. After the excitement had died down, he belittled Moseley's complaints by charging that the "frenzied unionists" had been a few children and "loose women,"[59] ignoring the fact that the demonstration had acted in his organization's name. Moseley let the matter drop. Nevertheless, it illustrated the difficulty of holding the people to a policy of law and order, particularly at a time when a demonstration of passion was most advantageous for the Union's cause. It was a tribute to his moral ascendancy that Attwood's followers did not more often cross the narrow line which divided peaceful exuberance from lawlessness.

Grey's victory in the country at large became clear a few days later. The government's majority stood between 130 and 140 depending on whose reading of the independent members one took. As the nation collectively breathed again, Attwood took a few days off in Ramsgate. There was really no time, however, to relax. Economic collapse might yet drive the government from office and destroy all hopes of reform.

On 24 June Russell reintroduced the second Reform Bill. Both sides in the Commons were now unanimous in wanting a reform measure of some kind. Both were also nervous. The Whigs were fearful that the radicals would not be satisfied and, led by the political unions, would proceed to demand manhood suffrage. Hunt was already proclaiming that expectation in London and had alleged that Birmingham was of like mind; a lie which Attwood moved swiftly to deny. Moreover, there had been violence. On 3 June strikers and troops had fought in Merthyr Tydfil and twenty-five people had died. Farther afield, the O'Connellites were not making matters any easier. In this atmosphere of fear the committee stages were again likely to prove difficult.

Attwood's tactic was to wait, but now the waiting was not born of indecision. The Union must be careful, "if we hold no meetings the anti-reformers say we are indifferent. If we hold small meetings they say we are insignificant. If we hold large meetings they say we wish to intimidate them."[60] His patience was soon rewarded. The new bill included a clause which required the £10 franchise holder to pay his rates at half-yearly or longer intervals. Presumably Althorp, the leader of the House, was unaware of the effect of such a stipulation. It had been introduced merely to placate some members of the cabinet who wanted a higher borough qualification. Attwood was more alert. He estimated that in Birmingham less than 10 per cent of potential electors paid their rates at such long intervals. Without delay, the council drew up a memorial to Grey, forecasting that if the clause were left unmodified there would be trouble.[61] Grey replied by return of post. The offending regulation would be withdrawn, it had been "inadvertently inserted."[62] Elated, Union members counted it a coup even though they had not been alone in their protest. Others agreed. Ellenborough was sure that the reversal had been "conceived in the basest spirit of concession to the Birmingham Union and to the low press." In the next general meeting of the council, Attwood used it as the keynote to his speech and as a shining example of the power of unity and legality.[63]

Three weeks later, the council's commitment to the bill was tested. Three London delegates of the National Association of Working Classes appeared to beg support for a greater extension of the franchise. The council demurred, using the totally Attwoodian argument that it was pledged to the bill and could not now renege. It was not so united, however, as this public stance would suggest. Some members had been unhappy at the refusal, whereas others wished for an unambiguous avowal of endorsement for the bill. At this point Attwood's skill at finding compromises came into play. To satisfy the latter faction, a petition was drawn up renewing the commitment. Included, however, was a strongly worded denunciation of opponents in Parliament clearly designed to placate the ultra-radical elements in the alliance: "... the petitioners had observed with disgust and indignation the factional and puerile opposition made to a majority of that Honourable House, and to the demands of an oppressed and insulted people, and, with feelings of nearly similar character they contrasted the rapidity with which measures of penalty and spoliation had been enacted by former Parliaments and extraordinary tardiness at present displayed in completing a wholesome and healing measure of wisdom, justice and conciliation."[64] Daniel O'Connell was given the task of insulting the House by presenting these sentiments. The Commons response was gratifying. The Speaker ordered it thrown out as "grossly disrespectful and directly tending to violate the privileges of parliament."[65] Attwood had not anticipated such a strong reaction but was not displeased. The object of the Union's activities was to gain notice and if that notice enjoined a touch of notoriety, so be it. The benefits far outweighed the losses in both Birmingham and London. Cobbett later attributed "the amazing dispatch" of the Commons in dealing with the bill after this date to Birmingham's intemperance.[66] He was quite wrong, but the recognition from a man who often found pleasure in belittling Attwood's efforts was welcome.

Throughout August and early September, the Union held to its course. A variety of amendments, including the Chandos clause to enfranchise the £50 tenants-at-will in the counties and thereby add to the power of the landowners, passed by without complaint, despite newspaper and general radical criticism of such concessions. Only William IV's coronation on 8 September persuaded the council to arrange a public meeting. Attwood presided over a stage-managed dinner at the Globe Inn in which the expressions of political opinion were kept to approbation for the monarchy.[67] Attwood was firmly in control. The stream of mementoes, souvenirs, and commemorative plaques that celebrated the Union now became a flood. On all, Attwood's name and picture was the dominating feature. One very popular item was a lithograph portrait which Attwood modestly admitted was flattering if not a particularly good likeness.⁶⁸ His speeches were widely quoted and it was virtually impossible to speak a word against him. From the few who dared, angry supporters quickly won a retraction.⁶⁹ He knew that whenever he called the Union would gather. But, for the moment, he preferred to leave Parliament to work out its own salvation; for maximum effect the power of public opinion needed to be used judiciously and with the nation's attention focused on Westminster there was no need for further excitement.

By the middle of September the debate in Parliament was in its final stages. Attwood, anxious to be in at the moment of triumph, for he did not for a moment expect the bill to be defeated, hurried to London to attend the last three days of debate. He took rooms overlooking Westminster Palace Yard where he could watch the excited crowds, milling around from dawn to dusk, without undue risk, but he was rarely there. Getting into the visitor's gallery was almost impossible, but since all opinions were immediately relayed outside there was no need to be physically present. Early in the morning of 22 September, cheers echoed through the streets. Everyone seemed to know, almost without being told, that all was well. The Commons had passed the Reform Bill 345–236.⁷⁰ The relief was overwhelming. By daybreak the news was being carried across the country. Attwood did not return to Birmingham to celebrate; his people on the council were now sufficiently in control to make sure that no "outrage" occurred. He happily journeyed on to Ramsgate to bring his family the proof that Elizabeth need not have worried about the outcome of the debate.

The pleasures of family life, away from the constant pressure of leadership in Birmingham, gave him time to think. What were the options? Although he did not confide in Elizabeth, he was not deceived into thinking that the struggle was over. The House of Lords, the stronghold of the Tories, still stood in the way. It was not yet time to think about disbanding the Union as his wife expected. Its participation in the battle to win reform was likely to be greater than ever as the struggle shifted to new ground, Lords versus Commons. The claim to be a real union of the middle and working classes had been invested with greater significance.

The government held the same view and hoped that popular pressure, in part channelled through the Political Union, would persuade the upper house to accept the revised bill. Precautions nevertheless needed to be taken. The question of the creation of additional peerages had been broached with the king. Already as many peers had been created as seemed "decent" in the coronation honours list, but it was clear that many more might be needed. The difficulty would lie in getting William to agree.

They were right to be concerned. The duke of Wellington did not believe that the threat of a flood of new peers was particularly convincing. The king would not so dilute the peerage as to make a mockery of the social order. Moreover, the duke and his aristocratic friends were not men to be overawed by spectacles in the provincial towns and they did not expect others to be so either. Thus the government would be defeated in the Lords and the Whigs forced to think again. In the duke's opinion popular support for reform had already begun to wane. Meetings at several towns had not been quite as well attended in the days after the passage of the bill in the Commons. What he failed to understand was the common belief that nothing stood in the way of final approval and that such demonstrations were unnecessary. It was his mistake to confuse satisfaction with apathy.

By the middle of September, the council was anxious about the bill's chances of success in the House of Lords. Attwood's London sources urged that he contact Grey to express the Union's disquiet. Recognizing the reluctance of the cabinet to give official approval to the political unions, he determined to approach the prime minister in his capacity as a long-standing critic of the monetary system. A memorial was drawn up which pressed for an immediate expansion of the currency; if this were not done, it declared, the Reform Bill might be passed too late to prevent widespread violence.

His desire to talk to Grey on this point was quite genuine. For some months he had been visiting Nicholls, the Bank of England's agent, late at night.[71] Ostensibly the visits had been made to obtain advances for a few days on the security of good trade bills. But that could have been done by a clerk. Nicholls was well aware of Attwood's real interest – to discover the opinion of the Bank of England on the economy. The Bank was experiencing a drain of bullion and inadvertently Nicholls had revealed that confidential information; if the Bank in consequence chose to rein in its discount of bills, Attwood knew that business would immediately suffer a severe decline. He was therefore concerned to make sure that the cabinet was prepared for such an eventuality. Attwood and four others presented the memorial to the prime minister on 22 September. Grey was pleased to see them. The ostensible cause for their approach, the economy, was rapidly dismissed, although a few reassuring words were reserved for Attwood. Grey was much more anxious to ascertain their views on the state of public opinion and the consequences if the bill were to be defeated.[72] He also hinted that the Union should no longer remain quiet. This was no time for reticence.

Attwood welcomed the advice and returned to Birmingham determined to give the Whigs a spectacular demonstration of popular support. Planning had to be particularly careful because this was to be no ordinary show; it was to be an example of partnership whereby public opinion would be used to complement, not challenge, cabinet policy. Beardsworth's Repository had served up to this point, but now it was time to move outdoors, to the arena of the radicalism of twelve years before – Newhall Hill.

Organization had to be impeccable. There must be no hint of disorder which could discredit the enterprise, yet it had to be sufficiently impressive to command the attention of London. The immediate problem lay in getting the various sections of the Union to arrive in an orderly fashion and to disperse in the same manner. No one was quite sure how many people would attend. Invitations to unions in the surrounding counties were sent and most promised delegations. The ironworkers and colliers presented a special worry because their temper was uncertain and their commitment to Attwood's brand of agitation unknown. The council had also to make a concerted effort to persuade a few of the town's wealthier inhabitants to appear as an illustration of the unity of opinion in the district.

The weather on 3 October was ideal. Church bells gave the signal at 10 A.M. for the people to gather.[73] Along the route street hawkers and entertainers kept the spectators amused. The Union band led the main body, headed by the council, from the town centre slowly to Newhall Hill. It took one and a half hours for all to arrive at the half-circle of wagons in the centre of the amphitheatre. New banners were sewn to provide colour and exhortation: "Attwood, Union, Liberty and Peace," "William the Fourth, the People's hope," "Earl Grey," and other equally patriotic slogans dominated. The number of participants was of course disputed. The Union claimed 100,000 and later raised it to 150,000; the anti-reformers admitted "perhaps 15,000" and many of those "only women and children." The Staffordshire Unions were there in force and a large contingent of the "dangerous" colliers and ironworkers marched in. Attwood was delighted. Clad in the fox fur-collared coat that had become his sartorial trademark, he attacked the oligarchical "junta" which had usurped the power of the crown, Parliament, and the people and spoke of the right of every man to "abundant wages" and of the necessity to remain within the bounds of the law. As he and other speakers presented the resolutions for the petition, the multitude shouted and clapped in delight notwithstanding the fact that many could not have heard all that was said. For the most part the speeches were moderate with only one or two echoes of the radical rallying cries so common at meetings elsewhere. After about three hours the crowds dispersed quietly. The whole affair had been a brilliant display of organizational skill.

On 4 October Brougham presented the petition, in company with seventy-nine others, to the House of Lords. Among so many it might easily have been overlooked but the council had made sure of publicity. The *Times* had included a notice of the spectacle on the same day and the editor had warned the aristocracy not to oppose such a formidable combination. The next day the newspaper had a copy of the proceedings, as did the *Morning Chronicle*, and devoted three columns to its publication. Some members of the upper house criticized the language used by some of the speakers and both Grey and Brougham, in what Attwood took to be an endorsement of the partnership, replied in defence of their Union supporters.[74] Other papers in London and the provincial towns carried condensed versions and the whole country was soon aware of Birmingham's example. The debate on the Reform Bill lasted another three days. Then, early on the morning of 8 October, all Attwood's hopes were crushed when the second reading was lost by 41 votes.[75]

Birmingham knew of the coming vote and throughout Saturday everyone anxiously awaited the arrival of the London papers. Crowds milled around the newspaper offices in Union Street until the papers came at 5 P.M. Despair and fear for the consequences were the immediate response in the streets and public houses. All that night the church and chapel bells peeled, muffled in "a dirge of the oligarchs re-echoing in the heart of England."[76] Attwood acted quickly. Within hours the council put out an address:

Friends and Fellow Countrymen – The Bill of Reform is rejected by the House of Lords! Patience! Patience! Patience! Our beloved King is firm – the House of Commons is firm – the whole nation is firm. What, then, have the people to fear? Nothing; unless their own violence should rashly lead to anarchy and place difficulties in the way of the King and Ministers. Therefore, there must be no violence. The people are too strong to require violence. By peace, by law, by order, everyone must rally round the Throne of the King. The small majority of the Lords will soon come to a sense of the duty which they owe to their Country and to the King; or some other legal means will be devised of carrying the Bill of Reform into a law without delay. Fellow Countrymen – be patient – be peaceful – be strictly obedient to the laws, and everything is yet safe. God bless the King.[77]

The address was posted in all parts of the town and had some effect in reassuring the people that all was not yet lost. Elsewhere there were few groups or individuals who could command such moral authority. Among the more violent responses were riots at Derby and Nottingham and the castle belonging to the duke of Newcastle was burned. Birmingham did not escape completely. An attempt to haul down a black banner from the steeple tower of St Philip's Church on Monday led to an altercation in which the Reverend Eckersall was abused. A small mob broke several windows in the High Street and Union Street and there were several minor arguments which required police action.[78] But the disturbances were uncoordinated and without direction.

At the regular meeting of the council on the following Tuesday everyone wanted to know what Attwood intended to do. The crowd overflowed from the room into the passages and outside into the streets. Attwood and Edmonds abandoned any plan to discuss policy and chose to speak from the windows of the tavern. Their message was unchanged – peace and patience. Luckily they possessed three letters from Westminster which suggested that they had reason for optimism. Lord John Russell, Lord Althorp, and Sir Gray Skipworth had written to Attwood on 8 October thanking him for the praise showered on them at the outdoor demonstration five days earlier. Russell's letter was by far the most important in that he included the sentence, "It is impossible that the whisper of a faction should prevail against the voice of a nation."[79] The sentiment expressed the council's appreciation of the situation exactly. When relayed to the Unionists it hinted that their leaders were in close contact with the government, that the partnership was intact, and that reform had not been abandoned. These soothing messages were all that he could offer for the moment. Attwood, well aware that he had to maintain control at this most dangerous time, moved carefully. Any act, however innocuous, might precipitate a sequence of responses that would damage the Union's credibility. Mob action would destroy any chance of a genuine union of all classes. Conversely, too compliant a role would drive Birmingham's masses into the arms of the extremists. In the weeks which followed, Attwood's standing in the nation rose in direct proportion to the degree of discipline he was able to impose on his people in contrast to events in other places. Lord Wharncliffe and a few of his fellow peers helped. They denounced Russell's letter as demonstrating the subserviency of the cabinet to the Birmingham Union.[80] The minister's reply was that he was only thanking the chairman of a meeting of 150,000 people was marvellous publicity for Attwood and he used the endorsement vigorously.[81]

In London, Grey had reaffirmed his commitment to reform and had successfully demanded the removal of Earl Howe, the queen's chamberlain, who had voted with the opposition, but the cabinet was reluctant to press ahead with the creation of peers.[82] There were suggestions that Grey might settle for a conciliatory bill. Attwood kept abreast of all developments through his friends at Westminster and on 13 October persuaded the council to send a strongly worded petition denying the right of the House of Lords to interfere in any way in the election of members for the Commons. A second address a week later called for the formation of political unions throughout the country whose main task would be the support of the Whigs. These calls apparently had some effect. By the end of October, the council had received fifty requests for its rules from would-be founders of political unions and a number of organizations were actually instituted on the Birmingham model. Success, however, created its own problems and, at home, Attwood was under pressure as others sought to capitalize on the town's newly acquired eminence and to steal control of affairs.

The attack came from two directions. Always jealous of Attwood's assumption of authority, Parkes and the old but still notorious Whig cabal had never ceased struggling to undermine him. Parkes continued to tell his friends that he "guided" the council in all its deliberations, but in reality he worked, at second hand, through Scholefield. For a man of Parkes's ambition this was not good enough and he had concluded that in the confusion it would be opportune to seize control of the middle ground. The Tories were invited to join in calling for a town meeting to support political reform and were bribed with the promise of places on the platform. The Political Council was alert and succeeded in getting a few seats, but Attwood himself was absent. When there was an attempt to get a vote of thanks for his past endeavours, Parkes pressed that it be withdrawn on the ground that "[it] may disrupt the unity of the proceedings."[83] The chairman of the Birmingham Political Union, it was implied, was not the man to unify opinion in the town and Dee's Hotel was not the place for histrionics. No one could mistake Parkes's objective. The second assault came from the extremists among the rank and file members of the Union, who resented their exclusion from the inner council and saw that the partnership with the Whigs would rupture if Grey retreated. Attwood, at his best when under attack, judged that something dramatic was again needed to fix the Union and himself in the nation's eye and so curb the tendency to splinter. He also intended to remind the Whigs that in a partnership there had to be trust on both sides.

Following the riots and "outrages" which had greeted the rejection of the Reform Bill by the House of Lords, several prominent newspapers including the *Times* and the *Morning Chronicle* had suggested the creation of a national guard to protect the householders from the mobs.[84] One ex-MP, Otway Cave, had urged the Political Union to give a lead but the council merely noted the request and refused.[85] A few days after the suggestion had been made, half of Bristol had been burned and there were reports of more than 400 casualties. Everywhere the demand for a national guard suddenly became insistent. The idea of a middle-class guard on the French model to act as the urban counterpart to the yeomanry had great appeal. People of all opinions had become afraid, and some noblemen barricaded doors and drew up cannon to their gates.[86] Every Birmingham shop had its complement of weapons. This arming was perfectly legal, an ancient right of freeborn Englishmen.[87] Attwood, however, under attack and determined to snatch the initiative, decided to take the whole question one stage further.

Events at Bristol constituted a direct threat to the whole thrust of Attwood's campaign. That city had a union but it had been unable to curb its wilder elements and the boast that the unions stood for law and order was undermined. The *Standard* even claimed that Birmingham Unionists had instigated the riots in the first place.[88] Attwood had feared such a pass and believed that such lies would be used to excuse repression, even leading to a military government under the command of Wellington. To counteract this adverse propaganda and to reemphasize the Union's control he recommended that it organize on military lines: "The effect of the contemplated organization will be, that if riots should occur in Birmingham, ten or fifteen thousand men will, in the short space of two hours or less, be prepared, irresistibly to vindicate the law, and restore the peace and security of the town."[89]

Stated so simply, it seemed a thoroughly good idea, certain to secure even greater authority for the council.

The plan itself was based upon the Anglo-Saxon unit of the tithing. The town was divided into seven districts.[90] Each district contained groups of ten men under the command of a tythingman. The latter reported to a constable of the hundred and the ten constables to one of ten marshalmen, who, in their turn, would attend the alderman of the district delegated by the Political Council.[91] Ideally, any disturbance would quickly be reported through the chain of command to council while the tythingman's section dealt with the immediate problem. There was no provision for arms; however, nothing was said to prevent individual members from purchasing their own weapons. Although an anonymous informant of Melbourne suggested that the plan included a section for subscriptions to buy muskets for those unable to afford their own, there is no evidence that Attwood ever countenanced such a step.[92]

The news of Birmingham's proposals spread quickly and naturally aroused fear and opposition. While it purported to be a device to keep the peace, the creation of private armies under the control of extraparliamentary organizations threatened to usurp the authority of the state.[93] Attwood might act responsibly, but what of the others who would be tempted to follow his lead? Within days, news of unions elsewhere proposing similar schemes was reported to the home secretary. No one knew the extent to which their activities were coordinated and what might be the eventual outcome if these were allowed to proceed unchecked. Countergroups might be formed and civil war ensue. The newspapers that had been most vocal in their calls for a national guard now began to retreat and to find fault with the whole concept.[94] Melbourne asked the law officers for an opinion on the legality of the Birmingham plan.[95] Their conclusion that the scheme implied the use of arms in disturbances identified as such by the leadership of the unions left the government with little choice except to intervene. Moreover, Grey heard that Wellington had advised the king to suppress the Birmingham organization; it was a direct hint that if Grey was unable to do so, Wellington was prepared to form a government that would.[96]

Wellington was writing to a number of peers and gathering information on the readiness of the militia in the expectation of civil war. Birmingham was, in his opinion, the centre of the danger: "He [Thomas Attwood] has given them, however, an organization which is neither more nor less than that of the United Irishmen, and evidently intended for military purposes. I have told Lord Grey that if they have not arms they are prepared to receive them, and organize to use them when their leaders please ... If we do not put these unions down with a firm hand, they will destroy the country."[97]

Under such intense lobbying the Whigs had to act and they agreed to issue a proclamation against the proposed military organizations. The task was to convince the Unionists, at the same time, that the government was still committed to the Reform Bill. Attwood in particular needed to be reassured and, if at all possible, persuaded to drop his plan before the proclamation was made public. The law officers had recommended just this course. Although the cabinet could not approach Attwood directly with such a request there was a compliant messenger at hand, Joseph Parkes. Althorp secretly asked Parkes to speak to Birmingham's leader on behalf of the government.[98] Working through Scholefield, he did so and appeared before the council on 22 November to explain the legal objections. At the end, with a show of reluctance, the councillors abandoned the plan.[99]

The sequence of events strongly hints that Attwood never seriously considered putting the scheme into practice. The three weeks of discussion had been made as public as possible. Proofs had been sent to public officials for approval and at the open council meetings he had always taken great care to emphasize his personal confidence in the king and the Whigs. Delays in the implementation of the plan at the end of each debate were introduced by his son, Bosco, or by an equally trusted friend. There is some evidence that Grey and Attwood had already been in communication on the subject. Lord Holland had been shown the first draft of the proclamation and had been assured "that ... the framers of it acknowledge that there were some technical illegalities in their scheme."[100] Attwood was sending a reminder to Westminster of the strength of the Union and its ability to resist oppression should a Polignac emerge as the leader of an anti-Reform government. It was all so much shadow-boxing but it served as the dramatic gesture he had been seeking. Attention was drawn to Birmingham at a time when the movement threatened to disintegrate into factions. By placing the Union at the head of a fashionable and popular cause, its ability to lead would be less likely to be questioned. The ploy was of course hazardous. Grey might have taken fright and stepped back from the Reform Bill. Wellington, for one, hoped that there would be a breach between unions and government, thus strengthening Wharncliffe's hand in is attempt to force

Grey to compromise on the bill.[101] Moreover, extremists might have become similarly emboldened. Attwood was relying on Grey's appreciation of the Union's usefulness at a time of excitement and it seemed logical to believe that the government would prefer to avoid confrontation with a reliable partner. The difficulty lay in recognizing the moment when the value of notoriety began to be outweighed by the need of the ministers to show strength to an angry king and a nervous Parliament. Hence the very public campaign and the carefully chosen mixture of bellicosity and deference in every one of Attwood's speeches.

There was nothing new in his approach; Attwood had always used such juxtapositions to make his points. But it was the first time these verbal thrusts had been given any tangible form. No avenue for conveying the real purpose of the ploy to the cabinet was left unexplored. Evening tête-à-têtes with Nicholls at the branch bank invariably drifted from business to that of the Union's plans. The agent was amazed by Attwood's "frank and candid" assessment of the situation. He should not have been. Nicholls's daily letter to London and the governor's contacts with members of the cabinet were common knowledge.[102] It was a tactic that Attwood pursued reluctantly because Attwoods & Spooner was engaged in technical negotiations with the Bank of England regarding the possibility of relinquishing its own notes in favour of the latter's circulation. He feared the governor's distaste for the involvement of bankers in radical political activity. Events were to confirm the validity of those fears when the Bank rejected the application. For the moment, however, Attwood believed that the winning of reform was worth any sacrifice. The proclamation against the arming of the unions was issued on the same evening that Birmingham abandoned the plan. Immediately both sides began to reap dividends. The Union under Attwood's direction received it as a friendly warning and took pride in their ability to coordinate their policy with that of the cabinet, whispering of secret correspondence and consultation. The government, although unable to ignore the military preparations, had been forced to recognize its dependence on the "respectable" Union, "who must stand between us and the plundering mobs of Hunt and Bristol."[103] For observers in either camp, it confirmed the national importance of the Birmingham organization, encouraging emulation by other radicals and calls for suppression by the bayonet if necessary from anti-reformers.

The pace of the reform movement began to pick up. Unions appeared "in every county and almost every parish in England" and most affected some connection with Birmingham and Attwood.

The latter could justly claim that his creation was no longer the junior partner in the relationship with the Whigs but enjoyed equal weight. "Grand meetings" were regularly advertised and the trappings of pomp and circumstance which attended those at Birmingham were slavishly followed. Unions nearby often sought fame by association and issued invitations to Attwood to preside over a special meeting.[104] On such occasions an open-air banquet and speeches whose tone, style, and content conscientiously aped those of Attwood were mandatory. The identification of the man with the movement was virtually complete. Yet this sense of national unity was more in the realm of illusion than fact. The ultra-radicals of London and the north considered his willingness to give the government time ill-conceived.[105] The moderates among the middle class continued to distrust him as he preferred to keep the Birmingham model separate and unencumbered. For its part, the Union kept public contact with its counterparts elsewhere to a minimum. To do otherwise would, in Attwood's opinion, court illegality and thus destroy the moral base of his crusade. Nevertheless, there was undoubtedly a degree of communication between the various groups. Councillors from Birmingham often attended neighbouring union meetings; if pressed the chairman would have argued that each acted on his own behalf, but it is fairly certain that they had been formally deputed to the function. Melbourne at the Home Office may also have known of and condoned these activities despite their clear illegality.[106] For outside observers, however, much of this was hidden.[107]

The cabinet recalled Parliament for 6 December. Some Tories were disappointed that it was not for the purpose of suppressing the unions. The Whigs, however, were convinced that the state of the country required a new Reform Bill as speedily as possible. Delay, Melbourne for one feared, would "subvert the whole power of the constitution and throw the whole island into confusion."[108] It was all very well to issue a proclamation against the arming of the Political Unions, but if the government was believed to be vacillating on the question there was no guarantee that the restrictions would be obeyed. The safest course was to recall the House and to proceed as before. To underline their concern, Grey successfully resisted William IV's desire to include a few condemnatory remarks on the subject of the unions in the speech from the throne. There was no need to antagonize Attwood and his creation unnecessarily.

In the days following the proclamation Attwood led the council cautiously. On his own initiative he held back a petition to the king on the subject of the creation of peers, on the grounds that Birmingham's notoriety needed no further or immediate reinforcement. The lull was temporary. Once Parliament had met, such quiescence might be misconstrued as apathy. To be effective the council had to be active. So, early in December, Attwood asked his colleagues to reaffirm the petition and to request that he deliver it himself to Grey.[109] There were two reasons for a personal call on the prime minister. Letters from friends were no substitute for first-hand impressions and Attwood needed to catch the mood of the capital if he was to march the Union in a popular direction. Secondly, and more importantly, the acceptance of his leadership on both the national and local scene required evidence of power and influence. Reports of private consultations with the prime minister were ideally suited for the purpose.

Attwood arrived on 30 November. Although he did not stay with his brother, he did have dinner with him. Matthias Attwood was his most trusted source regarding the intentions of the opposition. As a Tory himself and an anti-reformer, Matthias had had several meetings with his party leaders. His own seat, Boroughbridge, was one of those set down in Schedule A of the Reform Bill for total disenfranchisement. The brothers had always been frank with one another and Matthias made no secret on this occasion of his wish that the bill would be defeated in the House of Lords. Thomas was heartened on one point. The Union's about-face on the question of organization had been put down to his influence and even the Tories recognized his sincerity and honesty. But it was the visit to the prime minister's office which was the most reassuring event. Grey gave two extremely valuable promises: the unions would not be further circumscribed by law and a new Reform Bill would shortly be introduced.[110] Attwood was particularly delighted by the latter promise; to have kept Birmingham quiet until the new year without such a guarantee would have been impossible. In the present climate of uncertainty anything could happen.

Following the interview with Grey, Attwood hurried back to Birmingham. It was fortunate that he did so. His brief absence had allowed the wilder elements on the council to gain undue attention and even McDonnell, a reasonably loyal lieutenant, was impatiently trying to force through a number of specific reform proposals which would, in effect, prejudge the Whig's new bill.[111] There was also unrest in the neighbourhood caused by the harsh economic conditions, leading to a demand that the Union support the colliers, nailworkers, and others in their labour struggles. To do so, Attwood feared, would be tantamount to suicide for it would alienate the middle classes. He therefore worked to have the notion set aside, arguing that the Union must remain within the law and dissociate itself from violence however just the cause.[112] He had good reason to be careful. The Home Office was gathering information and preparing to act swiftly in the district if there were disturbances. Special constables had been sworn at Harborne and the troops had been put on alert in all their barracks including Birmingham.[113] At all costs provocative action had to be avoided if the relationship with the government was not to be compromised.

For some weeks the bill had been under review in the cabinet as a way was sought to conciliate the opposition. The early date for the recall of Parliament meant that decisions had to be reached quickly. On 12 December Russell introduced the result of their deliberations, "a neat blend of aristocratic and popular elements."[114] It had been a nervous few weeks for Attwood, whose primacy in the council had been under constant attack. Fortunately, Grey's earlier pledges, which had been reported to the council, were now redeemed and opposition was for the moment routed. Attwood led the Union in an enthusiastic endorsement of all points. The response in the Commons and from the country districts was equally favourable. Even Cobbett thought it an improvement on the July edition. Six days later the bill passed second reading in the Commons by 324 to 162. The number against reform had fallen by 69 since the summer. The improved margin of victory, however, did not tell the whole story. Most of those who had changed their vote had not joined the reformers. They had merely abstained. Everyone knew that the battle was to be fought once more in the House of Lords and few members of the cabinet were optimistic.

Prior to the second reading of the bill, which Attwood expected would be a formality, the council concentrated on drawing up a declaration in which the slurs cast on his character in the last few weeks were refuted. There was also time to turn to other matters. Currency and the gold standard had again become a subject of debate in London, and Attwood, with reform well in hand, wanted Birmingham to redeclare its interest in the question. Friends were once more urged to correspond with newspapers. There was also more time for the partners to sit in the bank and talk about their common interest. Together they drafted a letter to Brougham. Spooner signed it but its language clearly reflects a joint approach.[115] Attwood, moreover, felt free to pursue a personal interest – the freedom of Poland. Exiled Poles had been touring the country publicizing their loss of independence at the hands of the Russians. The Political Council and Attwood now took time to listen carefully to their grievances.[116]

The only affair in the new year to trouble Attwood was instigated by McDonnell. Daniel O'Connell, the Irish leader, planned to visit Birmingham and the Catholic priest wanted a public reception. Attwood opposed Union involvement because he feared further identification in the public mind with the United Irishmen. That body had been useful in the early stages of the organization but at this time its history of violence was contrary to the desired image. McDonnell, understandably, refused to accept the situation and persuaded the council to allow a scaled-down welcome that would not involve the Union officially. George Muntz, a strong anti-Catholic, noisily resigned in protest.[117] Although he was to return to the council in May, his temporary absence weakened Attwood's position because for all his bombast Muntz had been loyal.

At this stage the chairman was not too worried. His popularity within the Union was again high and direct challenges were rare. Others on the council were equally confident. Edmonds and Scholefield reached a gentleman's agreement on their respective positions regarding the second seat Birmingham was to obtain once the Reform Bill became law.[118] The first, of course, was generally acknowledged to be Attwood's seat. The weekly meetings of the council were spent amicably in discussing future initiatives. Despite earlier protestations that their sole objective was parliamentary reform, the members set up committees to inquire into the reform of the criminal code, conditions in Ireland (McDonnell's influence in the absence of Muntz was increasing), and the need to help Poland.[119] Moreover, their control of local politics grew stronger because the leaders had time to deal with every grievance. Their public image was also sharpened through the purchase of the *Birmingham Journal* by Parkes and Scholefield, although it could not always be counted on to present Attwood himself sympathetically.

The rank and file took advantage of the lull in public activities to circulate an address and petition expressing their appreciation of the council's efforts. They wanted a special general meeting at which the address could be presented. The council was flattered but did not wish to be seen courting the working class alone since the district's economic problems continued and it would not take much to spark violence. Attwood had no intention of allowing division now that the achievement of their objective was so tantalizingly close. Consequently, as a compromise, an extraordinary meeting of the council rather than the Union as a whole was called for 20 February. Despite Attwood's precaution some apprehension lingered in the town about the tone of the whole affair. The address was discovered to include a personal pledge of obedience to Attwood; a development many believed to be unconstitutional, provocative, and potentially dangerous. Reputedly signed by 25,000 men, it threatened to put teeth in a renewal of the quasi-military organization of the previous November. For this reason, the council prudently allowed only fifteen deputies to present their pledges. The spokesman, Ansen, was not, however, to be denied his moment of glory: "Attwood, whose name *alone* is a tower of strength to the patriots of these realms ... his abilities are transcendingly bright, his sentiments just and noble, his policy sound, wise and judicious ... We will emulate our revered Founder of Political Unions, and walk in his light."[120] Highly gratified, the chairman counted this tribute the fourth great moment of his life.

For appearances' sake the council insisted on cutting out the pledge of obedience from the published version of the address. It might have formed grounds for future prosecution as an illegal oath. To compensate, the fifteen deputies were invited to dinner.[121] Later the council reemphasized its concern for the well-being of the workers by issuing a number of declarations sympathizing with their fears. One prayed that cholera, then plaguing most of the country, would not visit the Birmingham area. These gestures seemed to be enough and the district remained peaceful.

At Westminster, the efforts of the Whigs had been directed towards promoting a climate of opinion favourable to the creation of additional peers if the House of Lords again proved recalcitrant. By the middle of January, the king appeared to have accepted the idea in principle, although he was clearly unhappy with the situation. Pressure on Grey to compromise was unrelenting. A group (the "waverers") led by Wharncliffe had been negotiating with the prime minister for some time to get a more "acceptable" bill; they threatened to oppose the second reading if additional peers were made. Attwood followed the debate with concern. It was difficult to know how best to support the government. The cabinet was urged by letter to secure the second reading by every means at its disposal, but he generally feared to call a demonstration for that purpose in case the "waverers" were stampeded into the arms of the "diehards." Grey was not making matters easier by insisting on gambling that all would be well.[122] Attwood, perforce, followed suit and feigned confidence: "he thought the time had arrived when they should determine never again to petition that House [Lords] on the subject of Reform."[123] In private he was not nearly so sure, but he did recognize, in company with most moderate radicals, that any such move would in all probability be counter-productive.

The bill passed third reading in the Commons on the morning of 24 March and was carried up to the Lords two days later. Grey spoke to the king on several occasions before the second reading in the upper House, urging agreement on the creation of fifty to sixty peers if the government were to be defeated. William was himself wavering and out of a list containing eligible names consented only to forty. The cabinet knew that would not be enough and reflected that the only option on defeat would be resignation. The second reading debate in the Lords began on 9 April and lasted four nights. Finally the division gave the government a majority of nine, 184 votes to 175.

During the debate in the House of Lords, the council sat, virtually continuously, in the newly acquired committee rooms in Great Charles Street.[124] Many workers took time off from work and clogged the streets, anxiously trading the latest rumours. A pamphlet, "Defensive Instructions for the People," sold well. When the news of the successful passage of the bill reached Birmingham, joy was muted. Almost everyone guessed that the Tories planned to decimate the bill in its committee stage.

As the days passed these fears began to multiply. Grey needed to be sure of the strength of the political unions and there were some disturbing signs of division among the reformers. In a roundabout way, Cobbett had learnt that Parkes had been talking about compromises with both Grey and Attwood and leapt to the conclusion that the Birmingham Union was conniving in a sell-out.[125] He printed a circular, "To the People of Birmingham and the Reformers in all the Great Towns," and sent copies to the unions and the newspapers.[126] The message was simple – do not trust the Birmingham leadership! Attwood had to reply. The council's behaviour required no apology, but it was true that the members had been silent for too long. Not only Cobbett seemed to doubt their sincerity. A few Tory newspapers were claiming that popular support for reform had dwindled and their inactivity did nothing to refute that lie. The answer to both criticisms and some reassurance for Grey would be provided by another meeting on Newhall Hill. One was already at the planning stage and set to coincide with the first day of the committee sitting in the House of Lords, 7 May. The objective would be the approval of a petition to the king requesting a massive creation of peers. The whole of the Union's resources were to be put into gathering a huge display of enthusiasm that would capture the attention of the country. Moreover, as a contingency, Attwood set up a working party to draft a reform bill of their own; the Union would not accept a crippled bill.

Each member of the council was assigned a specific task and invitations were issued to every union in the area to send delegations. The response of Attwood's twenty-one year-old son, Aurelius, was typical. He was chairman of the small Halesowen Political Union and he threw himself into the spirit of the occasion. Days were spent examining the route to be marched into Birmingham, setting out the duties of the marshals, and even in cooperating with his sisters in constructing impressive banners. Thomas Attwood himself worked almost non-stop. If the demonstration was to be effective it had to be peaceful; hence the arrangements had to be impeccable.

Excitement mounted on the Saturday and by Sunday a steady stream of people were on the roads leading into the town. As soon as it was light on Monday morning officials began to take up their stations. Mounted guides wearing their sashes of office waited on the roads to bring the marching unions in. The weather was glorious and spectators thronged the streets. At 10 A.M. the march to Newhall Hill began. For some two hours thereafter the streets were thronged as each division wound its way to its appointed space. One observer estimated the Grand Northern Division, which included unions and delegations from Wolverhampton, Bilston, Sedgeley, Willenhall, Wednesbury, Walsall, Darlaston, and West Bromwich, at 100,000 people and four miles in length.

Attwood's arrival at the wagons in the centre of the amphitheatre was the signal for a loud and spontaneous ovation.[127] The first speech would be of critical importance and he had spent days drafting his remarks. As ever, the problem was to bring together the ideas that would evoke the greatest response to his continuing and, he had to admit, unexciting plea for patience and peace. The substance had to be less than the sound. From all accounts he achieved a masterpiece. His ability to play on emotions had never been more finely tuned. A trumpet called for silence and proclaimed the importance of the speaker. His commitment was absolute; he "would rather die than see the great Bill of Reform rejected or mutilated." The dangerous question was put, "had not you all rather die than live the slaves of the boroughmongers?" Daring references to the civil war of the seventeenth century and the fate of Charles I who had ignored the will of the people abounded. These were the challenges that the people wanted to hear and their reply to each rhetorical question left no doubt as to whom was master. Few cared that in the end they had merely authorized a petition and agreed to "PEACE, LAW, ORDER, LOYALTY, UNION."

Various speakers followed to build upon Attwood's foundation. Finally, the crowd was broken up once more into its component parts. The council had been careful to make the dispersal as orderly as the gathering. The second phase of the operation was now put into effect with the aim of gaining the maximum publicity. The *Times* had sent two of its own reporters, but most papers had to rely on the Union's authorized version published in the *Journal*. Copies were rushed to London so that sympathetic newspapers like the *Morning Chronicle* could print the story the following day. Apart from the estimate of the attendance, 200,000 according to the official tally, less than half that number according to others, the report could hardly be faulted. However, in London events were moving rapidly. As Attwood worked that evening to make sure that his words had been accurately transcribed, the government failed to defeat a motion by Lord Lyndhurst to postpone consideration of the disenfranchising clauses in the bill. Grey, after some debate in the cabinet, felt he had no alternative but to ask the king to create new peers or to accept his resignation.

The speed of events took Attwood by surprise. When the express coach arrived in Birmingham on the morning of 8 May, he was eagerly awaiting news of the reaction in London to his monster meeting. He had known of Lyndhurst's motion but along with most observers had not expected the "waverers" to join in sufficient numbers to effect its passage.[128] As the news spread through the town, business immediately ceased. Attwood called the council members together and they debated most of the day. They could not agree on a response and, for the first time in months, Attwood was indecisive. Consequently, some of the town's ultra-radicals, aware of his unease, began to plan their own protest. Russell printed placards declaring, "No Taxes Paid Here Until the Reform Bill Is Passed," for display in shopkeepers' windows. The chance that Attwood would lose control suddenly became a distinct possibility.

The king accepted the cabinet's resignation and Lyndhurst was asked to approach anyone who might be willing to bring in an "extensive" Reform Bill. In reality that meant an appeal to the duke of Wellington and Robert Peel. Reports of the decision reached Birmingham on 9 May. Attwood had always taken care to emphasize the loyalty of the people to William IV. Now sentiment immediately changed and no one was more reviled. Even public house signs which contained references to the king were removed or hung upside down. Paradoxically this radical anger strengthened Attwood's position. For the past two days a trickle of "respectable" townsmen had come forward to join the Union. On the news of resignation it became a flood. Five hundred merchants, manufacturers, solicitors, and others walked in procession to the committee room to offer their support.[129] Attwood was perceived by them to be the only man who could hold the radicals in line, maintain order, and still offer hope that reform would be carried.

The absence of solid support from the town's middle classes had long been a point of weakness. Attwood's annoyance at their behaviour on one occasion had driven him to describe them as being "as full of vice as an egg is full of meat; we are servile to our superiors, arrogant to our inferiors, jealous towards each other, and malignant towards all."[130] Now their appearance was very welcome. Attwood was under extreme pressure to make some gesture of defiance. Crowds of working men milled around outside the Union's offices in Great Charles Street and some of them were openly decrying Attwood's caution. All day long the tension increased. Some cheering tale was needed to lighten the mood of despair which left violence as the only recourse. With the declaration of support from the five hundred in hand, Attwood could and did argue that all was not lost. The Tories were becoming isolated and could not long prevail against the full weight of the nation. It was not much, but since every word now carried weight he hoped it would hold his more volatile members in check. The next step was to ensure that all knew that the Union would fight on. Notice of a meeting that afternoon on Newhall Hill was given. To appease those who now abjured the king, all were instructed to remove their Union medals because they bore the legend "God save the King." Instead the ribbon of the Union Jack or a simple blue ribbon was to be worn.

The council retired to a private room to draft speeches.[131] There was no time for careful reflection or planning. The inner core's practice of presenting programs to the larger group could not be followed. In consequence, the debate was fierce. Fortunately, confidence had returned to Attwood and he fought vigorously to keep the temper even and the recommendations moderate. He even defended the king, using the time-honoured subterfuge of "bad advisers." The emphasis of the speeches should be placed, in his opinion, on an appeal to the House of Commons. The members of that House had the power to prevent a Tory administration and until evidence of weakness emerged the Union must stick by them. If passed, Lord Ebrington's proposed motion of confidence in the outgoing ministers, he told the councillors, would stop Wellington. Actually, Attwood must have known that the motion would resolve nothing. Wellington's government could function long enough to achieve its goals without the sanction of the Commons. The mere fact of the motion, however, would give the uninitiated the impression that Parliament was at least trying to meet their demands.

To buttress the appeal a clause warning that, if attacked, the people had the right to resort to arms – a clear reference to the November scare – was added to the proposed petition.[132] Attwood was again using the carrot-and-stick form of argument, but this time he was taking a far greater risk. If Wellington did succeed in forming a government, his foremost antagonist outside Parliament would surely be among the first to be arrested. Other tactics, such as no tax payments and runs on the savings banks, were to be kept out of the petition. Attwood barely won the debate. Only the fact that the more extreme radicals on the council were equally nervous allowed his approach to prevail. As it was, he had to agree to the inclusion of references to the alternatives proposed by the ultra-radicals in one of the speeches. Muntz, who could be trusted to stick to the script, was deputed to convey approval in principle for such measures but at the same time was to make clear that they were not as yet official policy.

At three o'clock Newhall Hill was blanketed with people. It was a sombre gathering. Banners and flags from Monday were draped in black and few of the workers were disposed to listen to the usual appeals for moderation. They had come to hear one man, Attwood. If he had issued a call to arms, there can be little doubt that they would have responded. A few days later, a deputation claiming to represent 1,500 armed men were to offer their services as "protectors" for the council, an offer that had to be gently refused.[133] The villagers of Harborne had already arranged their own unapproved bodyguard for their most famous resident and kept watch on all approaches to his house. Tales of swords being sharpened in barracks and ammunition parcelled out to the regular troops abounded. The rumours had some foundation. There were 250 infantrymen at the Weedon Barracks ready to march on the town in support of the resident Scots Greys at the first sign of trouble.[134] Daily, sometimes hourly, rumours of the mood in other towns and in London circulated. Civil war was being talked about openly and some even spoke of a possible change in the dynasty.[135] In such a highly charged atmosphere Attwood's speech was critical. Fortunately he kept his head and chose to emphasize the personal nature of the battle: "the new Government ... might kidnap him ... (No, No), but thousands, he doubted not would follow him to his imprisonment." The fight would be continued whatever the personal cost. It was a simple appeal – trust him. The petition won approval and the crowd, apparently satisfied, dispersed quietly.

A coach and four carrying Scholefield, Parkes, and Green set out for London to deliver the petition to O'Connell for presentation in the Commons.[136] Attwood realized that his place was in Birmingham where he alone could maintain order. He also announced that letters had been sent to Wallace of Glasgow and to his brother Charles in Newcastle inviting each to come to him so that they could confer on a joint course of action.[137] The challenge to the Tories, if it had to come from the provinces, must encompass as wide an alliance as possible. During the next few days, meetings in emulation of Birmingham were held all over Britain and a close eye was kept on the leader of that town's reform movement.[138] The *Times* sent its own reporter so as to be the first with the news of his next move. While the three delegates were in London, Attwood convened the council each day to give at least the appearance of action.[139] Each councillor was required to choose a deputy so that if any suddenly disappeared the command structure would remain in place. Outside, excitement was such that the slightest disturbance sent the workers pouring into the streets. Very little work was accomplished as wild schemes were concocted to thwart the Tories. Even the names of streets were changed; Wellington Street, for example, became Attwood Street. All night long the bells rang the death knell and men began to drill.

In London, the duke of Wellington and Lord Lyndhurst were busy. It was proving more difficult to form a new cabinet than expected, yet, few MPs doubted that one would eventually emerge. Ebrington's motion had passed, but the vote had not been overwhelming. The greatest stumbling-block to a resolution of the impasse was proving to be Peel's refusal to join Wellington on the ground that he did not wish to bring in a Reform Bill as the king required.[140] Manners Sutton, the Speaker and an alternative leader in the Commons, also expressed reluctance, but for him the argument that the king needed him was likely to prove conclusive.

News that Wellington was getting close to forming a government reached Birmingham late on Saturday night (12 May). The council was shocked. It had just finished celebrating the earlier tidings that Ebrington's motion had succeeded and the mood in the town had picked up considerably. An address to the king (which he refused to accept) had been sent off in the expectation that Wellington would admit his defeat.[141] It had respectfully asked for the recall of the Whigs. All that day the council had been reassuring various delegates of the improved chances of a peaceful resolution to the question; now prospects were again reduced to unrelieved gloom and the council knew the danger that dashed hopes might pose to the peace.

The next day, Scholefield returned with the information that Grey despaired.[142] The Whig leader's only recommendation had been to obey the laws and await Wellington's bill. Perhaps it would be as good as that just rejected. Once again Attwood's response was critical. Some of the newer middle-class members of the Union wanted to follow Grey's advice. Attwood, however, recognized the wider constitutional applications. If the House of Lords could throw out the Reform Bill and the cabinet and make new ministers of its own, the notion of popular government would be lost and the "spirit of the people would be utterly broken."[143] Before that unhappy state was reached, there would almost certainly be civil war and the constitution would be destroyed. Attwood had fought long to avoid the latter calamity and believed passionately in the right of the people to protest against government action in an open society. Feverishly, he cast about for some means to thwart Wellington. He knew there could be no turning back. A government against the people, a government without legitimacy, wold inevitably turn to repression. The Union and its chairman had to be ready to lead and to take the consequences.

Scholefield gave his official report to the council on Monday. People packed the rooms and their temper was rising. They demanded more dramatic action. The ideas of tax-withholding and a run on the savings banks gained supporters. In response Attwood proposed a "Solemn Declaration against the Duke of Wellington." It was a tactic that had precedent and, if one were selective in choice of example, a fair history of success. In particular, Attwood was well aware of its links with the Civil War of two hundred years before. It was to be a threat as well as an appeal. Eight points highlighting the duke's incompetence culminated in a request that William IV reject any administration led by that peer and recall the Whigs. Every reformer in the country would be asked to sign in an echo of the Solemn League and Covenant of Scotland of the seventeenth century. It would then be presented to the king as a "National document." In the meantime it could be printed and sent to London with the councillors' signatures as an indication of intent.[144]

If the situation was chaotic and tempestuous in Birmingham, so too was it in London. The *Morning Herald* frightened its readers by proclaiming that soldiers, the Scots Greys, had joined Attwood and there were many reports that the country was close to insurrection.[145] In the Commons, there was a great deal of anger that some members, purely for the sake of office, were thinking of joining a government which would bring in the very thing that they had been opposing – reform – and all MPs feared the temper of the people.[146] Gradually, Wellington was being forced to recognize that an administration which he headed had no chance of governing peacefully and that the majority in the Commons would not accept reform from him. It was exactly what Attwood had hoped.[147]

Attwood was the reverse of a revolutionary conspirator. He instinctively acted on a principle later defined by John Stuart Mill: "The people to be in the best state, should appear ready and impatient to break out into outrage *without* actually breaking out."[148] Everything was still being conducted in the open to gain the maximum publicity. Attwood had no wish to destroy the system. If he had been forced to mobilize his followers, their chances against a determined government would have been slight and he knew it. Broadsides and pamphlets issued in Birmingham with his approval spoke of the need for barricades but took care to emphasize that they would be employed only *in extremis*. Francis Place's recollections of revolutionary conspiracies, with Birmingham "the place in which to hoist the standard of revolt," can similarly be put down to hyperbole.[149] There may have been some plans and lists of the names of people who would be useful in the event of revolution, but it is hard to believe that Attwood was party to it. The threat, however, had to be made in order to raise the spectre of British troops firing on the British people. It had happened before and it could happen again, but it was Attwood's fervent desire that such a calamity should be regarded only as a last resort. While options remained open, it was unlikely to occur. If Wellington had persisted and had proceeded against the unions, Attwood would have been pushed into a difficult position. At that stage he could not have backed down.

Wellington finally bowed to public opinion and informed the

king of his failure. He recommended that Grey and the Whigs be recalled. Parkes immediately returned by the night coach to Birmingham. On the way he distributed leaflets urging "spontaneous" demonstrations of support for the Whigs. The unions were needed. No one could now dispute Althorp's forecast, made some time before, that "without an irresistible amount of popular support, no Reform Bill of any value could pass into law."[150] The information Parkes put about was that Grey had already been recalled and was in office – an exaggeration, to be sure, but the object was to produce a popular expression of joy which would leave the king no choice. Parkes arrived about six o'clock in the morning of 16 May. Quickly he set about telling the council members; the first to hear was Charles Jones, and by 7 A.M. people were pouring into the streets.[151] The bells were set ringing and decorations to celebrate the "victory" were attached to the towers. Parkes meanwhile had set off for Harborne, four miles distant. After a moment's delay caused by the protective circle of villagers he gained admittance to Attwood's house. The "most important man in England" was still in bed but the women were up and about. The relief of the household was immense. Arrest had been expected at any time.

After a quick breakfast, Attwood and Parkes set about drafting resolutions for a meeting that day in celebration. Other councillors drove out to join them and by eleven o'clock the lanes around the village were jammed with well-wishers. Attwood then started back to Birmingham. After some rapid and effective organizing, the bulk of the people who had milled around the committee rooms in Great Charles Street were directed to meet him at Five Ways turnpike gate; a place that offered a little space where a crowd could gather. Following a few brief speeches these joined the procession which had come with Attwood from Harborne in a march to Newhall Hill. Close to 40,000 eventually gathered. The speeches were understandably self-congratulatory; as Attwood remarked with pride, "I cannot but express the great delight I feel in Birmingham having been mainly instrumental in the accomplishment of this glorious consummation."[152] Other speakers chose to emphasize the chairman's role. Modestly, in reply, he attributed all to God, the king, the law, and the courage of the people of the town. An address to Grey and various resolutions of thanks to reformers elsewhere who had made common cause against Wellington were adopted. A few hours later a deputation appointed by and including Attwood set off for London to deliver their decrees.

The trip to the capital took longer than expected. At each town and village they were met by cheering inhabitants. Upon their arrival in London, however, they found to their dismay that they had been deluded. Although Grey had been recalled, there was as yet no guarantee that the Reform Bill would be passed. William IV still had not agreed to create peers, preferring to induce the duke of Wellington and his friends simply to end their opposition and to say as much in Parliament. On the day that Attwood came into London that project failed. The Tory peers had stamped out of the House of Lords without making the declaration.[153] Clearly Attwood could not yet rest and in addition to meeting with various members of the Whig cabinet, he began to discuss an appropriate response with the London Political Union. That group seemed willing to bow to his expertise; they adopted the badge of the Birmingham Union and plans were set afoot for a monster meeting on Hampstead Heath. However, the public demonstrations and the threat of even greater unrest if opposition to the bill persisted, persuaded the king, still reluctantly, to give his unconditional consent to the creation of peers. The announcement of commitment was sufficient. The opposition gave way and on 4 June the bill was passed.

In his assessment of the impact of the unions on this decision, Michael Brock is equivocal.[154] There is a great deal of evidence that much of what was decided rested on parliamentary calculations and not on the excitement in the country. Nevertheless one cannot ignore the maelstrom in which these calculations were made. As Russell was later to admit, those days were "the only time in my political life in which I felt uneasy as to the result." Although the Union leaders and particularly Attwood were proving remarkably successful in keeping control – his "troops" reportedly appeared disciplined and "as yet obedient"[155] – one estimate given to the Home Office put the armed force at his command at over 1,000 men and the magistrates told the local army commander that he could not count on any help in the form of special constables if trouble broke out.[156]

To compound the fears there were few examples of those expressions of discontent – riots – that because of their chaotic character were easily put down. Every report suggested that all was gathered for a "tremendous explosion" if the bill were lost. If that occurred, and even if the army responded to the call to fire (a far from foregone conclusion), the country would collapse economically and the resulting unemployment would ignite those few who had remained quiet. In economic terms, the calls for a run on the banks and a tax revolt were already creating a crisis of confidence. The Consolidated Funds, a barometer of financial prosperity, had fallen from 85 to 83 $\frac{1}{2}$ in under two weeks. It did not take much imagination to project the trend and recognize the danger. Thus while Wellington and Grey pirouetted with William IV, the pressure from without added a strident note that dictated both the pace of the measure and the ground covered. However, to go one stage further and argue that there was a real threat of revolution would be a mistake. Joseph Hamburger's contention that Britain did not face a "revolutionary crisis" in 1832, although overstated, is probably correct.[157] Certainly neither Attwood nor the Union had, despite their rhetoric, prepared for such an eventuality. Only the promised letters to Charles Attwood and Wallace suggest that the question of a coordinated national leadership was discussed at all. If Wellington had chosen to stay in office and face the ensuing disorder, reform might still have been defeated.

But on 19 May 1832, when it became clear that the bill would pass, such calculations did not have to be made. The opinion of a majority in Parliament, society, and in the streets was that Attwood and Birmingham were primarily responsible for the success of Grey. The man of the hour was equally certain and was convinced that the Union was now the senior partner in the Whig/Birmingham alliance: "Our meetings in Birmingham have been like claps of thunder bursting over the heads of our enemies, and our Declaration against the Duke of Wellington has sealed the door of his party forever ... I am afraid some of us men from Buttonland will get proud and puffed up with worldly pride."[158]

Rumours circulated that he had been offered ennoblement or a large pecuniary reward by a "grateful government." There may have been some truth to the report; if so, sensibly, he refused both. His proud claim that he was merely the servant of his country would not be sullied by crass opportunism. After all, there was still currency reform to be won.

London glittered in the heady days that followed. The *beau monde* competed with an unending stream of workers' organizations in displaying Attwood, as the "man most responsible" for preventing revolution, at their soirées, luncheons, dinners, and the other myriad excuses for the city to advertise its importance. "If we [the deputies] do not leave London shortly," he told his wife, "we shall have more to fear from the dinners than from the barricades and the cannonballs."

Not everyone offered their congratulations. The day after the bill had passed Althorp met him by chance. "If the people don't get their belly full after this," Attwood remarked, "I shall be torn to pieces." "And so much the better, you deserve it" was the minister's robust reply. On 19 May he had spoken to Grey and Holland at the Treasury, told them that economic reform was next on the agenda, and was exceptionally gratified to hear from the prime minister himself, "we owe our situation entirely to you." Grey's private observations were less complimentary.[159] Attwood and his friends had appeared in full Union regalia which suggested to outsiders that the cabinet was offering recognition of an extraparliamentary organization.[160] Attwood, of course, had put on the trappings of office with exactly that object in mind. He intended to remind Grey that he was not an individual of temporary fame but the leader of a powerful interest group whose influence did not end with one victory. On most occasions, however, Attwood simply walked the stage, enjoying the spotlight. George Grote, one of society's genteel radicals, probably summed up best the sentiments of those who gave him so much attention:

If, Gentlemen, I were required to name a person whose services I appreciate the highest, and whose feelings I envy most, through this momentous period, I should not hesitate to pronounce the name of Thomas Attwood. It is to him, more than any other individual, that we owe the success of this great measure. He has taught the people to combine for a great public purpose without breaking any of the salutary restraints of law, and without violating any of the obligations as private citizens. He has divested the physical force of the country of its terrors and its lawlessness, and has made it conducive to ends of the highest public benefit.[161]

The keywords of this fulsome praise are contained in the last sentence. It was to be his most lasting memorial, an achievement which others strove to emulate for the remainder of the century.

Grote's remarks were made at the event which for the Birmingham leader was the highlight of the whole triumphant whirl – a specially convened court of the Corporation of London. The idea originally grew out of his own request for a moment of the corporation's time to deliver Birmingham's vote of thanks, agreed at the 16 May meeting, to the people of the capital for their steadfast support of reform. To his delight the lord mayor took advantage of the celebration to move that the freedom of the city be bestowed upon him. An honour, Attwood immodestly informed Elizabeth, only previously given to "Kings, Emperors, Generals, Ministers and Statesmen." One or two objections came from the floor on the ground that it implied recognition of an illegal body, but they were easily brushed aside. Attwood gleefully agreed with the protesters: "To see these ancient and powerful corporations thus fraternizing as it were, with our new political societies may well be supposed to cut off all hope from our opponents."[162] His eye was still much on the future. After the formalities, dinner in the sumptuous Egyptian room of Mansion House crowned a truly memorable evening.

Notwithstanding the pleasures of being lionized, within a few days other pressing business appeared. Parliament's collective mind was turning to new issues and on 22 May a committee was appointed to inquire into the Bank of England's charter. Among those selected to serve was Matthias Attwood; surely an omen that this time Parliament was ready for change. Thomas Attwood at once became much more purposeful and turned every conversation whatever the occasion to the subject of the currency: "They had scotched the snake not killed it."[162] With his brother in a position of authority he daily expected a call to appear before the committee. It had been no secret that Parliament was preparing to examine the subject and he had come to London prepared with copies of his old pamphlets and new ideas scribbled on scraps of paper. As he had told his friends on leaving Birmingham for the triumphal drive to London, the time had now arrived for realizing their project as to a change in the currency.[163] Was it not fortuitous that it came at the height of his popularity and that the cabinet appeared exhausted: "The Banking Comm[itt]ee seems likely to fall into my hands. In that case you will see, my dear, that I shall have been a great instrument in giving Liberty, Prosperity and *Virtue* to a distressed and oppressed people."[164]

The committee did not request his attendance in the first few days of its deliberations, but from every side came assurances that the invitation would not be long delayed. Spooner and Taylor were in town to represent Birmingham on the general committee of country bankers and they kept him apprised of conditions.[165] Spooner's absence from the Union had now become an advantage because it allowed the war to be fought on two fronts. These were the days of high optimism. Only time would tell that one success did not inevitably beget another.

The return home was as triumphal as the departure. The council had planned a "grand entry" but the eventual reception was more than they could have dreamed. The route from London to Birmingham was akin to a royal progress. Ladies and labourers decorated themselves with blue ribbons and cheered Attwood and his friends through every village and hamlet. Often they had to halt, give speeches, and receive tokens of appreciation. At Coventry, they were taken from their coach and escorted into town; a delay which meant that when they finally were freed they had to travel at "a dangerous pace" if the council's advertised timetable in Birmingham was to be kept. While still several miles from home, the cavalcade was greeted by outriders and gradually was slowed to a walk. The complicated schedule of speeches at various points as they entered the town had to be abandoned.

Eventually the crowd of well-wishers arrested the progress of the carriage completely. The centre-pole and harness broke and the coach was pulled, almost carried, for the remainder of the journey. As the procession approached Market Street it was greeted with musket shots, the ringing of church bells, and deafening cheers. It has been planned to proceed to the open area at the Five Ways turnpike gate where galleries had been erected, but as it would have taken several hours more, at a conservative estimate, to travel the two miles to that point and it was getting dark, the principals decided to make their speeches from the Hen and Chickens Hotel. Never one to withhold praise for their achievements, Attwood told "his" people on this occasion, "the final knell of despotism has tolled – the bright day of our liberty and our happiness is beginning to dawn."[166] As such it was a victory for Europe as well as England. Late in the evening he was finally released by his admirers and travelled the last few decorated miles to Harborne. On this day and after this extraordinary week of universal acclaim Attwood, in truth, deserved the nickname Cobbett was derisively to bestow upon him – "King Tom."

CHAPTER TEN

A Stranger in the House

The adulation of Thomas Attwood reached embarrassing heights in the days after the parade. People pursued him in the streets, reverently trying to touch his clothes or begging to shake his hand. Outside his house at Harborne there was a constant vigil by countryfolk seeking a glimpse of their hero. Calls for the erection of a statue, for civic dinners in his honour, and for an immediate declaration of support in the forthcoming election were commonplace. Towns throughout the country tried to present him with testimonials and requests that he stand for this or that constituency littered his table. Legends began to be built, telling tales of daring and defiance.[1] Mementoes of the campaign sold handsomely. A new Union medal was faced with the head of Attwood instead of the crown. More to the chairman's taste were the blue garters for the ladies, declaring "Attwood for ever!" Mugs, pipes, and all manner of other items that the imagination of Birmingham's entrepreneurs could devise appeared with the image of "King Tom" prominently displayed. Within the Union itself, however, the unity of purpose which had marked the final drive towards reform was crumbling.

The union of the middle and working classes had been an artificial device designed for a single purpose. Once that had been accomplished the strains of conflicting expectations proved unbearable. Within days of the bill's passing, 170 prominent manufacturers and merchants published a notice of withdrawal. They urged that the Union be disbanded on the ground that it was too dangerous an instrument to be left to the "less-respectable" inhabitants of the town. More critically, an unsavoury wrangle between two wings of the organization became public.

Both Scholefield and Edmonds put in a claim for the second

seat awarded under the bill to Birmingham – the first was of course still conceded to Attwood. When the topic had been debated some weeks earlier, Scholefield had been the council's choice and Edmonds had bowed to the decision. However, when the former's wife, a chronic invalid, had become very ill and appeared near death, he had withdrawn his acceptance. Edmonds had then claimed the nomination and had announced that he had Scholefield's support. By this time Mrs Scholefield was recovering. Her husband angrily denied such an endorsement and demanded that the original Union pledge be fulfilled. Letters were exchanged and eventually published.[2] In the end Attwood had to arbitrate. Scholefield, the vice-president, won, but relations were so soured that he withdrew from the council and maintained his distance until 1837 when there was some doubt that he could defeat the Tory candidate.

No sooner was this unpleasantness out of the way than Henry "Orator" Hunt suddenly reappeared with the avowed object of forming the Midlands Union of the Working Classes. Attwood and the middle-class leadership were to be abandoned; the workers were now capable of mounting their own campaigns. The presence among the new Unionists of the Reverend Dr Wade, still ostensibly a member of the Political Council, exemplified the widening gulf between the more radical elements and the moderate reformers represented in Attwood's creation.[3] Furthermore, yet another group, "Committee of Birmingham's Non-Electors," had already decided to break away. For still others, Owenism was proving attractive to those who sought a more complete reform of society and a cooperative conference was held in Birmingham under the direction of another councillor, William Pare. A Home Office report that many of Birmingham's citizens believed that "Attwood is asleep and doesn't go far enough" underlined the general awareness of his problems.[4]

The chairman, in the midst of his glory, was unconcerned and indirectly confirmed the complaints by refusing to allow open debate on national issues. Only the Irish and Scottish reform bills and one increasingly popular topic – the Polish question – were excepted. With the former he could hardly do otherwise; they were simply extensions of the English campaign. The Irish bill in particular required attention as it was soon apparent that it would not be as strong as the English or Scottish versions. O'Connell had for the past twelve months generously reduced Irish agitation and lent his weight in support of Grey's bill. The Union could not now in all conscience abandon him. A petition and a Newhall

Hill meeting were the least they could do. However, although there can be no doubt as to Attwood's sincerity, there was simply too much happening to allow time for the careful planning that had attended such affairs in the past few months.

When they met at the Hill on 25 June, the pageantry and excitement were missing.[5] Attwood gave a rousing speech which dealt more with currency than it did Irish reform, but the effect was minimal. The London newspapers hardly noticed Birmingham's intervention and the Irish bill passed unadulterated. As for the other issues, Poland's agony was debated but action was put off till the annual general meeting at the end of July. Apart from these concerns the council was told to keep to local matters and to organize self-congratulatory celebrations. The sitting of the select committee on the Bank of England's charter, for example, was "not a Newhall Hill affair." There was no ambiguity in Attwood's position. He was living up to his oft-stated principles and awaiting the "honest endeavours of the new parliament."[6] It did, however, diminish the sense of purpose of the council and gave their weekly meetings overtones of redundancy.

These internal squabbles meant little to Attwood. His attention was focused on Westminster and the return, in the forthcoming election, of as many currency "mono-maniacs" to the Commons as possible. As their leader he had confidence in his ability to change the policies of the government. The Union's role was to be subsidiary to his own. It was to be a channel for expression of public opinion as he worked to restore "a state of permanent prosperity."

The first assignment for the Union was to give support to those parliamentary candidates in the districts who promised aid in Parliament. George de Bosco, Attwood's eldest son, was put up at Walsall.[7] Then defiance from a not unexpected quarter in Birmingham emerged. To separate the sheep from the goats in other constituencies an idea raised during the Reform Bill campaign was revived – pledges on a variety of radical proposals. A subcommittee of the council had been set up to consider the question. Attwood had been missing when the decision to examine the issue was taken, but since Bosco had been in the chair it would seem likely that it had his approval. He was under the impression that the pledges demanded would apply only to the currency.[8]

It was at this point that the deterioration in internal affairs, largely of his own making and the first real challenge to his post-Reform Act ascendancy appeared. Russell, the perennial critic, in proposing the list from the floor, added the demand that Attwood, who was "once a great Tory," be among those to pledge. Attwood was outraged and reacted emotionally: "It would be disgraceful to adopt such tests – it showed a mean dastardly suspicion – which was likely to destroy the Union, and clearly proved there was treachery in the camp ... your demanding a pledge from me, therefore wounds me to the quick ... To take Pledges from such men [himself and Scholefield] ... he would say was to gild refined gold, to paint the lily – to throw perfume o'er the violet."[9] This display of "royal" temper led to a prolonged and acrimonious debate. Russell, a few days later, published a "full account to defend his character." In reality he sought to blacken Attwood's name and drive him from the Union. Cobbett picked it up and scathingly headed his editorial, "Puddle in a storm, or King Tom in his tantrums."[10] If all were not to be lost Attwood had to apologize, a difficult act of self-effacement for a man of his temperament. After some urgent conversations with Edmonds he did so. But he chose the easy way out and apologized for the language not the substance of his remarks.[11] This partial explanation was naturally accepted by the council at large and the crisis, for the moment, was resolved. Nevertheless, the position of Attwood as arbiter of public opinion in Birmingham had been weakened. It is unlikely that, with the Bank of England's charter under review and his reputation in London unsullied, he was much concerned.

Preparations for Attwood's return to London had begun as soon as he had arrived home. With his popularity at its height he anticipated no obstacles to an early appearance before the select committee then examining the Bank of England's charter. But the summons to London failed to materialize. Angry and disappointed, he went to see George Nicholls. The nightly letter to the governor of the Bank of England or a private letter to Peel might achieve what personal entreaty had not. Carefully he assured Nicholls that the Union was to kept on for "the Restoration of the Country to a State of Permanent Prosperity." Grey and Althorp had promised an early call to give his evidence, but since that had not come he could only conclude that "Ministers were afraid to place him before the Committee." Nicholls was suitably impressed and entreated the governor to persuade Althorp to call Attwood.[12] Indeed, Nicholls found it hard to understand why Attwood had not yet been examined. The man was sincere and his testimony would be "boldly frank without the least reserve." If Attwood were to be questioned intelligently, it should be easy to make him "negative his own propositions," for although his ideas were "ingenious" they were still "lamentably wrong." The argument persuaded the governor and the letter was shown to Althorp. Almost immediately, the latter agreed to write to Attwood assuring him that he would be called. To make doubly certain that Attwood felt wanted, Althorp, through the governor, authorized Nicholls to tell the Union leader unofficially that the invitation would not be long delayed.[13]

For several days Attwood had been anxious to join his brother's campaign among the merchants and bankers of London as Matthias conjured up a stream of witnesses and propaganda in support of currency reform. Since every salon was open to the leader of the Birmingham Political Union, his presence and eloquence would be of great help. Some urgency was added by the need to refute an argument which had lately gained some circulation. Oliver Mason, the leading local Tory and sometime high bailiff of Birmingham, had recently given evidence to a House of Lords committee whose task was to examine the London-Birmingham Railway bill. Keen to prove the viability of such a railway, Mason had contrasted the population increase in the town with the decline in poor relief – proof, he believed, of its growing affluence. The figures had been seized by those who wished to discredit Attwood, to challenge his contentions regarding the damage done by Peel's Act.[14] It was a simple point, without qualification, and hence the ploy was proving effective. In fact the decline in indoor relief, the figure quoted, had been more than compensated by the growth in outdoor relief, but London preferred to believe otherwise and some missionary work was essential if the damage to the currency school's case was to be limited. On a happier note there was one additional inducement to bring him to town. A civic dinner, given by the corporation of London, was planned. Grey and Althorp were to be granted the freedom of the city. As a recent freeman himself Attwood would have an honoured place at the celebration.[15] With the added encouragement of Nicholls's report he set out for the capital.

He spent a little over a week in London. Although the excitement created by the passage of the Reform Bill had abated, his notoriety had not and the days and evenings passed delightfully. In his own biased opinion, he was making converts at every turn and defeating anyone who tried to oppose his currency arguments. For the first few days the only cloud was the aggravating absence of Althorp's oft-promised invitation to give evidence. However, he could not really complain too bitterly; the committee's engagement book was clearly full and others were similarly held in suspense. For a few days it was amusing to hear Matthias boast that he had destroyed this or that witness during each sitting.[16] Then, just when it seemed that Althorp had chosen to ignore him, a further letter arrived. This time the promise was unequivocal; it gave a personal guarantee that Attwood would be asked to appear.[17]

In his absence the Political Council had recirculated his "Memorial on the Currency." In the previous November five days and nights had been spent in council deliberating on the major points in this admirable summary of his basic arguments.[18] Plans had also been set on foot to make the third annual general meeting a forum on the economy. Initially, Attwood had wanted to forgo this on the grounds of expense and the official day, the first Monday in July, had been allowed to pass unmarked. But the splintering of the Union and the need for extraparliamentary agitation in support of his ideas had changed his mind regarding the need for another "Newhall Hill affair." On other fronts, various councillors, on his insistence, had been writing to sister political unions, urging that they continue to follow Birmingham's lead and agitate for monetary reform. Declarations and addresses were prepared and made the rounds for signatures.[19]

Attwood made a flying visit back to Birmingham to organize and speak at the meeting. But he had come too late and it was poorly organized (Edmonds was unenthusiastic); in any event, general interest in the Union was low. A small crowd gathered on 30 July to hear him and his most trusted lieutenants. The speeches were restricted, on his personal order, to his economic ideas and lacked the usual fire that such occasions normally inspired.[20] It is doubtful that the meeting had any effect in London or even in Birmingham. However, coincidentally, the summons to Westminster was at last delivered.

Attwood entered the committee room on 2 August with some trepidation. Matthias had become ill at a most inopportune moment and was unable to attend. Moreover, Mason's figures regarding Birmingham's prosperity were still being talked about and although he could question the interpretation the numbers were irrefutable. Attwood could only hope that he was sufficiently prepared to satisfy the sceptical and that at least one of the members would be sympathetic.

The examination began coldly and clinically. Questions relating to the role and record of the Bank of England's branch banks sought information rather than opinion. Nicholls's conjecture that

Attwood was now a friend of the Bank was confirmed, although he naturally insisted upon expressing his usual reservations respecting gold.[21] The committee thereupon turned its attention to the subject of foreign exchanges. In the interrogation which followed, Attwood was subjected to heavy pressure from those who had been swayed by the evidence of previous witnesses. Horsley Palmer had been given an early opportunity to present the Bank's interpretation of recent monetary crises and to explain the guidelines within which Bank policy operated. Contrary to Attwood's conclusion that Matthias had "demolished" those arguments during the hearing, Palmer's exposition had satisfied many of the committee members.[22] He had admitted a connection between Bank of England notes and the country bank issues, between bank notes and prices, and between prices and the exchanges. Attwood agreed with these statements.[23] Where they disagreed was in the definition of an overissue.[24]

The state of the exchange was, Attwood considered, a totally inadequate regulator. Indeed, he decried the whole discussion of overissue in those terms. He readily admitted that expansion in the currency supply would turn the exchanges against England,[25] but he argued that the subsequent bullion drain should be ignored – the home market would expand and absorb the slack.[26] When it was felt that the specie loss should not be disregarded, an Order-in-Council suspending an exchange of paper for gold could be passed. In both instances depreciation should be allowed to continue until "full employment is obtained."

Upon being pressed to define the term "full employment," Attwood referred to the year 1825 when, he believed, there was not a significant number of "industrious honest workmen" out of a job. To the Malthusian argument that there was only so much housing, clothing, and food, Attwood countered with his four times production hypothesis. The committee was, however, in no mood to accept these principles and returned a number of times to the same point, leading Attwood into the blind alleys of taxation and the ratio of consumption between the productive and nonproductive segments of society.[27] One questioner referred to Ricardo's theory of the capital fund to prove the inability of the medium of exchange to add to production. Attwood held to his view that whereas an additional issue of currency might not directly enlarge the capital fund, its stimulation of trade and the improvement in profit margins would allow capital to be used more productively. The fact that he viewed calmly the possibility of a

Bank restriction, i.e. by going off the gold standard, if his ideas were acted upon, whereas Horsley Palmer promised stability, condemned him.[28] Attwood's compromise proposal, which was irrevocably linked with the concept of depreciation, thereby constituted a moral affront. John Stuart Mill would later condemn "The gigantic plan of confiscation which at present finds such advocates – a depreciation of the currency... That men who are not all knowing in their private dealings should understand what the term 'depreciation' means and yet support it, speaks ill for the existing state of morality on such subjects."[29]

The report of the committee was short and largely noncommittal with the consensus in favour of a renewal of the charter. The disparities between Althorp's proposals and the Bank's counter-proposals on the question of terms were resolved in August 1833. Attwood was disappointed but not disheartened. The report had left many questions unanswered; it would now be up to the Commons and he would be there to give a lead. Moreover, public acclaim might well win what reasoned argument had lost: "Now if I succeed in getting the Currency rectified; I am afraid it will make you proud," he told Elizabeth. "Only think what a fine thing it will be to have assisted first in obtaining *Liberty*, second in preventing *Anarchy*, third in restoring *Prosperity*."[30]

The chance to capitalize on his reputation and gain publicity for his ideas came almost at once. Cobbett arrived in Birmingham to challenge the "mono-maniacs" to a debate on currency. About fifteen hundred people bought tickets and settled down to what they hoped would be a "grand fight." It did not prove much of a battle. Attwood began and spoke for four and a half hours. Everyone was so exhausted that the debate was promptly adjourned to the next day. His speech had been little more than a catalogue of past endeavours and a testament to the accuracy of his predictions. Cobbett and Charles Jones, the third pugilist, were equally boring. At the conclusion, a hand count showed that the Birmingham men had "won"; a result, given the location, which had never been in doubt.[31] Nevertheless, within days Attwood read a number of most commendatory accounts in the London newspapers. The *Morning Herald* hailed his oration as a "much more statesman like view of the subject than has ever occurred in the walls of Parliament."[32] It was welcome reinforcement of his stature as an economist and nicely complemented the reports of his evidence before the select committee which some admirers had publicly described as "masterful."[33] The only sour note came when Grey acknowledged the receipt of a copy of the Cobbett debate with the discouraging comment, "I fear that your opinions and mine will not agree as to the nature of the remedy."[34]

The uncontested election in Birmingham passed largely without incident. However, Attwood was not content with a quiet campaign. Radical discontent had undermined his authority and he intended to use the Union's ability to muster public opinion once he was in Parliament. In the last resort he could count on his popularity to pull the disparate elements together, but he knew that it was a well that could be drawn upon too often. He therefore publicized his sense of community. Dinners for the children of the poor, for factory workers, and so on were promoted. A committee did the rounds searching out concrete examples of distress. These would give reality to the figures contained in the petitions and addresses sent to Parliament and give the townspeople a personal stake in the reception of those appeals. Attwood was everywhere giving a lead and serving as the fulcrum for activity.

During the weeks prior to the election, gatherings of electors and non-electors, masters, workers, and the unemployed paraded to voice their support of both the man and currency reform.[35] Celebratory dinners and visits from the leaders of other political unions, all voicing their gratitude for his leadership, were noticed prominently in the local newspapers. The Bromsgrove Address, in which he was named as "the liberator of the people," had great propaganda value. Calls for a permanent memorial in his honour were regularly printed. Letters published in the London press on this or that point were republished, together with his rebuttals, to confirm his national standing. It was a masterly campaign in which Scholefield, linked by association despite his resignation from the council and Edmonds's enmity, was kept firmly in the background. There were one or two special events – the creation of a Polish Association and a march of the unemployed – to focus attention, but they were really not needed. Such was the degree of confidence that squabbles between various council members, including one over the church rate between Salt and Edmonds, occurred without noticeable effect.

Secure in Birmingham, the council spent a considerable amount of energy in promoting candidates elsewhere. When unable to make a personal appearance, Attwood wrote exhorting unionists to aid candidates from whom he had some hope of future assistance. The intervention had some effect, if in some cases only for the resentment it aroused.[36] Most attention was, however, focused on two contests nearer home, North Warwickshire and Walsall. The former counted numerous electors from Birmingham and the Union's concern was obvious. Dempster Heming, Attwood's preferred candidate, had some radical credentials and had two Tories for opponents.[37] Given the latter party's dominance in the county generally it was not altogether surprising when the campaign ended in defeat.

The interest in Walsall was much greater. Bosco was opposed by Charles Foster, a banker and an old opponent of currency reform. Foster later claimed that the young Attwood's candidacy was motivated by simple spite, as he had recently withdrawn his bank's account from Attwoods & Spooner of London. Since the Union's first thrust in June tempers had been rising. Societies and clubs of all sorts had become involved. Pitched battles had been fought in the streets between rival gangs. Both sides tried to use the threat of exclusive dealing and bribery to coerce the electors. Foster ignored Bosco in his speeches, recognizing that the father was his real opponent; on one occasion he referred to Thomas Attwood, not without some justification, as "the prophet of the unfulfilled evil."[38] Unfortunately, these tactics ensured that the Unionists felt bound to reply in kind and the violence escalated. The magistrates under pressure called in the newly created London police to try to keep order. On election day, 12 December, voters were pelted with mud from one side or the other and even with troops on the streets a full-scale riot appeared likely. Bosco was appalled, but there was little he could do except issue an appeal to his father.

Shortly after noon Thomas Attwood came. He had stayed in Birmingham only long enough to be elected unopposed. Word of his arrival soon spread and a crowd gathered to hear him speak. Regrettably, at that moment the Scots Greys chose to charge. Intimidated, the people scattered and polling came virtually to a halt. The intervention had been a disaster. It had ended in exactly the kind of chaos that Attwood had spent eighteen months trying to avoid. On the eve of his first appearance in the Commons, his claim that he stood for "Peace, Law and Order" had been discredited. Opponents would not soon forget. Moreover, Bosco was defeated by 73 votes, 304–231.[39]

In early January 1833 Attwood prepared to move to rented accommodation at 13, Abingdon Street in London. He drew up explicit instructions for the council on behaviour and responsibility during his absence, but how far Muntz, himself rather excitable, and young Bosco could carry them out was questionable. A public dinner with O'Connell gave him one last opportunity to issue warnings to his followers and with that done he departed.

As the day set for the opening of Parliament approached, the city of London became exceedingly nervous. Even some of the Reform Bill's most earnest advocates appeared to be having second thoughts; the Whigs had perhaps gone too far. The long period of political agitation by extraparliamentary associations suggested that the new House of Commons might be eccentrically radical. In that event, the government's carefully designed compromise aimed at satisfying middle-class needs while preserving the power of the aristocracy might be quickly overborne. In the opinion of the duke of Rutland, "Attwood and O'Connell will turn the scale in the end."[40] Sir John Graham uneasily forecast, "the Radicals will be stronger than we imagined; the destructives will overpower the Conservatives."[41] The expected Radical onslaught, however, never materialized. They failed to find common ground for action and the Whigs successfully defended the measure given royal assent the previous summer. That sentence of failure, in retrospect, can be easily explained, albeit in general terms. Radicalism in the early nineteenth century was by its very nature the province of the individualist whose imagination often ranged beyond the bounds of practicality and who found compromise irksome. Membership of the House of Commons was to prove a chastening experience for men like Attwood accustomed to the adulation of the common people. Rules of procedure and the traditional agenda so circumscribed these enthusiasts that energy became sapped and the sense of mission vitiated.

Such disillusionment was unthinkable, however, as Attwood stood on the steps of the Houses of Parliament on 29 January, the day of the speech from the throne. His self-confidence permitted no thought of defeat. He was the leader of "the most formidable combination in the country,"[42] the self-appointed spokesman for the urban manufacturing interest, the representative of a fourth political faction – the ultra Union party – which had been the most significant factor in the final, crucial stages of the campaign for reform. Early in the new session he would introduce a motion on the subject of distress and thereby raise the currency question. He would succeed or "the Whigs must follow the fate of the Tories."[43]

A letter from C.C. Western lay in his pocket. It had arrived just before he had left Birmingham. Western, who had pursued the will-o'-the-wisp of currency reform almost as long as Attwood, knew his friend and counselled caution. To win an early alteration in the monetary system:

> ... great care will be necessary in choosing the *moment* to moot it, and the man to do it. There are some men generally there [Parliament] who are most forward and unpopular, who will damn the best motion in the world, and as to the time, there is a time to drive a nail, and if that is not waited for and seized when it presents itself, in vain all reasoning and argument. You have a great deal to learn of the House of Commons, I mean all of you who have not tried it and mean to mix in the war of words. The good humour and favourable opinion of the House must be cultivated in order to get fair play for your argument.[44]

It was a warning to forget the open-air style of oratory and to adopt a new approach. The admonition went unheeded and Attwood's parliamentary career began on a course which was to lead to bitter disappointment and resignation in 1839.

The speech from the throne disgusted him by concentrating upon self-improvement and Irish suppression. The first he deemed impossible – were not the labourers already "working themselves to death?" The second was cruel and dangerous, for "Poverty has already made them madmen; by coercion you may make them devils."[45] His protests and those of the other Radicals were ignored. For the moment he had to be content with voting with O'Connell against the government. His time, he believed, would come.

Outside the claustrophobic atmosphere of the House matters seemed to be progressing satisfactorily. With Matthias and a cross-section of MPs and city businessmen to help, the gathering of forces to push monetary reform advanced rapidly. They had been planning for some months and anticipated that with his arrival the enterprise would quickly be pushed to a successful conclusion. There were rumours that he had already had "private interviews and communications" with the chancellor of the exchequer.[46] They did not know that these had merely been part of Attwood's impatient struggle to speak to the Bank charter committee. With hopes high they had naturally placed the best construction on events. Early in March they gave the movement a focus by organizing the "Currency Club" and actively solicited membership in the provinces as well as in London.[47] The tactic was designed to replicate the close-knit group which had spearheaded Attwood's drive to leadership in Birmingham.

Attwood learned that a private member's motion could be introduced only on Tuesdays and Thursdays and that there was no slot available until mid-March. After booking his time for a motion on the currency, he set about building the coalition that would carry it to victory.[48] Promises of assistance were commonplace; the fulfilment of his dream seemed tantalizingly close.

At this time his greatest enemy was his own impatience. Never a man to take criticism lightly, he daily expected malignant attacks on his integrity. In part, of course, he was right to be fearful. An incident at this time, blown out of all proportion by the press, was indicative of the kind of tactic used. A notice, printed in a number of newspapers, announced that he had been rejected as a member of the Literary Union Club.[49] He had been nominated, but a ballot of all members had been demanded, contrary to normal practice. The body of the membership then showed that they did not want him in their club. He would have been better advised to ignore the slight. Instead, he proudly replied in a letter to the *Morning Herald* that he had never applied to join and never would, being much too busy to waste time with such frippery.[50] The message was nevertheless quite clear. Respectable people found the Union leader unacceptable, others should take note. For the moment it was a minority view; constant reiteration might change that.

The Currency Club was similarly denigrated. A *Times* editorial was particularly dismissive, likening the participants to "beef-steak eaters, eccentrics, old fellows and gamblers." Nevertheless, the editor had to admit that over 100 gentlemen had been present; a formidable number given the composition of the new House of Commons, "loose Tories, loose Whigs, loose Conservatives, and loose Radicals, acknowledging no head, but wishing to become influential by some means or other not yet ascertained by them."[51] Pressure on the club and its most visible members was continuous. At Western's house some MPs felt obliged to make it quite clear that to form an "association" would not be "compatible with their duties as members of the legislature."[52] Independence was one virtue which the majority in the Commons publicly cherished; it was a convenient excuse for preferring a pledge of agreement to active membership. Meetings in public places, the Thatched House Tavern for example, had been poorly attended because MPs declined to be cast in the role of conspirators. In an effort to rally support, Burgess argued in his journal that it was wrong to think that the Attwoods intended to stampede MPs in an unknown direction; that they planned anything beyond the currency issue.[53] His plea was largely wasted. Prejudice ran too deeply to allow any interpretation but the worst to be placed on such activities.

In Parliament, Attwood was equally busy making his forthcoming task of winning a majority on the currency issue difficult. His son's complaint against Foster's election at Walsall had reached the House and a petition had been sent up for presentation by Attwood. His speech was to say the least provocative and ill-advised. Elections in which the military had been employed to keep the peace should, in his opinion, be declared null and void. If that was not done, citizens in future should "protect their own rights by going to the hustings with loaded pistols in their pockets and loaded rifles in their hands."[54] The House was properly shocked; such wild statements simply reinforced the view that he could not be trusted.

When Attwood's name was called on 14 March to present his scheduled motion on economic distress, he was absent. Earlier business had been dealt with more quickly than anticipated and his place on the list had been brought forward. Eventually he did appear, but due to the late hour and the small attendance the motion had to be postponed.[55] On 19 March he tried again, but the rules of the House prevented it. Not until two days later he was able to overcome the objections of Althorp, the leader of the Commons, who wished to continue a debate on Ireland, and move "that a Select Committee be appointed to inquire into the causes of the present distress existing among the industrious classes of the United Kingdom and into the most effectual means of relief."[56]

With the indulgence of the Speaker he gave a long rambling address, touching all manner of subjects. He began with an accusatory catalogue of Parliament's actions since early February and ended with the claim that he was a moderate reformer who now sought "Household Suffrage, Triennial Parliaments and Vote by Ballot – the same message given in a victory speech to his constituents a few weeks earlier. On Newhall Hill, in front of his own people, his speech would have won high praise. Within the confines of Westminster the histrionic style of oratory Cobbett was to call "round-towel" found few admirers. Moreover, although many MPs possessed strong accents, for some reason his provoked laughter. Like many of his fellow citizens, he invariably omitted to pronounce the letter "h." Thus he spoke of "'appy 'omes" and his "'opes." His enemies – his word for those who opposed him – never tired of their derision and made it difficult for Attwood to hold the attention of the House. It was a reaction he found it difficult to excuse.

The debate and division which followed was claimed as a victory by both sides but the reality was that Attwood lost. From the chaos which attended the tally it was clear that Attwood and his friends had not followed Western's advice and chosen the right moment or the right man. The *Times* reported that many in the House had been anxious to postpone the question until time allowed a more extensive discussion.[57] The division itself had startled those used to a more sedate pace of business. Some MPs had been absent under the impression that there would be no count. Others, including the marquis of Blandford, had been inexplicably shut out.[58] With respect to the second half of Western's instruction, Attwood's reputation as a rabble-rouser was too strong for some Whigs as well as many Tories. Thus, notwithstanding their inclination to vote for the motion on general principles, they had abstained. Perversely, Attwood in his desire for kudos had fanned this prejudice by alluding to the political unions several times in his speech – organizations which many still considered unconstitutional. The council, at home, had compounded the ill-advisedness of this course by issuing a number of provocative and ill-timed statements. Bosco had announced at one meeting that "the people had been sold and betrayed," and several speakers had warned Grey against attacking "their Union."[59] All such boasts were faithfully reported in the newspapers and the reaction in London was predictable.

Still, the defeat had been narrow, 158–192. About half the agricultural members and more than half of the conservatives had voted for it. It could be argued, and was by Attwood's friends, that with greater care victory could have been won. Indeed, they believed that it was only a matter of time before a similar motion was passed. Some of their opponents agreed. Their coalition was "becoming so strong in the House of Commons that they will forcibly carry their point."[60] Further support for this view came from chance remarks in the corridors. Praise for Attwood's argument was heard in unexpected quarters. Althorp, for one, now agreed that "a gross robbery was committed by Mr. Peel's bill in 1819." The fact that he continued to reject Attwood's prescription on the ground that repeal would commit "a similar robbery" was no cause for despair.[61] Perhaps, if the case was presented by someone else, Althorp would not be so adamant. Peel, apparently, was also convinced that the motion marked a turning-point in the combinations within the House. Currency would be the new focal point and he expected the Ultra-Tories and Radicals would unite, leaving him no option but to counterattack in conjunction with the Whigs.[62] The tide seemed to be running with the currency school.

While Matthias Attwood and his friends set about organizing the next division on the motion, Attwood took the opportunity to visit his constituency. The council in the absence of its master had been experiencing some difficulty in holding the sympathy of the town. A meeting in Beardsworth's Repository to debate the Irish Reform Bill had not been a great success. Complaints that Grey was proving unfaithful were increasingly heard wherever working men gathered and the councillors, in their daily rounds, were being asked pointed questions about the Union's inactivity. Graffiti, a popular outlet for radical displeasure, increasingly included attacks on the prime minister, in one instance declaring "Damn Earl Grey's bloody head off."[63] The councillors had begged Attwood to come back to explain.

They met with their chairman on 9 April and were delighted with his insider's account of the proceedings in the Commons. He treated the crowded council room to a detailed analysis of his disappointment with the government's legislation: "At one period he had looked around the Reformed House of Commons, and he had almost regretted that he had ever lent his humble assistance to the formation of it."[64] However, as the session had worn on his opinion had softened. The removal of the worst coercion measures from the Irish bill, the divisions in favour of the bill "to protect infants in factories," in support of tax readjustment, against flogging in the army, and above all the close vote on his own motion on distress attested to a growing sense of justice among MPs. Hence, he stated, it was still possible that prosperity might be restored by this Parliament; plans were already afoot for a motion. He asked those present to indicate whether they wished to pursue further reform at once or wait until prosperity was achieved. The answer was never in doubt, in spite of Attwood's admission that "the Reform Act, great as it was, did not give them more than one-half of their real political and constitutional rights." They chose prosperity.

Encouraged by the continuing acceptance of his leadership, Attwood returned to Westminster prepared to press his argument. Matthias Attwood was chosen to reintroduce the subject. It was thought that his Tory affiliations would attract those who had abstained or had voted with the government out of dislike for the Political Union's leader. Matthias tried to introduce the motion on the 19th but Althorp took precedence by producing the budget.[65] Finally, Matthias found an opportunity to rise. Thomas Attwood prudently remained in the background throughout the debate and did not speak. The House was crowded and there was an air of excitement which many compared to the night that the Reform Bill passed. The Whigs were immensely nervous, fearing that the prestige gained by their carrying of Reform was about to be lost.[66] Some wanted to head off the vote through a preemptive call for a commission whose task would be to inquire into the causes of distress; the commission's members would be directed to pay particular attention to the culpability of the currency system. Althorp, however, would have none of this and pressed for a vote. He had read the House accurately. To Attwood's chagrin the motion was lost 139–331, a much heavier defeat than that of the previous month.

It was a tremendous shock; success which had seemed assured had been snatched away. The *Times*, the *Morning Chronicle*, and the *Examiner* attributed the defeat to the poor quality of the introductory speech by Matthias Attwood.[67] In fact the size of the "No" vote derived from intense government canvassing and a general scepticism on the part of the average member regarding the extent to which the country suffered from depression. Peel had worked with Althorp to create the "No" vote and his strong speech in the debate had sealed the alliance. The Attwoods' calculations had been based upon optimism rather than a careful assessment of their chances. They had assumed, for example, that they could count on the country gentlemen whose complaints of distress had all too often claimed the attention of the Commons in the past. They might have been correct a few years earlier, but in 1833 there had been some improvement and the gentleman farmers were less inclined to rock this ministerial boat and hazard displeasure.[68] Similarly, individual pledges had proved worthless.[69] Even some of those who had voted with them were "unreliable" and had been less than wholehearted in their speeches of support.[70] Worse was to follow. On 24 April a resolution was approved which was intended to close the question to further discussion: "Resolved that it is in the opinion of this House, that any alteration in the monetary system of the country which would have the effect of lowering the standard of value would be highly inexpedient and dangerous."[71]

Aurelius Attwood, speaking for his father, lamented: "the prospects of poor Britain are now more gloomy and discouraging than they have been for a long time – much more so than when Boney threatened to invade her."[72] Immensely disappointed by yet another demonstration of what he regarded as the venality of MPs, Thomas Attwood, after writing a number of angry letters to the *Times* to refute some of its more scandalous allegations, fled Parliament to seek solace among his Birmingham friends. The reason for the continued existence of the Political Union had never been more apparent. What could not be achieved through the normal constitutional channels might still be accomplished by other means. In fury, he called a meeting for Newhall Hill on 20 May; the object was to petition the king for the dismissal of his ministers. Although the reformed House was scarcely five months old, Attwood's personal political education in the Commons was over. Rarely in the ensuing years did he manifest any serious inclination to come to terms with the national assembly on any issue.

An attendance of well over 100,000 by Union estimates, or some 20,000 according to governmental observers, verified the enduring magnetism of Attwood in the Birmingham district and the hope of some new initiative. For his part, Attwood announced that he was glad to be back among "the brave, the just, the generous and patriotic people of Birmingham."[73] He had gone to Westminster determined to support the ministers in their efforts to retrieve prosperity and confirm the liberty of the British people. He had been "grievously deceived"; they were not interested in the voice of the urban centres of provincial England. The Whig cabinet must be replaced, by whom he knew not. O'Connell followed and put the weight of the Irish people behind the Birmingham petition. Benjamin Hadley, the council's secretary, presented facts and figures on poverty in the town culled from a variety of independent and Union surveys. How could the minister deny the existence of poverty in the face of such evidence? Both he and his fellow speakers answered by alluding to the criminality of the affluent in a paraphrase of eighteenth-century mercantilist wisdom, "the degradation of the poor is, in fact, the aggrandisement of the rich." Dismissal of the king's ministers, vote by ballot, annual parliaments, and, endorsed in the excitement of the moment, universal suffrage, were the only solutions. Cobbett welcomed Birmingham back into the ranks of the "honest" reformers at the first opportunity.[74]

The effect of the meeting proved to be much less dramatic than Attwood had anticipated. He had known, of course, of the splintering of opinion that had accelerated in the last few months. Even McDonnell had resigned over a question of debts. Those who remained in the Union were often at cross-purposes. The rump of the radical faction ceaselessly agitated for a greater say in Union activities and had succeeded in getting annual parliaments and universal suffrage tucked into most of the Union's less official announcements. The credibility of the Union's claim to represent the town as a whole had been further strained by a petition designed by the "respectable inhabitants" to counter Union "pretensions" and circulated in April. While in Parliament Attwood had been sufficiently occupied to ignore such distractions. Moreover, he laboured under the assumption that upon his return such divisions could be healed simply by appealing to all sides to rally behind his leadership. Nevertheless, he had been sufficiently concerned to make sure that the preparations for the 20 May affair rivalled those of twelve months earlier. A large attendance would confound the predictions of impotence.

Regional unions were invited (about thirty attended), flags, banners, and patriotic signs were made, special constables enrolled, and a carefully scheduled procession to the scene of past glory, Newhall Hill, publicized. An open carriage carrying Attwood and his special guest O'Connell, was the centrepiece. Yet at the end of the day even Attwood had to admit that something was missing. The crowd had been large, according to Union figures, but the enthusiasm had been that of a holiday and not of a political occasion. Homage had been paid, but in the streets afterwards few seemed inclined to pursue the argument. Even the councillors continued to bicker as the radicals pushed for direct action – the nonpayment of taxes for example – while his lieutenants counselled faith in their leader. Attwood did not help by dashing away. He should have stayed to heal the breaches and to reassert his dominance. Instead, he left on Tuesday for London, carrying the "voice of the people" to the Commons with him.

In the next few days and weeks virtually all the news for his campaign was bad. The London papers almost uniformly deprecated the Birmingham meeting. A caricature in the *Argus* depicting Attwood and O'Connell with their arms around each other and both embraced by the devil was much admired. For once, no one in the capital seemed anxious to hear his version of Birmingham's latest demonstration. He presented the petition in the House without much fuss but its reception elsewhere was hostile. Lord Fitzwilliam, to whom it was sent for presentation to the king, declined to help and returned it accompanied by a twelve-page letter criticizing its negative approach. They next tried Lord Melbourne, the secretary of state for the Home Department, but he was similarly unsympathetic.[75] Reaction elsewhere was equally disappointing. Attwood had hoped that Birmingham's example would be followed in other parts of the country. But only Sheffield held a public meeting to debate a resolution for the dismissal of the

Grey government.⁷⁶ Petitions of a related nature were submitted to the Commons, but there was no unanimity, particularly on the question of the currency.⁷⁷

The greatest problem, however, was the Union's deteriorating relationship with the government. During the reform crisis Attwood had counted on the sympathy of the Whigs and they, although never easy with the relationship, had been equally trusting. It was this liaison which had given the Union's activities a kind of legitimacy; that was no longer the case. To the government, Attwood and his friends were simply a nuisance. Melbourne had been writing to the town's magistrates for some weeks. In his opinion, Birmingham's radicals had been granted too much license in the past. Warnings should be issued, troops must be on call, and any hint of sedition prosecuted immediately. Part of the trouble was, he told his correspondents, the weakness of the civil force. The Union acted as a law unto itself. It must mend its ways.⁷⁸ The threat was given more tangible expression in a clause of the Irish coercion bill. Outdoor meetings were to be severely restricted in that country; Attwood had little doubt that its implementation could easily serve as a precedent for England.⁷⁹ Attwood's constant harping on the continuing importance of the Union had clearly been counter-productive and the Whigs were sufficiently secure to dispense with the notion of partnership.

Through the following months Attwood attended the House every day and earnestly sought to win the members to his side by "honest argument." In May, with the help of Matthias, he secured an appointment to a select committee directed "to Inquire into the Present State of Manufacturing, Commerce and Shipping." One of those examined, T.C. Salt, a close associate in the Union, faithfully recounted the currency views of his mentor.⁸⁰ Attwood, however, refused to follow procedure with other witnesses asking questions the committee as a whole deemed improper and which therefore had little effect.⁸¹ He had been forced to adopt this line of questioning by the nature of the evidence presented. The economy was recovering and even Salt was unable to deny it. Witnesses concentrated upon this aspect and the responses Attwood hoped to elicit were not forthcoming. Impatiently, he tried to force witnesses to provide the answers he required; the routine of committee work, so different from his role at Union meetings, was alien to his mercurial nature and he harmed rather than furthered his cause. Attwood was chosen to sit on only one other committee during his parliamentary career – a select committee on Public Walks.⁸²

A variety of attacks were made during the summer on the attempts of the government to enact the new charter for the Bank of England. Attwood was present at every debate. He worked with a well-organized lobby, put together by Burgess and often led outside Parliament by Spooner, to remove those clauses which most affected the operations of the country banks. In this they were successful and the cabinet was eventually forced to yield. From all accounts Althorp, who was the main architect of the original bill, came close to resigning.[83] Yet it was a Pyrrhic victory. In Attwood's opinion it did little more than maintain the status quo that he had laboured so hard to overturn. Nevertheless, this success did nurture a glimmer of hope that a more extensive reform of the currency was possible if the right combination could be found.

For the remainder of 1833, and when the new session began in February 1834, Attwood struggled to interest the Commons in the currency question in the manner recommended by Western but rarely without some oratorical embellishment whose extravagance defeated its purpose. He recounted tales of suffering and foretold revolution. Several times he warned that if the government persisted in its policies, the gunmakers of the nation would be unable to meet the demand for their products. With "riot," "revolution," and "catastrophe" among his favourite words, he earned a reputation as a prophet of doom. But he saw no alternative and later was driven to beseech his friends: "If you ever can pick me up a tale of misery, injustice, and ruin, I shall be glad, I am like Mrs. Radcliffe, always looking out for horrors, and a pretty lot of them I have collected."[84] The improvement in the state of trade soon became obvious to all, so that even the complaints emanating from disaffected gentlemen farmers dwindled. Without their support he became increasingly unable to command the attention of the House.

The loss of respect which accompanied that of notice was accelerated by Attwood's refusal to adjust to the needs of the moment. The business of the Commons had expanded rapidly since the Napoleonic Wars and required strict timetables. Attwood believed correctly that much of the work was routine and should be transferred to other agencies; at present, the "great principles of legislation" were neglected.[85] To compensate, Attwood introduced his pet subject, one of those "great principles," at every opportunity, even when it was completely unrelated to the question at hand. He had still not adapted his style of oratory to the new forum, and once begun he found it difficult to stop. The problem was compounded by unflagging emphasis upon the merits of the Birmingham organization whose pretensions to primacy in the realm of public opinion were becoming notorious. In retaliation, a motion had been introduced in June to declare such unions illegal on the grounds that they formed a ministry of their own with Thomas Attwood as, rather ludicrously, "First Lord of the Treasury."[86] With these handicaps no subject would have been well received. Currency reform had very little chance at all. The government particularly disliked his threats to use his "ragged" following to circumvent Parliament and watched Birmingham very carefully indeed. Attwood was even appointed to the new Warwickshire Peace Commission in the vain hope that it would, as Parkes said, "put a muzzle on his mouth."[87]

In the latter part of the session Attwood added a second area of claimed expertise upon which to lecture the Commons. He began to raise the question of the dispossessed Poles in England and the danger to liberty in Europe presented by Russian ambitions. Many assumed that he was using the subject to promote the Napoleonic Wars' answer to the economic strains imposed by conflict – a paper currency. They were wrong. One of the "important issues" upon which Attwood had allowed debate within the Union twelve months before had been that of Poland. Often well-known Polish leaders enjoyed the hospitality of his home. His concern was tied to his fervent nationalism and jingoistic belief in the responsibilities of the position of world leadership that was Britain's heritage. National pride needed to be gratified and a nation's ideas to be exalted. Only on this highest plane, he claimed, could individual selfishness be submerged in social character, providing the stimulus for the development of human life. Attwood might have found a kindred spirit in Kipling some seventy years later, but Palmerston, the foreign secretary, had little sympathy for such sentiments.

In July 1833 Attwood had introduced a motion to withhold recognition of any redistribution of Polish territory contrary to the Treaty of Vienna.[88] It was defeated 177–95; the loss was not, however, overwhelming and with judicial management of opinion in the House something for the Poles might have been managed. Such tactful lobbying was, unfortunately, beyond Attwood's capabilities. Instead, he followed the instincts that had served him well in other situations but were useless in the Commons. He became more intemperate in his demands and harped on the need for a "preventive war" with Russia to "crush the bully to dust." It was far too extreme a demand and his involvement in a motion on any aspect of foreign affairs soon came to be regarded as a sure indication of its eventual defeat.

A further example of the refusal to compromise that cost him the sympathy of other members was his support for Cobbett's motion that Sir Robert Peel be dismissed from the king's councils because of his part in bringing in the resumption legislation of 1819. For the majority of the Commons such criticism was unacceptable. Peel was a respected member and his integrity unquestioned. Only five offered Cobbett their support – Fielden, Lalor, Roe, John O'Connell, and Thomas Attwood. Two hundred and ninety-eight voted against. A motion "that the proceedings on this resolution be expunged from the minutes" was immediately introduced and carried by a similar majority.[89] Identification with such a group, in such a cause, was not the best way to cultivate the "good feeling" of the House. On this occasion even his brother was critical of his behaviour.

By the spring of 1834 the House had become very impatient with Attwood's constant polemics. The expressions of displeasure were led by Stanley, who at the end of one of Attwood's tirades on the currency – the debate was in fact concerned with malt duties – called for "an end to this useless discussion."[90] More critically, the ubiquitous Joseph Hume, who saw himself, even if no one else did, as the leader of the Radicals, publicly rebuked the banker during a discussion of free trade observing that he saw "no connection between the question of currency and the subject under the consideration of the House."[91] Hume and his "Philosophical Radical" friends of the Grote circle, whose praise had been exceedingly fulsome in 1832, disliked the "depreciation crotchet" but routinely included him in their calculations of potential supporters. They had therefore been careful to treat him kindly. Recently, however, they had become aware of Attwood's lack of interest in Benthamite principles of economy and efficiency. During an exchange over the army estimates Hume asked, "was not the hon. Member returned to promote economy?" Attwood shouted, "No." Hume, *Hansard* reported, was "shocked."[92]

For the next few months Attwood suffered indefatigable harassment on all manner of subjects notwithstanding his consistent support for the Radicals' moderate parliamentary reform principles.[93] The crowning insult of this session came in early July. Attwood had made several attempts to bring forward a motion of which he had given notice for the first time in February. It was designed to allow the continued issue of notes under £5. Each time he had been frustrated by the pressure of other business. Finally, on 3 July, Attwood overcame objections and introduced his motion. He had not proceeded very far when he was interrupted by a request that the House be counted; it was suspected that there was not a quorum. Attwood protested but was gratified to find that forty members were present. He continued. Once more he was interrupted. Rigby Wason moved that the House be recounted. While Attwood had been speaking several members had left, a quorum was lacking, and the House adjourned.[94] Wearily, he wrote to his brother, "I am quite tired of politics."

Notwithstanding his preoccupation with monetary matters, Attwood's speeches on a profusion of subjects often contained penetrating observations and demonstrated a consistency in reflecting his radical predilections which many might well have envied. It was unfortunate that the views he expressed found little favour with the House; in divisions he rarely voted on the majority side, an identification with failure which handicapped his hopes for currency reform before he even began to speak.[95] In each debate he supported principles which paralleled those that determined his economic prescriptions. The state had the responsibility of ensuring the economic well-being of the people through a conscious policy of price maintenance and stabilization by means of a managed currency. If that well-being was not achieved and there was no work, the people had the right to unemployment benefits which the government was obligated to provide without let or hindrance. Thus, for example, the Poor Law amendment bill contradicted the constitution.[96] Attwood fought this bill through every stage in the House.

On one occasion he remained in the House or its environs for almost five days in order to be present at every important debate and division. He believed that the attack on the old Poor Law was absurd given the increase in population and spoke vigorously in favour of out-door relief. He concluded, "if the people were prevented from living honestly, they would be justified in living dishonestly."[97] His opinion had not changed on this question in twenty years; work was a right whereas charity was only a gift. The labourer could not be expected, or allowed, to beg.[98] His efforts did not go unnoticed by the people he sought to protect. In one month in 1836 he was chosen to present some forty petitions from the agricultural districts of Suffolk, Cambridgeshire, and Bedfordshire complaining of the administration of the new Poor Law.[99] There was a proposal to add his name to the Commons committee inquiring into the legislation. The motion was defeated but it was not laughed out of court.[100]

At every opportunity he defended those he considered the victims of governmental mismanagement. On the sale of beer legislation he objected to the glib condemnation of the working classes and the assignment of unneeded power to magistrates. Furthermore, he asked, why should money rather than character be the standard for licence-holding?[101] In the debate on the South Australia colonization scheme, Attwood was the first to call for some provision of relief for emigrants in case of failure.[102] He opposed the 18th clause of the factory bill which directed that children in factories be taught to read and write, pointing out that the arrangement would in fact compel the children to work ten hours a day, since the two hours of tuition would be in addition to the eight hours of labour. The clause in effect, he declared, made the children pay for their own education; in his opinion, the state should be responsible and pay all expenses.[103] These sentiments found few friends in a House of Commons weaned on the free market approach of Smith and Ricardo.

On other points in the bill he joined with his brother Matthias in utterly condemning a strict interpretation of the principles of political economy in their application to the labour market. As Matthias Attwood eloquently argued, "The question was not a mere question of the feelings of Englishmen, but a question of the feelings of humanity – a question of the grossest injustice – of utter destruction, inflicted upon the feeble and the unprotected. It was not a question of pounds, shillings, and pence; it was not a matter to be settled on the grounds of mercantile advantage."[104] Thomas Attwood voted consistently to have the ten-hour regulation (older children were then expected to work eleven and a half hours a day) extended to the age of eighteen, but the amendment was defeated.[105] Conversely he opposed the growing mood of centralism at Westminster. Although the steadying hand of the government was necessary in dealing with the welfare of the poor, control should remain in the grasp of those closest to the problem. Birmingham was quite capable of managing its own affairs without the help of appointed commissioners from London or parliamentary committees. The administration of government needed a thorough overhaul. Sinecures should be abolished and without a doubt the tax system required amendment.[106]

On 15 September 1834 his pent-up frustration and bitterness after so many defeats was vented at a dinner for 3,000 in Birmingham, in a speech containing a litany of complaints very different from that of the previous year. The Commons was devoid of integrity. One half consisted of "Jews of Change Alley and Monks of Oxford"; the other half was composed of lords and gentlemen too rich and too far removed from the masses to have any common feeling with them.¹⁰⁷ As a result he added payment of members to his list of required political reforms, so that ordinary people could join the "Club" and be sufficiently independent to remain above the petty corruption of government. He had also recognized at last that opposition to his views was of a personal nature that went beyond the confines of Westminster. The press of London had been routinely hostile and he read into that hostility the antiprovincial bias which he had encountered years before. Observations he had made in jest were reported as in earnest. Conversely, serious commentary had appeared in newspapers as humorous asides; often they ignored him altogether. "I entertain serious thoughts of resigning," he told his Birmingham audience.

To a degree Attwood's catalogue of complaint was justified. Prejudice and partiality in the Commons were two barriers that he was not alone in failing to surmount. Of course, he himself was not blameless. He preferred to play the role of the outsider hammering away at the gates of privilege. He also liked to think of himself as the only true prophet of industrial Britain and was rarely willing to compromise on any issue. But it is also true that there had been no real effort to give Attwood and his constituents in the industrial centres, electors and non-electors, a sense of participation in the business of government. The extension of the party system of organization in the Commons since 1832 had followed pre-Reform alignments. Thus Attwood was condemned to fight his battles largely alone and on terms dictated by his opponents who had the advantage of number. It was a task he found onerous and his friends were dismayed at the end of each session by the depth of his disillusionment.

The change in government in November 1834 offered some cheer. To be free of the "false, perjured and cruel Whigs" seemed like a victory of sorts. "Lady Jersey gives out that he [Wellington] will certainly rectify the currency," Attwood told his wife.¹⁰⁸ At first sight this assessment appears remarkably naive. Actually, it derived from a careful analysis of the strength of the new Tory government. Attwood was no longer disposed to believe the promises of politicians and their familiars, but he foresaw that out of weakness Wellington and Peel might accede to popular measures to retain office and thus be persuaded to give the country prosperity. Moreover, he had called for the removal of the Whigs some months before and they had to be replaced by someone.¹⁰⁹ Hence, despite his misgivings about the collective intelligence of the Commons, Attwood sought reelection.

It was the first real campaign the Union had had to fight, the Tories having succeeded in persuading Richard Spooner to stand. The friends had discussed the possibility for several months and it had been with great reluctance that Spooner had yielded to the Tory party's invitation. Spooner's challenge, of course, was not to his partner but to Scholefield. Attwood remained virtually untouchable for he had grown somewhat larger than life for the ordinary "Brummagem." The position of his fellow MP was a different matter. He had cut no sort of dash in the town since the argument with Edmonds and had not offered a single opinion in the Commons. Still, Attwood valued personal loyalty and had done his best to dissuade Spooner from making the challenge.

During the election Scholefield let Attwood make all the running and trusted that most voters would not split their choices and "plump for the B.P.U. men."[110] For his part Attwood concentrated his attack on the Tories, preferring to damn Spooner by association with that "Scourge of God, Attila," otherwise known as Sir Robert Peel. There was never any doubt as to the result and Spooner, the "out-of-date" Tory, went down to heavy defeat.[111] Such popularity was not, however, translated into support for the Union. It had become increasingly ineffective despite such useful, if perennial, rallying cries as the church rate. The editor of the *Birmingham Journal* several times lamented the apathy of the town and during the election campaign Edmonds felt obliged to claim that the Political Union was "reposing not sleeping"; it merely waited for Attwood to wave his magic wand.[112] It is clear, however, that neither the majority of those who professed faith in the viability of the Union nor the general populace honestly shared that optimistic appraisal.[113]

Before the newly elected House of Commons met, the Whigs actively courted the Radicals in order to present a more coherent opposition. There is no evidence that Attwood was consulted directly by either side, although he was aware of the Whig determination to contest the speakership. They had persuaded James Abercrombie to oppose Charles Manners Sutton, the Speaker for the previous eighteen years.[114] Attwood informed his constituents, the day before the Whigs and Radicals met at Lichfield House, that he intended to vote for Abercrombie, but that was as far as his participation went. Meetings at Lichfield House between the various factions continued during February and March.[115] Attwood did not attend. He was almost completely isolated.

The "unjustified" panegyrics contained in the address from the throne encouraged a short burst of enthusiasm as he tested his theory that the Tories might be pushed towards a revaluation of the currency systems. But his hopes were quickly dashed. Peel, in the Commons, was as intransigent as ever and would clearly rather resign than move one step towards Birmingham's position. In the ensuing weeks Attwood voted on major divisions with Russell and the Whigs, without, one suspects, giving his vote much thought save that it was registered against Peel. Rarely did he join in the debate itself. Instead, he quietly withdrew into himself and concentrated on furthering the affairs of his cousin John in the interminable court case, an effort which left scarcely a "moment's leisure." The administration collapsed in April but the change did not lift his spirits. The new prime minister, Melbourne, had enjoyed ample opportunities to demonstrate his enlightenment in the past two years and had failed the test miserably. So he continued to maintain a low profile and spoke moderately, evidently with the intention of improving his standing in the House.

In the summer months he found very few issues of interest. One arose in June when an old friend, Cayley, proposed that a committee be appointed "to inquire into Agriculture Distress, and the Propriety of Establishing a Silver Standard." The idea had been mooted on several earlier occasions but nothing had been done. Huskisson had been one of the major advocates before his death in 1830, and even a governor of the Bank of England, Jeremiah Harman, had reportedly favoured a bimetallic standard. Attwood had flirted with the idea but had always been convinced that it would be too complicated to operate, especially when compared with his own much simpler panacea, a revision in the official price of gold. Lack of success now forced concession: "my object is, that a larger Bank circulation could more safely exist on a silver, than on a gold, standard." He noted the anomalies that had arisen in the implementation of Palmer's principle. The Bank directors had allowed their desire for profit to override their caution and sense of duty: "what is their situation at the moment, their liabilities are near £30,000,000 while their bullion is only £5,000,000." A number of speakers followed and supported Attwood's position, but the motion was lost, 126–216.[116] Nevertheless, it was an interesting debate and Attwood wondered if further capital might not be made of the approach at a later date.

Not all of his time was spent in London during this parliamentary session. He had a minor role in the movement at home to apply the Municipal Corporations Act to Birmingham and in the spring of 1835 there was a concerted movement to persuade him to reactivate the Political Union. An advertisement called on the

Union to "AWAKE, ARISE AND PUT FORTH THY STRENGTH." A requisition, signed by 3,000, led to a special meeting of the council.[117] Edmonds carefully made it clear that Attwood had "no communication whatever on the subject."[118] It was a point he had been told to make. The requisition had originated in the "sectional rooms" – vestiges of the old organization at the workers' level – and had a clear class bias. Attwood could not afford to be associated with such groups unless the drive was a success. Otherwise it would simply end in the alienation of the registered voters and the end of all hopes. Moreover, it was obviously designed to split the coalition created by Parkes in the Whig campaign for the municipal corporation bill, a coalition that included the workers. Since the proposal threatened division rather than unity, the council stalled. Nothing could be done without "the Chairman." The leaders of the sectional rooms had expected that answer and had some bait to offer – the promise of sufficient paid subscriptions to allow a complete range of activities. The promise was tempting. Muntz hurried to London and came back with the news that Attwood would return to see for himself.[119]

From the moment he stepped from the coach the requisitioners sought to show that his authority in the town was undiminished. Every public utterance was an excuse for loud applause. Every appearance in the streets was a signal for crowds to gather. The meetings he addressed were packed and he was unceasingly urged to declare the Union "alive." But Attwood was now a man of experience and was not easily carried away by the noise of the crowd. Private talks quickly proved that the enthusiasm was indeed limited to the working men. It was true that issues of the moment, municipal incorporation and the problems of the Irish Church, did provide an opportunity for confrontation. Liberals, a few middle-class Radicals, and Whig lawyers were cooperating to challenge the conservatives and they had made promises to the common people.[120] But as Derek Fraser has argued, it was in many respects a "struggle for supremacy within the urban middle class."[121] The issues were obviously a vehicle of convenience without the sense of commitment which had marked the enthusiasm for the Political Union. The very attempt of the working men to reactivate the old organization demonstrated its fragility. Attwood could see that it hardly provided a suitable base upon which to build even if he cared to contest the local leadership of the coalition. Nevertheless, his perennial dilemma of credibility remained and he was virtually forced to pursue the idea, if only to prevent the working men turning to another more compliant leader. He therefore agreed with Muntz and Edmonds that it would be expedient to let the initiative develop slowly. Each step had to be controlled, premature enthusiasm contained, and private discussions held with any interested parties in order to broaden the base. The time, he knew, was not right – the economy was strong – and despite disappointment he had not yet abandoned the "respectable" route to monetary reform.[122]

An opportunity for a more aggressive stance occurred in August 1835 when the House of Lords began to mutilate the municipal corporations bill sent up by the Commons. A reform of the upper house was the kind of issue that promised unity – the Lords were far from popular – and to champion such a change would not involve a challenge to those pressing for the incorporation of Birmingham itself. Yet his response to this suggestion underlined his lack of enthusiasm for any reactivation of the Union at this time. At a town meeting, held to protest the arrogance of the Lords, he arrived late and gave a conciliatory speech in favour of a number of mild resolutions. Moreover, he did not endorse the pretensions of his followers to retain control of this issue.

Pressure from his rank and file followers for the Union "to be active" would not, however, relent. Almost in desperation he authorized a public meeting in his name for September. It would satisfy the workers' desire to be doing something and would allow resolutions recommending reorganization to be put and tested. There was, however, one crucial reservation. He would not attend. Close identification with such an attempt would be worse than no liaison at all. Until real strength and an enduring commitment could be ensured, no confidence could be placed in the movement.

The town hall was crowded on the day chosen by the Political Union for the test.[123] Representatives from the hinterland attended and the resolutions were passed enthusiastically. It seemed much like old times and the council in delight wrote to tell him so. But Attwood refused to be impressed. Prosperity continued and, in retrospective analysis, he had long concluded that the earlier success had in part derived from the weakness of the economy and its attendant unemployment. The price of forge pig iron had risen dramatically and Birmingham was more affluent than at any time since 1825.[124] Thus the message returned from London remained, "tread warily." As for himself, he was enjoying a mutually delusive second honeymoon with the Whigs at Westminster and for the only time in his parliamentary career he was gratified to hear his observations on the conduct of the House of Lords greeted with cheers from the ministerial benches.[125] Relations with the government remained good and he was not disposed to embark on a pointless crusade.

Attwood's advice proved to be sound. Once a deal had been struck between Commons and Lords over the corporation bill and all sides appeared satisfied, the calls for the revival of the Political Union in Birmingham rapidly abated. The operatives' interest in national questions was not strong and in local affairs there was not much to occupy them. They had only wanted a resurrection to thwart Tory initiatives and to assert their desire to be a major part of any process strengthening local government.[126]

The old council, however, now took its turn. The councillors had enjoyed the revival of their prominence. The workers' call promised a return to the exciting days of 1832 and, with municipal elections at some point in the future, its members intended to keep their names before the public. When Attwood returned home in November hoping for a well-earned rest, he suffered innumerable visitors, seeking to persuade him that his duty again lay in local politics. Once more, he bowed to their pleas that he resume his leadership, even if it was to be in name only and despite the fact that he did not like some of the men now claiming to speak for the town any more than his friends did. In January the council, claiming to be well prepared, called a meeting to approve an address to the king offering qualified support for the corporation bill and pressing for a reform of the House of Lords.[127]

It was a clever combination. The first matter reflected the general opinion of the town and was unexceptional except in its point of origin. The second, however, had a much more radical tinge. It echoed the mildest of the workers' demands and caught the grumblings of the middle classes who still resented the changes made by the Lords to bills, including that of incorporation, sent up from the Commons. Attwood, who had been prevailed upon to participate directly, had long advocated both ideas but had always ended his remarks in the past with the injunction that the reformed Parliament should be allowed to stumble on; it would reach the desired goal in the end. In this speech, however, he indicated his willingness to go one step further. If prosperity began to falter as a result of the "boroughmongers'" tricks it must immediately be concluded that the Reform Act of 1832 had failed: "[Then] ... you must raise five thousand pounds ... send delegations throughout the kingdom to call meetings of the people in a hundred districts ... you must offer to lead them and to guide them legally and peacefully into the measures necessary for their redress ... rally under the standard of the Political Union."[128] The speech had been carefully constructed. It was not yet time to mobilize, but the dangers were growing and should be recognized. If and when distress did reappear, a precise timetable had been set.

During the next few weeks and months, every opportunity was taken to press the same thesis: at an expensive Grand Reform Dinner attended by a few Radical MPs including Joseph Hume, Sir William Molesworth, and others of the Grote circle, and Daniel O'Connell;[129] at a meeting of shopkeepers, manufacturers, and merchants; in the union hall of journeymen printers; and even at vestry rate meetings. Conservatives in the town were sufficiently concerned to begin a round of dinners of their own to try to find ways to prevent the reanimation.[130] They need not have worried. Attwood had been right. While business prospered the council's plans had little chance of success. It did not matter what was done; the level of support stayed maddeningly low. Not even a change of name to "The Birmingham and Midland Reform Association " in a forlorn attempt to broaden their appeal did anything to help.[131] The experiment had failed and Attwood, exercising his option with some relief, slipped away, without much eagerness, to his Commons duties. On 8 February 1836 Russell introduced a motion for a select committee to inquire into agricultural distress. Pointedly, he took the precaution of reading the anti-currency reform resolution of 1833 as an instruction and looked directly at Attwood. The banker was unperturbed.

A week later Attwood presented Birmingham's petition in favour of a reform of the Lords. It was a further sign of his weakened position that even Joshua Scholefield did not give his wholehearted support. Dugdale, the county member for Warwick, with whom Attwood had been at odds many times over the years, sneered: "The petition was said to come from a body called the Birmingham Political Union, but it was well-known to every man in that House, that that body had bled to death a long time ago, and he believed it was out of the power of the hon. Member for Birmingham with all his eloquence, ingenuity, and ability to bring it again into existence."[132] He attributed the signatures gathered by the petitioners to be those of "low persons and children." This latter claim was certainly erroneous, but Attwood did not try to deny that the life had gone out of the Union as an agent of national reform. When George Edmonds stated in Birmingham that he too considered the body "defunct," it appeared that the obituary notices could be written.[133]

Attwood implicitly accepted the decision by seeking to renew his liaison with the agricultural interest. Sixteen years earlier he had wooed farmers through their own organizations and newspapers by letter and lecture. He had achieved moderate success, but the intermittent nature of the support given his policies in the Commons by country members attested to their limitations as a pressure group. Throughout 1835 and 1836 Attwood lectured on currency to the Central Agricultural Association. From the laudatory remarks of several speakers in the Commons it would seem that his efforts were not completely wasted.[134]

Similarly discouraged by the failure of direct action in the Commons, several of his intimates reverted to their 1820s policy of persuasion.[135] Matthias Attwood succeeded in gaining appointment to the committee deputed to look into the cause of agricultural distress in February 1836. Richard Spooner petitioned to be accepted as a witness before both the Commons and the Lords committees.[136] Muntz followed shortly thereafter. Both now advocated the immediate adoption of a double standard, gold with silver, and a depreciation of approximately 6 per cent.[137] Undoubtedly, despite recent parliamentary election differences, these calculations closely reflected Attwood's current assessment of what was needed. Still, these tactics were stop-gap expedients that had failed in the past and were unlikely to produce much change. If the only notice was to be singled out by Benjamin Disraeli in a witty if silly diatribe in the third of his *Letters of Runnymede*, then it had all been for nothing. Attwood continued to haunt the rooms of the select committees, "wasting" their time (so they complained) by inquiring into the state of agriculture and the operation of the joint-stock banks. Few members bothered to listen. All too often when they did so, he was pushed into the defence of matters which he personally considered secondary: the price of corn or the frequency with which directors of joint-stock banks borrowed on the shares they owned. He began to ask himself more and more why he bothered.

In his fifty-third year he was beginning to feel old. Bosco was engaged to Mary Medley, eldest daughter of William Medley, of Westminster, JP for Middlesex and Buckinghamshire. Angela, his eldest daughter, was preparing for marriage to Daniel, the son of Edward Gibbon Wakefield, and possible emigration to Australia. In his current state of depression, Attwood thought the latter plan was one any young man of industry might do well to emulate.[138] Relatives and friends seemed to be dying with disconcerting regularity. His father, who had seemed eternal, died on 24 November 1836, aged ninety years, his mother had died the previous year at eighty-three, and he began thinking more often about his own mortality. What would one say upon meeting one's Creator? Perhaps "ragged and barefoot children" could read a lesson over his grave.[139] It was all very sentimental but in perfect keeping with his sense of frustration. Even Matthias seemed to have confidence that the latest round of prosperity would continue. Joint-stock banks and the speculative promotion of everything from railways to plate glass had captured the country's attention. He began to think the unthinkable – perhaps his analysis was faulty: "All the Working Classes are very prosperous here. Your old friends the Boroughmongers have made the *money* equal to its duties. They have, as it were, let in the *Waters* into the *Pond* again, and thus the *fishes swim* about at pleasure."[140]

Around the dinner table conversation turned increasingly towards going home permanently. The cost of maintaining a house in London, a town that he had never liked, was all the more difficult to bear if it was all for nothing. Resignation was the simple answer. His daughter's prospective father-in-law, Wakefield, and a friend, Sir William Molesworth, were convinced of his sincerity. Both initiated addresses to the electors of Birmingham, soliciting votes in the expectation that he would not stand again.[141] The Reform Association also took the possibility seriously and sent his old friends Muntz, Hadley, Salt, Boultbee, and Douglas to London to ask what to do.[142] By the time they arrived, however, conditions had begun to change.

CHAPTER ELEVEN

Failure

Difficulties in the United States caused largely by speculative trading had begun to spill across the Atlantic in the autumn of 1836.[1] By November the iron producers in the midlands were experiencing problems. As usual when faced with falling order books, they started to cut back production, blowing out twenty furnaces in Staffordshire by Guy Fawkes Night. Several banks, particularly the newer joint stock companies which had been liberal in the provision of loans to merchants, similarly tried to reduce their commitments by refusing new loans and by calling for repayment of old ones.[2] Reduced demand for goods and the need for cash forced even more stocks out of the market and prices began to drop quite rapidly. Although as yet there was some optimism in the streets that the economy might soon recover, Attwood was certain that the crisis that he had long predicted had finally arrived.[3] Yet not all the signs were favourable for the reemergence of the Union.

Birmingham had changed dramatically since 1832. Prosperity had accelerated the urban sprawl. Gone were the gardens and walks of Attwood's youth, yet for a little longer the town remained a place of comfort. Grand public buildings and private houses, societies and institutions, carriages and planned suburbs attested to the increase in wealth. There were as yet no heaps of human beings huddled together in slums of unimaginable filth and disease. The inspectors of factories, appointed in 1833, had found the labourers and their children relatively unscathed by industrialization. Critically, however, the sense of common purpose had been lost.

The Union's inability to command support except when Attwood himself appeared and a plethora of other groups pursuing single purposes from anti-slavery to the repeal of the coercive measures for Ireland, from patent reform to a theatre for the arts, led to a cacophony of voices. Each claimed the right to speak and it had been beyond Attwood's powers in 1835 to draw these elements together. In 1829 a closely-knit group with some claim to leadership had used the issue of reform as a net to catch the masses. In 1836, although currency augmentation and a sense of social justice remained a common link, the disagreements were too fundamental. None was more critical than the gap between worker and employer. Although small workshops could still be found, factory size had increased. The harmony between classes in the town that had marked the earlier years all but vanished in the scramble for profits. The market had become more complex and the independence of the master which had allowed latitude in employment relationships had been eroded.[4] The incidence of strikes and lockouts, often reported venomously in the local papers, attested to the decline in the relationship; the decline was exacerbated by the exodus of the middle classes from the centre to the outlying villages and hamlets.

Attwood in his periodic visits had tried to reawaken his fellow-citizens' sense of identity, but those who applauded did so more because of their pride in recent history than their hope for the future. Yet he had to keep their attention. His authority at Westminster had been so depleted that only his right to speak for Birmingham won him any sort of hearing. The provincial challenge to London's dominance was unceasing and distinctive and so pervasive that no government could ignore any of its parts. That in itself was an achievement, owing in no small measure to Attwood's mobilization of opinion. Unfortunately, although each campaign won an audience, none achieved unity. Instead, personal animosities simply found new outlets for expression; moreover, as trade continued to deteriorate, hardship introduced its own element of ill-feeling.

The point was almost immediately underlined by a so-called deputation of the "principal Merchants and Manufacturers." They held a meeting and unilaterally decided to seek an interview with Melbourne to lay before him the dismal state of trade. Carefully, they let it be known that they would make no specific recommendations, particularly none respecting the currency. They went further, stating that "Thomas Attwood is specifically requested not to attend."[5] Although the initiative emanated from several merchants corresponding with the United States (men feeling the bite of the collapse in their trade) and was led by Charles Shaw, an old enemy of Attwood, it was unnecessarily vindictive. Angered, Attwood took a greater interest than he might otherwise have done. Muntz, who had been briefed and sent to act in Attwood's name, brusquely demanded and won a place on the deputation. Attwood instructed him to raise the currency question despite Shaw's directive, if Melbourne evinced the slightest interest in Birmingham's situation.[6] The whole episode ended, as might have been expected, in mutual recrimination.

In London, Attwood understood that while he could largely afford to ignore the snubs of Shaw and his cronies, he did need something to capture the imagination and appeal to the pride of Birmingham – to make his claim to leadership indisputable once again. In 1830 he had waited on others to attract the attention of the Commons and to provide a rallying point; this time he optimistically concluded that he could do it himself. The king's speech on 31 January 1837 had again been a disappointment. He had "walked two miles in a hurry" to hear it for himself, but the chamber was already full.[7] Reports, however, indicated that there had been nothing about the currency or Russia: the two issues, in his opinion, of current importance.

The opportunity to do something about the first and to focus opposition came quickly. A debate on one of the committee reports on joint-stock banks was scheduled for 6 February. It promised to be lively and Attwood spent hours composing a speech that would command attention, one full of statistics and, he believed, irrefutable logic. Regrettably, his reputation led the Speaker to recognize everyone but him, despite a prominent position on the benches secured by arriving early. This failure was annoying but not critical. The speech could be published in an open letter to Sir Robert Peel and circulated privately in a public way to MPs. The excuse for this approach would be the need to refute some of Peel's more "idiotic" remarks.[8]

The letter and the speech from which it was taken were clever productions. For the past three years the country had enjoyed prosperity because there had been a temporary depreciation of the currency; a depreciation created by the Bank of England and its foster-children, the joint-stock banks, through the unconscious adoption of policies long recommended by the Birmingham school. It was an argument difficult to challenge, particularly as others, including some Ricardians, had been making the same point although with a pejorative rather than commendatory purpose. Attwood went on to argue that the government should now apply his ideas more coherently. Currency and interest rate management would lift the economy out of its crisis. Reaction to the publication on the whole was positive, probably more so than if he had presented the argument encumbered by unnecessary verbiage in the chamber.⁹ It was unlikely that he had changed anyone's mind – three months later the Commons refused to hear a motion on the currency – but that had not been the object of the exercise. The letter and the newspaper interest it aroused were given maximum attention in Birmingham and became a major talking-point.

In Birmingham his friends picked up this lead. Every issue, local or national, which could attract attention and engender the sense of excitement that had made the reform movement in 1832 so memorable was carefully revived. Muntz and the others knew that the unconditional support of the people must be one of the first priorities if a repeat of the débâcle of twelve months earlier was to be avoided. Each worked in the manufactories, among those whom he knew best. They had to woo the operatives, to steal them from the trade unions and the little secret meeting groups that had become too popular in the town to allow unanimous action.¹⁰ With unemployment or underemployment becoming widespread the task was not too difficult; most working men remembered their days on Newhall Hill. At a crowded meeting on 18 April, a carefully primed deputation from the floor interrupted the proceedings of the Reform Association's regular, usually neglected, meeting to demand that the Association change its name to Political Union. References to the days of past glory and to the monetary prescription for prosperity were made with ritual formality.¹¹ Attwood's name and services were held up as a talisman under whose charm all could unite. His currency expertise again seemed to offer a way out of the economic crisis, while his demonstrated leadership qualities promised to provide the means for the implementation of his ideas.

The preliminary step had been taken. The task was now to build upon it. The Irish under McDonnell met separately and resolved to join the Union. Attwood's opposition in Parliament to the Irish municipal reform bill had been noted and they were grateful. The problem, however, was that the workers stood alone. Whereas Attwood commanded loyalty across class divisions, the idea of a Union did not. The majority of masters stayed aloof; some were outright hostile, refusing to allow their men to leave the workplaces to attend meetings. The pattern of 1830 had been similar, but then two factors had offered hope for a better end. The town had united behind the effort to win the East Retford seat and the gulf between the various classes was crossed by many bridges including the currency issue itself, although even then the gathering of opinion had been slow and the expenses heavy. Such happy conjunctions were noticeably absent in 1837.

The absence of harmony worried Attwood and his growing lack of confidence made him question the wisdom of proceeding further. Was there not a chance that party strife could be submerged in the demand for the rectification of the currency?[12] Cooperation of this kind would be infinitely preferable to the rebirth of a Union clad solely in working-class clothes. Eventually he was persuaded that the desired cooperation was unlikely in that the working classes would insist on a political dimension. Finally, against his better judgment, Attwood accepted the recommendation of Robert Douglas, the editor of the *Birmingham Journal*, that quarterly membership tickets be issued at 6d each, to be paid on joining the organization. At this figure the Union would need about 4,000 members to be financially viable. He agreed to become chairman if the goal was achieved.[13] The question of an appeal to the middle classes was left for future consideration. The bargain was an enormous gamble and from the outset his heart really was not in it. To lead only a portion of the population was a negation of his basic philosophy, his vision of a society in harmony, of the interdependence of mankind. The source of his pride had been the unanimity of opinion in Birmingham in 1832, of his vanity the belief that he spoke for the nation. Agreement to Douglas's plan was a mark of his despair.

Enrolment proceeded slowly, but by early June Edmonds and the others decided that there had been a reasonable demonstration of support. Still 300 short, they declared that the Union was reconstituted and asked Attwood to accept the nomination to be chairman. With a little of his old panache he bravely replied that he had never deserted the Union and was ready "to do my duty."[14] In private he continued to be relatively unenthusiastic, but there was no viable alternative.

While arrangements had been completed in Birmingham he had been battling in Parliament on two fronts. Daily he expected some sort of announcement regarding Russia. For weeks he had been forecasting that "war was imminent" yet the government procrastinated.[15] Not even that affront to British power, the *Vixen* affair, had convinced the Whigs of Russia's malignancy: "what a horrible shame that we who crushed Napoleon should tamely submit to be insulted by Nicholas."[16] He regretted that he had no time to pursue the matter personally, but the threat to prosperity was now too serious to be ignored.

As the economy collapsed his sense of mission strengthened,

leading him to declare that "a great political change *shall* take place." After several weeks of waiting his new motion on the currency found a place in the schedule. Modestly he warned his friends not to expect too much as he was sure the ministers would find some way "to burke the motion."[17] In fact, the rebuff was worse than that. On the appointed day there were not enough MPs in the House to form a quorum and he was counted out. To get the motion rescheduled legitimately would mean a wait of several more weeks and by then it could be too late. "I shall try to force my motion," he told Elizabeth.[18] It might not be the way to win the good opinion of the Commons but at least he would be heard.

His opportunity came on the following Monday, the fifth of June. Lord John Russell moved that the House form itself into a committee to debate the Poor Law relief (Ireland) bill. Attwood caught the Speaker's eye and rose to introduce an amendment. Once launched he spoke for three hours.[19] Although the audience occasionally roared with laughter at the wrong time, he was heard with "very creditable patience and attention."[20] Some fifty did leave during the course of the monologue but weariness and the demands of other business, he charitably decided, might have been the cause. Muntz later told him that in an interview with Lord Melbourne, the prime minister had evinced admiration for Attwood's perception of the economic crisis.[21] Lord John Russell's immediate response was more pertinent; he protested that the member for Birmingham had given no prior notice of his intention to bring the subject before the House. Such a practice was "incompatible with public convenience."[22] The Commons agreed. Only twenty-four MPs could be found to vote with Attwood.[23]

The tone of Attwood's speech had been deliberately offensive and seemed almost perversely to invite ridicule. He had begun by comparing the cabinet with Nero who fiddled while Rome burnt. Oxford and Cambridge scholars, he charged, controlled the House and laced their speeches with literary allusions divorced from reality. They scorned the representatives of "honest buttons and buckles," preferring to attend Ascot races than listen to the voice of commerce and manufacturing. He bitterly noted that since 1833 he had been unable to join a single select committee – he had made himself too great a nuisance on his first. Having vented his frustrations, he proceeded to regale the House with his interpretation of the events of the past twenty years, reciting a list of errors which the House had already heard on countless other occasions. He joined with other theorists in concluding that the strains upon the money market in 1836–7 has been caused by the Bank's late and rapid imposition of stringency.[24] This action had been unnecessary and demonstrated, he declared, the need for a new set of rules for the Bank to follow – rules drawn up with the interest of the labouring classes in mind. The House should be careful: "They should repeal the Poor Law, their Corn Law, and the Money Law Bills. If they were not relieved by law, the people would relieve themselves ... if relief were further withheld a civil war ... with all its incalculable calamities, might be the consequence."[25] He left no doubt in their minds regarding the side upon which he would stand.

These statements were, of course, part of Attwood's usual high-flown rhetoric. He venerated the monarchy and the constitution and would brook no criticism of the nation's figureheads. But he genuinely believed that he had been treated as an "outcast" and made the butt of unnecessary ribaldry. Much of this speech was punctuated with sniggers and laughter at what he considered quite innocent passages.[26] The laughter probably derived from his melodramatic style of oratory and nothing more; others were similarly treated, but he took it personally. If Parliament wanted no part of him and those whom he considered his constituents, then he would look beyond for support and comfort. The hostility of the new industrial society to the old governing alliances had never been more bitterly voiced. Attwood's miscalculation lay in his assumption that, given his wholehearted attention, the rifts between the ranks of the divergent groups in Birmingham could be healed and the weapon of public opinion reforged. He prepared to return home, shorn of all political pretensions as a member of Parliament, condemned to adopt an increasingly radical stance in order to control the forces he had, in part, let loose. The situation of 1830–2 had been reversed. Then the Union and its legions had been a useful though not indispensable instrument to be discarded at will. Now the new Union's radical supporters were in a position to use him and, when the time came, they would prove that they had learned their lesson well. When his objectives no longer matched their own he would be abandoned.

The reelected chairman arrived in Birmingham on 16 June without any definite plans. A few days earlier, expectations of unanimity had been raised by a meeting reputedly of "all creeds and political shades."[27] Unfortunately, the only point of unanimity had been the desire to decry the Union. Political discussion had been barred during the deliberations and one attempt to raise the question of reform had been shouted down. Auguries elsewhere were also discouraging. Letters to the *Birmingham Advertiser*, the *Philanthropist*, and *Aris' Birmingham Gazette* had generally deplored its revival. Predictions of class warfare and diminished investment abounded, on the assumption that the activities of 1832 would be repeated and that this time there would be opposition. Nonetheless, Attwood could not now back down even if his working-class supporters would have let him. Much of the activity of the past few weeks had been haphazard, without the sanction of the council.[28] Perhaps all that was needed was his "magic wand."

Newhall Hill was chosen as the site for the rebirth of the Union in the hope that it would awaken pleasant memories. Past success was similarly emphasized in every placard: "Meet us Monday next, at the OLD PLACE, under the OLD LEADER, for the OLD cause. Peace, Law and Order! Be this your watchword!"[29]

The council elected on 7 June, "better and stronger than ever," included only fifteen from that of the former time.[30] Most noticeably absent were Charles Jones, whose fortunes had declined and who had retired from the political arena, William Pare, now much more respectable as the superintendent registrar of marriages and deaths, and Bosco, who was busy elsewhere and disillusioned about politics. Of the newcomers among the thirty-four, councillors Douglas and P.H. Muntz were influential. The latter, brother of G.F. Muntz, had become the family's local spokesman since George had moved to Wales to attend more closely to business interests. The remainder were mostly small businessmen and not close to Attwood. Surprisingly, despite the reliance on working-class support, there were no working men on the governing body. It was as yet Attwood's Union and his hold was going to be difficult to pry loose.

The procession which left the Union's offices in Moor Street was colourful but less numerous than had been hoped. Not until the radical workers from the ironworks and coalpits of Oldbury, West Bromwich, Bilston, and Wednesbury arrived did the crowds swell to the proportions expected.[31] Estimates of numbers were as wild as before, from 15,000 to 150,000, depending on the observer's affiliation. Attwood had as usual prepared carefully and his speech employed all the tricks learnt over the years; it won a tremendous response. With Muntz as his seconder he proposed a new assault upon the House of Commons through the medium of "Household Suffrage, Vote by Ballot, Triennial Parliaments and the Abolition of Property Qualification."[32] It was not an ultra-radical program for there were signs that his overtures to the middle class were enjoying some success. Tindal, the agent of the Bank of England, spoke for many in the town when he told his directors, "the currency question serves as a safety valve for the escape of high pressure steam." This interpretation was not unreasonable. Attwood's motives were well known and his leadership as a moderate could be welcomed just as it had been in 1832.[33] Hadley, Salt, and Muntz were appointed as a deputation to London to plead the Union's cause. As Attwood saw it, "Our deputation goes to London tomorrow [25 June] to offer the *Olive Branch* or the *Moral Sword* to Lord Melbourne."[34]

Notwithstanding scepticism in the newspapers about the viability of the movement and the distractions caused by the death of William IV, Attwood ploughed on with a variety of public appearances. Victoria's accession to the throne, which required a proclamation procession, was an ideal opportunity to seize attention. He described the occasion for Elizabeth: "The young and interesting Queen was quite forgotten; and I a simple citizen of Birmingham without flag or banner, or distinction of any kind, and walking alone *immediately behind the Clergy* and Magistrates, was received with ten times ten thousand shouts of 'Attwood for ever'; throughout every street, during a 3 hours progress. At the end of this triumphant procession I addressed 30,000 *men* in New Street ... you would have been delighted with the wild frenzy of the people. The old men burst through the soldiers to shake me by the hand, and the young women acted in a still more gratifying and tender way."[35]

Afterwards he harangued an enthusiastic crowd from the bank's window.[36] The contrast between this type of reception and that accorded him by the Commons encouraged him: "Whenever I die, I think I shall be buried in the new burial ground of Harborne Church, unless, perhaps, I may prefer Newhall Hill. Both will be near enough for my faithful *Buttons*, with their wives and daughters, to make a little *Becket* of me."[37]

Apart from a brief visit to London to present an address of congratulation from the Political Council to Queen Victoria, "who looked quite pretty," and a day or two in Ramsgate to visit his family on holiday, Attwood remained in Birmingham, attempting to repair his neglect of the Union's structure.[38] The change in the monarchy required an election and, despite his recent disappointments in the Commons, he decided, optimistically, that it would be better to lead the new radical movement from inside the corridors of Westminster.

Regrettably the sense of pride in the old organization and its leaders could not be sustained. What little remained of the attempt to create an all-party spirit under the aegis of currency reform vanished under the pressure of the election campaign. The Tories put up a relatively innocuous candidate, A.G. Stapleton. Attwood, in good spirits, had no doubt he would defeat the "mere tool of jealous neighbours." Still, he saw that the Union had to be mobilized to ensure the reelection of the incumbents and for the moment other objectives must be held in abeyance. Scholefield, whose seat was again the more vulnerable, began to appear at Union functions after an absence of five years. The Political Council then made a significant mistake; it unwisely urged the rank and file to participate in every aspect of the campaign. As a result, Birmingham experienced the ugly side of early nineteenth-century parliamentary contests. And, as at Walsall in 1832, Attwood was unable to remain untouched.

The unpleasantness began when some Tories were threatened by rowdy Unionists outside their hotel and some windows were broken. The commander of the Dragoons, Colonel Wallace, brought out his men. Seeking to defuse the situation without resorting to force, he asked for and received, or so he thought, the permission of Stapleton to bring Attwood to the hotel so that he might disperse the crowd. Attwood accompanied by Scholefield arrived and addressed the people from the balcony of Stapleton's room. Stapleton's committee objected, presumably on the ground that the speech had a political objective, and some of his supporters began to manhandle Attwood. With help of his friends Attwood fought his way back outside; eventually, the people dispersed but not before the riot act had been read and several arrests had been made.[39] A verbal battle ensued, each side blaming the other for the fracas. From the evidence of the troop commander and the magistrates it would appear that Attwood had acted correctly and the Tories badly. But that was of scant comfort, since the episode embittered relations between the rival groups and made future cooperation on any political question extremely unlikely.

Attwood and Scholefield easily defeated Stapleton.[40] Election results elsewhere were, however, disappointing to Attwood and he concluded that monetary reform would not be popular in the new House. Within the town prospects were equally discouraging. It was only the relatively innocuous demand for local relief that could command bipartisanship. It was an issue, Attwood acknowledged, that demanded priority. Unemployment was at such a peak and the demands on charity so great that even he, whose largesse had become legendary, had printed a handbill telling those who sought help that he could give no more. Commendably, masters and men, Whig, Tory, and radical, were willing to cooperate in seeking a solution. The only caveat was that there should be no formal organization. Attwood willingly accepted the condition. A town meeting – not on Newhall Hill, said the Tories – was scheduled for the end of September. A petition would be sent from Birmingham as a whole to the Whig ministry.[41]

A committee on distress which had been charged with organizing the meeting worked hard. However, enthusiasm for the project waned as doubts began to surface as to the advisability of including the unemployed in the actual debate and the subject of political reform was introduced by some of the Unionists, contrary to Attwood's explicit orders. The number of Tories at the planning sessions rapidly diminished as the sense of community vanished even in the face of such misery, a victim of crude self-interest. Attendance on the day was disappointing, only 4,500 and these were mostly operatives; only five Tories and twelve Whigs appeared. The discussion was desultory, the end inconclusive, and, indeed, the reverse of what Attwood had expected. Those who spoke "incredibly" chose to voice a lack of confidence in the efficacy of monetary reform. Only the force of Attwood's personality and a rousing speech won the acceptance of the unexciting memorial drawn up by the committee in the expectation of all-party support.[42] Now its combination of Tory, Whig, and radical ideas hardly reflected the mood of the meeting and there was a great deal of grumbling about time wasted.

There would be no great combination of the "industrious classes" this time. The gulf was too great to be crossed by abstract appeals to principle. The majority might still prefer Attwood's analysis of the economy but it was not their primary concern. Politics and the question of social order divided master and man on a much more fundamental level. One crumb of comfort for the Union emerged from this débâcle. A deputation composed mostly of Attwood's friends had been appointed to present the petition. It was to visit Lord Melbourne and would claim to represent the people of Birmingham. The leaders of the Union would be kept in the public eye. Privately, however, the council agreed that the whole exercise had been futile. For Attwood it realized his worst fears. In 1830 he had turned to radical reform to rally the town. Now the same cause would divide it.

Matters were not much better in the Union itself. Tickets were not going well and the working account was very low. Something had to be done to ginger up the general populace. Parkes, whose personal ambitions required ultra-radical connections to be eschewed, happily announced that Attwood was thinking of urging the end of cabinet government and a return to sworn privy councillors – a proposal that, Parkes considered, proved the banker "as mad as a March hare."[43] Whatever the truth of the matter, Attwood did not pursue that course. Instead, on 17 October, he publicly admitted his mistake in trying to ally with the Tories. He had come to what he believed was a most significant conclusion: "they must raise the standard of universal suffrage."[44]

Earlier declarations of commitment to that standard had usually been made as oratorical flourishes and had been abandoned on reflection. Many probably expected a similar retreat on this occasion. But a week later Attwood elaborated on the idea. To obtain prosperity through currency reform Parliament must be thoroughly purged. This could only be achieved by organizing a gigantic out-of-doors campaign backed by the strength of at least two million men.[45] Dramatically, he reiterated an older proposal: "Missionaries must be sent out to other towns to gather support."[46] Birmingham should lead not simply by example but by direction; if a roar of disappointment was needed then it should be one voice and not a chorus. It was a dangerous approach that virtually guaranteed a riposte from the government, but expediency dictated that the Union should appeal to the common people, "the final refuge of the constitution," who must be brought forward to vindicate "Liberty and virtue, the prosperity and happiness of all."[47] The sentiment could be applauded yet there was an air of calculation in his sudden announcement and most of his listeners were aware of it.

Birmingham's artisans generally found the discovery of "natural right" unconvincing; particularly since he had cloaked the idea in his 1822 assumption that selected representatives of the middle class would still lead. The artisan was being told to fight for the franchise but that once it had been won he must use his vote in the service of others and chance that he would not be forgotten. It was a qualification that was immediately challenged. Edmonds assured Attwood that he was still the undisputed leader but times had changed. He would have to choose one side or the other; a simple statement was not enough. Attwood was sufficiently a realist to recognize that there really was no choice. The Union which he had agreed to lead was in reality an instrument of working-class radicalism and nothing more, despite his best efforts to broaden its appeal. If he did not become attuned to the new direction, his authority would be challenged and he might well be replaced. The council was instructed to make overtures to radicals elsewhere. If it were to be a working-class movement it would have to have as broad a base as possible; otherwise the government would have little difficulty in crushing it.

One of the first manifestations of the new commitment came at a meeting of the council on 11 December. A delegate from the London Working Men's Association, Hetherington, applauded the stand on universal suffrage and pledged closer cooperation between the two groups.[48] The event was particularly significant because it was just such a liaison that Attwood and his friends had previously avoided. The direction in which the Union was moving was further emphasized two days later. Daniel O'Connell came to town in the company of Scholefield and McDonnell. He held a meeting in the Town Hall and tried to persuade the audience that they should support the Whigs. Such support, he said, would eventually help both Ireland and England and he advocated the formation of a National Reform Association.[49] The Unionists were there in strength. Led by Hadley, Muntz, Salt, and Edmonds, they, who two years before had pledged his health, attacked O'Connell's integrity. Finally, the latter cut the meeting short and left in "high dudgeon."[50] The "present Political Union" wrote the editor of the *Philanthropist*, was "not the same kind of thing as that whose name it bears, which existed in 1832."[51]

The speech from the throne in November 1837 offered Attwood little cheer. The ministers clearly hoped that Tory weakness would keep them in power without a major policy shift. He voted for an amendment relating to the ballot, for an extension of the suffrage, and for changes in the duration of Parliament. It was lost, 20–509. His fellow members had not changed, remaining "ignorant as asses and as obstinate as hogs." Earlier hopes that Melbourne was at least in part following his advice with regard to a managed currency were dashed; England was a "doomed and God *abandoned* land." "Birmingham's boat" offered Melbourne his only chance.[52] Attwood's capacity for self-delusion remained as strong as ever. Sadly, he had become the prisoner of his one great achievement.

He ventured into the arena only once in December, when he spoke for one and a half hours on the subject of Russian aggression. Laughter punctuated his remarks and Palmerston chose to reply with a number of sneering remarks relating to Attwood's true constituency.[53] Badly hurt, thereafter he left Parliament for the most part to its own devices, contenting himself with daily attendance and the occasional vote.

Life in the capital was much more than just Westminster, however. His spirits were buoyed by a plethora of social engagements which ministered to the sense of his own importance. The Polish Association was particularly active and, as he was recognized as one of the leading Russophobes in the House of Commons, the Poles were full of compliments. There were various members of his family in town with whom to spend a pleasant evening. Angela, now the wife of Daniel Wakefield, lived nearby (they were soon to move in with Thomas and Elizabeth when Wakefield's career as a barrister failed), as did Bosco, who worked in a nearby bank. Moreover, he could always take a few days off in Ramsgate where his wife was resting and where Marcus nursed his leg. The latter's condition was a continual source of anxiety for Attwood was a very caring father. "I compare it [my life] with his," he told Elizabeth; "pleasure and pain; happiness and misery; hope and despair; the wild enjoyments of love and the melancholy anticipation of death – form a solemn and most painful contrast."[54]

Attwood returned to Birmingham shortly before Christmas and endorsed all the decisions that had been taken by the council in his absence. Their resolve to establish relationships with such groups as the London Working Men's Association and to shun the Whigs and Radical allies was, he declared, sensible.[55] There was little else he could do. Despite his new commitment few new subscriptions had been sold and the town was quiet. In the following weeks he rarely attended council meetings, dividing his time between Westminster and Ramsgate.

The winter of 1838 was extremely cold. A sheep was roasted on the ice at Hammersmith and people could walk across the Thames near the Tower. Attwood kept busy by helping his cousin John in winning what proved to be the final decision in the Small v. Attwood case. The bill to obtain incorporation for Birmingham was also nearing the statute book and he acted as host for the deputations from the town and escorted them to various ministers' houses.[56] Even Parkes received a visit. In the House, Attwood loyally but unavailingly fought to prevent O'Connell being reprimanded over a breach of privilege matter.[57]

Early in March his wife's mother died after a long illness and Attwood went to Harborne for the funeral. His visit was brief and he did not bother to meet with the council. Marcus was again gravely ill and had been left behind in London with his brother Algernon. The amputation of his leg was necessary and there was no guarantee that his son would survive the operation.[58] In all these months there is little to suggest that Attwood gave much thought to the Union and the state of its initiatives in Birmingham. Neither is there any evidence that he made contact with Hetherington and the London Working Men's Association or tried to advance the spirit of cooperation between the two groups. His continuing friendship with O'Connell suggests that he did not entirely sympathize with the council's ultra-radical tendencies and that the commitment to universal suffrage in December had been less than wholehearted.

The councillors had continued to find it difficult to rouse the town. In January the Working Men's Memorial Committee declared their alliance with the Union but there were few tangible results.[59] Reorganization and decentralization did not improve the financial position or produce enthusiastic support. A plan to encourage political unions in eight other towns by sending delegations from Birmingham similarly failed. Working men were more interested in forming associations on the London model and the middle classes wanted nothing to do with either.[60] Finally, the council recognized that it must adopt a new procedure. Salt outlined two proposals. The first was to journey through the North and Scotland, where distress was believed to be greater, actively promoting the Union and its program of reform, including a national petition. In order to do this effectively, advance publicity was essential. Salt proposed to suspend the Political Council meetings while the itinerary was prepared.[61] His second plan was equally innovative. At the close of that day's meeting he had arranged to meet a number of women with the object of forming a Women's Political Union. Its members would agitate for improved conditions of labour for women and encourage their husbands and sons to become actively involved in the larger organization. The proposal would show that the council accepted the need for dramatic changes in the social as well as the economic order. Both plans were approved.

Salt did fulfil his promise by visiting Lancashire. The most sterling missionary work, however, was accomplished by John Collins, an operative and lately a member of the Political Council. He toured the West of Scotland including Glasgow and everywhere met enthusiastic audiences. Scottish reformers were told that a deputation from Birmingham would arrive in the near future to seek their cooperation in the drive towards reform.[62] Immediately, preparations were begun by the Scots to receive their guests and to publish expressions of solidarity. Indeed, Collins was forced to restrain his converts from "using too strong language, and from recommending too strong measures." A committee was established in Glasgow and it issued a formal invitation to Attwood and "such friends as you may think most favourable to the cause" to attend a meeting on 21 May.[63]

Attwood had been watching Collins's progress closely. He was concerned that the delegate might promise something that Birmingham could not deliver; or worse, propose an illegal enterprise. The invitation allayed his fears. Collins had done his job perfectly: the request was for individual participation. Without hesitation, Attwood accepted and he proposed that a meeting be held in Birmingham after the return of the delegates from Scotland. By that means they could capitalize upon the excitement engendered in the north. To his chagrin the proposal was debated. Absence and the failure to consolidate his rule as chairman had weakened his authority. After some deliberation is advice was rejected by the council and plans for a "great send-off," rather than a reception, proceeded.[64] Attwood's friends, Salt, Edmonds and Douglas, succeeded in getting their more radical colleagues to accept the need to correspond with Attwood on the point but they had to agree that "the opinion of the majority should govern." It was not the first time that Attwood had been criticized in the council but the frequency of such criticism was increasing.[65] At this meeting it was tentatively agreed, also without his prior approval, to stage a National Convention in London, at which each delegate was to represent one town, or at least 20,000 people. Attwood recognized the weakness of his position and capitulated. Nervously, he restated their motto, "PEACE, LAW, ORDER, LOYALTY, and UNION," and entreated the organizers in Scotland to see that the watchwords were followed.[66]

A town meeting, the Union's perennial disguise, was held on 14 May. Attwood, P.H. Muntz, Hadley, Edmonds, Salt, and Douglas were appointed to the deputation to Glasgow. The inner core of his supporters were still strong enough to win the occasional gesture to the memory of 1830–2. The "great send-off" was not well attended even by the deputation itself. Attwood was still in London, Hadley was away, and Salt was at a funeral. The procession to the railway station had to be abandoned for lack of interest. Salt and Attwood caught up with the rest at Manchester. From there the deputation, somewhat depressed, travelled together to Hamilton and Glasgow. Immediately, their mood changed. Everywhere they were met by admiring crowds and cheering radical reformers. On 21 May, in Glasgow, a procession two miles long, forty-three bands of music, and countless banners rekindled all the old enthusiasm despite the pouring rain. Attwood was particularly well received as the father of reform, and responded by advocating universal suffrage and a national strike if their demands were not heeded.[67] Later that day a banquet was held in their honour. Attwood was able to attend only one more meeting, at Paisley on 22 May. He had been unwell and the illness of Marcus was never far from his mind. The other members of the deputation took it upon themselves to recommend that he return home with Edmonds while they continued their tour through Scotland.[68] He journeyed by steamer to get the benefit of the sea air.[69]

The deputation had company throughout their "triumphal" progress. A group from the London Working Men's Association, led by Tom Murphy of Marylebone, had travelled north to add London's voice to that of Birmingham in Scotland. Moreover, they carried with them copies of the bill – the Charter – which Francis Place or, as some historians have argued, William Lovett, had drafted.[70] At the banquet on the evening of the 21st Attwood proposed a toast to "Universal Suffrage, Annual Parliaments and Vote by Ballot" in accordance with the five points of the national petition brought by the Birmingham deputation. The second item in that triad replaced what had hitherto been the preference of the Union leadership, triennial parliaments. In the absence of evidence to the contrary, it must be concluded that the Birmingham deputation had been swayed by the need for unity and consistency within the movement. Birmingham's own ultra-radicals had favoured short-term parliaments, but Attwood had originally vetoed the proposal. There was one major point of difference between the petition and the Charter. Attwood omitted the demand for equal electoral districts. He had calculated that such a change would give Ireland the right to return 200 members to Parliament, while England, Wales, and Scotland would "elect but 400" altogether.[71] This upset the historic balance and notwithstanding his sympathy for Irish causes he never doubted the justice of English claims to primacy. The two groups discussed the disagreement, but with Attwood intransigent Murphy wisely refrained from forcing the issue.[72] The need to create enthusiasm and unity outweighed other considerations.

From the Political Union's point of view the foray into Scotland had been a huge success. The deputation was greeted on its return by large crowds and the council was gratified to discover that general interest in the Union had increased. Collins continued to quarter the north and his weekly reports from Leeds, Newcastle, and other major towns served to keep excitement high. Signatures to the petition numbered 32,680 by the end of June. Visitors from

London became a regular feature and all kept to the theme of unity and moral force. "They [Birmingham's Unionists] may not agree with us in detail," wrote one, but "the best public feeling prevails."[73] Pierce, a councillor, noted that "they were going for the cardinal points recommended by the Working Men's Association of London."[74] He trusted that the men of the metropolis would respond with whole-hearted support. The first meaningful concession to the centres of working-class opinion outside Birmingham had been made. It was to lead to the Union's destruction.

Attwood recovered slowly from his illness, attended Parliament irregularly, and did not appear in Birmingham until July when his need to reassert control over the Union became imperative. At council meetings and, indeed, everywhere he went in the town he was greeted rapturously.[75] Nevertheless, he was well aware that not all the omens were favourable. Feargus O'Connor was praising Attwood and Birmingham for their "manly qualities" and leadership, but the threat of violence was increasingly mentioned by the press. Although O'Connor invited delegates from Birmingham to attend "Reform Banquets" and to participate in the formation of the Grand Northern Political Union, only Collins was brave enough to attend. The others nervously feared guilt by association. On the other hand, the council was being forced to yield the leadership of the moderate elements to Lovett and the London Working Men's Association. Birmingham was slowly but surely being squeezed.

To forestall a total eclipse, Attwood and the council set about preparing a mammoth demonstration on 6 August. On Attwood's insistence moral force was emphasized at every opportunity. Holloway Head was chosen to be the site now that Newhall Hill was built upon. The surrounding districts were canvassed thoroughly to ensure a large gathering and the Union set out to make it as colourful as possible.[76] On the day in question it was variously estimated that between one hundred and two hundred thousand people came to hear the speeches of Attwood and the delegates from Ireland, Glasgow, London, Leeds, and other towns. In the main, the assembly was as orderly as those of earlier years and all the speakers respected Attwood's call for legality. Attwood and London's principal speaker, John Vincent, emphasized the motto of the Political Union.[77] Only Feargus O'Connor went a little further and advocated that the people be ready to resort to other means.[78] For the moment, however, he hastened to add that he was a devoted follower of Thomas Attwood and friends with everyone. For the first time in years Birmingham had captured the attention of the country. The *Morning Advertiser* had sent four reporters and all newspapers carried accounts in the following days. The call for the creation of a National Convention in London, to be held early in the new year, ensured that the momentum would not be lost. To pay for it a "National Rent" was to be levied upon all Chartists. It sounded attractive and Birmingham's delegates were chosen with great fanfare.

Other meetings were held around the country to select deputies. In each instance the Political Union sent delegations. Yet the demands which accompanied each selection were diverse. The movement was losing what little unity of purpose it had and Attwood was not sure how to hang on. Edmonds, sent by Attwood to attend a radical dinner in Liverpool, felt obliged to declare that Attwood was giving up his "hobby-horse currency" to win universal suffrage.[79] A number of radicals, particularly in the north, began to urge their supporters to practise military manoeuvres and to arm themselves.[80] In London, O'Connor defended their right to do so and was frequently at odds with Lovett and the Working Men's Association. At the end of September the council in Birmingham debated the question of physical force and the following week condemned O'Connor and the Reverend Joseph Rayner Stephens who had recently given an inflammatory speech at Norwich.[81] Salt, Attwood's closest friend on the council, led the censure debate and was clearly acting for the absent chairman. Attwood, however, remained optimistic that differences could be settled and "universal suffrage won within twelve months.[82]

On 13 November O'Connor arrived in Birmingham, unannounced and uninvited, to attend a council meeting. He angrily attacked the council and Salt in particular. Attwood, he claimed, had in the past advised physical force if other means failed; his observations had been marked by a difference only in the letter, not in the spirit. O'Connor's ill-temper led him to question the council's sincerity in its pursuit of reform; it had adopted universal suffrage only lately and now it had become "squeamish." He concluded by challenging Salt to a public debate "to see who shall be abandoned by the people."[83]

O'Connor continued his onslaught through the columns of his paper, the *Northern Star*, while the Union, for its part, regularly denounced violence despite the use of the rhetoric of violence in its spokesmen's earlier speeches. At meetings in the north, O'Connor played upon the rumours that the Birmingham organization sought to deflect the agitation against the Poor Law Amendment Act and thus serve the purposes of the Whigs.[84] An open debate was held between the protagonists on 26 November. By then differences had been papered over, thanks to the mediation of Collins, and it was hoped that a semblance of unity could be restored. The council expected too much. O'Connor, still determined to wrest the initiative from Attwood, departed without making many of the conciliatory gestures that he had promised.[85]

At this time, very little seemed to be going well for the Union, except that with incorporation now completed it was able to dominate the new town council. The National Rent scheme in which Attwood had great hopes was failing to produce much in the way of revenue despite a variety of ingenious collection schemes. In addition, the central committee that had been set up to manage the affairs of the Union found it difficult to communicate with the rank and file. The workers in the rapidly growing town no longer acknowledged the patriarchal system traditional in the small workshops. Many believed that they could act alone and O'Connor's constant criticisms of the council had encouraged that view. Attwood responded in much the same way as he had in 1832, a tactic involving part bluster, part the coopting of critics. Five working men were added to the council in this way after they had protested the arbitrary election procedure.[86] Elsewhere in the country the bickering was equally fierce and plans went ahead for the convention without much reference to Birmingham and none at all to Attwood.

One problem that the Union often faced was the absence of its leader. A rumour circulated in November that Attwood was dead. Nothing had been heard from him for some time and three letters on the currency he had published in London newspapers omitted the question of reform entirely, suggesting that they had been drafted many years earlier. On hearing of the rumour he finally responded. A letter from Ryde in the Isle of Wight commended the council's diligence and begged them to continue their emphasis upon moral influence. For the moment he could not journey to Birmingham on account of "the indisposition of myself and my family."[87] The town had no other political figure of Attwood's stature and suffered accordingly. Edmonds and Salt had opposed O'Connor in Attwood's name but without his authority. Often they were reduced to the plaintive declaration that, they were "sorry he [Attwood] was not here."[88]

On New Year's Day 1839 Attwood came to a council meeting. The affection with which he was regarded by the people of Birmingham had apparently not diminished and for the first time in several weeks the room was crowded. Yet he had nothing new to offer. His remarks concentrated upon the need for peaceful agitation, "to talk of arms is utterly useless."[89] Thereafter he followed the round of dinners and speeches that had characterized his visits to Birmingham during the last two years. Perhaps the only difference this time was his taking tea with the ladies of the Female Political Union. At every opportunity, he attacked the Northern radicals for their "wickedness" in sowing dissension and for their "wrong-headed" advocacy of physical force. Everywhere he repeated his conviction that universal suffrage would be achieved in less than twelve months. The council endorsed his position enthusiastically. Along with leaders in other parts of the country, even O'Connor, its members had become concerned about the divisions and knew that only a united voice could hope to command attention.

The National Convention was a disappointment to the Birmingham delegates from the first. Although as a mark of honour to the town Douglas was made chairman and, with P.H. Muntz, authorized to collect and administer the National Rents, the appointment signified nothing in terms of power. Birmingham was not to be the arbiter of opinion on this occasion. O'Connor and the northern delegates were well entrenched and the language of the speeches became increasingly violent. The truce that had emerged in January had been based upon O'Connor's impression that to gain anything the moderates had to be participants. Now it was collapsing under the strain of conflicting expectations.

Since the need to obtain more signatures for what Attwood had termed "the National Petition" was the most pressing business, roving agitators were appointed to tour the country districts. Salt, Hadley, Pierce, Muntz, Douglas, and O'Connor journeyed to Wolverhampton and Coventry but failed to rouse anything other than curiosity. At Kenilworth, "where there had been much life in 1832," they were unable to organize a meeting at all.[90] At the convention, the Unionists had tried to join with Lovett and the Working Men's Association in order to outvote the O'Connorites. For a time it appeared they might make some progress and Attwood, whose knowledge of events derived almost exclusively from the Birmingham delegates, was quite happy, calling the missionaries his "good shepherds" and daily expecting news of an enlarged flock.[91]

Early in March Salt reported that the convention was at last making headway. Lovett wrote to Place that "the blood and thunder heroes are being done up." However, on the same evening that this letter was written a number of northern radicals met at the

Crown and Anchor Inn and rededicated themselves to the use of physical force if it became necessary. As the news of this commitment spread, the moderates began to despair and question the value of continuing. Anything they might achieve would be instantly undone by the rhetoric of confrontation even if it emanated from a minority. A nervous government would not have to search for an excuse for repression. At the end of the month Salt, Hadley, and Douglas had lost all interest and announced their resignations: "the Peace, Law and Order resolution has been defiled in spirit and letter."[92]

The defection of three of Birmingham's councillors from the convention highlighted a division of opinion that had appeared in the town. The council met on Tuesdays and the Working Men's Committee on Thursdays and their conclusions did not always agree. Every evening meetings had been held in the Bull-Ring to hear reports of the convention's deliberations. On 3 April convention missionaries from London combined with this faction to hold a meeting on Holloway Head. It censured the Political Council and the three who had resigned. All kinds of slurs were made on their integrity, which would have been inconceivable a few years earlier.[93] The Union or what was left of it was now almost totally out of control.

Attwood had been in London since the beginning of February attending the new session of Parliament. Debates on the Corn Laws and Russia occupied him. From his letters he appears to have deluded himself into believing that the "mad-caps" were largely tamed and reform would surely come.[94] Even as late as 21 March, he was still defending the Chartists from charges of intemperate language in the House of Commons. He assured his fellow parliamentarians that the labourers of England would only use peaceful means to achieve their ends.[95] News relayed by Salt from Birmingham, relating to the split in the ranks of the Unionists, horrified him: "... my faithful battalions in Birmingham, worn out, and borne down by long and unregarded sufferings, and by hoarded injuries of many kinds, are at last, as you fear, listening to the wild advocates of *physical force*. I will not believe it. Other parts of the country may have been led astray, but Birmingham has never been deceived."[96] He did not want to believe that Salt was telling the truth. Salt had been overcritical of the "many noble and high minded men in the Convention." Attwood urged the council to be cautious, "the times are out of joint"; Birmingham was "the hope of England." The letter was read aloud at a council meeting on 9 April that had been invaded by a large group of pro-convention workers. If Attwood had been present to hear the laughter and jeers which greeted his strictures on legality and peacefulness, he would not long have held such hopes. At the end of April he was still doggedly expressing his conviction that the Chartists would continue to act within the law. That was, however, for public consumption, in private he was having second thoughts: "I do not mean to be made either a fool or a scoundrel." Yet he was not ready to give up "my ragged battalions are a little restive, but I shall bring them into strict order."[97]

The National Petition, taken to Attwood on 7 May, contained 1,286,000 signatures. He had agreed to present it after accepting a rather ambiguous disavowal of physical force by the convention five days earlier.[98] Relations with the Chartists were, however, far from amicable. On one occasion he had gone to the convention's rooms to reiterate his doctrine, "Peace, Law and Order," and he had been treated with "insult and contumely." The members of that assembly, he decided, were brutal and stupid – a very different description than that given to Salt. The manner in which the petition had been brought to him was in itself rather singular. Two delegates had leapt from a cab and accosted him while he took a leisurely stroll to the Commons on the 6th. Caught unprepared, he told them to bring the petition to Fielden's house. The next day he had been surprised to see a procession of fifty-two delegates escorting a wagon draped with a Union Jack, and looking to all intents and purposes like a funeral hearse, draw up before the house at the appointed time. From one of Fielden's bedroom windows he gave a short speech.[99] By this time he had his thoughts in order and he carefully refused to guarantee that a bill would be subsequently introduced. As he had told Lovett, the petition was constitutionally valid, but the bill's inclusion of a sixth point, equal electoral districts, was not. Moreover, he had no wish to subject himself to the division of the House: "If I find there is hooting, and laughing, and crowing, and all sorts of botheration, when I present the petition – if I have a regular sickening of it, then I'll promise nothing."[100]

In the face of such fundamental differences of opinion Attwood's agreement to face the House in support of the National Convention and the petition would have been surprising, were it not for the peculiar position in which he was placed. Clive Behagg has argued convincingly that the middle-class members of the Political Union had obtained their immediate goals by the reform of local government.[101] For men like P.H. Muntz that was undoubtedly true.[102] The decline in councillors' attendance on Tuesdays in 1839 confirms that loss of interest. That argument cannot, however, be made to explain Attwood's participation. The petition had been drawn up by the council of the Birmingham Political Union under his direction. It was so phrased that acceptance of the political recommendations necessitated the acceptance of his currency theories. The preamble demanded a "fair day's wage for a fair day's work" and complained of economic distress. To refuse to present the petition would have constituted a denial of his own handiwork.

There was an additional factor. Six years of experience in the House had not taught him to observe the rudimentary rules of procedure or to moderate his language. Attwood remained unable to obtain support within the House for any of his own motions. He had introduced a motion regarding the strength of the navy on 15 March and had neglected to ascertain if anyone would be willing to second it. Not until the Speaker requested a name from the floor and Attwood had gazed around looking "for some honest man" was a seconder found.[103] Eleven days later he gave a speech which was to take up twelve columns of *Hansard* proposing that the navy be expanded. This time no support could be found despite his pleas and "it fell to the ground."[104] On 30 May Attwood called the attention of the House to the large exportation of gold and proposed that the House of Commons interfere. His speech was again long and despite cries of "No, No" he insisted upon recapping the events of the previous twenty-five years. The motion did not come to a vote.[105] As a result of these rebuffs and countless others often of a more subtle nature, a new House chosen by universal suffrage had become Attwood's last rather forlorn hope.

His conduct in the debates tacitly acknowledged his hopeless position. Hume's perennial motion for household suffrage received its usual endorsement from the member for Birmingham but in a style so offensive that it contributed to the bill's defeat. Regularly repeating his charges of 1837, he indulged his feelings of frustration in intemperate attacks on virtually every group and individual in the House, "I put it to the Whigs for I think little of them, I put it to the Tories, and I think little of them too. I put it to the Radicals in this House – and of all three factions I think them the worst."[106]

In the event, presentation of the petition had to be delayed. On the same day that it was passed to him the government resigned. No one knew what would happen. Attwood expected that the Lords Normanby and Durham would be approached.[107] Others, better informed, knew that the queen would have to ask Peel. The refusal of Victoria to allow Peel to dictate the personnel of her bedchamber added complications and Parliament had to be adjourned.

This drove all thoughts of petition and Charter from his head. Changes of government, either in whole or in part, usually provided small groups with an opportunity for influence. For one of the few times in his political life he now became caught up in a Westminster "plot." On 12 May fifteen self-proclaimed "Radicals" met at Molesworth's house. The sources of their radicalism differed but for the moment they saw advantage in cooperation.[108] Attwood joined the others in signing a note to Melbourne telling him that they would withhold their support if he tried to form a new government unless he agreed to "liberalize largely."[109] For the next few days Attwood rhapsodized on the possibilities and thought the little group's ultimatum must be accepted. With this and the solicitation of his vote for a new Speaker his natural optimism had revived. The euphoria subsided quickly. Victoria's support was more important than that of a few Radicals. The Charter had to be moved back to the centre of his stage.

The National Petition was brought before the House on 14 June. He had taken the precaution of showing it to the Speaker first and had been relieved to discover that it would not be tossed out on the grounds of illegality. Attwood introduced it soberly but spoke at length transgressing recently established procedural rules for such occasions. His sympathy for the movement was made clear and he ended with a personal disavowal of the use of physical force.[110] It was in fact one of his better parliamentary performances.

The National Convention had in the meantime adjourned, much to his chagrin, to Birmingham. He had told his wife that he would keep them out of the town. There it conducted disorderly meetings in the Bull-Ring, one of which ended in a clash with the police sent from London to control them. Attwood did gain one small victory. As a result of the 3 July clash a requisition was circulated by a number of alarmed middle-class citizens asking Attwood and Muntz to unite the lower and middle classes in behalf of reform.[111] Under the Birmingham Political Union all had been orderly. Attwood replied that he was pleased by the "confidence and affection" of the townsmen. However, he made no promises, no doubt well aware that the lower orders were still enamoured of the more extreme elements among the Chartists.

The motion to implement the resolutions of the petition was made on 12 July by Attwood. Riotous behaviour had not endeared the Chartists to the Commons or Attwood and the latter chose to concentrate upon the currency question rather than reform in his supporting speech. It was a subject on which he had spoken at length four days earlier during a debate on a motion to inquire into the activities of the Bank of England.[112] Lord John Russell countered by showing the House a placard. Although it openly rejected the currency thesis and had been signed by every member of the General Convention, Attwood had been unaware of its existence. Paper money, it stated, was a corrupting influence which had defrauded and robbed labourers of "three-fourths of their labour."[113] Attwood's destruction was complete and final: "Here was an argument I could not answer ... I was paralysed. I had created the General Convention. It was the very offspring of my own brain. I was surrounded by enemies on every side ... At this moment, *out of my own camp*, a mortal weapon was directed against my heart. I leave you my friends to judge my feelings. For twenty-five years I have wasted my life in incessant labours."[114] The motion was defeated 46–235.

Russell's well-conceived insertion of the placard into the Charter debate extinguished the last vestiges of blinkered optimism that Attwood had so carefully nurtured during these difficult months. It was an indication of his desperation that the public repudiation of his theory came as a surprise. As early as August 1838, a deputation from Lancashire had attended the convention with the announced purpose of vetoing any attempt to include the paper money schemes of the Birmingham leader in the petition.[115] His friends must have apprised him of their presence and the promises that had been given. Moreover, O'Connor's dislike of what he called "rag-botheration" was well known. To proceed in the belief that the convention could ultimately be won over was clearly unjustified; it suggests that in his then state of mind Attwood was losing touch with reality. His immediate decision was to retire; if the whole world were not "raving mad," then he was. Years of labour both within and outside the walls of Parliament had produced "but little good." He had failed.[116]

CHAPTER TWELVE

The Final Years

Attwood's depression in June 1839 was understandable, but not all the portents were as ominous as he had persuaded himself they were. Melbourne's position was weak; Shaw-Lefevre had been elected Speaker by only eighteen votes; and radicals of all persuasions might expect greater attention then they had heretofore enjoyed. Outside the Commons the divisions both within the ranks of the Chartists and in Birmingham certainly prevented any chance of a united front. Yet of all the leaders he continued to be the most universally admired. Riots in Birmingham in July underlined the growing propensity of the urban workers to violence, but they had gathered on the strength of a rumour that he would shortly appear to address them. The only speaker of note had come from their own ranks and his exhortations contained the essential features of Attwoodian economics. The middle-class reformers of the town, in the guise of a Peace, Law, Order Committee, held meetings in which the name of Attwood was spoken as a charm to heal all rifts. From several quarters came the suggestion that the town present him with some mark of esteem.[1] Even more complimentary was the perpetuation and extension of his currency doctrines through both official and unofficial channels. When discussing the propriety of dispatching a deputation to present the town's views to the newly appointed select committee on the Bank of England, the mayor said: "it was admitted by all the people of Birmingham, with few exceptions, that to the present defective monetary system was to be attributed the present very great distress."[2] A "Currency Committee," set up to coordinate their efforts in this sphere, held frequent discussions in the town hall. The most commonly articulated opinions were those that had originated in the pamphlets of Thomas Attwood. In 1844 the publication of the *Gemini Letters* restated most of his ideas. He remained Birmingham's favourite son, yet to Attwood such calculations no longer mattered. He was tired and the continual raising and dashing of his hopes had drained him. Without a sense of commitment he could not continue. His disillusionment was complete, as he informed Sir George Sinclair: "the labour, the time, the expense have quite exhausted my patience. I abandon all hope of doing good, and am content at last to let the Devil take his own."[3]

For the moment he stayed at Westminster, partly to avoid a trip to his constituency in the continuing turmoil: "Mischief of some kind would probably be produced and that mischief, whatever it might be, would most certainly be laid at my door."[4] In Parliament he spoke more regularly than had been his habit of late, his favourite topic being the Birmingham police bill; a bill that if passed would cover all England, he warned, "with ten thousand arms," limiting the liberties of the people.[5] Most of his other speeches lacked his old fire and concentrated upon a forlorn reiteration of his views on all manner of subjects. On occasion, he launched into flights of imagination which only served to emphasize his sense of injury. "Bad men" had been at work urging the people to violence in order to injure the cause which they "falsely professed to serve." Possibly, he told the House, they were the agents of Nicholas of Russia or conversely some Conservative "partisans of the right hon. Baronet, Peel."[6] The flashes of temper elicited by the personal nature of Commons' debates in other years became less frequent. Only when Peel ridiculed Attwood's economic expertise did Attwood protest; that interjection was greeted with laughter.[7] Increasingly, with thoughts of retirement uppermost, Attwood concentrated upon the defence both of himself and his associates.

A petition from Birmingham in opposition to the police bill had been attacked on the ground that it emanated from a corporation dominated by radicals and violent men. Edmonds was singled out for special mention. Attwood steadfastly denied all the allegations, declaring that "a more worthy upright man never lived."[8] With regard to physical force he maintained that he had done nothing of which he should feel ashamed.[9] His concern for the welfare of the poor and distressed remained a redeeming feature of all his endeavours; few of his fellow-parliamentarians could say as much. Labour was the most "sacred" form of property and nothing should interfere with the worker's "constitutional right of living fairly and honestly by his own labour."[10] If in times of economic depression that were not possible, then the state should be obliged to provide relief.

Attwood abandoned London as soon as the session ended and travelled to Samaris Manor House, Jersey, in the Channel Islands, a haven used earlier by him for physical and spiritual regeneration. The Parliament of Great Britain had not been kind and clearly he had not enjoyed his seven years of service. Even at the end he showed that he still failed to understand parliamentary procedure by applying to the wrong office for the post of Steward to the Chiltern Hundreds – the only way to resign from the Commons. The personal reputation he left behind was relatively creditable. In reply to a request for a letter of introduction in 1842, Peel, then prime minister, wrote: "I have always heard your name mentioned (so far as private Character and Conduct are concerned) even by your strenuous opponents, with sentiments of esteem and good-will."[11] Letters to prominent politicians received considerate inspection and rarely was he ignored. But it was in his public life that the measure of his failure must be sought.

Lord Melbourne indicated the source of Attwood's parliamentary problems: "I differ from your opinions, from your views and still more from the measures you have taken to accomplish them."[12] The means Attwood had used were unconventional. In the Commons, Villiers enlarged upon that objection: "there was something so singular in the matter and so eccentric in the manner of the hon. Gentleman, that he continued to throw discredit and ridicule on almost every question he touched upon in the House."[13] Much of this criticism was valid. Too often Attwood allowed himself to be deflected into the realms of politics and philosophy, neither of which he understood. His flamboyant and undisciplined style coupled with a penchant for self-righteous morality and doom-laden prognostication was contrasted unfavourably and sometimes unfairly with the cool and measured but equally polemical tracts of Ricardo and other economists. The failure of the Reform Act to fulfil his expectations of a "rational" House drove Attwood into "distasteful" alliances in which he was never completely happy. His concept of "Union" had created a vehicle for agitation which could incorporate all manifestations of discontent only under exceptional conditions and concerning relatively simple and readily definable issues. Once the protest itself became more sophisticated the strains proved intolerable. Society in Birmingham and England grew too complex for the kind of artificial framework envisaged by Attwood. His concept of the nature of the world in which he lived did not change, but his palliatives were under attack from a new and unexpected quarter. The various attempts to reanimate the Union consequently failed and he was left with only memories of old victories. Alone in the House with but inconsistent support from his constituents, despite their adulatory behaviour in his presence, Attwood faced the choice of all institutionalized radicals – conformity or rejection. He chose the latter and retired, "my health broken down," in confusion.[14]

The winter of 1839–40 was spent quietly by Attwood recapitulating his mistakes and trying to understand the nature of his failure: "Standing on the rocks of Jersey, or wandering over its most beautiful hills and most happy vallied [sic], I have had the leisure to reflect upon the course which duty requires."[15] The time for thought was tragically interrupted by the sudden death of his wife, aged fifty-five. She had never been strong and one of the reasons for the choice of Jersey as his retreat was the mildness of its climate. Her death on 26 April 1840 added enormously to his sense of desolation; she had been his chief confidante and one of the pillars of his life.

As the summer passed Attwood's naturally active mind was unable to avoid the further contemplation of the causes of his failure. Discussions with the Reverend Charles Foster of St Clement's Church, in whose churchyard his wife was buried, helped to clarify the subject.[16] After a few months he set about writing a history of the "Second Movement of the Birmingham Political Unions."[17] Essentially, it was a philosophical document designed to enable "some future, and perhaps abler, politicians to avoid the rocks upon which the public cause had been wrecked in my hands." Pessimistically, he believed that the chance would not come again for several years; the public had been frightened by the excesses of the Chartists and he doubted that "political agitation upon a large and efficient scale" was practicable any more.

His prescription for a successful movement had not changed: "WISDOM, VIRTUE, and INTEGRITY in LEADERS ... CONFIDENCE and UNLIMITED OBEDIENCE to those LEADERS ... COMPETENT WEALTH to defray the necessary expenses, in their hands."[18] As a result of the fiasco caused by the "irrationality" of the convention's demagogues, Attwood had become convinced that the first prerequisite, leadership, would have to come from the politicians who "commence the MOVEMENT." This assumption led inevitably to the preeminence of the middle classes. Obedience was to be won by "a species of MORAL DICTATORSHIP." The last point reemphasizes his unusual grasp of the value of publicity. Money was the key to success; without that commodity control could be lost and leadership entrusted to "unknown, untried, ignorant and rash hands." With it success was assured: "They should have influenced the PUBLIC PRESS, so as to have all their proceedings efficiently published, and to keep the *public mind* in a sound and healthy state, properly instructed in the measures necessary for success, and properly guarded against those which *must* lead to failure. The NATIONAL PETITION would have been signed by more than two million men within a few months; and that petition would have been followed ... by probably ten thousand other petitions."[19] The analysis was made on the basis of a comparison between the campaigns of 1830–2 and 1837–9. The merits of the former highlighted the defects of the latter. Unfortunately, Attwood had failed to allow for the changes in circumstance between the two periods. While he held fast to a concept of society that was applicable to the earlier time, the working class in particular had moved on.

Various attempts were made by friends in the winter of 1840–1 to woo Attwood from the tranquillity of Jersey but in each instance he resisted. He did visit his old constituency briefly at the time that his brother Charles was trying to develop a national movement for reform, and there was some expectation that he would use his influence to win support for the project. To the disappointment of Charles and his old allies, only social engagements were accepted: "I have given up politics totally."[20]

There were also renewed efforts by this friends to obtain a testimonial of some kind for him from the town. The inhabitants of Deritend and Bordesley tried hard but could produce only £100 – a pitifully small amount.[21] Another group, led by Scholefield, met in January 1841 to organize a second attempt to build a monument to Attwood.[22] The town council was approached but declined to participate. In the end nothing was done.[23] The problem, Attwood was told, lay in the state of the economy and the proximity of a general election. The real reason, of course, was that for an influential number in the wealthier classes his participation in the Chartist agitation blotted out any of the good that he had achieved earlier. The Loyal and Constitutional Association of Birmingham applauded a speech by the earl of Dartmouth in which the violence and the threat of armed insurrection posed by the Chartists was laid at Attwood's door.[24] The latter remonstrated by letter but was rebuffed.[25] This was not an isolated attack. Attwood, put on the defensive, included a postscript to his "History" defending the inflammatory speeches he had made in 1831–2 and 1838.[26] He also wrote a letter to be read at the Low Bailiff's Dinner in which he stated that his prime concern had been the prevention of a recourse to arms.[27] It was a waste of effort. In politics, party advantage determines what is accepted as truth. The Tories of the town sought to damn Scholefield and George Muntz, the current MPs, through their association with Attwood. In such a climate and given the poverty of the workers, the failure of his friends to carry through their testimonial plans was predictable.

Attwood returned to Birmingham in June 1841 in a somewhat better frame of mind. The pain resulting from the loss of his wife had begun to diminish and he recognized that he could not languish in solitude for ever. Moreover, it went against his combative nature to leave the field entirely to his enemies. His reappearance coincided with the parliamentary campaign for the reelection of his old friends, and he joined in. Simply by appearing with them he reminded people of the great days of the past and made the unspoken promise that Birmingham's voice was still potent. The experience was remarkably pleasant. Notwithstanding the turmoil of the rest of the country and the imminent collapse of the Whig government, the hustings in Birmingham were comparatively uneventful. Attwood spoke frequently but without anger and there was little of the personal abuse which had characterized earlier contests. In terms of policy, Corn Law reform attracted his support; this move may have astonished some in Birmingham who lamented Manchester's failure to appreciate the origin of all distress, the currency. Attwood's endorsement, of course, stemmed form this oft-repeated contention that the Corn Law was one means by which the agricultural interest had been deluded into supporting the Act of 1819.[28]

The return of a Tory government headed by Sir Robert Peel prompted Attwood to send a private letter to the prime minister.[29] Peel had heard the catalogue of errors and missed opportunities on many other occasions but promised Attwood his most careful attention out of his respect for "the disinterested motives which have actuated your conduct in public life."[30] In a second letter Attwood again forecast calamity if a paper issue were not implemented.[31] Despite the international fame and internal tranquillity which Attwood envisaged as the rewards of action, Peel closed the exchange with a short, crisp note.[32]

Shortly thereafter Peel received another letter from Attwood. The subject was however very different; it asked for a letter of introduction to the colonial secretary, Lord Stanley. He had been thinking carefully about his future. Disappointment and rejection, together with his wife's death, had persuaded him that it would be better for him to leave England and start anew. With a group of friends, he proposed to emigrate to Western Canada.[33] Why Western Canada was chosen is difficult to discern. His son-in-law was in New Zealand, and the young man's father, Edward Gibbon Wakefield, had been a consistent advocate of the colonization of South Australia. One of his old friends, Benjamin Hadley, had gone to South Africa. Possibly Attwood wished to avoid all inadvertent contact with his past life beyond that which was to be allowed by choice. Attwood's decision to emigrate was not illogical; it followed advice he had given others over the years. With the resignation of his seat in the House he was for the moment directionless. Moreover, as Wakefield's recollection of him at this time suggests, he was a man still in his prime.[34] He lived with two daughters at his old home, Grove House, but the younger could easily travel with him and the elder was again planning to depart for New Zealand. Of his sons, George de Bosco was the secretary of the Bank of British North America in London; Aurelius managed the estates of an uncle; Edward Marcus was a barrister at Gray's Inn, although the loss of one leg made practice difficult; and Algernon worked in their London bank. All were apparently reasonably independent and presented no obstacle to his plans. Consequently, following a favourable reply from Stanley, Attwood set out to liquidate his assets. He immediately experienced a new shock.

Most of his business activities prior to entry into the political arena had been conducted on behalf of his father. Day-to-day expenses had been met from the profits of the bank and the other family enterprises. Out of this income the household at Harborne had lived well but not extravagantly. Life could have been easier and money saved if the Attwoods had not insisted upon translating theoretical concern into practical philanthropy. Whereas Thomas sought to improve the welfare of the people on a national scale, Elizabeth Carless Attwood earned the gratitude of the poor in their own village. The amount and scope of the charity dispensed at the Grove was well known and the unemployed of Birmingham would sometimes walk to Harborne to request aid. Elizabeth had inherited £20,000 shortly after their marriage and the annual income from its investment (the capital was unavailable) had always been required to meet the family's expenses. Wakefield, who later lived with Attwood, doubted whether "anyone of his fame and fortune ever lived in so poorly furnished a house."[35]

The drain of extravagant charity upon his resources had been bearable until the desire to achieve monetary reform thrust him into politics. The two movements of the Birmingham Political Union had proved expensive. Subscriptions totally failed to meet the expenditures the leaders deemed essential for success. Not until 1835 had the debt accumulated between 1830 and 1832 been paid off.[36] The memory of this financial drain had proved one of the biggest barriers to the resurrection of the Union in 1835.[37] Attwood attributed the failure of the movement to this lack of funds. It had driven the Union into the hands of the publicity-gathering extremists; his own meagre purse had been unable to remedy it.[38]

During the 1830s household costs had escalated alarmingly. Attendance at Westminster necessitated the maintenance of two homes. The family had also grown as a result of the marriage of Angela to the impoverished Daniel Wakefield. They and their subsequent offspring lived for some time with the Attwoods at the Grove. Moreover, the long drawn-out illness of Marcus had been attended by mounting medical expenses. Beset by bills, Attwood more than once enjoined his wife to prefer "economy to expense," to choose accommodation in London that was both "moderate and cheap."[39] A further burden had been the stream of emigré Poles who arrived at Harborne with letters of introduction, most of which urged that he "do" something for them — doubtless few were disappointed. As a result of these handicaps and the failure of a number of business enterprises including the cotton mill in France, he had been unable to accumulate any capital. For a new life in Canada, money was essential. He therefore approached his eldest brother, George, anticipating a cash settlement for his share of his father's estate.

When Matthias Attwood died on 24 November 1836, George was made the residuary legatee and devisee of all his estates. The acquisition of coal and iron businesses by the father and the varied activities of his sons had been financed by the two banks in which he was a partner. George had been instructed to liquidate debts by the sale of those enterprises but had disobeyed these instructions. The London obligations had been covered only through further loans from the Birmingham branch upon the security of the family estates. It seems clear that in 1842 Thomas Attwood approached the bank expecting to find the books balanced and the steel mill and other industries operating at a profit. The fact that his brother had adopted a more affluent style of life since their father's death supported that conclusion. Due to his parliamentary duties Thomas had not found time to examine the state of the family's affairs personally. Upon inquiry he discovered that the majority of their enterprises were operating at a loss and only frequent unsecured interest-free loans kept them in production at all.

Attwood was crushed. Instead of finding credit he had discovered liability. Debts stood to his name; the sum of £12,286.10s.3d., which he had acquired as part of earlier profit distribution, was listed as recoverable asset. At once the plans to emigrate were abandoned.[40] With the limited means at his disposal repayment of what was now booked as a loan was out of the question. His only alternative was an arrangement with his friends and partners whereby he withdrew from the bank and gave up all claims to a share of the family holdings. In return the debt was to be written off. Nine years after his death, when those who had been privy to the agreement were also dead, Thomas Attwood's name was lumped with that of his brother George and covered with unjust abuse. Unfortunately, the debt had been left on the books, although it is almost certain that he had been given to understand that it had been buried. He told his children that "he owed the bank nothing,"[41] an improbable assertion if he had known that future events were likely to prove otherwise. The answer to this conundrum can probably be unearthed in the delinquency of his brother George. It later became known that he had mismanaged his own affairs and those of the bank. George had needed to list every "asset" whether recoverable or not in order to balance the books.[42]

Attwood, another dream unfulfilled, was obliged to live on at Grove House with two daughters, Angela and Rosabel, the children of the elder girl, three dogs, a macaw, and a cockatoo. Almost totally withdrawn from life in Birmingham, his time was occupied with an old stand-by, letter-writing. The *Times, Morning Post, Morning Herald, Circular to Bankers,* and Lord Palmerston among others received further bulletins on the state of the economy and the Attwoodian cure. To ensure publication Attwood used his strategically located son, Algernon, to hawk the letters from newspaper to newspaper.[43] The only planned amusement was the spending of part of each "season" in lodgings in London to be with old friends and to watch Parliament.

Old colleagues, many of whom had connections with Birmingham's town council, were told to forget him. The "old man" was tired. They listened and obeyed but they were sceptical. No matter how much he protested they knew that he had not given up hope of seeing the monetary system reformed. If the right circumstances came about, would he be able to resist a call to arms? His friends understood him better, perhaps, than he did himself. On several occasions they sought to catch his interest. When the Birmingham police bill threatened in July, they had some success; perhaps because he had begun the opposition to it as his last act as an MP. A series of all-party petitions was sent to London and on one of his visits to the metropolis he spent some time lobbying on its behalf.[44] He quickly tired of the exercise, but friends were pleased, nevertheless; at least he had been drawn back into the town's affairs.

The winter of 1842–3 was hard and strikes and other forms of confrontation did little to lighten the gloom. Consequently, in the summer of 1843, he was tempted by simmering provincial discontent, particularly in Ireland and Wales, to make one final assault on entrenched opinion. The *Birmingham Journal* on 15 July contained a notice of a rumour abroad in the town to the effect that Attwood was about to come out of retirement to lead a great popular movement which would concentrate upon a single object in the "interests of all and opposed to the interests of none."[45]

Attwood plotted with a number of associates, including T.C. Salt, to produce a "spontaneous" demand that he "return" to lead a popular movement; a demand to which in good conscience he must respond positively. The low point reached by the economy during the past winter promised to provide the springboard. For two months all went well. Meetings in a number of wards expressed their collective delight at the news and tentatively endorsed Attwood's plan whatever it might be. Old friends whose help had been spurned for many years rallied to his call. Richard Spooner, supported by George Attwood, led a middle-class oriented group in a discussion on the state of the country.[46] A general meeting, held on 29 September, prepared a carefully worded requisition and a deputation was appointed to present it. Fifteen thousand signed the document in a few hours. The next day the deputation noisily tramped to Harborne to solicit his help. Graciously he consented to lead.[47]

The groundwork done, his task was now to translate talk into action. In the end that was to prove impossible. Difficulties and dissension inevitably appeared, much as they had done in 1838. The Chartists had been meeting in Birmingham to discuss the question of land reform. Upon hearing of his resolve to recommence political agitation many of their supporters had signed the requisition but they also sent a deputation to call upon him to urge that he adopt the People's Charter. He was horrified. Memories of their "betrayal" in 1839 were undimmed. Salt warned him to be careful. Their rank and file must be part of his movement if it were to have a chance of success. So he tempered his anger with an attempt at reasonableness, and refused their recommendation ostensibly on the same grounds that he had split from them in 1839 – their propensity to violence and advocacy of the "unconstitutional" equal electoral districts provision. To be sure that they understood, however, he explained what he thought was his role in the new movement: "I was in no want of advice; that, if I interfered at all in any public movement it would be my duty to teach and to guide, and not be taught and guided."[48]

The episode illustrated the dilemma that he had faced many times. To win currency reform a broad, national coalition was essential. Yet such a coalition could not be formed under the banner of currency reform. Unfortunately, the choice of any single issue or group of issues behind which his economic proposals could be concealed would, on this occasion, similarly prevent genuine consensus. His program would thus have to be very different from that of the Chartists or indeed any other current pressure group.[49] When the actual "Plan" was unveiled on 26 October the language was deliberately vague. Some national newspapers took it seriously, probably out of respect for its author and the continuing Chartist agitation. The *Times* devoted several leaders to a careful analysis and reached the predictable conclusion that the "Plan" was merely a cover for Attwood's currency schemes.[50] Reactions closer to home were, however, more important. The sponsors were disappointed. Even the editor of the normally sympathetic *Journal* damned it with faint praise.

Two further meetings were held on 13 and 16 November to consider the future, but enthusiasm was fading. The working classes were alienated by the disavowal of their brand of reform and Attwood's declared intention to rely upon the electors and richer classes who "can influence Parliament."[51] The fact that the latter had the wealth to defray the necessary expenses of the movement, given his own impoverishment, must have been a significant factor in this spiritless decision. Those at whom he aimed his appeal were unimpressed. His contention that the time was now right for such a movement was categorically denied by some.[52] Soon Attwood's supporters had all but deserted him for more fruitful endeavours and he subsided unnoticed into the comfortable but deadening world of the Grove. Only the occasional published letter generated a little excitement. As a Birmingham satirist put it: "soon, soon, the gorgeous schemes decay, Attwood like Jones has had his day."

The national career of Thomas Attwood was finally over and he recognized that fact. Despair compounded by the insecurity of his financial position eroded the last vestiges of his treasured independence and he abandoned one of the principles of a lifetime – he wrote a very private letter to Peel requesting political patronage:

> I am perfectly sensible that I have no claims whatever on you. But my recollection of the friendship with which your venerated father was pleased to honour me, and my sense of the kind consideration, which, although a political opponent, I have always experienced at your hands, induce me to write this letter, for the purpose of respectfully saying, that if you should possibly deem it consistent with your duty to recommend me to some Foreign Appointment, under any Department of the Government, in which you might think my integrity and capacity would be useful, I will take that you shall never have cause to regret any recommendation.[53]

It was the letter of a proud man driven upon hard times and Peel replied gently. The supplication was refused with regret on the ground that "I really have not the power."[54] It was a half-truth. Such positions were reserved for favoured candidates. But the reputation acquired by Attwood over the previous thirteen years prevented concession. Not even Peel's good offices could have overcome the enmity of the prime minister's Tory colleagues toward the Birmingham "mono-maniac." Shortly after this last hope for useful employment was destroyed Attwood was afflicted by what Wakefield described as "the first symptoms of Paralysis Agitans," probably Parkinson's disease.[55]

In the spring of 1844 Attwood's health was still reasonably good and he continued to read everything about the economy that he could find. On 24 May the *Morning Post* printed his latest thoughts on the subject of the currency, "What is the Pound Sterling." More importantly, on 30 June, Attwood at the age of sixty married again. His second wife was Elizabeth Grice, the only daughter of Joseph Grice of Handsworth Hall, near Birmingham. The ceremony was held at St John's Parish Church in Paddington. Their union was one of convenience. As we have seen, since his first wife had died his two daughters had cared for him, but the elder, Angela, was at long last leaving for New Zealand, and the younger, Rosabel, might conceivably marry and also depart. The Grices had been friends of the Attwoods for many years and Elizabeth happily accepted the arrangement.[56] The Grice family were not poor so that in addition to the settlement of the question of companionship, the financial problems were partially resolved. Nevertheless there was not much spare cash. When Benjamin Hadley, an old friend and fellow ex-councillor, begged for financial help from South Africa, Attwood had to refuse, although it distressed him to do so.[57]

The newly-weds departed for their honeymoon in Belgium and Germany, presumably to visit the famous health spas. It was the first time he had journeyed to the continent since his business trip to France twenty years earlier. His interpretation of what he saw did not, however, change. The people in these nations were both prosperous and free: "not like the Irish and the English who are slaves."[58] Upon their return they stayed only a short time in Harborne, moving on to the resort town of Scarborough on the Yorkshire coast. There they resided in a small house called Grove Villa overlooking the sea. At this time he was still strong enough to take walks across the north sands to Selby Mill and back.[59]

Occasionally Attwood was consulted by his friends. One old Political Union colleague, John Betts, asked him to return to Birmingham for a meeting on the subject of Corn Law repeal. He declined the invitation; this time his retirement from active agitation was quite final.[60] Nevertheless, he wrote a carefully reasoned letter signifying his support for their objectives: "discord between the *oppressing* classes at last gives hope to the oppressed classes." The letter was printed in the *Birmingham Journal* and at the meeting to discuss the Corn Laws three cheers were given for Attwood.[61] He had not been totally forgotten. In 1846 the Attwoods moved to York and lived in an old house close to Micklegate Bar. In the autumn they continued their tour of the north and chose another renowned spa, Higher Harrogate, for their winter quarters. Eventually the allure of home became too strong and early in 1847 they returned to the environs of Birmingham. There they lived quietly at Fern Lodge on the Heathfield Road, Handsworth. Visitors were few but some, including General Bem, soon to be famous for his exploits in Hungary, had fascinating tales to tell.[62]

Attwood appeared in public only once more before his death. It was perhaps fitting that this appearance provoked almost as much controversy as had his earlier activities. At the election for North Warwickshire in 1847 he voted for the two Conservatives, Newdegate and his own lifelong friend Richard Spooner.[63] By so doing he openly abandoned his Political Union associates who supported the Whig/Radical candidates.[64] His choice was immediately placarded by Conservatives as a great triumph for their cause. The Radicals attributed it to a failing of his mental powers. This latter contention cannot be accepted. He was continuing his correspondence with other currency advocates at this time to their apparent satisfaction.[65] Moreover, in letters published in the *Morning*

Post his old ideas were set forth in his usual style. Indeed, he added a further element to his analysis of the theory of money by shrewdly pointing to the multiplier effect of the "Railway mania" on the circulation.[66]

Attwood's own explanation of his vote was equally unsatisfactory. He said that he would not have considered the Conservative candidates as members for the borough but for the county they were eminently suitable. Given his oft-stated objective for the reform movement – the creation of a House of Commons responsive to the needs of the manufacturing interest – the constituency for which the members were elected was plainly irrelevant, although it must be admitted that he also favoured balance. Attwood's support for his lifelong friend, partner, and fellow currency advocate, Spooner, required no explanation. There had been disagreements, particularly in 1841 when the Loyal and Constitutional Association, led in part by Spooner, had opposed the plans to erect a statue of Attwood. Spooner had been very hurt by an angry letter from his friend. The quarrel had been patched up and Spooner had been an eager co-worker in the movement in 1843. They had lived in close proximity for too many years, even in London where Spooner's house was only a few doors away, for enmity to last.

The choice of Newdegate might be considered odd, although he was the sitting member, having been first elected in 1843. However, Attwood's political sympathies had long followed an erratic course. In old age he had settled firmly upon a conspiracy theory to explain the lack of action by successive governments and the lack of interest of the opposition regarding the gold standard: "I had not devil enough in my composition 30 years ago, to enable me to discover that it was *guilt*, and not *ignorance*, which we Currency Men have had to contend with. The Members of the Government and all the public men always knew that the tale of '4 percent' was a lie; but it suited their purpose to support it."[67] Disillusioned and bitter, he had returned to the kind of blanket indictment of those who administered the affairs of the nation which he had favoured in the first flush of idealistic youth. Only catastrophe would bring about the desired changes in attitude. On political questions he did, however, allow that not all his criticism had been valid. Given such views, the choice of Newdegate may simply have been based on personality and a desire to demonstrate that he felt an obligation to no one.

Only two further letters on the subject of money, as far as can be ascertained, were written before Attwood completely succumbed to the disease which was to incapacitate him for the last seven years of his life.[68] In both Attwood applied the reasoning and marshalled the facts which had become almost a trademark of his argument. The Bank Charter Act of 1844 and the other fiscal measures adopted during the previous fifteen years were ignored. Lord George Bentinck was told to consider "the present crisis" in the light of that of 1825, some twenty-two years earlier."[69] G.F. Muntz was asked to introduce three resolutions virtually identical to those submitted for the consideration of Davenport in 1822 and similar in object to some of his own questions in the House in 1834.[70] Clearly, whereas his understanding of the nature of each successive crisis had been sharpened by experience, his conception of the underlying principles had undergone no modification since the "great act of confiscation" in 1819.

In July 1848 the Attwoods moved from Handsworth to the village of Allesley, where he took a pretty stone house near the church. But now physical deterioration proceeded rapidly. Within twelve months he became "a thin, wasted and decrepit old man."[71] Nature walks became impossible. Wakefield sadly recalled that "Long before I left him his hand shook so much that he was scarcely able to raise glass of wine to his lips."[72] By 1854 he was a mere wreck of his former self, unable to shake hands. Nevertheless, he lingered for two more years, witnessed the deaths of this two elder brothers and his eldest son, and the marriages of Algernon in 1853 and Rosabel in 1855.[73] Occasional visits to Umberslade Hall where Dr Johnson operated a water-cure establishment offered temporary ease, but these last few years were very hard. Elizabeth struggled to keep him entertained but it was not easy. Christmas was usually a cheerful occasion spent roasting oysters on the eve and with a visit to the bell-ringers. Occasionally at parties he would repeat in his best Newhall Hill voice some lines from Hamlet. Eventually he became too weak even for that.

In October 1855 he made his last move, to Ellerslie, Great Malvern, where Dr Johnson kept a small clinic. On 6 March 1856 he died. He was buried in Hanley Castle churchyard, where the gravestone is a simple slab of polished granite carrying only the dates of his birth and death and those of his first wife. He left only £1,500 to his widow.[74] His remaining assets were few: the silver cup presented by the workers to the young miracle-worker, a gold chain and medal presented by the Union, the oak box with gold trimmings given by the Corporation of London, and his old house in the Crescent which sold for £800. In a material sense it was not much after a lifetime of effort. Obituaries appeared in a number of newspapers including his old enemy, the *Times*. Sufficient time had elapsed for the political antagonisms roused by the mention of his name to have become less intense. A public meeting was held at the Town Hall on 21 April 1856.[75] Out of this debate developed the resolve to erect a statue in his honour. Eventually and with some difficulty £800 was raised, and the work commissioned.[76] It was unveiled on 7 June 1858; on the base was inscribed, "Thomas Attwood, Founder of the Birmingham Political Union." The marble statue, after two moves, now stands on the site of the house in which he lived when first married, The Larches, Sparkbrook, Birmingham. In 1983 the bicentenary of his birth was commemorated in the city. A plaque was placed on the site of his house in the Crescent and the city council cleaned up his statue and its surroundings.

The modest inscription that can be found upon the statue of Attwood erected in Birmingham paraphrased his own assessment of his achievement. Some time before his death he had written: "Whenever it shall please Almighty God to call me to the grave the greatest compliment which my friends can pay me will be to inscribe upon by tomb, "HERE LIES THE FOUNDER OF POLITICAL UNIONS."[77] With Attwood's departure from the political arena numerous tributes were offered by a variety of commentators to the same achievement. All alluded to the significance of his practical demonstration of the force of public opinion and the irresistibility of moral persuasion sensibly applied. Despite the failure of the second movement of the Birmingham Political Union, the Reform Act of 1832 remained as tangible and irrefutable evidence of accomplishment. Yet, at the same time, the acceptance of this evidence as the measure of his life's work denoted, for Attwood, failure and defeat. He never wavered from the point that his political labours were subsidiary to one object – the "rectification of the currency."[78] His test of the usefulness of political reform was primarily the adoption of a "sound" monetary policy. In this he had "toiled in vain," and at his death he seemed to expect that it would be forgotten. His pessimism and sense of failure were unjustified.

Attwood's merit as an economist had been obscured by the struggle for recognition in which he had been forced to engage. Yet, as Britain moved through a series of crises in the first half of the nineteenth century, their worst effects were often staved off by a last-minute application of palliatives previously suggested by Attwood.[79] His analysis, although apparently unheeded, was often proved accurate. Strip Attwood's work of its superfluous language, and one is left with an explanation of banking and the nature of currency together with an extrapolation of business behaviour from the Birmingham model which entitle him to respect within the field of political economy.

Attwood's defeat in 1839 stemmed from his inability to recognize the diverging patterns of protest of the Victorian era – not from his quality as an economist. The original problems that let to his complaints remained unresolved. Thus, despite the withdrawal of its founder, a recognizable school of economic thought which took many of its basic precepts from his work continued to exist in Birmingham.[80] It avoided a political orientation and operated as a pressure group, in the style of Attwood's own efforts before 1829, rather than as part of a general movement. The part played by the "school" in the Bank Act debate of 1844 attested to the continued strength of Attwood's thesis in its new guise.

Slowly, the ideas themselves came to permeate all aspects of both theoretical and institutional deliberation upon the subject of money. Attwood's conception of a managed currency as a positive aid to economic growth was the precursor of twentieth-century monetary doctrine. Keynes may never have read any of Attwood's pamphlets, but the sources he did use undoubtedly owed a measure of inspiration to the Birmingham banker.[81] Above all else, both Attwood and the school he founded were indefatigable propagandists. Although the changes they had sought had not materialized in statute form, an intellectual accommodation had been made and Attwood's long campaign had not been, as he believed, "in vain."

Given the evidence available to Attwood, however, his choice of epitaph was not unreasonable. He had never regarded the adoption of his prescription for economic distress as an end in itself. His recommendations were intended to secure the prosaic "bread, beer, and meat" platform of prosperity. Cabinet inertia and recalcitrance in the face of need had been the stimulus for his initial onslaught on orthodoxy. The failure to win a change in policy from those with power spurred the movement to restructure the legislature. The nature of Attwood's philosophy therefore depended upon a socio-economic concept of the nation at large in which it was the duty of the governing body to consider the welfare of all sections of the community and to act with justice and humanity. The Birmingham Political Union had been the most visibly successful instrument designed by Attwood to win his argument. Thus in the proposed epitaph he had singled out one element of his radicalism instead of another. Only within his personal scale of priorities can either one be said to be subsidiary.

Each stage of Attwood's career illustrated further facets of an unorthodox reading of the social, economic, and political events of the day. The radicalism he embraced changed over time, in concert with the disappointments he suffered and the exigencies of the moment. His public life spanned those decades when Britain was changing in character at an unprecedented rate. Attwood's career in large measure reflected this development and laid particular emphasis upon the Birmingham experience.

Notwithstanding the movement in his philosophy, both temporal and linear, there were identifiable common factors in Attwood's radicalism. Although in 1812 he acted only as a spokesman for one sector of the economy, the letters Attwood then wrote to Lord Liverpool warning of the danger to the crown if public opinion were not heeded clearly contain the rudiments of the Birmingham Political Union. Similarly his analyses of parliamentary failure in those years differ only marginally from the angry speeches directed at both sides of the House in 1838. In each instance, Attwood looked to the industrial centres to provide the direction and leadership which he considered was so clearly absent from Westminster.

Attwood had decided in 1817 that the government did not operate on principles of "eternal and immutable justice,"[82] and within two years he had virtually conditioned himself to equate cabinet policy with incompetence. That he did not become identified with the radical reformers prior to 1829 can be attributed to his peculiar sense of individualism combined with more than a touch of arrogance.[83] Only when he came to recognize the inability of the individual to affect national policy did Attwood accept the logic of his position and seek the enfranchisement of the people for whom he professed to speak. As Rev. Charles Foster astutely recognized: "He knew the people – he felt their wrongs, ... [he] became their head and their heart and their hand."[84]

Thomas Attwood was indisputably a radical, but his radicalism was that of the middle classes in the new industrial provinces. He was a radical because the questions he asked and the answers he provided differed from those of the established order. His economic gospel favoured the urban manufacturing interest over the commercial, financial, and agricultural sectors. Politically, his program was designed to secure the accommodation of that interest within the framework of the constitution. Attwood's inspiration came from Birmingham, and he served her with "desperate fidelity."[85] In return the town became his willing disciple. Neither had real cause for regret.

NOTES

INTRODUCTION

1 W.L. Burn, *The Age of Equipoise* (London: Allen and Unwin 1964), 19.
2 D. Ricardo, *The High Price of Bullion: A Proof of the Depreciation of Bank Notes* (London: J. Murray 1810), 45–50.
3 1 *Hansard*, 19, 7 May 1811, c. 986–1011; E. Cannan, *The Paper Pound, 1797–1831* (London: King 1919), containing a reprint of the Bullion committee's report.
4 R. Southey, "Parliamentary Reform," *Quarterly Review* 16 (October 1816): 260.
5 A. Briggs, "The Social Structure and Politics in Birmingham and Lyons (1825–48)," *British Journal of Sociology* 1 (1950): 67–80; "Thomas Attwood and the Economic Background of the Birmingham Political Union," *Cambridge Historical Journal* 9 (1948): 190–216.
6 D. Ricardo, *The Works and Correspondence of David Ricardo*, ed. P. Sraffa, 10 vols. (Cambridge: Royal Historical Society 1951–5), 5: 384–5.
7 2 *Hansard*, 5, 19 April 1821, c. 96; H. Thornton, *An Enquiry into the Nature and Effects of the Paper Credit of Great Britain* (London: J. Hatchard 1802). This book was one of Attwood's favourite studies of economic theory.
8 2 *Hansard*, 6, 11 February 1822, c. 252; speech of H. Brougham.
9 T. Raikes, *A Portion of the Journal Kept by Thomas Raikes, 1831–1847*, 2 vols., 2nd ed. (London: Longman, Brown, Green and Longman 1856), 1: 34–5.
10 The expression was first used in an editorial by the *Times*, 4 October 1831.
11 E.G. Edwards, *Personal Recollections of Birmingham and Birmingham Men* (Birmingham: Midland Educational Trading Company 1877), 60.
12 T. Raikes, *Private Correspondence with the Duke of Wellington and other*

Distinguished Contemporaries, ed. H. Raikes, 2 vols. (London: Richard Bentley 1861), 1: 34–5, reporting a remark made by the duke of R[utland] to Lord W[harncliffe].

CHAPTER ONE

1 Eleven children were born, of whom ten survived: Mary, b. 17 April 1776, d. 14 February 1777; George, b. 19 December 1777, d. 24 May 1854; Matthias, b. 24 November 1779, d. 11 November 1851; Mary Ann, b. 14 October 1781, d. 29 July 1872; Thomas, b. 6 October 1783, d. 6 March 1856; James Henry, b. 25 July 1785, d. 14 July 1865; Susanna, b. 6 November 1787, d. 29 October 1819; Edward, b. 22 February 1789, d. 19 October 1866; Charles, b. 25 January 1791, d. 24 February 1875; Rachel Maria, b. 26 April 1792, d. 9 August 1881; Benjamin, b. 31 July 1794, d. 22 November 1874. C.M. Wakefield, *The Life of Thomas Attwood* (London: Harrison and Sons 1885), 2.
2 J. Robinson, *The Attwood Family* (Sunderland: by author 1903), 5–6. The Attwoods had a distinguished lineage, which included a Dudley and a Plantagenet. The original surname, later anglicized, was De Bois, reflected in one of the given names of Thomas Attwood's eldest son, George de Bosco.
3 The estate was purchased in 1750. Wakefield, *Attwood,* 7. George Attwood had been born at Haden Cross in 1720 or 1721.
4 Family Estate Papers contained in a trunk at Lloyds Bank, Birmingham.
5 *Birmingham Commercial Herald,* 5 June 1809. This issue contained notice of the dissolution of the partnership.
6 *Pye's Directory of Birmingham,* 1788 edition, does not include the Adelphi whereas that of 1797 does.
7 B.L. Johnson, "The Charcoal Iron Industry of the West Midlands" (MA thesis, University of Birmingham, 1951). The Spooners also owned a farm.
8 George Attwood, Jr, Matthias's eldest son, joined the Birmingham office after graduation from Oxford University. He was followed by his brother Matthias, Jr, later sent to London when a branch was opened there in 1801. Thomas, the third male offspring, and Richard Spooner, one of Isaac's ten children, were also added to the complement in Birmingham. Of the four remaining sons of Matthias, three, Charles, Edward, and Benjamin, moved to the North-East and were established by their father in the soap and glassmaking industries. The fourth, James, became a merchant dealing with Russia and spent much of his life in that country.

9 *Gentleman's Magazine* 191 (February 1852), obituary of Matthias Attwood, Jr.
10 *English Law Reports*, House of Lords 7, Clarke and Finnelly, vols. 4–7, Appeal from the Court of Exchequer in Equity, 664–89. The division of George Attwood's estate meant that James received most of the coal and iron holdings while Matthias gained the banks.
11 Leasowes cost £20,000 and was kept in the family until 1865 when it had to be sold to cover a portion of their debts when the bank failed. A bridge was built over the Stour by Matthias Attwood to connect the two parts of the estate.
12 The figure was placed upon the holdings by William Marshall, a partner in the bank at the time, during the investigation of the affairs of Attwoods & Spooner following the death of George in 1854.
13 Wakefield, *Attwood*, 2.
14 W.C. Aitken, "Brass and Brass Manufacture," in *Birmingham and the Midland Hardware Districts*, ed. S. Timmins (London: Robert Hardwick 1866), 328.
15 *Birmingham Journal*, 8 March 1856.
16 Wakefield, *Attwood*, 6; *Birmingham Journal*, 8 March 1856.
17 George Attwood, reputedly the "handsomest man in Oxford," was a student at University College. He matriculated on 2 April 1794, received his BA in 1798 and MA 22 May 1802.
18 Edwards, *Personal Recollections*, 50. The fact that he was deaf did not help his reputation. A request for a statement to be repeated is often attributed by the more fortunate to stupidity rather than deafness.
19 G. Mander, *The History of Wolverhampton Grammar School* (Wolverhampton: n.p. 1913), 203–10.
20 Wakefield, *Attwood*, 7.
21 T.S. Ashton, *Iron and Steel in the Industrial Revolution*, 2nd ed. (Manchester: University Press 1924), 227–9; P.L. Cottrell, *Industrial Finance 1830–1914: The Finance and Organisation of English Manufacturing Industry* (London: Methuen 1980), 15; L. Pressnell, *Country Banking in the Industrial Revolution (Oxford: Clarendon Press 1956)*, 291.
22 Bank of England Letter Books (hereinafter Letter Books), 28 November 1831.
23 Ibid., 27 February 1832. For a detailed analysis of banking practice in Birmingham, see D.J. Moss, "The Bank of England and the Country Banks: Birmingham 1827–33," *Economic History Review* 34 (November 1981): 540–53.
24 Estate Papers, Lloyds Bank, Birmingham.
25 J. Langford, *Century of Birmingham Life*, 2 vols. (Birmingham: Osborne 1868), 1: 311.

26 Aitken, "Brass," 359.
27 Edwards, *Personal Recollections*, 47.
28 Letter Books, 29 June 1827.
29 W.C. Gill and A. Briggs, *A History of Birmingham*, 2 vols. (London: Oxford University Press 1952), 1: 92.
30 Langford, *Century*, 1: 1–2; R.B. Rose, "The Priestley Riots of 1791," *Past and Present* 18 (1960), 68–88.
31 *Birmingham Journal*, 9 April 1832.
32 Anon., *A Brief History of Birmingham* (Birmingham: n.p. 1797), 58.
33 Langford, *Century*, 1: 105–7. Relief measures continued to be needed throughout the winter. *Morning Chronicle*, 6 January 1801.
34 Edwards, *Personal Recollections*, 52.
35 Attwood Papers, 28 June 1808, T. Attwood to Elizabeth Attwood. The papers are held privately by Mrs Priscilla Mitchell, Earl's Court, London, and Totnes, Devon. Further information about banking practice in the midlands can be found in *Report from the Select Committee to Inquire into the State of the Bank of England*, House of Lords Papers, 1819, 111, Q. 12–13.
36 Attwood Papers, 28 August 1806, T. Attwood to Elizabeth Carless.
37 Wakefield, *Attwood*, 381.
38 *Daily Mail*, 17 December 1879, Birmingham Reminiscences; Robinson, *Attwood Family*, 81–3; Wakefield, *Attwood*, 17–18. Elizabeth was born in 1784.
39 Wakefield, *Attwood*, 9.
40 Langford, *Century*, 1: 178–81. R.R. Dozier outlines the background to this government-sponsored but privately funded militia in *For King, Constitution and Country: English Loyalists and the French Revolution* (Lexington: University of Kentucky Press 1983), 133–71.
41 Attwood Papers, 2 June 1804, T. Attwood to Elizabeth Carless.
42 Wakefield, *Attwood*, 10.
43 Ibid., 12; Attwood Papers, 9 June 1805, T. Attwood to Elizabeth Carless; Langford, *Century*, 2: 240–1.
44 The resignation took effect on 8 March 1805.
45 Attwood Papers, April, 1805, T. Attwood to Elizabeth Carless.
46 Wakefield, *Attwood*, 17.
47 Wakefield, *Attwood*, 19; Attwood Papers, 3 February 1807 and an undated letter, both to Elizabeth Attwood. Western became a good friend of the Attwoods and was a fellow currency zealot.
48 Attwoods & Spooner's Cash Book, Lloyds Bank, Birmingham.
49 R.B. Prosser, *Birmingham Inventors and Inventions* (Birmingham: n.p. 1881), 191.
50 Ibid., 88.
51 Ibid., 184.
52 Wakefield, *Attwood*, 21.

CHAPTER TWO

1 One of the first tasks of Attwood as high bailiff had been to dispatch a petition to the House of Commons in November to protest the high price of grain. *Aris' Birmingham Gazette*, 27 January 1812.
2 Langford, *Century*, 1: 224–5.
3 A Commercial Committee had been founded in 1783 to monitor government taxation policy and to guard "public interest," but its meetings had been infrequent. Deputations had waited on the prime minister in 1786 and again in 1796 with little success. The committee became inactive after 1798. G.H. Wright, *Chronicles of the Birmingham Chamber of Commerce 1813–1913* (Birmingham: Chamber of Commerce 1913), 11–47.
4 *Aris' Birmingham Gazette*, 6 June 1808.
5 Their perception of the growth of executive power was undoubtedly well-founded. A.D. Harvey, *Britain in the Nineteenth Century* (London: Batsford 1978), 334–7; C. Emsley, *British Society and the French Wars 1793–1815* (London: Macmillan 1979).
6 F. Crouzet, *L'Economique Britannique et le Blocus Continental (1806–13)*, 2 vols. (Paris: Presses Universitaires de France 1958), 2: 563–640.
7 The London papers supported this view and reported editorials elsewhere, *Times*, 21 December 1811, 17 April 1812; *Sun*, 5 March 1812; *Morning Post*, 23 March 1812; *Courier*, 29 February and 3 March 1812.
8 *Morning Chronicle*, 29 January 1812; H. Brougham, *Memoirs of the Life and Times of Lord Brougham*, 3 vols. (London: W. Blackwood and Sons 1871), 2: 11–13.
9 Gill and Briggs, *Birmingham*, 2: 115. The association of Spooner with this group is rather surprising in that they were largely liberal dissenters, and identified with the "Friends of Peace" movement. J.F. Cookson, *The Friends of Peace: War Liberalism in England, 1793–1815* (Cambridge: University Press 1982), 215–37. This alliance identified the degree of Spooner's radicalism at this time.
10 *Liverpool Mercury*, 28 February 1812. A letter from Birmingham, signed "Mentor," reported a petition then in circulation with approximately 50,000 signatures.
11 *Staffordshire Advertiser*, 7 March 1812.
12 *Liverpool Mercury*, 20 February 1812. There was a note of personal animus towards Brougham in this decision.
13 *A Report of the Meeting held at the Royal Hotel, Birmingham, 31 March 1812, on the subject of the Orders in Council. And a letter to the Editor of the Midland Chronicle on the same subject. Also an Appendix containing the Speech of Thomas Attwood Esq. on the East Indian monopoly with the Resolutions of the Meeting held March 4th 1812* (Birmingham: n.p. 1812), 3–4.

14 C.H. Phillips, *The East India Company 1784–1834*, (Manchester: University Press 1940), 181; *A Report ... March 4th 1812*, 17.
15 Lord Valentia was an Irish peer. Sir George Staunton had accompanied Earl MacCartney and his own father on a journey to China to establish the embassy in 1797.
16 *A Report ... March 4th, 1812*, 17–20.
17 Attwood Papers, 28 April 1812, T. Attwood to Elizabeth Attwood.
18 *Liverpool Mercury* 20 March 1812. The editorial commended the Birmingham speakers for their opposition to the renewal of the charter but added that the supporting arguments of Attwood were erroneous. One month later the *Mercury* noticed a petition from Kingston upon Hull which specifically complained of the monopoly of the port of London and no more.
19 Ibid., 3 April 1812.
20 *A Report ... March 4th 1812*, 2–8. Spooner targeted the license system as representing the unfairness of the government's approach. This regulation allowed trade in certain commodities and by certain ships to continue irrespective of the Orders-in-Council. Forgery, corruption, and a black market network compounded the unfairness of the system.
21 *Midland Chronicle*, 3 April 1812; *Aris' Birmingham Gazette* 6 April 1812.
22 Attwood Papers, 6 April 1812, T. Attwood to Elizabeth Attwood.
23 Ibid., 10 and 28 April 1812, T. Attwood to Elizabeth Attwood.
24 Buckinghamshire had succeeded Melville in March. Between 1789 and 1794 he had been governor of Madras and at odds with the Court of Directors of the Company.
25 Charter Papers, 138, 25 April 1812; quoted by Phillips, *East India Company*, 182.
26 Attwood Papers, 24 April 1812, T. Attwood to Elizabeth Attwood.
27 Liverpool Papers, British Library, Add. Mss. 38410, f.87, 18 September 1812.
28 Wakefield, *Attwood*, 24.
29 Attwood Papers, 2 May, 1812, T. Attwood to Elizabeth Attwood.
30 *East India Debates*, 1 May 1812, quoted by Phillips, *East India Company*, 184.
31 Liverpool Papers, Add. Mss. 38410, f. 81, 9 May 1812.
32 Phillips, *East India Company*, 182, n. 3.
33 Wakefield, *Attwood*, 23; Liverpool Papers, Add. Mss. 38410, f.87, 18 September 1812.
34 *Courier*, 23 and 24 April 1812; *Leeds Mercury*, 25 April 1812.
35 *Royal Proclamation*, 21 April 1812.
36 *Parl. Papers*, 1812 (210), 111, "Minutes of Evidence taken before a Committee of the Whole House to whom it was referred to consider the several Petitions which have been presented to the House

in this Session of Parliament against the Orders-in-Council," Q. 2–15.
37 Cookson, *Friends of Peace*, 234.
38 *Parl. Papers*, 1812 (210), 111, "Minutes of Evidence ... Orders-in-Council," Q. 29, Evidence of T. Potts; Q. 43, evidence of J. Shaw; Q. 100, evidence of J. Scholefield.
39 *Times*, 9 May 1812.
40 *Morning Chronicle*, 8 May 1812.
41 Brougham discusses the delays and difficulties in detail. H. Brougham, *Memoirs*, 2: 13–21.
42 *Sun*, 17 June 1812.
43 *London Gazette*, 23 June 1812. There can be little doubt that the revocation was a tribute to the remarkable spirit of cooperation displayed by the most important manufacturing regions of the country. For a further analysis of the point, see Cookson, *The Friends of Peace*.
44 *Staffordshire Advertiser* 27 June and 11 July 1812; *Leeds Mercury*, 27 June 1812; *Felix Farley's Bristol Journal*, 9 May 1812; *Aris' Birmingham Gazette*, 29 June 1812.
45 *Aris' Birmingham Gazette*, 6 July 1812; *Leeds Mercury* 11 July 1812.
46 *Staffordshire Advertiser* 4 July 1812; *Liverpool Mercury*, 3 July 1812.
47 Edwards, *Personal Recollections*, 22.
48 Attwood Papers, 15 November 1838, T. Attwood to Elizabeth Attwood.
49 There had been a large number of meetings in May and June at the Public Office, chaired by the high bailiff, seeking means to relieve public distress.
50 One other matter of town improvement came in the same period – the bill for enlarging the powers of the Street Commissions was passed on 14 May. 52 Geo. 3 c.113. Attwood was made chairman of the new body.
51 *Courier*, 7 May 1822.
52 *Midland Chronicle*, 30 May 1812.
53 *Aris' Birmingham Gazette*, 22 June 1812.
54 Attwood Papers, Summer 1812.
55 He accepted the 128-ounce plate at a special dinner on his birthday, and was to count it one of the four great days of his life. The plate had been designed by Mr Lines, Sr, the founder of the Birmingham School for Art. Apart from the monetary value, 200 guineas, the piece was prized because it was the first presentation plate designed, modelled, and executed in the town. *Midland Counties Herald*, 13 March 1856.
56 *Aris' Birmingham Gazette*, 29 June 1812.
57 *Sun*, 12 May 1812, paid advertisement; *Morning Chronicle*, 22 May 1812, letter to the editor signed "A Birmingham Manufacturer."

58 Attwood Papers, 17 and 30 April 1812, T. Attwood to Elizabeth Attwood; *Liverpool Mercury*, 17 July 1812. At a second meeting to applaud the repeal of the Orders in August, the charges were repeated with even greater vehemence. *Morning Chronicle*, 11 August 1812.
59 *Sun*, 19 August 1812.
60 Liverpool Papers, Add. Mss. 38410 f.87, 18 September 1812.
61 Ibid., f.183, January 1813.
62 *Speech of Thomas Attwood, Esq. at the Town's Meeting against the Revival of the East India charter held at the Royal Hotel, Birmingham, Friday, January 8th, 1813* (Birmingham: O. and H. Smith 1813). A report of the whole meeting was given in the *Midland Chronicle*, 16 January 1813.
63 Attwood Papers, 11 February 1813, T. Attwood to Elizabeth Attwood.
64 Ibid., 15 February 1813, T. Attwood to Elizabeth Attwood.
65 Ibid., 19 February 1813, T. Attwood to Elizabeth Attwood.
66 Liverpool Papers, Add. Mss. 38410 f.116, 20 May 1813. Liverpool did promise to take Birmingham's interests into consideration.
67 Phillips, *East India Company*, 190. The request was made on 20 May.
68 1 *Hansard*, 26, 31 May 1813, c. 407.
69 Phillips, *East India Company*, 191–2.
70 For the contrary argument, see J. Money, *Experience and Identity: Birmingham and the West Midlands 1760–1800* (Manchester: University Press 1978).

CHAPTER THREE

1 *Cornish's Strangers' Guide through Birmingham* (Birmingham: Cornish Brothers 1849), 59.
2 Attwoods & Spooner's Cash Book.
3 Attwood Papers, 17 July 1815, T. Attwood to Elizabeth Attwood; *Birmingham Journal*, 1 April 1865. The estates were bought with bank money. In 1825 they were transferred to Richard Spooner for £20,000.
4 Ward, president of the Board of Trade in 1815, estimated that £4,500,000 had been spent in Birmingham since 1793 on the production of war materials. 1 *Hansard*, 36, 20 May 1817, c. 763. In the hand-made nail trade orders from the Admiralty had averaged 600 tons per annum and employed 50,000 workers.
5 W.O. Henderson, ed., *Industrial Britain under the Regency* (New York: F. Cass 1968), "T. Bodmer's Diary, 1816–17," 80–95.
6 T. Attwood, *A Second Letter to the Earl of Liverpool on the Bank Reports* (Birmingham 1819), 26–7; Attwoods & Spooner's Cash Book.

7 For a description of the political manoeuvring, see A. Mitchell, *The Whigs in Opposition* (London: Clarendon Press 1967) and Boyd Hilton, *Corn, Cash and Commerce* (Oxford: University Press 1978).
8 It had been agreed in 1811 that upon the conclusion of the war the gold standard would be reimposed. See R. Southey, "Parliamentary Reform," *Quarterly Review* 16 (October 1816): 260, for a contemporary view.
9 *Aris' Birmingham Gazette*, 13 March 1815.
10 Ibid., 13 January 1817; Wakefield, *Attwood*, 61. He did assist in the drafting of the petition.
11 Attwood did draw up a petition in 1816 to protest the practice of unproductive labour as a means of relieving the poor. It was left in public places and in a few days was signed by 17,000 people. Parliament chose to ignore it and thereby confirmed in Attwood's eyes its ineptitude. *Birmingham Journal*, 9 April 1816.
12 Attwood Papers, 30 May 1816, T. Attwood to Lord Liverpool. An earlier version of this section was published in D.J.Moss, "Banknotes versus Gold: The Monetary Theory of Thomas Attwood in His Early Writings, 1816-19," *History of Political Economy* 14 (1981): 19-38.
13 He was repeating an opinion common at the time. *Annals* 4 (1794): 266-9.
14 T. Attwood, *The Remedy; or, Thoughts on the Present Distresses*, 2nd ed. (Birmingham 1817), 5-7; *Observations on Currency, Population and Pauperism* (Birmingham 1818), 11. Other commentators had made the same observation and deplored deflationary policy that could only increase the wealth of the fundholder. Cf. J. Eyre, *A Letter to the Right Honourable Lord Rolle* (London: n.p. 1817), 17, J. Hoare, *Tracts on Our Present Monetary System* (London: n.p. 1814), and the views persistently expressed by William Cobbett in his *Political Register*.
15 *Prosperity Restored or Reflections on the Causes of Public Distress and on the only means of Relieving them* (Birmingham 1817), 43-4.
16 T. Attwood, *A Letter to the Right Honourable Nicholas Vansittart on the Creation of Money and on its Action Upon National Prosperity* (Birmingham 1817), 6.
17 *Observations*, 186; *Letter to Vansittart*, 83.
18 *Letter to Vansittart*, 86.
19 *Observations*, 74.
20 Ibid., 266.
21 *Prosperity*, 24-6.
22 *Prosperity*, 32; *Remedy*, 2nd ed., 67.
23 As an example he looked to the Clearing House technique whose

business he put at £4 million a day. *Remedy*, 2nd ed., 67. For a more detailed analysis see *Prosperity*, 32.
24 *Remedy*, 1st ed., 8; *Prosperity*, 126.
25 *Observations*, 229.
26 Ibid., 159. In his examination of the causes of the price during the war and its relationship to gold, Attwood correctly noted the additional strains placed on the bullion supply; strains created by foreign loans, the blockade, and the continental proclivity for hoarding. All increased demand and consequently the commodity price of gold. *Prosperity*, 65–6.
27 Ibid., 227 and 138, also *Letter to Vansittart*, 94.
28 Ibid., 226.
29 *Prosperity*, 194. Cf. H. Thornton, *An Enquiry into the Nature and Effects of the Paper Credit of Great Britain* (London: J. Hatchard 1802), 312.
30 *Prosperity*, 177.
31 *Remedy*, 2nd ed., 37.
32 *Prosperity*, 129.
33 Ibid., 61, 207.
34 *Letter to Vansittart*, 31.
35 *Remedy*, 1st ed., 10; *Observations*, 17; *Letter to Vansittart*, 27.
36 *Remedy*, 9.
37 *Prosperity*, 126; *Observations*, 192.
38 This theoretical analysis accurately described the course pursued by the Bank during the Napoleonic Wars. See the relevant chapters in E.V. Morgan, *The Theory and Practice of Central Banking 1793–1913*, new ed., (London: F. Cass 1965).
39 *Remedy*, 1st ed., 7.
40 He examined bullion market problems in his analysis of the depression, 1816–17. *Observations*, 153, 247; *Prosperity*, 167.
41 *Prosperity*, 40–1.
42 *Letter to Vansittart*, 69; *Prosperity*, 78. Attwood was willing to acknowledge that an "equitable adjustment of contracts," as promoted by Cobbett, Lord Stanhope, and others, would accomplish the same purpose but argued that currency augmentation would create less dislocation.
43 *Prosperity*, 165–6.
44 *Letter to Vansittart*, 69.
45 *Remedy*, 1st ed., 647; *Observations*, 153.
46 *Prosperity*, 40.
47 *Observations*, 162.
48 *Remedy*, 1st ed., 7; *Observations*, 154. On these points Attwood was broadly in agreement with Rev. T.R. Malthus, "Depreciation of the Currency," *Edinburgh Review* 17 (February 1811): 355.

49 *Observations*, 31; *Prosperity*, 163–4.
50 J. Law, *Money and Trade*, new ed. (Glasgow: n.p. 1750), 20–3.
51 Malthus, "Depreciation," 365.
52 G. Berkeley, *Complete Works*, ed. A.C. Fraser, 4 vols. (Oxford: Clarendon Press 1901), 4: 422–4; J. Bentham, "Proposal for the Circulation of a New Species of Paper Currency," in *Jeremy Bentham's Economic Writings*, ed. W. Stark (London: Allen and Unwin 1952–4), 2: 151–200; D. Stewart, *Collected Works of Dugdale Stewart*, ed. W. Hamilton, 11 vols. (Edinburgh: T. Constable 1954–60), 8: 397–8; M. Lauderdale, *An Inquiry into the Nature and Origin of Public Wealth*, ed. M. Paglin, 2nd ed. (New York: August M. Kelly 1962).
53 *Remedy*, 1st ed., 63; *Observations*, 152.
54 W.J. Copplestone, *Memoir of Edward Copplestone* (London: by author 1851), 85; *Observations*, 204.
55 *Prosperity*, 102.
56 *Observations*, 247.
57 *Remedy*, 2nd ed., 26.
58 D. Hume, *The Philosophical Works of David Hume*, ed. T.H. Green and T.H. Grose, 4 vols. (London: T.H. Green 1878), 1: 131–15, 365; J. Massie, *An Essay on the Growing Causes of the National Rate of Interest* (London: n.p. 1750), 136–8; D. Ricardo, *Reply to Mr. Bosanquet's Practical Observations on the Report of the Bullion Committee* (London: n.p. 1811), 45–50.
59 *Remedy*, 2nd ed., 50–4.
60 *Prosperity*, 129–35.
61 *Parl. Papers*, House of Commons, 1821 (668), 10. "Report from the Select Committee to whom the Several Petitions complaining of the Distressed State of the Agriculture was referred," Q. 252.
62 *Observations*, 200.
63 Ibid., 196–8.
64 *Prosperity*, 179–85.
65 *Letter to Vansittart*, 38–43, 101–3.
66 *Observations*, 174.
67 Ibid., 142.
68 Ibid., 214–15.
69 Ibid., 166–70.
70 Ibid., 224.

CHAPTER FOUR

1 M. Attwood, *Observations concerning the Distress of the Country* (London: T. Wilson 1817).
2 *Prosperity*, 139.

3 Langford, *Century*, 1: 338–9; 414–16; *Aris' Birmingham Gazette*, 4 November 1816. Edmonds, an acquaintance of Attwood, organized a Hampden Club and held mass meetings on Newhall Hill.
4 *Prosperity*, 117.
5 Langford, *Century*, 1: 420–1.
6 *Aris' Birmingham Gazette*, 12 May 1817.
7 Ibid., 10 February 1817; Langford, *Century*, 1: 345.
8 Attwood Papers, 6 July 1818, T. Attwood to Elizabeth Attwood.
9 Ibid., 2 and 6 March 1817, T. Attwood to Elizabeth Attwood.
10 Attwood made a similar assessment of his success at the beginning of one of his letters to Young in 1818. The Exchequer expended an additional 15 million pounds sterling in 1817 and that, he claimed, added five times that amount to the "nominal national riches," scattering "life and contentment." *Observations*, 212–13.
11 Attwood Papers, 2 July 1818, T. Attwood to Elizabeth Attwood.
12 Ibid., 4 July 1818, T. Attwood to Elizabeth Attwood.
13 Ibid., 2 and 4 July 1818, second letters, T. Attwood to Elizabeth Attwood.
14 *Aris' Birmingham Gazette*, 23 August 1819.
15 Langford, *Century*, 1: 421; *Aris' Birmingham Gazette*, 19 July 1819.
16 *Aris' Birmingham Gazette*, 2 August 1819.
17 A subscription was raised in Birmingham to help relieve those injured. *Aris' Birmingham Gazette*, 27 September 1819.
18 Attwood Papers, 1 March 1819, T. Attwood to Elizabeth Attwood.
19 Ibid., 28 February 1819, T. Attwood to Elizabeth Attwood.
20 Ibid., 3 and 5 March 1819, T. Attwood to Elizabeth Attwood. Attwood's views on parliamentary reform at this time were quite unequivocal: it was so much drivel that distracted the Whigs from the real issue of the economy. The candidates were respectively J.C. Hobhouse and George Lamb.
21 *Parl. Papers*, House of Lords, 1819 (291), 111, "Select Committee to inquire into the State of the Bank of England," Q. 5–32.
22 Attwood Papers, 29 December 1843, T. Attwood to Elizabeth Attwood.
23 1 *Hansard*, 38, 18 May 1818, c. 764.
24 Peel had, in fact, voted against Horner's resolutions in 1810 (those based on the Bullion Report) but was soon won to the side of the resumptionists in 1819.
25 J.K. Horsefield, "The Bankers and the Bullionists in 1819," *Journal of Political Economy* 57 (October 1949), 442–8.
26 *Parl. Papers*, House of Lords, 1819 (291), 111, "Select Committee," Q. 27.
27 *Annual Register*, 1819, General History, 11.
28 *Parl., Papers*, House of Commons, 1819 (202), 111, "Report of Select

Committee appointed to inquire into the State of the Bank of England."
29 1 *Hansard*, 40, 20 May 1819, c. 683.
30 Ibid., c. 602, part of a written declaration by the directors of the Bank of England.
31 Ibid., 40, 25 May 1819, c. 778.
32 *Parl. Papers*, House of Commons, 1819 (202), 111, "Select Committee."
33 Wakefield, *Attwood*, 71; *Times*, 25 May 1819. The editor wrote a scathing attack on the enterprise.
34 T. Attwood, *A Letter to the Earl of Liverpool on the Reports of the Committees of the Two Houses of Parliament on the Question of the Bank Restriction Act* (Birmingham 1819), 3.
35 Ibid., 15. Two years before the act was due to expire the market price of bullion should be ascertained and a coinage created conforming to that price. These coins would be issued at the Bank's discretion. If this was done imaginatively, the public would quickly become accustomed to their use and when full resumption finally occurred it would not be known whether the act had expired or not. In a postscript he repeated the opinion expressed on other occasions: a circulation of £25 million secured by exchequer bills would adequately serve the community.
36 59 Geo. 3 c. 49; 1 *Hansard*, 40, 14 June 1819, c. 1154.
37 T. Attwood, *A Second Letter to the Earl of Liverpool on the Bank Reports as Occasioning the National Dangers and Distresses* (Birmingham 1819).
38 Ibid., 50.

CHAPTER FIVE

1 His brother George had signed a declaration of loyalty which promised to bring to justice writers of "seditious or inflammatory writings."
2 *Birmingham Chronicle*, 30 December 1820. Scholefield was a merchant in the American trade.
3 Ibid., 6 January 1820.
4 Sir John Sinclair (1754–1835) was a Scottish country gentleman and agricultural innovator. He had sat in Parliament almost continuously from 1780 to 1811 and had been the first chief clerk of the Board of Agriculture in 1786. He wrote extensively on economics and many of his works had been read by Attwood.
5 *Farmers' Journal*, 8 January, 16 December 1816.
6 2 *Hansard*, 1, 12 May 1820, c. 339 and c. 342.
7 Attwood Papers, 19 May 1820, T. Attwood to Elizabeth Attwood.
8 *Farmers' Journal*, 15 May 1820, letter signed "Beds."
9 Ibid., 30 May 1820, letter signed Z.A.

10 Attwood had tried every tactic to overcome this suspicion. He even claimed to have supported the Corn Law of 1815; a lie which even a most cursory reading of his early pamphlets would have demonstrated.
11 *Birmingham Chronicle*, 8 June 1820.
12 Ibid., 20 July 1820.
13 A. Briggs, "The Social Structure and Politics in Birmingham and Lyons (1825–48)," *British Journal of Sociology* 11 (March 1950): 67–80, and *Victorian Cities* (London: Oldhams 1963).
14 Attwood Papers, 27 August 1820, T. Attwood to Elizabeth Attwood.
15 *Birmingham Chronicle*, 19 October 1820. Resolutions of the town meeting held on 15 October. Wakefield misdates Spooner's election bid, placing it in 1822. Wakefield, *Attwood*, 86–7. The election was notable for the ill-feeling aroused and several pamphlets were written at its conclusion defending the various parties. One by an anonymous writer, Philo-Veritas, *An Attempt to Defend Mr. Spooner and his Supporters* (Birmingham: n.p. 1820) was quite bitter about the whole affair.
16 There is a retrospective description of this election in the *Birmingham Journal*, 26 November 1864.
17 *Birmingham Chronicle*, 9 November 1820.
18 Attwood Papers, 7 November 1820, T. Attwood to Elizabeth Attwood.
19 *Birmingham Chronicle*, 16 November 1820.
20 Langford, *Century*, 1: 318.
21 *Birmingham Chronicle*, 17 May 1821.
22 *Parl. Papers*, House of Commons, 1821 (668), 10, "Report from the Select Committee to whom the Several Petitions complaining of the Distressed State of Agriculture of the United Kingdom were referred."
23 Attwood Papers, 13 April 1821, T. Attwood to Richard Spooner.
24 A.J.B. Hilton, "The Economic Policies of the Tory Government, 1815–1830" (D. Phil. thesis, Oxford University, 1973), 139–40.
25 2 *Hansard*, 4, 8 February 1821, c. 535.
26 *Agriculturalist*, 2 January 1836, address of T. Attwood to the Central Agricultural Society.
27 Attwood's attempt to counter this ploy by having one of his old essays on agriculture read into the minutes was savagely brushed aside. Huskisson correctly saw that Attwood sought to set the agenda. *Agriculturalist*, 2 January 1836.
28 Attwood Papers, 11 April 1821, T. Attwood to Elizabeth Attwood.
29 Ibid., 13 April 1821, T. Attwood to Elizabeth Attwood.
30 Ibid., 15 April 1821, T. Attwood to Elizabeth Attwood.
31 Ibid., 16 April 1821, T. Attwood to Elizabeth Attwood.

32 Ibid., 21 April 1821, T. Attwood to Elizabeth Attwood.
33 W.R. Torrens, *The Life and Times of the Right Honourable Sir James R.G. Graham*, 2 vols. (London: Ottley and Company 1863), 1: 170–1. John Rooke lived near Wigton in Cumberland on a farm named Ake-head and was of a group known locally as "states-men." Proudly independent and careful small farmers holding their land under a fee system, they had been sinking ever deeper into debt since 1815. Rooke had fought to improve his farm with the latest scientific innovations, some of his own design, but it had been to little avail. His response had been to take the opposite tack from Webb Hall and favour a free trade in corn. From that it was only a small step to recognition of the inequity of the currency regulations and the ready acceptance of Attwood's arguments, expressed in the *Farmers' Journal*. Cruttwell of Derbyshire was a friend of longer duration, having begun his campaign for monetary reform at the same time as Attwood.
34 *Parl. Papers*, House of Commons, 1821 (668), 10, "Report ... Select Committee," Q. 295–6.
35 D. Ricardo, "Letters to Hutches Towser," 4 July 1821, quoted by F. Fetter, *Development of British Monetary Orthodoxy* (Cambridge: Harvard University Press 1965), 104.
36 *Parl. Papers*, House of Commons, 1821 (668), 10, "Report ... Select Committee," 27–8.
37 2 *Hansard*, 5, 19 April 1821, c. 96.
38 Ibid., c. 140.
39 Ibid., c. 141.
40 Ibid., 6, 11 February 1822, c. 253.
41 T. Attwood and Sir John Sinclair, *The Late Prosperity and the Present Adversity of the Country Explained; the Proper Remedies Considered, and the Comparative Merits of the English and Scottish Systems of Banking Discussed in a Correspondence between Sir John Sinclair and Mr. Thomas Attwood* (London 1826), 91.

CHAPTER SIX

1 English Law Reports, House of Lords, 7, Clarke and Finnelly, Appeal from Court of Exchequer in Equity (235–8), 686–7.
2 Attwood Papers, 21 April 1821, James Attwood to T. Attwood.
3 Hilton, "The Economic Policies," 152–7.
4 Cf. J. Wheatley, *An Essay on the Theory of Money and the Principles of Commerce* (London: T. Cadwell 1822), 126.
5 A letter to Brougham from Attwood had been dismissed rather unkindly. Attwood Papers, 23 February 1822.

6 *Observations*, 23.
7 Mitchell, *Whigs*, 167.
8 Bromley-Davenport Papers, John Rylands Library, 27 April 1822, T. Attwood to Edward Davenport. Davenport had begun to correspond with Attwood some months before; they found a common interest in the currency.
9 Ibid., 2 and 27 April 1822. Attwood was endeavouring to persuade Davenport to publish a pamphlet on the subject. Three years later it appeared, but the author preferred to remain anonymous. Anon., *The Corn Question, in a Letter Addressed to the Right Hon. W. Huskisson* (1825).
10 Hilton, "The Economic Policies," 177.
11 Attwood Papers, 9 and 12 May 1822, T. Attwood to Elizabeth Attwood.
12 Ibid., 12 May 1822, T. Attwood to Elizabeth Attwood.
13 Ibid., 14 May 1822, T. Attwood to Elizabeth Attwood.
14 Miscellaneous Manuscripts, 6 MP 5151, Patent applications, Rouen Record Office. It has not been possible to find what exactly was meant by a "second class" engine.
15 Attwood Papers, 21 May 1821, T. Attwood to Elizabeth Attwood, Bromley-Davenport Papers, 9 June 1822, T. Attwood to E. Davenport.
16 Bromley-Davenport Papers, 9 June 1822, T. Attwood to E. Davenport.
17 2 *Hansard*, 7, 12 June 1822, c. 965; c.f. *Prosperity*, 25–35.
18 R.G. Hawtrey, *A Century of Bank Rate*, 2nd ed. (London: Cass 1962), 4.
19 *Birmingham Chronicle*, 25 July 1822.
20 Ibid., 26 September 1822, "Opinion of M. Say on our Agricultural Distress," letter to Henry James, 31 July 1822.
21 *Farmers' Journal*, 9 December 1822.
22 Ibid., 19 August 1822. The letter was reprinted in the *Birmingham Journal* 16 July 1831.
23 *Farmers' Journal*, 2 September 1822. The term "Jew," Attwood emphasized, was a category; it was not meant to refer particularly to men of Jewish extraction but to the "frailties" commonly associated with the word.
24 Ibid., 25 November 1822. A more detailed analysis was given in his pamphlet *Mr. Attwood's Letter and Tables showing the Unjust Payment from the Landed to the Monied Interest by the Present System with the Ruin of the Landlord and Tenant* (Stamford: n.p. 1822).
25 *Parl. Papers*, 1833 (690), 6, "Select Committee on Manufacturers, Commerce and Shipping," Q. 4146.
26 L.H. Jenks, *The Migration of British Capital to 1875* (New York: A.A. Knopf 1927), 53. Glowing press reports persuaded even the aged and normally cautious Matthias Attwood, Sr, to participate. He

joined in the formation of a company with a nominal capital of £1 million to reopen some Mexican silver mines.
27 T. Attwood and Sir J. Sinclair, *The Late Prosperity*, Introduction.
28 D.J. Moss, "The Private Banks of Birmingham, 1800–1827," *Business History* 24 (1982), fig. 1, 87. Statistics in Attwoods & Spooner's Cash Book offer proof that Attwood did as he promised.
29 K.E. Richardson, "The Life and Times of Thomas Attwood" (PHD thesis, Nottingham, 1965), 233 ff.
30 Attwood Papers, 19 November 1822, T. Attwood to Elizabeth Attwood.
31 *Aris' Birmingham Gazette*, 15 September 1832.
32 Attwood Papers, 26 October 1824, T. Attwood to Elizabeth Attwood.
33 Wakefield, *Attwood*, 93.
34 *Birmingham Chronicle*, 17 June 1824.
35 Rail 886, 8, 14 January, 14 May, and 10 December, 1824, Public Record Office, Portugal Street.
36 *Aris' Birmingham Gazette*, 13 September 1824.
37 Ibid., 13 and 20 September 1824.
38 Bromley-Davenport Papers, 17 January 1825, T. Attwood to E. Davenport.
39 *Aris' Birmingham Gazette*, 20 December 1824.
40 Langford, *Century*, 1: 461.
41 Attwood Papers, 9 February 1825, T. Attwood to Elizabeth Attwood.
42 Ibid., 23 February 1825, T. Attwood to Elizabeth Attwood.
43 Ibid., 28 February and 5 March 1825, T. Attwood to Elizabeth Attwood.
44 *Aris' Birmingham Gazette*, 26 September 1825.
45 Ibid., 12 and 26 June 1826.
46 Ibid., 28 August 1826.
47 Richardson, "Life and Times," 237. Periodically someone would suggest that the plans be revived, but a railway between Liverpool and Birmingham did not become a reality until it was taken over by the experienced and powerful Liverpool merchants and shipowners. The railway was completed in June 1837 without the assistance of Thomas Attwood. As for the Birmingham to London line, through careful negotiation and the payment of large sums to landowners the bill was eventually released from committee and passed in 1833. George Stephenson & Sons were chosen as engineers and the capital was put at £2,500,000; a sum which illustrated clearly the serious underestimation of costs by Attwood and his friends. The line was completed in 1838.
48 *Aris' Birmingham Gazette*, 3 January 1825. The company was founded 6 December 1824.
49 Ibid., 14 February and 21 March 1825.
50 Ibid., 18 July 1831, letter to the editor, signed "B."

51 Ibid., 25 March and 3 October 1825.
52 Ibid., 21 February 1825.
53 Ibid., 4 April, 23 and 28 November 1825.
54 Attwood and Sinclair, *Late Prosperity*, 12.
55 Moss, "The Private Banks," 89–90.
56 *Birmingham Chronicle*, 3 February 1825.
57 *Annual Register* (1825), 20.
58 Sir J. Clapham, *The Bank of England*, 2 vols. (Cambridge: University Press 1944), 2: 95–6.
59 2 *Hansard*, 12, 25 March 1825, c. 1194–6.
60 Ibid., 13, 27 June 1825, c. 1386, speech of Hudson Gurney.
61 *Morning Chronicle*, 2 May 1825.
62 Ibid., 1 August 1825.
63 Ibid., 16 August 1825.
64 A.E. Feaveryear, *The Pound Sterling: A History of English Money* (Oxford: Clarendon Press 1931). For a further discussion of the crises see E.V. Morgan, *The Theory and Practice of Central Banking 1797–1912*, new ed. (London: F. Cass 1965), 75–80; L.S. Pressnell, *Country Banking in the Industrial Revolution*, (Oxford: Clarendon Press 1956), 482–99; F.W. Fetter, *Development of British Monetary Orthodoxy 1797–1875* (Cambridge: Harvard University Press 1965), 111–25; and Hilton, "The Economic Policies," chap. 7.
65 *Times*, 23 November 1825.
66 *Morning Chronicle*, 20 December 1825.
67 *Birmingham Journal*, 3 December 1825.
68 Ibid., 10 December 1825.
69 Peel Papers, British Library, Add. Mss 40496, f.195, 3 December 1841, T. Attwood to Sir Robert Peel.
70 T. Attwood, *The Scotch Banker, containing articles under that signature on Banking and Currency* (London 1828), 162–5. The letter is not in the Liverpool Papers.
71 Hilton, "The Economic Policies," 235.
72 Wakefield, *Attwood*, 101–2. Matthias approached six banking houses; he was unable to get even one signature.
73 Peel Papers, Add. Mss. 40384, f.5, 10 December 1825.
74 Ibid., Sir Robert Peel's letter cross-hatched in Thomas Attwood's hand.
75 Hilton, "The Economic Policies," 236.
76 Peel Papers, Add. Mss. 40854, f.10, 16 December 1825.
77 Ibid., f.8, 16 December 1825.
78 Ibid., Add. Mss. 40384, ff.16, 18, 40–2, Robert Peel's letters to Sir Herbert Taylor, Henry Hobhouse, and Cornelius Buller respectively.
79 Ibid., ff.1–3, 16 December 1825.
80 Ibid., f.8, 16 December 1825.

81 Ibid., f.10.
82 Attwood Papers, 17 December 1825, T. Attwood to Elizabeth Attwood.
83 Bromley-Davenport Papers, 26 July 1827, T. Attwood to Edward Davenport.
84 *Birmingham Journal*, 6 April 1833. Republication of a letter to the editor of the *Times*, dated 28 March 1833.
85 *Parl. Papers*, 1831–2 (722), 6, "Committee of Secrecy on the Bank of England Charter," Q. 2217; Clapham, *The Bank*, 2: 99.
86 T.E. Gregory, *The Westminster Bank through a Century*, 2 vols. (London: Oxford University Press 1936), 2: 149–50. *Parl. Papers*, House of Commons, 1831–2 (722), 6, "Committee of Secrecy on the Bank of England Charter," Q. 602–5, 5012; *The Journal of Mrs. Arbuthnot 1820–1832*, ed. F. Bamford, (London: Macmillan 1950), 1: 426–8; A.G. Stapleton, *George Canning and His Times* (London: n.p. 1859), "Letter to Lord Liverpool," 235–6.
87 Hilton, "The Economic Policies," 237–9.
88 Peel Papers, Add. Mss. 40384, f.12, 16 December 1825.
89 Ibid., ff.55 and 67, 19 December 1825, letters from Robert Peel to Theodore Price and Isaac Spooner respectively.
90 Ibid., f.215, 26 December 1825.
91 Ibid., f.216, 28 December 1825.
92 *Parl. Papers*, 1836 (591), 9, "Report from the Secret Committee on Joint Stock Banks," Q. 802.
93 *Aris' Birmingham Gazette*, 19 December 1825; *Birmingham Journal*, 17 December 1825.
94 Taylors & Lloyds Letter Books, No. 323; *Birmingham Journal*, 24 December 1825.
95 Peel Papers, Add. Mss 40384, f.10, 16 December 1825, Robert Peel to Sir Robert Peel.
96 Ibid., f.8, 16 December 1825.
97 Letter Books, 2 November 1832, George Nicholls to R. Elsey.
98 *Birmingham Journal*, 24 December 1825.
99 Attwoods & Spooner's Cash Book.

CHAPTER SEVEN

1 W.D. Smart, *Economic Annals of the Nineteenth Century*, Reprints of Economic Classics, 2 vols. (New York: Augustus M. Kelley 1964), 2: 347. For further information on the debates, see Clapham, *Bank*, 2: 102–16; Fetter, *Monetary Orthodoxy*, 118–24; W.T.C. King, *History of the London Discount Market* (London: Routledge 1936), 35–101.
2 For example, note William Huskisson's retrospective analysis in 2 *Hansard*, 14, 17 February 1830, c. 455.

3 Hilton, "Economic Policies," 248–53. Two Acts were passed. The first declared that notes under £5 were to be withdrawn by 5 April 1829. A second Act authorized the creation of joint-stock banks outside a sixty-five mile radius of the capital and empowered the Governor and Company of the Bank of England to carry on a banking business in any place in England and Wales.
4 Attwood Papers, January 1826, Robert Peel to T. Attwood
5 *Birmingham Chronicle*, 22 December 1825. Chambers of Commerce in Exeter and Hull even sent letters to the Bank of England to urge the rejection of the government's plan to open Bank of England branches in their towns. Bank of England, BRA B560/1 Branch Bank Committee Book C.
6 *Birmingham Chronicle*, 29 December 1825; *Birmingham Journal*, 31 December 1825, 7 January 1826.
7 *Birmingham Chronicle*, 29 December 1825.
8 Attwood Papers, 21 February 1826, T. Attwood to Elizabeth Attwood.
9 Ibid.
10 Ibid., 27 February 1827, T. Attwood to Elizabeth Attwood.
11 *Aris' Birmingham Gazette*, 10 April 1826.
12 Other correspondents included Kirkman Finlay and John Gladstone. neither allowed the letters sent to them to be published. Finlay (1773–1842) was a merchant and textile manufacturer in Glasgow. He sat in the Commons for Glasgow, 1812–18, and Malmesbury, 1810–20. He resigned in 1820 and then stood in 1830 and 1831 for the same places, but each time was defeated. John Gladstone (1764–1851) was a factory owner in Manchester who had become friendly with the Attwoods during the campaign against the Resumption Act in 1819. He was, of course, the father of W.E. Gladstone. By this date he had changed his political affiliation from Whig to Canningite.
13 *Birmingham Chronicle*, 23 March 1826; *Birmingham Journal*, 25 March 1826.
14 *Birmingham Chronicle*, 3 August 1826.
15 Charles Jones had long been an avid propagandist for currency change and was a regular correspondent of the newspapers on the subject. He summed up his position in one letter that leaves little room for doubt: "the money price of commodities must always be regulated by the proportion which the circulating money of a country bears to its circulating commodities." *Birmingham Journal*, 17 May 1827, the last of a series of three letters to the editor. Salt was a small businessman, a lamp maker, who had been a friend for some years. The third deputy, Hadley, did not rush into print with the zeal of the others but he spoke regularly and authoritatively at town meetings on this and other subjects.

16 *Birmingham Journal*, 5 August 1826; *Aris' Birmingham Gazette*, 7 August 1826.
17 *Birmingham Journal*, 12 August 1826, letter to the editor. The memorial also illustrated the continued development of a single school of thought in Birmingham on questions of political economy. When Cobbett sneered at the "Little Shilling projects" of Birmingham he correctly referred to a group and not to the banker alone. *Cobbett's Political Register* 62, no. 15 (7 October 1826).
18 *Aris' Birmingham Gazette*, 13 November 1826; *Birmingham Journal*, 11 November 1826.
19 *Birmingham Journal*, 18 November 1826.
20 Ibid., 25 November 1826.
21 Attwood Papers, 4 September 1826, T. Attwood to Elizabeth Attwood.
22 Attwoods & Spooner had been appointed one of the overseeing banks in the winding up of Gibbins, Smith & Goode. It had been a melancholy business.
23 Attwood Papers, 7 September 1826, T. Attwood to Elizabeth Attwood.
24 Ibid., 18 September 1826, T. Attwood to Elizabeth Attwood.
25 The factory began operations in 1828. However, after several profitless years, notwithstanding the appointment of Attwood's eldest son as manager, the enterprise was sold.
26 Attwood Papers, October 1826, Robert Peel to T. Attwood.
27 Attwoods & Spooner's Cash Book.
28 Attwood Papers, 2 December 1826, Lord Liverpool to T. Attwood.
29 Ibid., 20 February 1827, T. Attwood to Elizabeth Attwood.
30 *Birmingham Journal*, 17 March 1824.
31 Ibid., 24 March 1827.
32 Attwood Papers, 21 March 1827, T. Attwood to Elizabeth Attwood.
33 *Birmingham Journal*, 31 March 1827; Attwood Papers, 2 April 1827, T. Attwood to Elizabeth Attwood.
34 2 *Hansard*, 17, 11 June 1827, c. 1287.
35 Bromley-Davenport Papers, 27 February 1827, T. Attwood to Edward Davenport. Attwood had been leading Davenport to this point for five years. Each had visited the other on several occasions and Davenport had written a pamphlet, anonymously, under Attwood's tutelage. Unfortunately, Davenport was lazy and indecisive and rarely repaid Attwood's trust.
36 2 *Hansard*, 17, 11 June 1827, c. 1283–5.
37 Ibid., c. 1300; ibid., c. 1287.
38 Attwood Papers, 14 March 1827, T. Attwood to Elizabeth Attwood. J. Horsley Palmer, a future governor of the Bank of England, was a director of the British Iron Company. This position in a company engaged in a law suit with the Attwood family may have contrib-

uted, in a small measure, to his hostility to Attwood's bank at a later date.
39 *Birmingham Journal*, 9 June 1827. Such discourtesy, for it could have been no more than that, would seem unlikely save on the part of one or two of the most intoxicated. No one was more patriotic than Attwood and despite his low opinion of the king's ministers, he would not have welcomed any demonstrations during what was in all respects a routine expression of loyalty.
40 It appears few men in Parliament thought that the issue was important. *Journal of Mrs. Arbuthnot*, ed. Bamford, 2: 171, 179, 187–9; M. Brock, *The Great Reform Act* (London: Hutchinson 1973), 51, 71–4; Mitchell, *Whigs*, 203.
41 Langford, *Century*, 1: 530.
42 *Aris' Birmingham Gazette*, 25 June 1827.
43 Bromley-Davenport Papers, 13 May 1829, J. Parkes to C. Tennyson; Wakefield, *Attwood*, 112.
44 Attwood Papers, 30 June 1827, T. Attwood to Elizabeth Attwood.
45 The agent was George Nicholls (1781–1865). He was an excellent choice in that he brought a wealth of business experience to the post. He had managed the Gloucester and Berkeley Ship Canal, later became a Poor Law commissioner, and in 1836 was sent to Ireland to report on conditions. He was eventually knighted. In Birmingham he quickly became a force for change in banking circles.
46 Letter Books, 24 November 1826, T. Attwood to George Nicholls.
47 *Circular to Bankers*, 25 July 1828.
48 Attwood wrote six letters in all, later published in the *Scotch Banker*.
49 Letter Books, 19 October 1827, George Nicholls to Henry Hase. Moillet & Smith also contributed.
50 Ibid., 21 September 1827, George Nicholls to Henry Hase: *Birmingham Journal*, 13 October 1827. The following year the privilege of compounding was extended to all banks.
51 *Aris' Birmingham Gazette*, 10 December 1827.
52 Attwood Papers, 25 and 27 February 1828, T. Attwood to Elizabeth Attwood.
53 *Scotch Banker*, 182, letter written 2 February 1828 and not published in the *Globe*.
54 Attwood Papers, 28 February 1828, T. Attwood to Elizabeth Attwood. An analysis of this struggle is given by Hilton, "Economic Policies," 266–75. Attwood found it most instructive for Herries represented the City interest and Huskisson was reputedly an "enemy" of the Bank of England.
55 *Times*, 22 and 23 February 1828; Wakefield, *Attwood*, 116–17.
56 Attwood Papers, 28 February 1828, T. Attwood to Elizabeth Attwood.
57 *Globe*, 14 March, 2 and 10 April 1828.

58 Ibid., 14 March 1828.
59 *Aris' Birmingham Gazette*, 11 July 1828.
60 *Birmingham Chronicle*, 23 June 1827. The figure, with characteristic extravagance, was expanded "to the whole population" when Attwood recapitulated his points at the end of the speech.
61 Ibid., 25 June 1827.
62 Birmingham's efforts were all to no avail. The government decided to limit its support to the transfer of Penryn to Manchester, but even that was thrown out by the House of Lords in the following May.
63 *Birmingham Journal*, 23 June 1827.
64 Attwood Papers, 19 March 1827, T. Attwood to Elizabeth Attwood.
65 C.W. Wynn to Lord W. Bentinck, 16 June 1829; quoted by Mitchell, *Whigs*, 216.
66 Attwood Papers, 12 March 1829, T. Attwood to Edward Davenport.
67 Ibid., 23 May 1829, T. Attwood to Edward Davenport.
68 *Report of the Proceedings at the Meeting of the Inhabitants of Birmingham Held on Monday the 25th of January, 1830, of a General Political Union, with a View of obtaining a Redress of Public Wrongs and Grievences* (Birmingham: W. Hodgetts 1830), 5.
69 *Aris' Birmingham Gazette*, 11 May 1829; *Birmingham Journal*, 9 May 1829.
70 Thomas Attwood, *Causes of the Present Distress, Speech of Thomas Attwood Esq. at the Public Meeting Held in Birmingham, on the 8th of May, 1829, for the Purpose of Considering the Distressed State of the Currency* (Birmingham 1829), 11–78. The newspaper reports and other published editions of Attwood's speech varied considerably in detail. The editor of the *Birmingham Journal* published, in pamphlet form, a version which he claimed had been given Attwood's blessing. Attwood denied this and published his record through Beilby, Knott, Beilby & Co. Later he admitted that even this version did not contain all the points he had made and in a letter to *Aris' Birmingham Gazette* he added to it. The confusion as to what was actually said was one reason for the careful vetting of reports of the Political Union meetings which were sent to London in 1830–2.
71 *Aris' Birmingham Gazette*, 11 May 1829.
72 *Birmingham Journal*, 18 May 1829, letter to the editor signed William Redfern. The letter was expanded and republished, 1 August 1829.
73 Ibid., 4 July 1829.
74 Attwood Papers, 24 June 1829, William Cobbett to T. Attwood; Wakefield, *Attwood*, 126.
75 *Scotch Banker*, 25.
76 *Cobbett's Political Register*, 16 May 1829.
77 Bromley-Davenport Papers, 23 May 1829, T. Attwood to Edward Davenport.
78 Attwood Papers, 18 December 1828, T. Attwood to Elizabeth Attwood.

79 *Birmingham Journal*, 16 May 1829; *Distressed State*, 13 and 39.
80 Bromley-Davenport Papers, 1 June 1829, T. Attwood to Edward Davenport.
81 *Aris' Birmingham Gazette*, 25 May 1829, letter to the editor signed "Peeping Tom."
82 Letter books, 22 May 1829, George Nicholls to Henry Hase.
83 Wakefield, *Attwood*, 124–6.

CHAPTER EIGHT

1 Letter Books, 12 January 1830,, George Nicholls to R. Elsey.
2 *Cobbett's Political Register*, 29 December 1829.
3 *Birmingham Journal*, 23 January 1836.
4 Wakefield, *Attwood*, 129; Hutton, *Century*, 1: 533.
5 *Birmingham Journal*, 23 January 1836, report of Attwood's speech on 18 January 1836; D. O'Connell, *Correspondence of O'Connell*, ed. W.J. Fitzpatrick, 2 vols., (London: J. Murray 1888), 1: 199–200. The danger lay in the inadvertent infringement of the laws of 1795, 30 Geo. 3 c. 79 and 1817, 57 Geo. 3 c. 19. By the first, secrecy was prohibited as was correspondence between societies. The second extended the prohibition. The constitution of the Union consequently avoided all reference to branches in correspondence and gave notice that it would only hold open meetings.
6 *Birmingham Journal*, 12, 19, and 26 December 1829.
7 *Causes for the Present Distress*, 79.
8 For a more detailed description see C. Flick, *The Birmingham Political Union, 1830–1839* (Connecticut: Archon 1978), 25–6. Briggs discusses the Owenite-controlled newspapers of the town in "Press and Public Opinion in Early 19th Century Birmingham," *Dugdale Occasional Papers*, no. 8 (1949).
9 *Birmingham Journal*, 31 July 1830, speech at dinner for Sir Francis Burdett at the Royal Hotel.
10 Letter Books, 25 May 1831, George Nicholls to Timothy Rippon.
11 Edwards, *Personal Recollections*, 80–8.
12 Langford, *Century*, 1: 531.
13 G.F. Muntz, *Letter to His Grace the Duke of Wellington* (Birmingham: n.p. 1830), 1.
14 Ibid., 24.
15 Letter Books, 23 May 1832, George Nicholls to R. Elsey.
16 *Birmingham Journal*, 16 January 1830, advertisement for the town meeting.
17 *Monthly Argus* 1 (September 1829): 65.
18 Ibid., 2 (April 1830): 449.

19 *Birmingham Journal*, 16 January 1830.
20 Ibid., 9 January 1830.
21 *Aris' Birmingham Gazette*, 11 January 1830.
22 Ibid., 9 January 1830.
23 3 *Hansard*, 24, 2 June 1834, c. 86–76, 49, 17 July 1839, c. 433.
24 *Birmingham Journal*, 9 January 1830.
25 Letter Books, 25 January, 1830, George Nicholls to R. Elsey.
26 *Report of the Proceedings ... 25th of January, 1830*, 8–10.
27 *Prosperity*, 113–18.
28 Brock, *The Great Reform Act*, 256.
29 Bromley-Davenport Papers, 25 February 1830, T. Attwood to E. Davenport.
30 Ibid., 60–1; Flick, *Birmingham Political Union*, 33–4; *Morning Chronicle*, 23 January 1830.
31 *Report of the Proceedings ... 25th of January, 1830*, 13–14.
32 This speech supports Thomas's contention that the Whig reformers had become "increasingly hesitant and tentative about popular reform by 1830." W. Thomas, "James Mill's Politics: The Essay on Government and the Movement for Reform," *Historical Journal* 12 (June 1969): 284.
33 Parkes later gloried in this reverse. George Attwood, he claimed, had yelled, "throw him over," but he himself had "never bowed my knee." It is this kind of remark which makes much of Parkes's evidence with regard to the Political Union suspect. George Attwood had not been at the meeting. Place Papers, British Library, Add. Mss. 35150 ff. 216, 219, 8 January 1837, J. Parkes to F. Place.
34 *Report of the Proceedings ... 25th of January, 1830*, 15.
35 Mitchell, *Whigs*, 217.
36 Attwood Papers, 24 October 1829. Later, on 16 March 1830, Davenport became to disgusted with his parliamentary friends' failure to support his currency motions that he almost broke with them. 2 *Hansard*, 33, 18 March 1830, c. 604.
37 2 *Hansard*, 32, 21 May 1829, c. 1672–9.
38 N. Gash, *Mr. Secretary Peel* (Cambridge: Harvard University Press 1961), 600. The *Annual Register* (1830) noted Blandford's activities and attributed them directly to the emancipation bill.
39 *Quarterly Review*, 42, January and March 1830, Article ix(i), R. Forsyth, "Political Fragments," 269–77.
40 *Report of the Proceedings ... 25th of January, 1830*, 13.
41 Sir L. Woodward. *The Age of Reform*, 2nd ed. (Oxford: Clarendon Press 1964), 77.
42 Attwood Papers, 24 June 1830, T. Attwood to Elizabeth Attwood.
43 For a further discussion of this debate see Mitchell, *The Whigs*,

chaps. 9 and 10; J. Milton-Smith, "Earl Grey's Cabinet and the Objects of Parliamentary Reform," *Historical Journal* 15, no. 1 (1972): 59.
44 2 *Hansard*, 22, 8 February 1830, c. 241–2.
45 Attwood Papers, 29 January 1830, Marquis of Blandford to T. Attwood.
46 *Annual Register* (1830): 18–19.
47 Ibid., 87; 2 *Hansard*, 22, 18 February 1830, c. 678.
48 It is debatable whether Blandford was aware of the extent of this concession.
49 Bromley-Davenport Papers, 25 February 1830, T. Attwood to Edward Davenport.
50 *Birmingham Journal*, 20 March 1820.
51 2 *Hansard*, 22, 18 February 1830, c. 698. This brevity can perhaps be attributed to Blandford's letter to the *Standard* in July 1829, in which he attacked part of the Utilitarians' reform platform: "I will never stand for the wild advocate of voting by ballot on universal suffrage; both these inventions of modern date, unfounded in reason."
52 Ibid., c. 714.
53 Ibid., c. 716.
54 Ibid., c. 706.
55 *Morning Journal*, 26 January 1830.
56 *Morning Advertiser*, 26 January 1830.
57 *Morning Herald*, 26 January 1830.
58 *Manchester Courier*, 27 January 1830.
59 *Times*, 26 January 1830.
60 *Cobbett's Political Register*, 6 February 1830.
61 2 *Hansard*, 22, 11 February 1830, c. 347–8.
62 Bromley-Davenport Papers, 25 February 1830, T. Attwood to Edward Davenport.
63 W. Thomas, *The Philosophical Radicals: Nine Studies in Theory and Practice, 1817–1841* (Oxford: Clarendon Press 1978), 250–1.
64 *Cobbett's Political Register*, 29 December 1829. Cobbett reported that he had visited Birmingham to discuss the economic situation and its possible improvement with a variety of artisans and labourers. The answers generally given to his questions had not pleased him.
65 *Report of the Proceedings ... 25th of January, 1830*, 15. Many "respectable" inhabitants were deterred from joining the Union by this statement of intent. They feared confrontation.
66 *Birmingham Journal*, 27 February 1830.
67 As individuals some of the new councillors had opposed the act at its inception the previous year. *Birmingham Journal*, 22 August and 21 November 1829.
68 Flick, *Birmingham Political Union*, 39–40.

69 The Political Council was fortunate in that Birmingham possessed two superb arenas in which oratorical skills could be displayed, Beardsworth's and Newhall Hill. The first meetings were held in Beardsworth's Horse and Carriage Repository in the centre of the market quarter. The Repository was the largest salesroom of horses and carriages in the United Kingdom. W. Hutton, *History of Birmingham* 4th ed. (Birmingham: Pearson 1809), 112; Birmingham Reference Library, Local Notes and Queries, c. 181/129. John Beardsworth rarely refused a request for the use of the facility even on the shortest notice. He was one of the best-loved characters in the town. His origins were comparatively humble – he had begun his career as a hackney cab driver – but he had been fortunate enough to marry an heiress who had ridden in his cab. Using her money he had built the Repository. The most useful feature was a glass-roofed central gallery measuring 324 by 150 feet. For the meeting of 25 January 1830, between eighteen and twenty-five thousand persons had been accommodated. When the size of the crowds became too great for even this enormous hall, the stage was shifted to Newhall Hill, the scene of a number of reform meetings more than a decade earlier. Here a natural amphitheatre, approximately twelve acres in area, provided a stage visible to one to two hundred thousand spectators. The task of supplying the audience to fill one or another of these theatres remained. In this the experience and expertise of George Edmonds coupled with Attwood's flair for the dramatic gesture proved more than adequate. Attendance figures vary, depending on the source. The official Union figures were generally much higher than those given by outsiders.
70 *Birmingham Journal*, 15 May 1830.
71 *Corrected Report of the Proceedings of The First Meeting of the Birmingham Political Union Held at Mr. Beardsworth's Repository on Monday, May 27th, 1830* (Birmingham 1830), 3; Wakefield, *Attwood*, 138–43.
72 A gold medal was presented to Attwood first and then each member of the Union was given a replica in white metal. The obverse depicted the British lion rising from slumber; the legend above, "The safety of the King and the people," the legend below, "The Constitution; nothing less, and nothing more." The reverse of the medal illustrated the royal crown of Britain irradiated; above was written "Unity, Liberty, Prosperity"; below it was the inscription, "Birmingham Political Union, 25th January, 1830." A ribbon, in the colours of the Union Jack, completed the insignia.
73 Wakefield, *Attwood*, 135.
74 *Midland Representative*, 3 December 1831.

75 Mass meetings were avoided by the London radicals precisely because they could be dangerous. G. Wallas, *The Life of Francis Place* (New York: Allen 1919), 306n1.
76 *Birmingham Advertiser*, 27 November 1834.
77 G.J. Holyoake, *Sixty Years of an Agitator's Life*, 3 vols., 3rd ed. (London: T.F. Unwin 1893), 1: 26.
78 Letter books, 31 May 1831, George Nicholls to Timothy Rippon.
79 Edwards, *Personal Recollections*, 141–54: *Birmingham Journal*, 9 April 1831; *Monthly Argus* 11 (1830): 29.
80 Holyoake, *Sixty Years*, 1: 31.
81 *Songs to be Sung at the Dinner of the Birmingham Political Union*, 11 October 1830 (handbill).
82 *Birmingham Journal*, 27 March 1830. The newspaper became one of the Union's strongest supporters, although relations with Attwood on a personal level became strained when control of it passed in February 1832 to Parkes and Scholefield.
83 Place Papers, Add. Mss. 27, 2793 f. 8. The *Times* sent its own correspondent to cover the meeting.
84 Home Office Papers, Disturbances, Correspondence, 40.29.
85 *Annual Register* 111 (1831): 281. The game with numbers was played by all, even those whom one would expect to be objective. See Letter Books, 12 October 1831, George Nicholls to R. Elsey.
86 Cf. J. Bright, *Public Addresses by John Bright*, ed. J.E. Thorold Rogers, 2 vols. (London: Macmillan 1879), 1: 197.
87 3 *Hansard*, 7, 12 October 1831, c. 596–624.
88 Bromley-Davenport Papers, T. Attwood to E. Davenport, 25 February 1830.
89 Wakefield, *Attwood*, 179–80: *Aris' Birmingham Gazette*, 15 October 1831.
90 *Annual Register*, 111 (1831): 283, reports of the speeches of Sir Henry Hardinge and Sir Richard Vyvyan.
91 Ibid., 285.
92 *Cobbett's Political Register*, 27 February 1830.
93 Ibid., 6 March 1830.
94 Attwood Papers, 25 June 1830, T. Attwood to Elizabeth Attwood.
95 Brock, *The Great Reform Bill*, 77.
96 Attwood Papers, 25 June 1830, T. Attwood to Elizabeth Attwood. Rivalries at Westminster prevented the promised appearance of Burdett, Hobhouse, and Davenport. O'Connell, *Correspondence of Daniel O'Connell*, 1: 199; *Coventry Observer*, 18 February 1830.
97 R.K. Hugh, "The Earl of Radnor and Free Trade," *Huntington Library Quarterly* 39 (1976): 152–4.
98 Attwood Papers, 23 June 1830, T. Attwood to Elizabeth Attwood.
99 Ibid., 24 June 1830. This unilateral decision by Attwood indicated the

degree of control he enjoyed over the Union. Burdett's motion to enfranchise Manchester, Leeds, and Birmingham had won 140 votes.
100 Lord Broughton, *Recollections of a Long Life*, ed. Lady Dorchester, 4 vols. (London: n.p. 1910), 4: 28.
101 2 *Hansard*, 23, 23 February 1830, c. 660.
102 Mitchell, *Whigs*, chap. 10.
103 Attwood Papers, 23 June 1830, T. Attwood to Elizabeth Attwood.
104 *Birmingham Journal*, 24 July 1830, letter of Edward Davenport.
105 Langford, *Century*, 1: 511–14.
106 *Birmingham Journal*, 31 July 1830. The council adopted a further series of resolutions on more specific points. One required that the enfranchised boroughs pledge themselves to support candidates at the forthcoming election who favoured reform. To ensure that those so inclined be known the fourth resolution requested pledges from candidates announcing their intentions. Ibid., 31 July 1830. This stipulation was to prove embarrassing for Attwood when he was proposed as a candidate in 1832.
107 *Cobbett's Political Register*, 17 July 1830.
108 *Morning Chronicle*, 9 July 1830.
109 A further factor, of course, was the impossibility of maintaining the early momentum which had been conceived in distress during a period of some improvement.
110 The membership still stood at only 5,000 – not a large enrolment given Birmingham's population of 144,000. The split in the radicals' ranks was further emphasized when Burdett was greeted by a shower of rotten cabbages and turnip tops as he began his personal reelection campaign at Westminster.
111 Grey Papers, Prior's Kitchen, Durham, 15 July 1830.
112 *Birmingham Journal*, 31 July 1830, Thomas Attwood's speech at the banquet in honour of Sir Francis Burdett.
113 Membership in the association would cost a penny a week. The money collected would fund a newsletter. Attwood was to give a free lecture once a week for twelve months.
114 2 *Hansard*, 22, 11 February 1830, c. 381–90. Actually Baring was a dubious conquest. Later, in an argument designed to refute the legitimacy of a single standard, he compared the use of gold to "a Birmingham mire of inconvertible rags." Lord Ashburton, *The Financial and Commercial Crisis Considered*, 3rd ed. (London: J. Murray 1847), 40.
115 *Birmingham Journal*, 7 August 1830.
116 *Dyott's Diary*, ed. R.W. Jeffrey, 2 vols. (London: Constable 1907), 2: 87.
117 *Birmingham Journal*, 14 August 1830.
118 Ibid., 28 August 1830. John Doherty, for instance, argued that "Univer-

sal Suffrage means nothing more than the power given to every man to protect his own labour from being devoured" – a most attractive argument which was difficult to refute. Quoted by A. Briggs, "The Language of Class in Early Nineteenth Century England," *Essays in Labour History*, ed. A. Briggs and J. Saville (New York: Macmillan 1960), 67.
119 *Birmingham Journal*, 25 September 1830.

CHAPTER NINE

1 Mitchell, *Whigs*, 232–5; Brock, *The Great Reform Bill*, 99.
2 H. Brougham, *Life and Times of Lord Brougham*, 3 vols. (London: W. Blackwood and Sons 1871), 3: 44–6.
3 Mitchell, *Whigs*, 239. Huskisson died after a railway accident on 15 September 1830.
4 Ibid., 244.
5 For an analysis of the riots see E.J. Hobsbawm and G. Rudé, *Captain Swing* (London: Lawrence and Wishart 1969), and Brock, *The Great Reform Act*, 111–13.
6 Gash, *Mr. Secretary Peel*, 647.
7 An associate of Attwood, Western, had struck exactly this note in August. *Morning Chronicle*, 7 August 1830. Most editors had played a similar tune.
8 *Report on Proceedings of the Dinner of the Political Union held at Mr. Beardsworth's Repository on Monday, October 11th, to Commemorate the French Revolution of July 1830* (Birmingham: Hodgetts 1830), 4.
9 *Report on Proceedings ... October 11th, 1830*, 7.
10 Attwood's control of the meeting was reported to the Home Office by George Nicholls. The whole episode, he wrote, "speaks well for the character of the people and shows also the influence which their leaders exercise over them." Home Office Papers, Correspondence Disturbances, 40. 32, 12 October 1830.
11 Place Papers, 35149 f. 117, J. Parkes to G. Grote, 25 October 1831. Even the most ambitious were enforced to recognize that fact. Joseph Parkes had followed the progress of the Union closely and had at various times tried to impose his own reform panacea, vote by ballot, upon the Union. When the changes in the political alignments at Westminster promised life to the Birmingham Political Union, he had considered establishing of an organization of his own in Birmingham. To this end he sought an overdraft of £85,000 from the Bank of England to launch it. Letter Books, 5 October 1830, George Nicholls to Timothy Rippon. But after 11 October no more was heard of this project until Parkes and Place tried, unsuc-

337 Notes to pages 186–8

cessfully, to organize the National Political Union of London in 1831. Parkes, in his letters to men of influence, often tried to depict Attwood as both foolish and cowardly.

12 *Birmingham Journal*, 13 May 1837.
13 *Report on Proceedings ... October 11th, 1830*, 5.
14 *Prosperity*, 43–4, *Observations*, 245; *Distressed State*, 46.
15 W.M. Torrens, *Memoirs of the Right Honourable William, Second Viscount Melbourne*, 2 vols. (London: n.p. 1878), 1: 34.
16 There were even hints of reactionary activity in relation to the situation in the Netherlands as a result of William's sympathy for his brother monarch.
17 3 *Hansard*, 1, 2 March 1830, c. 52–3.
18 Mitchell, *Whigs*, 245; Gash, *Peel*, 645–6; Brock, *The Great Reform Act*, 125.
19 3 *Hansard*, 1, 2 November 1830, c. 63–4.
20 Pare, who spoke for one faction in the Union, welcomed the violence, declaring that it "could enlighten their [ministers] pure minds." *Report of the Proceedings of a Town's Meeting held in Mr. Beardsworth's Repository on Monday 13th December, 1830. For the Purpose of Addressing his Majesty on the Dismissal of the Duke of Wellington's Administration* (Birmingham: W. Hodgetts 1830), 6.
21 Home Office Papers, Correspondence, Disturbances, 52. 11, 12.
22 *Birmingham Journal*, 13 November 1830.
23 *Report of the Proceedings ... 13th December, 1830*, 3.
24 Brock, *The Great Reform Act*, 128–30.
25 *Birmingham Journal*, 20 November 1830. The council rejected on 23 November an Irish proposal to repeal the Act of Union on the ground that with parliamentary reform the real ills of Ireland, oppression and economic distress, would be removed. Ireland could then enjoy with Scotland and Wales the fruits of common trade and justice. This typically English answer ended the dialogue between the respective groups.
26 Joseph Parkes disclosed that he had considered calling a town's meeting through a regular requisition to the high bailiff. He had discussed this with Scholefield and both had gone to lay the suggestion before Attwood. They discovered, however, that "a meeting of the inhabitants had already been decided upon, to be called by him as Chairman of the Political Union Council." Scholefield, one of the most prominent members of that council, had been unaware of the chairman's decision. At the end of the day the hope was expressed that Attwood would soon be returned as the member of Parliament for Birmingham. Attwood accepted that suggestion; no other names were proposed.
27 *Report of the Proceedings ... 13th December, 1830*, 3–4.

28 Ibid., 5–8.
29 In his speech, Attwood had pointedly thanked Blandford for his bill. *Report of the Proceedings ... 13th December, 1830*, 9.
30 Parkes had written to Place a few days before the meeting to lament that "the real friends of reform will not go." He further indicated that he would go to try to get some agreement "on the ballot." Place Papers, Add. Mss. 35145, f. 77, 5 December 1830.
31 *Birmingham Journal*, 8 January 1831; *Aris' Birmingham Gazette*, 10 January 1831.
32 Wakefield, *Attwood*, 165.
33 Flick, *Birmingham Political Union*, 57.
34 *Aris' Birmingham Gazette*, 2 May 1831.
35 D.E. Harton-Mole, "The Church of England and Society in Birmingham, 1830–1866" (PHD thesis, Cambridge, 1961), 97–8.
36 *Birmingham Journal*, 12 November 1825; R.K. Dent, *Old and New Birmingham*, 3 vols. (Birmingham: Houghton and Hammard 1879–1880), 3: 351–2, 409; Langford, *Century*, 2: 430. Then, between three and four thousand had marched in procession to Christ Church and had taken possession of the free seats. The beginning of the sermon, "submit yourself to every ordinance of man for the Lord's sake," had been the signal for all of them to rise, don white hats, and march out.
37 *Birmingham Journal*, 8 July 1831.
38 Charles Attwood, another of Thomas's brothers, lived at Wickham, was a glassmaker at Gateshead, and was to found the new town, Tow Law. The Newcastle Political Union had been formed during the summer. S. Middlebrook, *Newcastle Upon Tyne: Its Growth and Development* (Newcastle: Kemsley 1950), 173–9.
39 *Birmingham Journal*, 29 January 1831. These figures were those publicized by the Union and since they had propaganda value must be considered suspect.
40 It was entitled, "The petition of the Magistrates, Clergy, High and Low Bailiffs, Bankers, Merchants, Manufacturers and other Inhabitants."
41 Place Collections, Set 17, 11, 109a, cited by H. Ferguson, "The Birmingham Political Union" (PHD thesis, Harvard, 1959), 235; Home Office Papers, Disturbances Correspondence, 40. 28.
42 Home Office Papers, Disturbances Correspondence, 40.29, 43.41.
43 F. Hill, *An Autobiography of Fifty Years in Times of Reform*, ed. C. Hill (London: R. Bentley and Son 1894), 81. Printing costs were the biggest expense.
44 *Birmingham Journal*, 5 February 1831. These unions were established at Huddersfield, Almondbury, Honley, Kirkheaton, and Lepton.
45 Brock, *The Great Reform Act*, 135–6.

46 Ibid., 151.
47 Tennyson D'Eyncourt Papers, the Castle, Lincoln, 18 December 1830.
48 Brock, *The Great Reform Act*, 160–1.
49 *Birmingham Journal*, 9 April 1831; F. Hill, *Autobiography*, 80.
50 Attwood Papers, July 1831, T. Attwood to Elizabeth Attwood; Brock, *The Great Reform Act*, 165.
51 *Birmingham Journal*, 12 March 1831; *Aris' Birmingham Gazette*, 14 March 1831.
52 3 Hansard, 4, 2 July 1831, c. 1111–12. Matthias Attwood's own constituency was one of those targeted.
53 *Birmingham Journal*, 26 March 1831; *Aris' Birmingham Gazette*, 28 March 1831.
54 Tennyson d'Eyncourt Papers, 27 March 1831.
55 Brock, *The Great Reform Act*, 182–7.
56 *Birmingham Journal*, 30 April 1831.
57 Ibid., 7 and 14 May; *Aris' Birmingham Gazette*, 2 and 9 May 1831.
58 *Aris' Birmingham Gazette*, 9 May 1831; *Birmingham Journal*, 7 May 1831.
59 Attwood Papers, 11 and 16 May 1831, T. Attwood to Elizabeth Attwood.
60 *Times*, 9 May 1832.
61 *Birmingham Journal*, 2 July 1831.
62 Attwood Papers, 30 June 1831, Earl Grey to T. Attwood.
63 *Birmingham Journal*, 9 July 1831.
64 Ibid., 30 July 1831.
65 Wakefield, *Attwood*, 169.
66 *Cobbett's Political Register*, 6 August 1831.
67 Wakefield, *Attwood*, 235–41.
68 Attwood Papers, 8 August 1831, T. Attwood to Elizabeth Attwood.
69 For example, see the exchanges in the *Gazette* in July after a critical letter had been published.
70 Brock, *The Great Reform Act*, 235–41.
71 Letter Books, 14 and 18 June, 8 July, 5 and 8 October 1831, George Nicholls to T. Rippon.
72 *Copy of the Memorial Presented to Earl Grey in October, 1831*, broadsheet in Birmingham Reference Library; *Midland Representative*, 3 September and 1 October 1831.
73 *Report of the Proceedings at a Meeting of the Inhabitants of Birmingham held on Newhall Hill, October 3, 1831. Convened by the Council of the Political Union for the Purpose of Petitioning the House of Lords to Pass the Reform Bill.* (Birmingham: W. Hodgetts 1831).
74 3 Hansard, 7, 4 October 1831, c. 1119, 1309–29.
75 Brock, *The Great Reform Act*, 244.
76 Attwood Papers, 9 October 1831, T. Attwood to Elizabeth Attwood.

77 *Midland Representative,* 15 October 1831; *Birmingham Journal* 15 October 1831.
78 *Aris' Birmingham Gazette,* 17 October 1831; Letter Books, 11 and 12 October 1831, George Nicholls to Timothy Rippon.
79 Wakefield, *Attwood,* 179–80.
80 Ibid., 181.
81 *Midland Representative,* 15 October 1831.
82 Brock, *The Great Reform Act,* 244–5.
83 *Birmingham Journal,* 22 October 1831; *Aris' Birmingham Gazette,* 24 October 1831.
84 *Times,* 27 October and 1 November 1831; *Morning Chronicle,* 26 October, 5 November, and 5 December 1831; Home Office Papers, Disturbances Correspondence, 40.29.
85 *Birmingham Journal,* 29 October 1831.
86 Ibid., 5 November 1831; Home Office Papers, Disturbances Correspondence, 40.59.
87 Legal Opinion of the Law Officers, Home Office Papers, 49.7, 40.28; see also Grey, *Correspondence with William IV,* 1: 416.
88 *Standard,* 3 November 1831.
89 *Proposed Plan for the Organization of the Birmingham Political Union* (Birmingham: W. Hodgetts 1831), 3. Alternative plans had been debated at the weekly council meeting, 1, 8, and 15 November 1831. *Birmingham Journal,* 5, 12, and 19 November 1831. Attwood sent Lawley a proof of his speech on the plan. Howick Papers, University of Durham, 18 November 1831, Melbourne to Earl Grey.
90 The subdivision of the town had been made before by the Union to enable all of its members to dine. *Birmingham Journal,* 1 and 15 January 1931.
91 *Proposed Plan,* 4–8.
92 *Birmingham Journal,* 5 November 1837, Home Office Papers 41.11.
93 *Standard,* 8 November 1831.
94 *Morning Chronicle,* 12, 22 and 23 November 1831; *Times,* 23 November 1831.
95 Melbourne had taken the opinion of the law officers on the legality of the plan at the request of Grey. Grey, *Correspondence with William IV,* 1: 424.
96 Holland Papers, British Library, Add. Mss. 51867, f.204; Brock, *The Great Reform Act,* 258.
97 *Dispatches, Correspondence and Memoranda of Field Marshall Arthur, Duke of Wellington, C.G.,* ed. his son, 8 vols. (London: J. Murray 1850), 8: 75; *Three Early Nineteenth Century Diaries,* ed. A. Aspinall (London: Williams and Norgate 1952), 155, Lord Ellenborough's Diary, 19 November 1831. Peel agreed and wanted an armed association to

act against armed political unions. C.S. Parker, ed., *Sir Robert Peel from His Private Papers*, 2 vols. (London: J. Murray 1899), 2: 190–1.
98 Jessie K. Buckley, *Joseph Parkes of Birmingham* (London: Methuen 1926), 85–6. Flick, *Birmingham Political Union*, 68–9. Grey was persuaded to take this course by Althorp. Althorp Papers, 20 November 1831, Althorp to Grey.
99 Parkes concentrated on pointing out the infringement of 39 George 3 c. 79, and 57 George 3 c. 19. *Morning Chronicle*, 25 November 1831; *Birmingham Journal*, 26 November 1831.
100 Holland Papers, Add. Mss. 51868, f.219, 21 November 1831. It is possible that the ministers were simply putting their faith in Parkes's persuasiveness but it seems unlikely.
101 Brock, *The Great Reform Act*, 259–60.
102 Letter Books, 23 November 1831, G. Nicholls to T. Rippon.
103 Holland Papers, Add. Mss. 51868, f.201. The Birmingham Political Union had not been alone in its military-style organization and reports had inundated the Home Office, telling of potential trouble in almost every part of the country.
104 Wakefield, *Attwood*, 185–6.
105 Flick, *Birmingham Political Union*, 73–5.
106 Ferguson, "Birmingham Political Union," 133. Several pieces of legislation prohibited official correspondence or meetings between radical societies. Among the most strict were those passed to destroy the corresponding societies of the French Revolution period. The government could authorize the postmaster general to open letters of men considered "dangerous." Strictly interpreted, the law could have been used to ban the Union's demonstrations.
107 For example, see *Manchester Courier*, 12 November 1831.
108 Holland Diary, Add. Mss. 51868 f.210, 26 November 1831.
109 *Birmingham Journal*, 3 December 1831.
110 Ibid., 17 December 1831.
111 Attwood Papers, 3 December 1831, T. Attwood to Elizabeth Attwood.
112 *Birmingham Journal*, 3 December 1831. The colliers, nailworkers, and ironworkers had gone on strike in support of higher wages and had requested the Unions' support.
113 Home Office Papers, Disturbances Correspondence, 41.10, f.477, 10 December 1831.
114 Brock, *The Great Reform Act*, 264.
115 Brougham Papers, 9 January 1832, Richard Spooner to H. Brougham. this letter contains references to the earlier correspondence.
116 *Birmingham Journal*, 17 December 1831.
117 Ibid., 24 December 1831, 21 January 1832.
118 Tennyson d'Eyncourt Papers, 23 June 1831, J. Scholefield to C.

Tennyson; *Aris' Birmingham Gazette*, 2 July 1832, published correspondence between J. Scholefield and G. Edmonds.
119 Attwood Papers, 3 January 1832, Lafayette to T. Attwood.
120 *Birmingham Journal*, 25 February 1832.
121 Wakefield, *Attwood*, 191.
122 Brock, *The Great Reform Act*, 268–79.
123 *Midland Representative*, 17 March 1832.
124 *Birmingham Journal*, 7 April 1832.
125 Buckley, *Parkes*, 91–4; *Morning Chronicle*, 27 April 1832; Flick, *Birmingham Political Union*, 78. The compromise related to a change in the franchise which implied a rise in borough ratings. Joseph Parkes, who was used by Grey as a conduit to Attwood, had asked the latter's opinion and had been rebuffed. Thomas Attwood had followed the general radical line elucidated by his brother Charles of the Northern Political Union. *Tyne Mercury*, 24 April 1832. Middlebrook, *Newcastle upon Tyne*, 173–5; G.J. Holyoake, *Sixty Years of an Agitator's Life*, 3 vols. 3rd ed. (London: T.F. Unwin 1893), 1: 26.
126 *Cobbett's Political Register*, 21 and 28 April 1832.
127 The following description is based on *A Report of the Proceedings at the Grand Meeting of the Birmingham Political Union at NewHall Hill, on May 7, 1832* (Birmingham: William Hodgetts 1832) and *Birmingham Journal*, 12 May 1832.
128 Brock, *The Great Reform Act*, 290.
129 *Birmingham Journal*, 12 May 1832. Joseph Parkes presented their statement on 10 May 1832.
130 *Aris' Birmingham Gazette*, 18 July 1831.
131 J. Russell, *Report of the Immense and Instantaneous Meeting Held at Newhall Hill, May 10, 1832* (Birmingham: n.p. 1832); R.K. Dent, *Old and New Birmingham*, 3: 409: *Midland Representative*, 12 May 1832.
132 *Aris' Birmingham Gazette*, 14 May 1832.
133 *Birmingham Journal*, 19 May 1832; Wakefield, *Attwood*, 194; G. de Bosco Attwood's account.
134 Letter Books, 28 May 1832, G. Nicholls to T. Rippon.
135 *Three Nineteenth Century Diaries*, ed. Aspinall, Le Marchant's Diary, 10 May 1832.
136 Joseph Parkes claimed that he had not joined the Union earlier because he feared the loss of his position as Counsel of the King's Bench. *Birmingham Journal*, 26 November 1831. Presumably, he had overcome his fear.
137 This episode is something of a mystery as Wallace was already in Birmingham, *Birmingham Journal*, 28 April 1832, and Charles was busy in Newcastle. Ferguson, "Birmingham Political Union," 250–1.

138 Francis Place counted 201 meetings reported in *Times* and *Morning Chronicle,* 9–19 May. Place Papers, Add. Mss. 27, 794. 347. There are many sources concerning the leadership of the Union in this crisis. Ferguson, "Birmingham Political Union," 168–70.
139 A. Sommerville, *The Autobiography of a Working Man,* new ed. (Plymouth: Turnstile Press 1951), 244.
140 Brock, *The Great Reform Act,* 292–3.
141 *Birmingham Journal,* 12 and 19 May 1832.
142 The deputies had met with Grey and conferred with Place.
143 *Birmingham Journal,* 19 May 1832.
144 Wakefield, *Attwood,* 208–9. The declaration proved to be very popular, was translated into French, and circulated in France.
145 *Morning Herald,* 14 May 1832. Similar stories appeared in other newspapers. An analysis of the views of some MPs can be found in Brock, *The Great Reform Act,* 299–302.
146 Broughton, *Recollections,* 4: 74.
147 For this line of thinking in the Union, see a letter from Scholefield to Durham, 8 May 1832, Lambton Papers, University of Durham.
148 Fonblanque, *Life and Labours,* 29.
149 Place Papers, Add. Mss. 27793, 99. 10; Buckley, *Parkes,* 195–6.
150 Le Marchant, *Althorp,* 293.
151 Wakefield, *Attwood,* 209–10; H. Grote, *The Personal Life of George Grote* (London: J. Murray 1873), 78–80, J. Parkes to G. Grote, 18 May 1832.
152 *Birmingham Journal,* 19 May 1832; *Report of the Proceedings of the Public Meeting of the Inhabitants of Birmingham held in Newhall Hill, May 16th 1832. Convened by the Council of the Political Union for the Purpose of presenting an Address to Earl Grey on his Re-instatement to the Office of Premier* (Birmingham: William Hodgetts 1832).
153 Brock, *The Great Reform Act,* 303.
154 Ibid., 305–6.
155 Holland Diary, Add. Mss. 51869, ff. 480 and 484.
156 Home Office Papers, Disturbances Correspondence, 40.11 f.407, 14 May 1832.
157 J. Hamburger, *James Mill and the Art of Revolution* (London: Yale University Press 1963).
158 Attwood Papers, 19 May 1832, T. Attwood to Elizabeth Attwood.
159 Brock, *The Great Reform Act,* 314.
160 *Three Nineteenth Century Diaries,* ed. Aspinall, E.J. Littleton's Diary, 20 May 1832.
161 *Birmingham Journal,* 26 May 1832, report of the dinner given to Thomas Attwood by the mayor and aldermen of London, 23 May 1832. Earl Grey and Althorp were granted the freedom of the city at a separate diner.

162 *Birmingham Journal*, 29 September 1832, Attwood speech on 28 September; Attwood Papers, 23 May 1832, T. Attwood to Elizabeth Attwood.
163 Letter Books, 17 May 1832, G. Nicholls to T. Rippon.
164 Attwood Papers, 26 May 1832, T. Attwood to Elizabeth Attwood.
165 Letter Books, 25 May 1832, G. Nicholls to R. Elsey.
166 *Birmingham Journal*, 2 June 1832; Wakefield, *Attwood*, 229–42. McDonnell was never able to get close enough to Attwood to present an address from the council.

CHAPTER TEN

1 B.R. Haydon, *The Diary of Benjamin Robert Haydon*, ed. W.B. Pope, 5 vols. (Cambridge: Harvard University Press 1963), 3: 620–1. Charles Jones in one of the more dramatic incidents reputedly threatened to nail a tax-collector's ear to the door.
2 *Aris' Birmingham Gazette*, 2 July 1832.
3 The career of this remarkable clergyman is discussed by T.H. Lloyd, "Dr. Wade and the Working Class," *Midland History* 2, no. 2 (1973): 61–83. The Union attempted to expel Wade for his sins. *Poor Man's Guardian*, 10 November 1832. The objectives of this parallel union are examined in C. Behagg, "An Alliance with the Middle Class: The Birmingham Political Union and Early Chartism," in J. Epstein and D. Thompson, eds., *The Chartist Experience: Studies in Working Class Radicalism and Culture, 1830–60* (London: Macmillan 1982), 64–5.
4 Home Office Papers, Disturbances Correspondence, 40.30.
5 *Report of the Proceedings of the Great Public Meeting of the Inhabitants of Birmingham, held at NewHall Hill, on Monday, 25 June 1832* (Birmingham: William Hodgetts 1832).
6 For example, see his speech reported in the *Birmingham Journal*, 19 April 1832.
7 *Birmingham Journal*, 9 June 1832.
8 Letter Books, 29 June 1832, G. Nicholls to J.R. Elsey.
9 *The Substance of the Extraordinary Proceedings at the Birmingham Political Council on Tuesday evening July 3, on the Subject of Pledges and Mr. Attwood's Condemnation of the Person proposing the same* (Birmingham: J. Russell 1832).
10 *Cobbett's Political Register*, 21 July 1832.
11 *Birmingham Journal*, 14 July 1832.
12 Letter Books, 30 June 1832, G. Nicholls to J. Horsley-Palmer.
13 Ibid., 4 July 1832, J. Horsley-Palmer to G. Nicholls.
14 *Birmingham Journal*, 14 July 1832.
15 Attwood Papers, 12 July 1832, T. Attwood to Elizabeth Attwood.

16 Ibid., 14 July 1832, T. Attwood to Elizabeth Attwood. He counted this "a great day," since Matthias had reportedly "demolished" the testimony of Thomas Tooke, the noted economist, and Horsley-Palmer, the Bank of England's governor.
17 Ibid., 15 July 1832, Lord Althorp to T. Attwood.
18 *Birmingham Journal,* 21 July 1832.
19 Ibid., 28 July 1828.
20 Ibid., 4 August 1832.
21 *Parl. Papers,* 1831–2 (722), 6, "Committee ... Bank of England Charter," Q.5574, Q.5595.
22 The final report of the committee favoured an extension of the Bank's charter and suggested no specific regulations. Lord Althorp confirmed the government's intention to be the arbiter of monetary policy in his introductory speech regarding the appointment of an investigating committee. However, he allowed the Bank to retain its discretionary powers in more practical matters. 3 *Hansard,* 12, 22 May 1832, c. 1358.
23 *Parl. Papers,* 1832–2 (722), 6, "Committee ... Bank of England Charter," Q. 5619–21. The "Banking School" theorists, led by Tooke and Gilbert, believed otherwise with regard to the country note circulation. They contended that the issue depended upon the local volume of transactions for which the country notes were currently in use.
24 Ibid., Q.371, Q.678.
25 Ibid., Q.5619.
26 Ibid., Q.6532.
27 Ibid., Q.5697, Q.5704–5, Q.5709–22, Q.5750–4. These were questions answered inadequately by Attwood in his pamphlets.
28 Ibid., Q.5676, Q.57735, Q.5760–1, Q.5770, Q.5775, Q.5778, Q.5794. C.C. Western's description of the religious awe with which the standard was regarded by bullionists had become ever more relevant as the decade wore on. Years earlier he had written that "a degree of something like superstitious veneration has been created for what they [bullionists] called a *Sound Metallic Currency* at the *Ancient* standard of value; a sort of priesthood exercised by the learned on the subject; by which, as in the case of religious superstition, unassuming patient men are induced to believe that there are mysteries beyond the reach of common sense, and in like manner, give up the use of their own understanding, thus undergoing the fate of all common dupes." C.C. Western, *Second Address to the Landowners of the United Kingdom* (London: n.p. 1822), 73, Strip Cobbett's remarks of the rhetoric and demagoguery and one is left with the essence of Ricardo's contentions. Radicals differed only concerning the measure required to produce prosperity within that framework.

29 J.S. Mill, "The Currency Jungle," *Tait's Edinburgh Magazine* (January 1853).
30 Attwood Papers, 2 September 1832, T. Attwood to Elizabeth Attwood.
31 *Mansell and Co.'s Report of the Important Discussion held in Birmingham August 28th and 29th, 1832: Between William Cobbett, Thomas Attwood and Charles Jones, Esquires, on the Question Whether it is Best for the Safety and Welfare of the Nation to attempt to relieve the existing distress "by an Action on the Currency" or by an Equitable Adjustment of the Taxes, Rents, which now strangle the Industry of the Country* (Birmingham: Mansell and Co. 1832).
32 *Birmingham Journal*, 8 September 1832, copy of editorial in the *Morning Chronicle*.
33 *Edinburgh Evening Post*, 2 October 1832.
34 Attwood Papers, 5 September 1832, Lord Grey to T. Attwood.
35 *Birmingham Journal*, 18 and 25 August 1832; *Aris' Birmingham Gazette*, 27 August 1832.
36 Attwood Papers, 3 December 1832, Edward Ellice to T. Attwood.
37 *Birmingham Journal*, 29 September, 6 October, and 24 December 1832.
38 Ibid., 15 December 1832.
39 Wakefield, *Attwood*, 25. Bosco was soured by the whole sorry affair and never sought election again.
40 T. Raikes, *Private Correspondence*, 1: 34–5; report of remark made by the duke of R[utland] to Lord W[harncliffe].
41 *Early Correspondence of Lord John Russell, 1805–1840*, ed. Rollo Russell, 2 vols. (London: Fisher Unwin 1931), 2: 38. An earlier version of this section appeared in D.J. Moss, "A Study in Failure: Thomas Attwood, M.P. for Birmingham 1832–39," *Historical Journal* 21 (1978): 545–70.
42 The expression was first used by the *Times* in an editorial, 4 October 1831.
43 Attwood Papers, 9 February 1833, T. Attwood to Bosco Attwood.
44 Ibid., 21 January 1833, C.C. Western to T. Attwood.
45 3 *Hansard*, 15, 11 February 1833, c. 544–5.
46 Raikes, *Private Correspondence*, 1: 83.
47 *Times*, 7 March 1833.
48 He did present a petition from Birmingham which he had written and the Political Union had circulated, praying that the House would not pass the Irish coercion bill.
49 *Standard*, 11 March 1833; *True Sun*, 11 March 1833.
50 *Morning Herald*, 13 March 1833.
51 *Times*, 7 March 1833. The first notice had appeared the previous day in the column entitled "Money Market and City Intelligence."
52 Raikes, *Private Correspondence*, 1: 160.

53 *Circular to Bankers*, 281, 22 March 1833.
54 3 *Hansard*, 15, 26 February 1833, c. 1166–70.
55 *Birmingham Journal*, 16 March 1833.
56 3 *Hansard*, 15, 21 March 1833, c. 905–38. It was also published. *Speech of Thomas Attwood, Esq. M.P. on the State of the Country in the House of Commons on Thursday the 21st March 1833* (Birmingham: P. Ridgeway 1833).
57 *Times*, 31 March 1833.
58 *Morning Herald*, 22 March 1833.
59 *Birmingham Journal*, 23 February 1833.
60 Raikes, *Private Correspondence*, 1: 171.
61 T. Raikes, *A portion of the Journal Kept by Thomas Raikes* (London: Longman, Brown, Green and Longman 1856), 171–2; Attwood Papers, 2 August 1832, T. Attwood to his wife. In this letter Attwood states that he believed he was getting somewhere with Althorp.
62 Croker, *Correspondence*, 2: 205, Croker to Lady Hertford.
63 Grey Papers, Lord George Harvey to General Charles Grey, May 1833.
64 *Birmingham Journal*, 13 April 1833.
65 Raikes, *Private Correspondence*, 1: 181.
66 Broughton, *Dairy*, 4: 300, April 22–4, 1833.
67 *Times*, 23 April 1833.
68 Attwood Papers, 16 May 1833, T. Attwood to Elizabeth Attwood.
69 George Grote voted with Althorp as he had now decided that if public distress existed it should not be made "the cloak or stalking horse for bringing forward peculiar or individual theories." 3 *Hansard*, 17, 22 April 1833, c. 384–416.
70 *Parl. Papers*, 1830 (343), 17, "Minutes of Evidence taken before the Committee for Coin at the Board of Trade, 1828," 6–15; Lord Ashburton (A. Baring), *The Financial and Commercial Crisis Considered*, 3rd ed. (London: J. Murray 1847), 37–40.
71 3 *Hansard*, 17, 24 April 1833, c. 532.
72 Attwood Papers, 4 May 1833, Aurelius Attwood to his mother.
73 *Birmingham Journal*, 25 May 1833. Later, in the Commons, Attwood claimed an attendance of 150,000. 3 *Hansard*, 18, 24 June 1833, c. 1130. Union membership at this time stood at approximately 20,000.
74 *Cobbett's Political Register*, 25 May 1833. The applause was somewhat premature. Back in the Commons Attwood returned to his less radical suggestions of April and on occasion continued to support the House as it stood. 3 *Hansard,*. 19, 3 July 1833, c. 80.
75 *Birmingham Journal*, 29 June 1833.
76 *Times*, 23 May 1833.
77 3 *Hansard*, 18, 25 May 1833, c. 26.

78 Home Office Papers, Disturbances Correspondence, 40.11, f.405, 11 May 1833, f.407, 14 May 1833, f.410–12, 17 May 1833.
79 3 *Hansard*, 16, 15 May 1833, c. 672–80. He made several futile attempts to exempt meetings called to petition Parliament.
80 *Parl. Papers*, 1833 (690), 6, "Select Committee to Inquire into the Present State of Manufacturing, Commerce and Shipping," Q.4760–4.
81 3 *Hansard*, 38, 5 June 1837, c. 1194, gives Attwood's own account of his problems.
82 *Parl. Papers*, 1833 (448), 15 "Select Committee to Inquire into Public Walks."
83 *Three Nineteenth Century Diaries*, ed. Aspinall, Le Marchant's Diary, 342, 27 June 1833.
84 Attwood Papers, 6 October 1834, T. Attwood to Edward Attwood.
85 *Birmingham Journal*, 25 May 1833.
86 3 *Hansard*, 18, 26 June 1833, c. 426; *Staffordshire Mercury, Pottery Gazette and Newcastle Express*, 6 July 1833.
87 Brougham Papers, British Library, Add. Mss. 126333, J. Parkes to De Le Marchant, 5 August 1833.
88 3 *Hansard*, 19, 9 July 1833, c. 463.
89 *Staffordshire Mercury, Pottery Gazette and Newcastle Express*, 25 May 1833; 3 *Hansard*, 17, 16 May 1833, c. 1324–5.
90 3 *Hansard*, 21, 17 March 1834, c. 302.
91 Ibid., 22, 17 April 1834, c. 371. Attwood's response was equally forthright.
92 Ibid., 21, 3 March 1834, c. 1012. During the previous years Attwood had in fact supported many of Hume's attempts to force retrenchment through as reduction in public salaries and so on. 3 *Hansard*, 6, 7 March 1833, c. 353–6.
93 Attwood voted consistently in favour of motions for the secret ballot. 3 *Hansard*, 17, 25 April 1833, c. 664 was the first.
94 Ibid., 24, 3 July 1834, c. 1006.
95 Attwood was aware of the problem. 3 *Hansard*, 21, 17 March 1834, c. 299.
96 Ibid., 25, 11 August 1834, c. 1224.
97 Ibid., 11 August 1834, c. 1224.
98 *Observations*, 37; *Prosperity Restored*, 8.
99 Later he was in the minority for a vote to amend the Poor Law Amendment Act; the motion was lost 309–17. 3 *Hansard*, 40, 20 February 1838, c. 1416.
100 3 *Hansard*, 37, 6 March 1837, c. 1280–7.
101 3 *Hansard*, 17, 17 April, 1833, c. 204–5.
102 Ibid., 25, 31 July 1834, c. 794. Attwood was well acquainted with Edward Gibbon Wakefield's scheme. His daughter was married to the enthusiast's son.
103 Ibid., 25, 13 August 1834, c. 1285.

104 3 *Hansard*, 19, 5 July 1833, c. 247.
105 Ibid., 18 July 1833, c. 913–14.
106 3 *Hansard*, 15, 14 February 1833, c. 713–16, 16, 26 March 1833, c. 1118.
107 *Birmingham Journal*, 20 September 1834.
108 Attwood Papers, 19, 21 and 24 November 1834, T. Attwood to Elizabeth Attwood. He made a similar statement to his brother Charles, who subsequently engaged in a very public and noisy altercation with Lord Durham. Wakefield, *Attwood*, 275.
109 *True Sun*, 9 December 1834.
110 Each franchise-holder had two votes, since Birmingham was a constituency with the right to have two MPs.
111 Wakefield, *Attwood*, 286. The final poll was Attwood 1,718, Scholefield, 1,660, Spooner 915.
112 *Birmingham Journal*, 10 January 1835.
113 Ibid., 29 November 1834; Letter Books, 28 November 1834, C. Tindall to J.R. Elsey.
114 A.H. Graham, "The Lichfield House Compact," *Irish Historical Studies* 12, 3 (1960–1): 209–25.
115 For information on this attempt to "brigade the opposition," see Mrs M. Fawcett, *Life of Sir William Molesworth* (London: Macmillan 1901), 73; Buckley, *Parkes*, 135; Grote, *George Grote*, 99. Francis Place's account is in the British Library, Add. Mss. 35950, f.17–18.
116 3 *Hansard*, 28, 1 June 1835, c. 287–93.
117 Of those left in charge in 1833 only Bosco was absent.
118 *Birmingham Journal*, 30 May 1835.
119 Ibid., 7 and 13 June 1833.
120 Ibid., 22 August 1833.
121 D. Fraser, *Urban Politics in Victorian England*, (Leicester: Leicester University Press 1976), 115.
122 Conversations with friends proved that his assumed role as conciliator had impressed a number of people. Letter Books, 19 August 1835, C. Tindall to J.C. Turner.
123 *A Report of the Proceedings at the Great Town's Meeting Held in the Town-Hall in Birmingham on Friday, 4 September, 1835* (Birmingham: J. Webb 1835).
124 *Birmingham Journal*, 23 January 1836.
125 3 *Hansard*, 30, 22 August 1835, c. 866. The occasion was the presentation of a petition from Birmingham favouring corporation reform.
126 *The Reformer*, 10 September 1835.
127 *Birmingham Journal*, 8 and 22 January 1836.
128 *Proceedings of the Important Town's Meeting Convened by the Political Union and held in Birmingham Town Hall, On Monday, January 18, 1836* (Birmingham: J. Webb 1836).
129 *Philanthropist*, 4 February 1836.

130 *Birmingham Journal*, 30 January, 6, 20, and 22 February, 5 and 26 March 1836. *Aris' Birmingham Gazette*, 24 April 1826.
131 *Birmingham Journal*, 13 and 20 August 1836.
132 3 *Hansard*, 31, 16 February 1836, c. 442.
133 *Birmingham Journal*, 13 August 1836.
134 For example, 3 *Hansard*, 31, 8 February 1836, c. 155.
135 D. Spring, "Lord Chandos and the Farmer, 1818–1846," *Huntington Library Quarterly* 93 (August 1870): 268–87; Wakefield, *Attwood*, 293; *Agriculturalist*, 2 January 1836.
136 *Parl. Papers*, 1836 (465), 8, "Third Report of the Select Committee appointed to Inquire into the State of Agriculture," Q.15. and Q.569–615.
137 Ibid., Q.16 and Q.455. Matthias Attwood took time from his committee duties to appear before the House of Lords committee on the same subject. Ibid., 1837, 5 (464) "Select Committee of the House of Lords on the State of Agriculture."
138 Attwood Papers, 14 August 1836. Angela married on 1 September 1835 but her emigration was put off for several years because her husband was unable to acquire financial support for his schemes. Eventually he went to New Zealand and she joined him in 1844.
139 Ibid., 16 August 1836, T. Attwood to Elizabeth Attwood.
140 Sinclair of Ulbster Papers, National Library of Scotland, vol. 3, 7 October 1836, T. Attwood to Sir George Sinclair.
141 *Birmingham Journal*, 10 December 1836.
142 Ibid., 17 December 1836.

CHAPTER ELEVEN

1 For an analysis see R.C. Matthews, *A Study in Trade Cycle History* (Cambridge: University Press 1954); Fetter, *Development*, 166–8, and M. Levy-Boyer, "Central Banking and foreign trade: The Anglo-American Cycle in the 1830's," in *Financial Crises: Theory, History and Policy*, ed. C.P. Kindleberger and J.P. Laffargue (Cambridge: University Press 1982), 66–110.
2 Letter Books, 27 December 1836.
3 Sinclair of Ulbster Papers, vol. 3, 5 November 1836, T. Attwood to Sir George Sinclair.
4 The consequences of this change from the artisan's standpoint is cogently presented in Behagg, "An Alliance with the Middle Class," 69–71.
5 Letter Books, 7 March 1837, Charles Tindal to J.C. Turner.
6 Ibid., 8 March 1837, Charles Tindal to J.C. Turner.
7 Attwood Papers, 31 January 1837, T. Attwood to Elizabeth Attwood.

8 Ibid., 7 February 1837, T. Attwood to Sir Robert Peel.
9 Ibid., 14 February 1837, T. Attwood to Elizabeth Attwood.
10 *Birmingham Advertiser,* 9 February 1837, letter from Rev. McDonnell to J. Shea Lalor read aloud at a Rebellion Association Meeting.
11 *Birmingham Journal,* 22 April 1837.
12 Sinclair of Ulbster Papers, 1 April 1837, T. Attwood to Sir George Sinclair; *Birmingham Journal,* 29 April 1837.
13 *Birmingham Journal,* 22 April 1837.
14 Ibid., 10 June 1837. There was some competition for the attention of the workers. A Working Men's Memorial Committee joined with a group of unemployed to discuss the distress with their masters and the merchants. *Birmingham Journal,* 3 June 1837.
15 Attwood Papers, 10 March 1837, T. Attwood to Elizabeth Attwood.
16 Ibid., 7 June 1837. The *Vixen* was an English vessel which had been seized by the Russians on the Circassian coast.
17 *Birmingham Journal,* 18 May 1837.
18 Attwood Papers, 3 June 1837, T. Attwood to Elizabeth Attwood.
19 3 *Hansard,* 37, 5 June 1837, c. 805–1205.
20 Attwood Papers, 7 July 1837; T. Attwood to Elizabeth Attwood.
21 Ibid., 8 June 1837, T. Attwood to Elizabeth Attwood.
22 3 *Hansard,* 37, 5 June 1837, c. 1205.
23 The vote was 85–24.
24 Cf. R. Torrens, *A Letter to the Right Honourable Lord Viscount Melbourne* (London: Longman 1837); S.J. Lloyd, *Reflections suggested by a Perusal of Mr. Horsley Palmer's Pamphlet* (London: P. Richardson 1837), and more then forty others on the subject. The Bank of England had kept its discount rate too low in 1835 and 1836, thus encouraging the speculation which its policies were supposedly designed to discourage. The joint-stock banks had followed. Only the country banks like Attwoods & Spooner had been cautious; as Spooner said, the crisis of 1825–6 had "taught the bankers a lesson which they will not easily forget." *Parl. Papers,* 1836 (445), 8, pt. 2, "Third Report," Q.15708.
25 3 *Hansard,* 37, 5 June 1837, c. 1205.
26 Ibid., 15 June 1837, c. 1912; 39, 14 December 1837, c. 1095.
27 *Birmingham Journal,* 17 June 1837.
28 Letter Books, 14 June 1837, C. Tindall to J.C. Turner.
29 *Birmingham Advertiser,* 22 June 1837.
30 *Birmingham Journal,* 10 June 1837. Nostalgia rather than practicality dominated the decisions. The choice of Newhall Hill as the site of the meeting was particularly inept. Since 1832 the town had expanded and buildings encroached upon the natural amphitheatre so that it was hardly suitable for a mass demonstration.

31 A special invitation to join had been sent to them. Letter Books, 14 June 1837, C. Tindal to J. Turner.
32 *Birmingham Journal,* 24 June 1837.
33 Letter Books, 20 June 1837, C. Tindal to J. Turner.
34 Attwood Papers, 24 June 1837, T. Attwood to Elizabeth Attwood.
35 Ibid., 26 June 1837, T. Attwood to Elizabeth Attwood.
36 Letter Books, 27 June 1837, C. Tindal to J. Turner.
37 Attwood Papers, 2 July 1837, T. Attwood to Elizabeth Attwood.
38 Ibid., 14 July 1837, T. Attwood to Elizabeth Attwood.
39 Letter Books, 25 July 1937, C. Tindal to J. Turner; *Birmingham Journal,* 12 August 1837; *Philanthropist,* 10 August 1837; *Aris' Birmingham Gazette,* 14 August 1837.
40 The final count was Attwood 2,160; Scholefield, 2,132; Stapleton, 1,045.
41 *Birmingham Journal,* 2 September 1837; Flick, *Birmingham Political Union,* 121–2.
42 *Birmingham Journal,* 7 October 1837; *Birmingham Advertiser,* 5 October 1837. The *Advertiser*'s editor looked in vain for the promised attendance of "merchants and manufacturers."
43 Parkes Papers, Birmingham Public Library, Parkes to E.J. Stanley, 24 September 1837.
44 *Birmingham Journal,* 21 October 1837. Later he claimed that he had been driven to this conclusion by the queen's speech in November, but he had been toying with the idea for some time. *Birmingham Journal,* 23 December 1837.
45 Ibid., 28 October 1837. For a discussion of the reluctance of the middle-class members of the council to adopt this measure, see Behagg, "An Alliance with the Middle Class," 73–4.
46 Attwood Papers, 3 and 4 August 1837, T. Attwood to Elizabeth Attwood; *Birmingham Journal,* 5 August 1837.
47 Sinclair of Ulbster Papers, 1 January 1838, T. Attwood to Sir George Sinclair.
48 *Birmingham Journal,* 16 December 1837.
49 *Aris' Birmingham Gazette,* 18 December 1837.
50 Letter Books, 5 December 1837, C. Tindal to J. Turner.
51 *Philanthropist,* 21 December 1837.
52 Ibid., 21, 23, and 25 November 1837.
53 3 *Hansard,* 39, 15 December 1837, c. 1104.
54 Attwood Papers, 5 December 1837, T. Attwood to Elizabeth Attwood.
55 *Birmingham Journal,* 23 December 1837; *Aris' Birmingham Gazette,* 18 December 1837.
56 At one point Attwood stated that he endorsed the incorporation principle because it would "establish real Political Unions in every borough." *Bbirmingham Journal,* 4 November 1837. For further discussion of this point see N. Edsall, "Varieties of Radicalism: Attwood,

Cobden and the Local Politics of Municipal Incorporation," *Historical Journal*, 16, no. 1 (1983): 45–9; Attwood Papers, 3 February 1838, T. Attwood to Elizabeth Attwood. Sir Robert Peel as owner of the manor of Tamworth petitioned against the charter, putting the committee to extra expense.
57 3 *Hansard*, 41, 26 and 27 February 1838.
58 Attwood Papers, 9, 10, 11, 13, 14 March 1838, T. Attwood to Elizabeth Attwood.
59 *Birmingham Journal*, 27 January 1838.
60 Ibid., 17 March 1838.
61 This proposal was vetoed by the other members of the council. However, attendance at the succeeding meetings was described as "thin." Ibid., 3 March 1838.
62 Salt had in fact been responsible for the advance publicity.
63 Attwood Papers, 25 April 1838, A. Purdie to T. Attwood.
64 *Birmingham Journal*, 5 May 1838.
65 In 1837 several members had been most unhappy when he had not strongly supported in the Commons the council's petition demanding the dismissal of the Whig ministry. Ibid., 17 March 1837.
66 Attwood Papers, 5 May 1838, T. Attwood to A. Purdie.
67 *Birmingham Journal*, 26 May 1838; *Glasgow Gazette*, 22 May 1838.
68 *Birmingham Journal*, 2 June 1838, report to the Political Council by R.K. Douglas; Attwood Papers, 18 May 1838, T. Attwood to Elizabeth Attwood.
69 Attwood Papers, 21 May 1838, T. Attwood to Elizabeth Attwood.
70 Place Papers, Add. Mss. 27, 820, ff. 96–8. It appeared in pamphlet form. For the debate on the origin of the charter see D.J. Rowe, "The London Working Men's Association and the People's Charter," *Past and Present* 36 (April 1967): 73–86, and I. Prothero, "Debates: The London Workingmen's Association and the People's Charter," *Past and Present* 38 (October 1967): 169–73.
71 *Birmingham Journal*, 11 May 1839.
72 Ibid., 23 June 1838.
73 Vincent Papers, Transport House, London, 1/1/6, 18 June 1838, H. Vincent to T. Minikin.
74 *Birmingham Journal*, 21 July 1838.
75 Attwood Papers, 14 July 1838, T. Attwood to Elizabeth Attwood.
76 *Birmingham Journal*, 11 August 1838. Mark Hovell claimed that this meeting was the beginning of the Chartist movement. M. Hovell, *The Chartist Movement*, 2nd ed. (Manchester: University Press 1925), 107.
77 Vincent Papers, 1/1/8, 7 August 1838, H. Vincent to J. Minikin.
78 For an analysis, see J. Epstein, *The Lion of Freedom: Feargus O'Connor and the Chartist Movement, 1832–42* (London: Croome Helm 1984).

79 *Weekly True Sun,* 30 September 1838.
80 Vincent Papers, 1/1/10, 26 August 1838, H. Vincent to J. Minikin.
81 *Birmingham Journal,* 3 and 10 November 1838. For an analysis of Stephens, an ex-Methodist minister, see J.T. Ward, "Revolutionary Tory," *Transactions of the Lancashire and Cheshire Antiquarian Society* 68 (1950): 93–116.
82 Sinclair of Ulbster Papers, 2 October 1838, T. Attwood to Sir George Sinclair.
83 *Birmingham Journal,* 17 November 1838.
84 For O'Connor's attitude see Flick, *The Birmingham Political Union,* 151–62.
85 *Birmingham Journal,* 1 December 1838. O'Connor had arrived in Birmingham several days earlier and had again attended a Political Union council meeting where the argument had been renewed.
86 *Aris' Birmingham Gazette,* 13 August 1838; *Birmingham Gazette,* 11 August 1838. The latter newspaper reported seven additions.
87 *Birmingham Journal,* 24 November 1838.
88 Ibid., 1 December 1838; *Birmingham Journal,* 29 December 1838.
89 Ibid., 5 January 1839.
90 *Birmingham Journal,* 23 March 1839.
91 Attwood Papers, 4, 7, 18, and 20 February 1839, T. Attwood to Elizabeth Attwood.
92 *Birmingham Journal,* 30 March 1839.
93 *Times,* 11 March 1839.
94 Attwood Papers, 20 February 1839, T. Attwood to Elizabeth Attwood. The Political Union had opposed an effort in the town to start a separate anti-Corn Law campaign. This decision to work exclusively for the charter healed some of the rifts with the working men's groups.
95 3 *Hansard,* 46, 21 March 1839, c. 1100–1.
96 *Birmingham Journal,* 13 April 1839.
97 Attwood Papers, 1 May 1839, T. Attwood to Elizabeth Attwood.
98 Vincent Papers, 5/11, *The Western Vindicator,* 11 May 1839, "Life and Rambles of Henry Vincent."
99 Ibid., 5/12, 18 May 1839.
100 *Birmingham Journal,* 11 May 1839.
101 Behagg, "An Alliance with the Middle Class," 78–82.
102 Philip Henry Muntz, brother of the old councillor and future MP, G.F. Muntz, served as mayor in 1839 and 1840.
103 3 *Hansard,* 46, 15 March 1839, c. 802.
104 Ibid., 26 March 1839, c. 1186–97.
105 Ibid., 47, 30 May 1839, c. 1139–51.
106 Ibid., 26 March 1839, c. 1186–97; Ibid., 46, 26 March 1839, c. 1189.

107 Attwood Papers, 8 May 1839, T. Attwood to Elizabeth Attwood.
108 Ibid., 13 May, 1839, T. Attwood to Elizabeth Attwood.
109 Ibid., 14 May 1839, T. Attwood to Elizabeth Attwood.
110 3 *Hansard*, 48, 14 June 1839, c. 222–5.
111 *Birmingham Journal*, 6 July 1838; *Report of the Committee Appointed by the Town Council September 3rd. 1839 to Investigate the Causes of the Late Riots* (Birmingham: W. Hutton 1840). The Political Union had been dissolved in May.
112 3 *Hansard*, 49, 8 July 1839, c. 41–8.
113 Ibid., 12 July 1839, c. 274.
114 Wakefield, *Attwood*, 344, T. Attwood to his constituents, 17 July 1839.
115 *Birmingham Journal*, 20 July 1839.
116 Ibid., 17 July 1841. This was his own assessment.

CHAPTER TWELVE

1 *Birmingham Journal*, 1 February 1840. Efforts by the town council to provide a testimonial failed on political grounds. *Birmingham Advertiser*, 20 February 1840.
2 *Birmingham Journal*, 28 March 1840.
3 Sinclair of Ulbster Papers, 14 December 1839, T. Attwood to Sir George Sinclair.
4 *Aris' Birmingham Gazette*, 22 July 1839.
5 3 *Hansard*, 49, 23 July 1839, c. 707. He spoke on the subject on seven different occasions.
6 Ibid., 29 July 1839, c. 950.
7 Ibid., 2 August 1839, c. 1177.
8 Ibid., 29 July 1839, c. 950. Always loyal to old friends, in 1837 Attwood spent much time he might have devoted to the Union defending George Muntz in an assault case.
9 Sinclair of Ulbster Papers, 16 August 1839, T. Attwood to Sir George Sinclair.
10 3 *Hansard*, 50, 8 August 1839, c. 109. He included women's labour in this call for natural justice, on one occasion advocating an extensive overhaul of the legal system to improve the position of women. Whenever he visited Birmingham after 1837 he made a point of taking tea with the members of the Female Political Union.
11 Attwood Papers, 31 March 1842, Sir R. Peel to T. Attwood.
12 Ibid., 1 October 1839, Lord Melbourne to T. Attwood.
13 3 *Hansard*, 50, 9 August 1839, c. 173–4.
14 Sinclair of Ulbster Papers, 14 December 1839, T. Attwood to Sir George Sinclair. He was replaced as MP for Birmingham by G.F. Muntz, who became one of the "characters" of the House of Commons by

reason of his appearance, which "would promptly disperse a whole gang of banditti," rather than his views. He did, however, have one achievement. He persuaded the government to adopt the perforation of postage stamps. Edwards, *Personal Recollections*, 81, and J. Grant, *Portraits of Public Characters*, 2 vols. (London: Saunders and Otley 1841), 1: 87–93.

15 *Birmingham Journal*, 4 July 1840.
16 Foster published a series of articles in the *Jersey Gazette*, describing the rise and fall of the Political Union. These were reprinted in the *Birmingham Journal*, 19 and 26 September, 3 October 1840.
17 *Birmingham Journal*, 19 and 26 June, 17 July 1841. He completed the "History" by the end of August 1840.
18 Ibid., 17 July 1841.
19 Ibid., 26 June 1841. The "History" was dispatched to friends and acquaintances. See for example de Lisle Brock Papers, University of London, Ms. 643/7, 9 August 1841, Daniel de Lisle Brock to T. Attwood.
20 Sinclair of Ulbster Papers, 8 August 1840, T. Attwood to Sir George Sinclair.
21 *Birmingham Journal*, 12 December 1840. The final disposition of the £100 has not been discovered.
22 Ibid., 9 January 1841.
23 Wakefield, *Attwood*, 376.
24 *Birmingham Advertiser*, 24 December 1840.
25 *Birmingham Journal*, 9 January 1841. He published two long letters.
26 Ibid., 17 July 1841.
27 Ibid., 7 November 1840.
28 Ibid., 19 June 1841.
29 Peel Papers, Add. Mss. 40456, f. 195, 3 December 1841.
30 Ibid., f. 197, 7 December 1841.
31 Ibid., Add. Mss. 40497, f. 95, 10 December 1841.
32 Ibid., f. 79, 14 December 1841.
33 Ibid., Add. Mss. 40505, f. 181, 28 March 1841.
34 Wakefield, *Attwood*, 381–2.
35 Ibid., 321. On Elizabeth's death the capital, £20,000, reverted to the Carless family.
36 *Birmingham Journal*, 16 June 1835.
37 Ibid., 13 September 1835. Cf. speech of P.H. Muntz.
38 Ibid., 26 June 1841.
39 Attwood Papers, 20 May 1835, T. Attwood to Elizabeth Attwood.
40 Peel Papers, Add. Mss. 40551, f. 6, 6 September 1844.
41 Attwood Papers, 23 January 1843, T. Attwood to Algernon Attwood.
42 *Banker's Magazine*, May 1865; *Birmingham Journal*, 18 March, 1 April

1865. Isaac Spooner discovered the enormous deficit. George's personal debt was almost £400,000 in 1848–9 and proceedings were begun against him. However, he died before the matter could be concluded. It had thereupon been left to Richard Spooner, who like Thomas Attwood had neglected the bank, to insist upon the disposition of the family's holdings as originally outlined by Matthias Attwood shortly before his death. George transferred the assets to the bank which reduced the debt by £167,000. He accepted a pension of £1,500 per annum in lieu but only lived a few months, dying in May 1854. The Attwood family debt now stood at £253,000 plus the £12,286 still owed by Thomas and an additional £6,000 by Thomas Aurelius Attwood, Thomas's son.

Two new partners, George and Henry Marshall, had been brought in some years earlier. Neither had contributed much in the way of capital – they had previously been the bank's chief clerks and had relatives who were bankers in Walsall. By the end of 1864 only one partner, Henry Marshall, survived. At this time there was an attempt to amalgamate with the Birmingham Joint Stock Bank. It failed after an inspection of the books. The creditors then deemed that it was inadvisable for the estate to go through bankruptcy court because of the expense and its reputation for slowness. An attempt was made instead to get the London bank, then under the management of Wolverly Attwood, Matthias Attwood's son, to buy the estates owned by the bank above the market value and to cover some of his relatives' debts. Wolverly denied responsibility and would not go beyond an offer of £20,000 above the legal valuation. This was deemed unsatisfactory. Finally the property and assets of the bank were taken over by the Birmingham Joint Stock Bank which agreed to pay all creditors 11s. 3d. in the pound. The Spooners escaped most of the public opprobrium, having left a debt of only £3,000 compared to over a quarter of a million charge to the Attwoods. Nevertheless, all the partners were culpable to some degree either through misappropriation or negligence. The continuation of business after 1853 when the bank was beyond help was particularly criminal.

43 Attwood Papers, 23 January 1843, T. Attwood to Algernon Attwood.
44 Brougham Papers, Add. Mss. 30752, 29 July 1842, and Add. Mss. 25148, 10 August 1842.
45 *Birmingham Journal*, 15 July 1843.
46 Ibid., 29 July, 19 August, 30 September 1843.
47 Ibid., 4 November 1843, letter to the requisitionists from T. Attwood.
48 Ibid., 5 October 1843.
49 Ibid., 4 November 1843.

50 *Times*, 16 November 1843. The editorial was used by Attwood as an excuse for a new spate of letters to the editor. Between 7 November and 28 December, the *Times* published a total of seven letters from him and noticed him in editorials four times. The debate then in progress on the form of the proposed Bank Act undoubtedly contributed to the newspaper's interest.
51 *Birmingham Journal*, 7 October 1843.
52 Ibid., 18 November 1843.
53 Peel Papers, Add. Mss. 40551, f. 6, 2 September 1844.
54 Ibid., f. 8, 3 September 1844.
55 Wakefield, *Attwood*, 414.
56 Ibid.
57 de Lisle Brock Papers, 5642/9, 10 February 1843, Benjamin Hadley to T. Attwood.
58 Attwood Papers, 12 July 1845, T. Attwood to Algernon Attwood.
59 Wakefield, *Attwood*, 396.
60 Attwood Papers, 6 December 1845, T. Attwood to John Betts.
61 *Birmingham Journal*, 13 December 1845.
62 Wakefield, *Attwood*, 399.
63 He voted in the county election and not in Birmingham because his permanent residence was in the village of Handsworth.
64 He was not alone. Muntz refused to run with Scholefield or even to appear on the same platform. Edwards, *Personal Recollections*, 79–80.
65 Attwood corresponded with Sir Archibald Alison, of the Sheriff's Office, Glasgow, and was thanked for his comments on one of Alison's pamphlets on the currency.
66 *Morning Post*, 2 and 17 June, 1847.
67 Attwood Papers, 24 June 1847, T. Attwood to Algernon Attwood.
68 Ibid., 7 April 1865, Marcus Attwood to Angela Wakefield.
69 Ibid., 1 November 1847, T. Attwood to Lord George Bentinck.
70 Ibid., 27 March 1848, T. Attwood to G.F. Muntz.
71 Edwards, *Personal Recollections*, 50.
72 Wakefield, *Attwood*, 404.
73 Matthias Attwood died in 1851, George Attwood in 1854, and George de Bosco prematurely in 1855 at the age of forty-seven, leaving a widow with six children. Algernon married Emma Foulkes, of Wrexham, in August 1853; Rosabel married Henry Saunders of Kennington, Surrey, in August 1855.
74 He died intestate. Information on the administration of the estate is to be found in Somerset House, P.C.C. Admin Act Book (G.B. Moore), June 1856.
75 *Birmingham Mercury*, 21 April 1856.
76 Wakefield, *Attwood*, 428.

77 Lines written in the album of "Miss Pearman of Tennal Hall," cited by Wakefield, *Attwood*, 411–12.
78 Peel Papers, Add. Mss. 40496, f. 195, 3 December 1841, T. Attwood to Sir Robert Peel.
79 T. Tooke and W. Newmarch, *History of Prices and the State of Circulation form 1793 (to the Present Times)*, 6 vols. (London: Longman 1857), 5: preface, vi.
80 The *Gemini Letters*, first printed in the *Midland Chronicle* in 1843, were evidence of the existence of a school outside Attwood's immediate orbit.
81 Richardson, "Thomas Attwood," 165. This opinion was voiced by Sir Denis Robertson in conversation with Dr Richardson.
82 *Prosperity Restored*, 45–56.
83 Attwood Papers, 27 August 1820, T. Attwood to Elizabeth Attwood.
84 *Birmingham Journal*, 26 September 1840, extract from the *Jersey Gazette*'s articles by Rev. Charles Foster based on Attwood's conversations with him.
85 *Birmingham Journal*, 21 February 1840. These were his own words.

A Note on Sources

The varied nature and number of sources available for this study will be readily apparent from the notes. The main purpose of the following select bibliography, drawn from several thousand items, is to help the reader locate the most important primary materials. I have not included such obvious but essential references as *Hansard Parliamentary Debates,* the *Journals* of the House of Commons and the House of Lords, the *Sessional Papers* of both Houses, or the *Statutes of the Realm.* Space also precludes separate listing of relevant articles in the periodical literature of the Georgian and Victorian periods.

PRIMARY SOURCES: UNPUBLISHED

The most valuable collection of Attwood's letters and papers is held by Mrs Priscilla Mitchell, Totnes, Devon, a direct descendant of Thomas Attwood. Much of the correspondence and some of the printed material, in edited form, can also be found in a nineteenth-century biography of Attwood, written by his grandson, C.M. Wakefield; some of the material used by Wakefield has since disappeared. Attwood was a prolific letter writer as the private papers of many prominent men of the period attest. All major and many minor archives, including those in local record offices, were consulted. Among the most illuminating collections were the Bromley-Davenport Papers, John Rylands Library, Manchester; the Peel Papers, Place Papers, Brougham Papers, and Holland Papers, British Library; Russell Papers, Public Record Office; Birmingham Letter Books, Bank of England, Roehampton; Durham manuscripts and Grey Papers, Prior's Kitchen, Durham; Parkes Papers, in the Birmingham Library and at the University of London; Sinclair of Ulbster Papers, National Library of Scotland; and the Burdett-Coutts Papers, Bodleian Library, Oxford.

Birmingham Reference Library's holdings are extensive and were widely consulted. The Birmingham Town Book, the Commonplace Book on the Birmingham District as well as the scrapbooks of Broadsides, Sheets, and Handbills relating to the Birmingham Political Union were particularly useful. Similarly, the Public Record Office with its incomparable collection was worked through systematically.

PRIMARY SOURCES: PUBLISHED

Publications by Thomas Attwood, listed by date

Speech of Thomas Attwood, Esq., at the Town Meeting against the Renewal of the East Indian Company Charter, Birmingham: O. and H. Smith 1813.

The Remedy; or, Thoughts on the Present Distresses. In a letter to a public editor, 3 July 1816. London: Whittingham and Arliss 1816.

The Remedy; or Thoughts on the Present Distress. Second edition, with additions. London: Whittingham and Arliss 1816.

A Letter to the Right Honourable Nicholas Vansittart, on the Creation of Money, and its Action on National Prosperity. Birmingham: R. Wrightson 1817.

Prosperity Restored; or, Reflections on the Cause of the Present Distresses and on the Only Means of Relieving Them. By the Author of The Remedy, or, Thoughts on the Present Distresses. London: R. Wrightson 1817.

Observations on Currency, Population and Pauperism, in two letters to Arthur Young, Esquire, by Thomas Attwood, Esq. Birmingham: R. Wrightson 1818.

A Letter to the Earl of Liverpool, on the Reports of the Committees of the Two Houses of Parliament, on the Questions of the Bank Restrictions Act. Birmingham: R. Wrightson 1819.

A second Letter to the Earl of Liverpool, on the Bank Reports, as Occasioning the National Dangers and Distresses. Birmingham: R. Wrightson 1819.

State of Ireland: the Cause of the Present Disturbances in Ireland, as shewn by Mr. Attwood in his Seventh Letter on the Subject of the Currency, addressed to the Editor of the Farmer's Journal, and Inserted in the Paper on the 15th May 1820. London: n.p. 1820.

Mr. Attwood's Letters and Tables, Shewing the Unjust Payment from the Landed to the Monied Interest, by the Present System: with the Ruin of the Landlord and Tenant. Stamford: J. Drakard 1822.

A Correspondence Between Mr. Kitchen, Barford, and T. Attwood Esq., Birmingham, on the Subject of Returning to Cash Payments. Warwick: n.p. 1832.

The Late Prosperity, and the Present Adversity of the Country, Explained; the

Proper Remedies Considered, and the Comparative Merits of the English and Scottish Systems of Banking Discussed in a Correspondence between Sir J. Sinclair and Mr. Thomas Attwood. London: J. Ridgeway 1826.

Correspondence Between Kirkman Finlay, John Gladstone, Sir J. Sinclair and Thomas Attwood. No copy is known today but Wakefield saw copy endorsed by Attwood: "Printed by Sir John Sinclair, and afterwards suppressed by desire of Finlay and Gladstone." It is listed in *Memoirs of Sir John Sinclair,* 2: 414.

An Exposition of the Cause and Remedy of the Agricultural Distress. Hertford: St. Austin and Son 1828.

The Scotch Banker, containing articles under that signature on Banking, Currency, and republished from the Globe newspaper, etc. London: J. Ridgeway 1828.

Distressed State of the Country. The Speech of Thomas Attwood, Esq., on this Important Subject, at the Town's Meeting in Birmingham, held on the 8th May 1829. Birmingham: Beilby, Knott and Beilby 1928. This version was "revised and corrected" by Attwood. Another and shorter edition was published but was described by him as "very incorrect."

The Speech of Thomas Attwood, Esq., before the Lord Mayor and the Court of Common Council, on being presented with the Freedom of the City of London, May XXII, MDCCCXXXII. Birmingham: Broadside 1832.

Mansell and Co.'s Report of the Important Discussion held in Birmingham, August the 28th and 29th, 1832, Between William Cobbett, Thomas Attwood and Charles Jones, Esqrs. on the Question whether is it best for the safety and welfare of the nation to attempt to relieve the existing distress "by an action on the currency" or by "equitable Adjustment" of the taxes, etc. Birmingham: Mansell and Co. 1832.

Speech of Thomas Attwood Esq., M.P., on the State of the Country, in the House of Commons, on Thursday, the 21st of March, 1833. London: J. Ridgeway 1833.

Letter of Mr. T. Attwood to the Right Hon. Sir Robert Peel, Bart. London: Vacher and Sons 1837.

Other speeches on political and financial issues were published by a variety of printers. However, the accuracy of these reports is often questionable.

Attwood's evidence before parliamentary committees is contained in the following volumes:

Minutes of Evidence, taken before the Committee of the Whole House, To whom it was referred, to consider of the Several Petitions which have been presented to the House, in this Session of Parliament, relating to the Orders in Council. Parl. Papers, Commons, 1812 (210), 3:1–19.

Report from the Select Committee on the Petitions complaining of the Distressed State of Agriculture of the United Kingdom. Parl. Papers, Commons, 1812 (668), 9:242–63.

Report from the Committee on Secrecy in the Bank of England Charter; with the Minutes of Evidence. Parl. Papers, Commons, 1831–32 (772), 6:452–68.

Finally, letters were published in a variety of newspapers and periodicals. Among the most important are the series of ten letters to the *Farmers' Journal*, in a debate with George Webb Hall on the subject of the Corn Law, and those to the *Globe* which were subsequently republished as *The Scotch Banker*, listed above. Usually the letters were printed over his own name but occasionally over a pseudonym. Instances of the latter have been identified either by reference to his private correspondence or through the work of his grandson, C.M. Wakefield.

Other contemporary sources

Space precludes references to the range of nineteenth-century books, newspapers, and periodicals used in this study relating to the controversies, economic and political, in which Attwood became embroiled. These contemporary publications are cited in the text only when a discussion or interpretation is based primarily upon particular items.

SECONDARY SOURCES

Political history, monetary and banking development in Britain between 1783 and 1856 have been covered in the last sixty years by a large volume of literature. It is not the intention of this note to provide even a selection since the most useful books and articles are cited in the notes. The following items are of general interest.

For an introduction to the subject of monetary history in the period, F. Fetter, *Development of British Monetary Orthodoxy* (1965) is outstanding. There is a variety of more specialized but comprehensive monographs including E. Victor Morgan, *The Theory and Practice of Central Banking 1797–1913* (1965); L.S. Pressnell, *Country Banking in the Industrial Revolution* (1956); and R. Cameron, *Banking in the Early Stages of Industrialization* (1967). Among the articles, apart from my own, in which Attwood's specific approach to the economy is examined are A. Briggs, "Thomas Attwood and the Economic Background of the Birmingham Political Union," *Cambridge Historical Journal* (1948); and S. Checkland, "The Birmingham Economists, 1815–1850," *Economic History Review* (1948).

The course of the political reform movement leading to the Reform Bill has been extensively charted, although the debate about motives and the importance of the change is far from resolved.

Two studies of particular value are M. Brock, *The Great Reform Act* (1973), and, for the state of the Tory party, B. Hilton, *Corn, Cash and Commerce* (1978). Radicalism is well served by biography, although a definitive interpretation has still to be written. The role played by the Birmingham Political Union was recently surveyed in C. Flick, *The Birmingham Political Union and the Movements for Reform in Britain, 1830–32* (1978), but it lacks authority. Articles by A. Briggs, cited above and including "The Background to the Parliamentary Reform Movement in Three English Cities, 1830–32," *Cambridge Historical Journal* (1952), and by H. Ferguson, "The Birmingham Political Union and the Government, 1830–31," *Victorian Studies* (1960), have more positive conclusions. The latter's argument is more fully developed in his Harvard doctoral thesis, "The Birmingham Political Union, 1830–32" (1959), which was kindly made available to me.

Analysis of the Chartist movement is under constant revision and recent work on the background and motivation of the participants has been particularly interesting; see, for example, G. Stedman-Jones, "Rethinking Chartism," in *Languages of Class: Studies in English Working Class History, 1832–1982* (1983). With regard to the movement in Birmingham a recent article by C. Behagg, "An Alliance with the Middle Class: The Birmingham Political Union and Early Chartism," in J.A. Epstein and D. Thompson, eds., *The Chartist Experience: Studies in Working Class Radicalism and Culture, 1830–60* (1982), complements this biography. A study of Attwood's position might begin with M. Hovell's brief overview in *The Chartist Movement* (1918). Although it now appears simplistic, it is nevertheless stimulating.

Index

Abercrombie, James, 254
Abolition of property qualification, 269
Addison & Co., 141
Adelphi Steel House, 18
Agricultural distress: (1820–1) 95, 97; 101–4; (1829) 152, 157; (1836) 260
Agriculturalist lobby: (1819) 82; (1820–1) 87–8, 95–6, 97–9; 110, 135, 259–60
Allday, Joseph, 158
Allesley, 302
Althorp, Viscount, 143, 232; and Attwood, 224–5, 241; and Bank of England, 235, 248; and currency, 231–2, 242–4, 345n22; and political reform, 187; and Union, 175, 203, 207
Annual parliaments, 103, 158, 180, 245, 278
Annual Register, 117, 174
Antislavery, 112, 143
Aris' Birmingham Gazette, 115, 130, 131, 158, 269
Armaments industry, 5, 7, 35, 51, 73
Assignat, 67–8
Attwood, Algernon, 78, 275, 294, 296, 302, 358n73
Attwood, Angela, 260, 275, 294–6, 299, 350n138
Attwood, Ann (née Adams), 17, 20, 260
Attwood, Aurelius, 31, 215, 245, 294
Attwood, Benjamin, 23, 308n8
Attwood, Charles, 191, 219, 224, 292, 308n8, 338n38
Attwood, Edward Marcus, 71, 192, 195, 275, 278, 294–5, 308n8
Attwood, Elizabeth (née Carless), 29–31, 42, 48, 85, 116, 143, 192, 291, 294
Attwood, George, Jr, 21, 115–16, 118, 294–6, 297, 308n8, 309n17, 356–7n42
Attwood, George, Sr, 17–18, 309n10
Attwood, George de Bosco: as candidate for Parliament, 230–1, 237, 242; career, 260, 275, 294, 302; early life, 31, 112, 116; and Political Council, 207, 237–8, 269

Attwood, James, 18–19, 101, 308n8
Attwood, James, Sr, 309n10
Attwood, John, 100, 124–5, 128, 137–8, 142–3, 275
Attwood, Matthias, Jr: and Bank, 119; banking committee, 232–3, 345n16; currency motions, 104–5, 239–40, 243–4; economic analysis, 10, 11, 72, 79–81, 90, 181, 252, 260–1; Parliament, 32, 83, 86, 88, 98, 102, 137, 166; political reform, 76, 166, 194, 210; and Thomas, 54, 72, 107, 247
Attwood, Matthias, Sr, 17–20 passim, 111, 260, 309n10, 322–3n26, 356–7n42
Attwood, Rosabel, 100, 294, 296, 299, 302, 358n73
Attwood, Susanna, 87
Attwood, Thomas.
– agriculture, 66–7, 87–90, 94–7, 109–10
– analysis of economy: (1816–18) 84, 107, 109;

368 Index

(1825–6) 118–25 passim; (1827) 134–5; (1828) 145; (1833) 245; (1835–6) 261, 264–5, 268; (1840) 293; (1842) 297; (1847) 301–2
- annual parliaments, 278
- and Australia, 252, 260, 294
- Bank of England, 55, 59–61, 65–6, 79–80, 111, 119, 121, 124, 140, 142, 145, 234, 264, 265, 267, 268, 287, 319n35
- Bank Restriction Act, 9, 68–9, 83, 104
- Banking committee (1832–3) 226, 231–5 passim, 248
- Birmingham: creation of power base, 85–7, 113, 129–30, 138; economic activities in, 17–18, 27, 33, 116, 140–2; elections: (1832) 236; (1834) 253–4; (1837) 271; identification with, 25, 33, 49–50, 227; its economy, 64, 72–3, 110, 145; as high bailiff of, 5, 34, 36–48 passim; leader of, 4, 16, 48–50, 86, 110, 113, 152, 162–3, 227, 265, 288; loss of support in, 4, 115–16, 127–8, 158; memorial, 292–3, 302–3; as model, 31, 56, 57, 73, 144, 291; police bill, 289, 296–7; politics, 73, 78, 86–7, 129–30, 139–40, 293, 295; radicalism, 15, 34, 44, 50, 72, 76, 78, 110, 138, 297; social life, 27–8, 112; withdrawal from, 127–9, 296
- Birmingham school, 12, 15, 72, 85–7, 90–5, 111–12, 128–9, 135–8, 145

- Bullion committee (1810): 54–5, 83
- and Burdett, 76, 148, 155, 166, 168–9, 176–7, 179
- Catholic emancipation, 116
- charity, 74–5, 294
- childhood and education, 5, 21–2
- Church of England, 159
- Church of Ireland, 159
- and Cobbett, 75, 148, 163, 176, 214, 231, 235–6, 241
- commemorative plate, 46, 313n55
- Commons, 13, 47, 74, 92, 96–7, 135–6, 144, 153–4, 163, 245
- Corn Laws, 53, 268, 293, 300
- crisis (1825–6) 118–25
- currency management 9, 11, 57–60, 64–70
- and Davenport 102–3, 137, 145, 148–9, 165–6, 302, 322n9, 327n35, 334n96
- East India Company, 5, 30, 39–41, 43–4, 48–9
- East Retford, 139–40, 144, 146
- economic theory, 4, 55–6, 59–61, 62, 64, 69–70, 129, 319n35; agriculture, 66–7, 70; banking system: 27–8, 53, 54, 112, 119–20, 127, 129, 140–2 passim, 264, 268; capital fund theory, 234; contract adjustment 316n42; exchequer bills, 9–10, 54, 69, 122, 318n10, 319n35; full employment, 11, 58, 70, 234, 251; gold standard, 4, 10, 55, 57–60 passim, 83, 106, 107, 129, 234–5, 255, 269, 316n26;

inflation, 9–11 passim, 55, 63–4; international exchanges, 58, 97, 234–5, 285; international trade, 40, 43, 64, 234; labour theory of value, 57, 234, 289; money, 9–11, 57–60 passim, 64–70 passim, 211, 251; national debt, 65–6, 70; panacea, (1818) 63, 65–6; (1833) 69, 234–5; (1836–7) 264–5; price theory, 61, 68, 70, 234; productivity, 57, 64; taxation, 8–11 passim, 55, 62, 72, 109, 234; wage rates, 58, 64, 234
- faith in business, 56–7, 72, 84, 97
- family background, 17–18
- family life, 32, 71, 74–5, 78, 85, 92, 100, 111–12, 116, 143, 192, 195, 199, 260–1, 270–1, 275, 281, 291, 294–5, 296, 299–300
- Far East, 40–1, 43
- and France, 101, 105–7, 133–4, 295, 300
- House of Lords, 79, 154
- idealism, 153–4, 160–1
- illness, physical and mental, 4, 14, 20, 87, 92, 109, 156
- industrial revolution, 56, 110
- inventions, 33
- and Ireland, 145, 239, 265, 278–9
- Irish Catholics, 159–60
- Jews, 252, 322n23
- legal system, 30, 153
- lobbying, Westminster, 79, 89, 96, 114, 136, 142; London, 31, 44, 47, 48, 50, 55, 72–3, 76–8, 89, 96, 105, 114, 119, 237–8

369 Index

- and Lord Liverpool, 4, 11, 47, 54, 75, 83–4, 91, 106–7, 118–21, 128, 133
- Malthusianism, 11, 57–8, 234, 316n48
- member of Parliament: and Birmingham, 243, 263; colonization, 251–2; Currency club, 240; defence of friends, 289–90; English nationalism, 249, 328n39; factory acts, 251–2, 260; failure in Commons, 13–14, 254–5, 261, 264–5, 248–50, 267–8, 274, 285, 289; Literary Union, 240; motion on currency: (1833) 241–2; (1837) 267; and Navy estimates, 285; new approach to reform, 269–70, 273, 285–6; opinion of Commons 243, 244–5, 250, 252–3, 255, 258–60, 274; parliamentary committees, 247–8; plea for managed currency, 251; political expectations: (1833) 238–40; and Poor Law, 251; secret ballot, 189, 348n93; sense of accomplishment, 270; style, 241, 248; Warwickshire Peace commission, 249. See also Tory party (Commons); Whig party (Commons)
- Mechanics Institute, 116, 132, 136, 159–60
- merit as economist, 303
- military career, 29–30
- opinion of middle class, 92, 216–17
- Orders-in-Council: (1812–13) 38–40, 46–7
- Peel's Act (1819), 104, 109, 118–19, 268
- Political Union (1830–2): 9, 13, 93, 140, 147, 152–4, 157–9, 160–2, 220; affection of people, 198–9, 212–13, 218, 222; challenge to Wellington, 218, 221–2; and currency reform, 211; defence of king, 218; expense of, 170, 192, 294; French revolution (1830), 184–5; House of Lords, 199, 214, 216, 220; and Hunt, 190, 197; judicial system, 191; leadership of, 13, 171, 180, 185–6, 209–10, 216–17, 223; as moderate force, 203–4, 211, 221, 224; and O'Connell, 153, 166, 198; as public speaker in, 173; radicalism at time of Union, 146–7, 150, 186; radicals, 148, 150, 161, 189, 198, 209; rumours of rewards, 195, 224; Ultra-Tories, 164–6, 168; Warwick election (1831), 182
- Political Union (1835–9): approval of Council's radicalism, 275; attempt to create all-party union, 256–7, 270–3; Chartists, 14, 276, 278, 284; defence of, 283–4, 291, 297–8; equal electoral districts, 278, 284; increasing radicalism, 258–9, 268–9, 270–3; losing leadership, 263, 268, 277; moral emphasis, 277, 279, 281–2; Municipal Corporations Act, 255–8, 352n56; national convention, 277, 281, 283–5, 287; national petition (Charter), 284–7; national rent, 280–1; and O'Connell, 245, 246, 275–6; and O'Connor, 14, 279–81, 287; reform of House of Lords, 257–9; rumours of death, 281; and universal suffrage, 158, 273, 274, 278, 280
- physical appearance and character, 23, 28–30, 31, 32, 116
- and Poland, 211–12, 249, 275, 295, 275
- political reform: early opinion, 34, 42, 47, 318n20; 71–4, 76, 78, 86, 92–3, 103–4, 128–9, 138–9, 144, 150, 153–4, 163, 269–70, 273, 285–6
- and provincial opinion, 31, 47, 149
- pursuit of fortune, 33–4, 51–2
- railway promotion, 113–15
- retirement: appeal to Peel, 293–4, 298–9; assessment of his radicalism, 305–6; Belgium, 300; death of, 302–3; election preferences (1847), 300–1; financial situation, 294–6, 299–300; illness, 299, 302–3; memorial, 292–3, 303; and moderate reform (1842), 297–8; opinion on leadership, 291–2, 304–5; political failure, 290–1, 301; and Western Canada, 293–5
- Ricardianism, 9, 55–7, 61, 90, 234, 252
- and Ricardo, 6, 8–9, 11, 57, 67, 107–8, 290

– and Rouen, 101, 106, 133–4
– and Russia, 106, 143, 249, 266, 274, 283
– and United States, 38, 262
– world view, 186, 304–5
Attwood, Wolverly, 49, 357n42
Attwoods & Spooner (Birmingham), 14–15, 18, 23–4, 27, 32–3, 51–2, 75, 78, 101, 111–12, 114–15, 123–5, 128, 134, 140–2, 208, 294–6, 356–7n42
Attwoods & Spooner (London), 30–1, 52, 101, 115

Babbington, Matthew, 49
Bank Charter Act (1844), 12, 13, 302, 304
Bank of British North America, 294
Bank of England: and Attwood, 51, 140–1, 142, 233–4; and Attwoods & Spooner, 208; banking system, 9–10, 118–20, 264, 268, 352n24; branches, 128, 140–1, 326n3; as central bank, 55, 60, 79, 104–5, 117, 118–20, 126, 140–2; gold, 5–7, 53, 59–60, 80–2, 107–9; renewal of charter, 184, 226, 248
Bank of England branch (Birmingham), 128–9, 140
Bank Restriction Act (1797), 3, 13, 26–7, 67–8
Banking crisis (1824–6), 117–25
Baring, Alexander, 12, 98–9, 181, 335n114
Barnes, Thomas, 168–9
Baskerville, Thomas, 18
Beardsworth's Repository, 139, 146, 161, 201, 333n69

Beardsworth, John, 333n69
Bedfordshire, 251
Behagg, Clive, 284
Belgium, 184, 186, 300
Bem, General, 300
Bentham, Jeremy, 63–4
Bentinck, Lord George, 302
Berkeley, Bishop, 58, 63–4
Berlin-Milan Decrees (1806–7), 37, 44, 45
Betts, John, 154, 156, 300
Bibb, John, 172
Bielby, Robson, 170
Bilston, 215, 269
Bimetallism, 95, 181, 260, 335n114
Birmingham: administration, 25–6, 36–7, 74, 77; affection for Attwood, 227, 292–3, 296, 305; alienation from Westminster, 35, 47, 50; business structure, 25, 33, 35, 45, 52; Chamber of Commerce, 15, 87, 90, 128, 130–2, 311n3; charities, 94–5, 112; Chartists, 278–80, 283–4, 286; cholera, 213; and Corn Laws, 7, 53, 73, 130–2, 134–5, 268, 300; criticism of Attwood, 115–16, 127, 158; currency debate, 265; East Retford, 139–40, 143–4, 150; economy, 5, 7–8, 15–16, 25–7; (1812–15) 33–6, 44, 73–4; (post-war) 52, 73–4, 110–11; (1825) 118, 123, 127–8, 134, 142; (1829–30) 152; (1833) 247; (1835) 257; (1837) 271–2; (1842–3) 297; growth and population, 25, 162–3; and House of Lords, 202–3, 214; and

Ireland, 145; Loyal and Constitutional Association, 292, 301; Municipal Corporations Act, 256–8; political campaigns, 93–4, 195, 199; political opinion, 35, 38, 73, 78, 82–3, 90–1, 143, 149–50, 158, 159–60, 187, 203, 216, 218, 262–3; Poor rate, 190, 232; school of economic theory, 12, 15, 25–6, 72, 86, 91–4, 111, 127, 130–1, 136–8, 142, 156–7; social conditions, 8, 75, 82, 91–2, 122, 127–8, 245; trade unions, 211; unrest, 33–6, 216, 219; (1839) 288; Working-men's Memorial Committee, 276, 283. *See also* Birmingham Political Union
Birmingham (racehorse), 177
Birmingham (Radicals), 50, 73, 338n36
Birmingham Advertiser, 269
Birmingham and Midland Reform Association, 259
Birmingham Chronicle, 90, 109, 116, 118, 127, 130
Birmingham Currency Association, 181
Birmingham Investment Company, 115
Birmingham Irish Catholics, 159
Birmingham Joint-Stock Bank, 357n42
Birmingham Journal, 118, 130, 131, 138, 158, 172, 174, 175, 212, 216, 266
Birmingham police bill, 289, 296–7, 298
Birmingham Political Union, 3–4, 140, 157; abolition of property

qualification, 269; annual parliaments, 278; Attwood's control of, 186, 203–4, 217–19; Bank of England, 230; Blandford's bill, 167–9, 172; and Burdett, 180; and Captain Swing, 191; and Chartism, 14, 276, 278–9, 281, 283–4; comparison with Catholic Association, 168; and Corn Laws, 354n94; council (1837), 269; creation, 152–3, 158, 160–1, 168–9; criticism of Attwood, 277, 281, 284, 290; currency, 233; decline, 228–30, 245–6; division among leadership, 180–1, 192–3, 217–18; elections: (1831) 181–2, 196; (1832) 230–1, 236–7; (1834) 253–4; (1837) 271; equal electoral districts, 278, 284; explanation of 1832 success, 263, 265–6, 268; fall of Wellington administration, 188; financial organization, 171, 192, 294–5; first annual meeting, 171–2; French revolution (1830), 182, 184–6; government fear of, 187; House of Lords, 200, 204; household suffrage, 172, 189, 269; idea of revolution, 224; Irish reform, 243, 337n25; judicial system, 190–1, 330n5, 341n106; leadership of country, 208–9, 219, 220, 276; and London, 275, 278–9; mass meeting, 7 May 1832, 214–15; membership, 191, 335n110; middle-class membership, 217; military organization, 205–7, 211, 218; moderates' goals, 284–5; Municipal Corporations Act, 255–6; national convention, 282–3; numbers, 174–5; and O'Connor, 279–82 passim; opinion of Commons, 198; opposition in Birmingham (1833), 245–6; organization, 13, 160–1, 201–2, 219; pageantry, 171–4 passim, 201–2, 333n72; parish affairs, 169, 170, 179, 190–1, 204–5, 223; pledges, 230–1, 335n106; publicity, 168–9, 174, 175–6, 202, 216; reanimation (1835–6), 256–9, 262–3, 265–6; and reform of House of Lords, 258–9; religion, 174; Scotland, 276–8; support for first Reform Bill, 194; support for third Reform Bill, 215; as town meeting, 175; triennial parliaments, 269, 278; Ultra-Radicals, 176, 189, 210; Ultra-Tories, 172; universal suffrage, 158, 273, 274, 278, 280; weakness, 272–3, 276. See also Whig party (Birmingham) and (Commons)

Birmingham School. See Birmingham
Birmingham Waterworks, 115
Blandford, marquis of, 165, 166, 167–8, 176, 180, 242, 332n51
Bone-turners, 136
Bordesley, 292
Boroughbridge, Yorks, 88, 210
Boultbee, William H., 261
Brass industry, 25, 136
Briggs, Asa, 8, 91
Bristol, 41, 205, 208
Bristol & Worcester railway, 114
British Iron Company (court case), 124, 137–8, 142–3, 275
British Northern & Western railway, 114
Bromsgrove, 236
Brougham, Henry, 38, 45, 88, 102, 143, 187, 202, 211–12
Buckinghamshire, earl of, 43, 48
Buller, Cornelius, 120
Bullion Committee (1810), 6, 53–4, 55
Bullionists, 7, 54, 79
Burdett, Francis, 76–7, 148, 155, 166, 168–9, 175–6, 179, 334n96, 335n110
Burgess, Henry, 141–2, 240, 248
Burn, W.L., 4
Butler, William, 58
Button-makers, 25, 136, 157

Cadbury, Richard, 139
Cakemore, 20
Calico printing, 20, 33
Callington, Cornwall, 88
Canning, George, 80, 135, 139–40, 147
Captain Swing, 183–4, 187, 191
Carless, Sarah, 100
Cartwright, Major John, 77
Castlereagh, Viscount, 49, 80, 89, 147
Catholic Association, 116, 134–5, 137, 143, 158, 164, 168, 170
Catholicism, 106, 159–60
Cayley, Edward Stillingfleet, 255

Central Agricultural Association, 260
Chamberlain, Joseph, 3
Chance, William, 158
Chandos, Lord, 192, 198
Chartists, 14, 276, 278–80, 283–4, 287–8, 297–8
China, 40, 43, 49
Cholera, 182
Church of England, 20, 26, 159, 190
Church of Ireland, 159, 256
Circular to Bankers, 296
Classical economists, 4, 5, 8, 55, 61, 90, 132, 234, 252, 290
Coal industry, 17–18, 51–2, 100, 123–4, 145, 201, 269
Cobbett's Political Register, 169
Cobbett, William: and Attwood, 75, 148, 163, 214, 231, 241; and Birmingham, 327n17, 332n64; contract adjustment, 316n42; currency debate, 235; French revolution (1830), 184; opinion of third Reform Bill, 211; paper money, 8–9, 75, 110, 117, 129, 148–9, 170; and Peel, 250; and Ricardo, 345n28; Union, 169, 176, 179–80, 198, 245
Collins, John, 276–7, 278, 279, 281
Colmer's Hall, 18
Committee of Birmingham's non-electors, 229
Colquhoun, Patrick, 75, 88, 96–7
Copper industry, 18
Cook, Benjamin, 33, 47
Cooperative movement, 154, 156
Copplestone, Edward, 63

Corn Laws, 7, 53, 73, 130–2, 134–5, 268, 283, 300
Corn trade, 101
Corngreaves steel furnaces, 17, 137
Corporation of London, 225–6
Cotton industry, 101, 106, 133
Country banking, 7, 18, 23–4, 28, 32–3, 51–3, 56–7, 112, 120, 123–5, 126, 127, 128–9, 140–2, 226, 234, 248, 262, 295, 356–7n42
Coventry, 99, 180, 227
Cruttwell, Richard, 98, 321n33
Cullen, Sinclair, 175
Currency Club, 239–40
Currency Committee, 288–9

Darlaston, 215
Dartmouth, earl of, 292
Davenport, Edward, 102–3, 137, 145, 148–9, 165, 166, 177–8, 302, 322n9, 327n35, 334n96
Depression: (postwar) 52, 73–4, 78; (1825) 119–25; (1829–30) 151, 152, 157; (1836) 262–3; (1842) 297
Derby riots, 203
Deritend, 292
Dillon, Lord, 178
Disraeli, Benjamin, 260
Doherty, John, 182, 335–6n118
Douglas, Robert, 261, 266, 277, 283
Dudley, earl of, 19, 100
Dugdale, Dugdale Stratford, 88, 181, 259
Durham, Lord, 285

East India Company, 5, 30–1, 36, 39–44, 48–9
East Retford, 139–40, 143–4, 146, 150, 169, 265

Ebrington, Viscount, 218–20
Eckersall, Reverend, 203
Edmonds, George: approval of Tories, 164, 172; and Attwood, 78, 132, 273, 277, 280–1; Commons attacks on, 289; currency, 135, 233; and O'Connell, 274; and parish affairs, 170, 190, 236, 256–7; Political Council, 154, 157–9, 197; as public speaker, 173; radical agenda, 77–8, 91, 189; and Scholefield, 212, 228–9, 236, 254; Union organization, 159, 161, 171–2, 203, 231, 259
Education, 21–2, 252, 267
Ellerslie, 302
Ellice, Edward, 99, 169, 180
Equitable Loan Company, 115
Ernes, Josiah ("Pigmy"), 157
Evans, James ("Goose"), 157
Examiner, 244
Eye Infirmary, 112

Factory Acts, 252
Farmers' Journal, 87–90 passim, 95, 100, 102
Fereday, J., 51–2
Fielden, John, 250, 284
Finlay, Kirkman, 326n12
Firearms, 157, 205, 206, 218, 223, 248
Fitzwilliam, Lord, 246
Foreign trade, 37–45 passim, 47–9, 52, 64, 75, 234
Foster, Charles, 241, 291, 305
France, 37–8, 75, 105–7, 111, 133–4, 184–6, 295
Franchise, 144, 167, 189, 193

Index

Free Grammar School, 179
Free Trade, 55, 130–1, 134–5

Gas Light and Coal Company, 77
Gascoyne, General, 195
Gemini Letters, 15, 288–9
General Steam Navigation Company, 111
George III, 88
George IV, 179
Gibbons, Smith & Goode (bankers), 118, 122, 124, 127
Gilt "toys," 25, 33, 35
Gladstone, John, 326n12
Glasgow, 41, 42, 276–9
Glassmaking, 24, 308n8
Globe, 141
Gold standard, 5, 6, 7, 10–12 passim, 53, 55, 81, 129
Gooch, Thomas Sherlock, 95
Graham, John, 148, 238
Grand Junction & Northern railway, 114
Grand Northern Political Union, 279
Grey, 2nd earl: and Attwood, 197, 210, 225; and currency, 231, 235, 242; forms government, 188; leadership of Whigs, 177–8, 187, 222; and Union, 202, 204, 206–8, 209, 220; and William IV, 223
Grice, Elizabeth, 299, 302
Grice, Joseph, 299
Grote, George, 225, 250, 259, 347n69

Hadley, Benjamin, 131, 147, 274, 277, 294, 326n15; and Attwood, 170, 245, 261, 270, 299–300; and parish affairs; and Political Council, 154; resignation, 283
Halesowen, 5, 17, 20, 21
Halesowen Political Union, 215
Hall, Geoffrey Webb, 87, 89, 95–6, 98
Hamburger, Joseph, 224
Hamilton, 277
Hampden Club (Birmingham) 53, 77, 87, 93, 139
Handsworth, 300, 302
Harborne, 31, 112, 128, 218, 222, 227, 228, 270, 275, 294–7 passim, 300
Harman, Jeremiah, 255
Harrowby, 1st earl of, 80
Hawne House, 17, 19, 21
Heming, Dempster, 237
Herries, John Charles, 328n54
Hetherington, Henry, 274, 276
Higher Harrogate, 300
Hilton, Boyd, 105, 122
Hobhouse, Henry, 177, 334n96
Hobhouse, John Cam, 318n20
Holland, 3rd Baron, 225
Holloway Head, 279
Home Office, 123, 184, 206, 209, 223, 246, 247
House of Commons, 13, 14, 44, 47, 53; and Birmingham, 149, 198, 248–9; currency reform, 80, 98, 126; (1833) 245; opinion of Attwood, 240–1, 250–1, 253, 274, 285; and reform, 102–3, 199, 238, 253, 285–7
House of Lords, 48, 80–1, 154, 214, 257–8
Household suffrage, 172, 189, 269
Howe, 2nd earl, 204
Hull, 41
Hume, David, 64–5, 69

Hume, Joseph, 167, 250, 259, 285
Hunt, Henry, 49, 76, 171, 189–90, 197, 229
Huskisson, William, 43, 69, 80, 96–9, 105, 120–1, 126, 137, 169, 183, 255, 320n27, 328n54

India, 40, 43, 48, 49
Imperial and Continental Gas, 111
Industrial relations, 136, 201, 265, 272, 281, 290, 304
Industrial revolution, 6, 8–9, 19, 27, 52, 110, 253, 304–5
Inflation, 5–6, 8, 11, 34, 61–3, 83
Ingot plan (Ricardo) 107
Insurance, 24
Ireland, 145, 195, 197, 245, 278, 297
Irish coercion bill, 243, 247
Irish Reform Bill, 229–30
Iron and steel industry, 18, 24, 35, 38, 51, 73, 110, 123, 124, 137, 145, 201, 257, 262, 269

James, Henry, 11, 86
Japanners, 25, 136, 157
Jersey, 290–2
Joint-stock company promotion, 110–11, 113–15, 116; banks, 262, 264
Jones, Charles: economic reform, 131, 135–6, 139, 235, 326n15; Political Council, 154, 156; political reform, 147, 150, 222; retirement, 269, 298
Joplin, Thomas, 122

Keynes, John Maynard, 4, 9, 303
King's Norton, 18
Knatchbull, Edward, 166
Knight, Henry, 170

Lalor, Patrick, 250
Lamb, George, 80, 318n20
Lamp industry, 25, 136
Langford, John A., 74
Lauderdale, 8th earl of, 63
Law, John, 63–4, 67
Lawley, Francis, 181
Leasowes, 19, 32, 309n11
Ledsam, Daniel, 139
Leeds, 278, 279
Legal system, 95, 153–4, 191
Leisure activities, 21, 28, 76–7, 182, 267
Lewis, Frankland, 80
Lewis, William Greethead, 77
Lichfield House, 254
Literary Union Club, 240
Littleton, Edward John, 80, 97
Liverpool, 41, 113, 117, 280
Liverpool, 2nd earl of, 136; and Attwood, 45, 47, 54, 75, 120–1, 126, 134, 147, 304; and economy, 11, 80, 95, 103–4, 117–18
Liverpool-Birmingham railway, 113–15, 323n47
Locke, John, 66
Lodge Forge Estate, 17
London Political Union, 163, 223
London Workingmen's Association, 274–6, 278–9
London-Birmingham railway, 113–15, 232, 323n47
Lovett, William, 278–9, 284
Loyal and Constitutional Association, 292
Luckcock, Felix, 157
Luckcock, Urban, 157
Lyndhurst, Lord, 216–17, 219

Maberly, John, 167
Macclesfield, 145
Mackintosh, James, 80

Macon's Act (1810), 37
Maddox, Charles, 77
Malthus, Thomas Robert, 57, 63–4, 89
Manchester, 77, 139, 145, 293
Manchester Courier, 168
Mansion House, 226
Marshall, George, 357n42
Marshall, William, 309n12
Mason, Oliver, 232–3
Massie, J., 65
McCulloch, John Ramsay, 67
McDonnell, Thomas, 159–60, 210, 245, 265, 274
Mechanics Institute (Birmingham) 116, 129, 132, 159–60, 164
Medley, Mary, 260
Medley, William, 260
Melbourne, 2nd viscount: and Attwood, 186, 274, 286, 288, 290; and Birmingham, 263–4; currency, 255, 267; on need for reform, 209; Union, 206, 246–7, 270
Mercantilism, 64, 68–9
Merthyr Tydfil, 197
Metropolitan Political Union, 189
Middleton Hall, 18
Midland Chronicle, 46
Midland Counties Herald, 15
Midlands Union of the Working Classes, 229
Mill, James, 67
Mill, John Stuart, 15, 235
Moillet & Smith (bankers), 123
Molesworth, William, 3, 5–7, 259, 261, 286
Money markets, 27, 68, 72, 109, 111, 117, 121, 224, 252
Monthly Argus, 158
Mordaunt, Sir Charles, 92
Morning Advertiser, 168, 279

Morning Chronicle, 42, 118, 149, 164, 202, 203, 216, 244
Morning Herald, 221, 235, 296
Morning Post, 296, 299, 300–1
Moseley, Thomas, 196
Municipal Corporations Act, 255–6
Muntz, George, 95, 269; and Attwood, 218, 264–5, 355n8; and Commons, 261, 267, 293, 302, 355n14; business interests, 155, 269; and Catholicism, 212; character, 155–6, 173–4; economic ideas, 156, 260; and Union, 154–5, 170, 172, 190, 237–8, 256–7
Muntz, Philip, 269–70, 274, 277, 284–6
Murphy, Tom, 278

Nail industry, 17
Napoleon, 31, 35, 37, 38, 51, 266
Napoleonic Wars, 5, 33–4, 35, 51
National Association for the Protection of Labour, 182
National Association of Working Classes, 197
National Convention, 277, 280, 283, 287
National Guard, 205, 206
National Petition (Charter), 286
National Political Union, 336–7n11
National Reform Association, 274
National Rent, 280–1
Netherton, 19
Newcastle, 278
Newcastle, 4th duke of, 88
Newdegate, Charles Newdigate, 300–1

375 Index

Newhall Hill, 77, 201, 215–16, 218, 222, 230, 241, 245–6, 265, 269–70, 272, 279, 283, 333n69, 351n30
Nicholas I, 266, 289
Nicholls, George, 139–41, 200, 208, 231–2, 328n45
Non-Intercourse Treaty, 34
Norfolk, duke of, 49, 88, 93
Normanby, Lord, 285
North Warwickshire, 237
Northern Political Union, 191
Northern Star, 280
Norwich, 280
Nottingham riots, 203

O'Connell, Daniel, 162, 166; and Attwood, 238, 245–7, 275–6; Birmingham, 212, 219; and reform, 166, 239, 259; and Union, 153, 198, 229–30, 274
O'Connell, John, 250
O'Connor, Feargus, 14, 279, 280, 287
Oldbury, 269
Orders-in-Council (1806–7), 7, 36–8, 44–5
Osler, Timothy, 170
Owenism, 154, 156, 229
Oxford, 252, 267

Paisley, 278
Palmer, Horsley, 234–5, 255, 327–8n38, 345n16
Palmerston, 3rd viscount, 249, 274, 296
Pare, William ("Snuffy"), 154, 156, 158, 171, 229, 269
Parkes, Joseph, 139, 160–1, 222, 256; and Attwood, 164, 186, 204–5, 223, 249, 272–3, 275; and Grey, 193, 214; and Scholefield, 204, 212, 337n26; and Union,

169, 189, 207, 219, 331n31, 336–7n11, 337n26, 338n30, 342n136
Parliamentary procedure, 239–40, 241, 248–9, 267, 285, 290
Parnell, Henry, 188
Parsons, Thomas, Jr, 157
Patents, 33
Peace, Law, Order committee, 288
Pearse, John, 82
Peel, Robert: agricultural committee, 96–7; asked to form government (1832), 217–19; and Attwood, 134, 264–5, 289, 290, 293–4, 298–9; and Birmingham, 116; crisis (1825–6), 120–2; currency, 80–2, 242, 244–5; formation of government (1834), 253–4; resignation (1830), 187–8; and Union, 182, 340–1n97; and Victoria, 285–6
Peel, Robert, Sr, 82, 97, 115, 119
Penryn, Cornwall, 139, 143–4, 329n62
Perceval, Spencer, 39, 43
Perkins, Thomas, 191–2
Peterloo, 78, 85, 173, 190
Phoenix Assurance Company, 111
Philanthropist, 269, 274
Philanthropy, 20, 23, 74–5, 116, 294
Philosophical Radicals, 250
Pitt, William (the Younger), 73–4, 102
Place, Francis, 189, 221, 278, 336–7n11
Plymouth, 41
Poissards, 76
Poland, 211–12, 229–30, 249, 275, 295
Pole & Thornton, 120
Polish Association, 236, 275

Political unions, 176, 192, 208–9, 215, 245
Poor Law Amendment Act, 268, 280–1
Poor Law relief (Ireland), 266
Pratchet, Richard, 36, 112
Press, influence of, 47, 109, 127, 138, 149–50, 159, 168–9, 174–5, 205–6, 212, 216, 219, 244, 253
Price, John, 112
Price, Theodore, 123
Priestley, Joseph, 26
Protection of Trade Association, 95
Provincial Bank of Ireland, 111
Provincial discontent, 5, 8, 13, 35, 43–4, 47, 50, 86, 91, 103, 253, 267, 305

Quantity theory of money, 7
Quarterly Review, 8–9, 165, 192

Radicals (Birmingham), 73, 78, 90, 300
Radicals (Commons), 254, 285–6
Radnor, Lord, 176, 191–2
Ramsgate, 195, 199, 270, 275
Redfern, William, 147–8, 161, 164, 169–70
Reform Association, 265
Reform Bill: first, 193–4; second, 197; third, 210–11, 223
Restriction Act (1797), 6, 26–7, 53, 69
Resumption Act, 1819 (Peel's Act), 11–12, 79–83 passim, 86, 95, 99, 104–5, 109, 111, 116, 126, 129, 232, 242, 293
Revolutionary conspiracy, lack of, 206–9 passim, 221, 224

376 Index

Ricardo, David, 3, 6, 7–9, 55, 59, 61, 65–7, 69, 79, 81–2, 89, 98, 101, 107–8, 252, 290
Riots, 26, 34, 44, 182, 183, 187, 197, 203, 205, 208, 271, 288
Robinson, George, 98, 112, 117, 129
Rooke, John, 98, 321n33
Rose, George, 39
Rothschild, Nathan Meyer, 121–2
Rotten boroughs, 139, 167, 176
Rowley Regis, 17–18
Russell, Joseph, 154, 158–9, 191–2, 230–1
Russell, Lord John: and Attwood, 14, 177–8, 255, 287; currency, 259, 267; and reform, 102–3, 145, 193, 197, 211, 223; and Union, 175–6, 203–4
Russia, 101, 106, 143, 212, 249, 266, 274, 275, 283
Rutland, duke of, 238
Ryde, Isle of Wight, 281
Ryland, John, 93

Salt, Thomas Clutton, 110, 131, 135–6, 326n15; and Attwood, 277, 281, 283, 297–8; Birmingham's economy, 247; and O'Connell, 274, 280; Union, 147, 153–4, 155, 188–9, 236, 270, 276, 283
Savings Bank and Friendly Institution, 138
Say, J., 109
Scarborough, 300
Scholefield, Joshua: Attwood memorial, 292–3; council, 172; and Edmonds, 212, 228–9; election (1832), 236; (1834), 254; (1837), 271; and Birmingham school, 86, 88, 91–3, 138, 145–6; and O'Connell, 274; and Parkes, 204, 212, 337n26; Union, 147, 152–3, 156, 180, 219, 220, 231, 259
Scotland, 276–9
Scots Greys, 218–19, 221, 237
Scottish Reform, 167, 185, 229
Secret ballot, 158, 180, 189, 191, 269, 278, 348n93
Sedgeley, 215
Shaw, Charles, 139, 263–4
Shears, Henry, 137
Sheffield, 41, 246
Sinclair, John, 87, 111, 129; career, 319n4
Sinclair, George, 289
Sinking Fund Commissioners, 70
Skipworth, Gray, 175, 203
Small, Robert, 137
Smith, Adam, 37, 48, 57, 69, 252
Smith, Timothy, 139, 170
Society for the Promotion of Christian Knowledge, 116
Society of Arts, 94
South America, 37, 40, 109, 116
Southey, Robert, 10–11
Sparkbrook, 31, 303
Spooner, Isaac, 18, 42, 78, 123, 143
Spooner, Richard: agriculture, 92–3, 260; and Attwood, 38, 54–5, 78, 100, 113, 297; Attwoods & Spooner, 142, 226, 351n24, 356–7n42; Birmingham, 87, 91–2, 138; business activities, 51, 113, 116; and Catholic emancipation, 116, 143; in Commons, 88–90; early radicalism, 37, 38–9, 45–6, 48; economic analysis, 53, 55, 72, 86, 211, 248, 260; election (1834), 254; (1847), 300–1; formation of Birmingham school, 86; political campaigns, 86–7, 88–9, 92–4 (1820), 93–4, 132–3, 320n15; political reform, 50, 87, 102, 138–9, 145–6, 155; Union, 154–5, 159, 180–1
St Martin's Church, 190
St Philip's Church, 203
Stafford, 132–3
Staffordshire Assizes, 138
Standard, 203
Stanley, Edward, 139, 250, 293, 294
Stapleton, A.G., 270
Staunton, George, 312n15, 316n42
Stephens, Joseph Raynes, 280
Stephenson, George, 114
Stewart, Dugdale, 63
Stuckey, Vincent, 122
Suffolk, 251
Sumner, Holme, 89, 96
Sussex, duke of, 97
Sutton, Charles Manners, 219, 254
Sweden, 18

Taxation, 9–10, 55, 62, 72, 95, 101–2, 110, 216, 217
Taylor, Herbert, 123
Taylor, James, 226
Taylor, John, 137
Taylors & Lloyds (bankers), 123, 142
Tennyson, Charles, 139, 195
Thomason, Edward, 33
Thornton, Henry, 12, 59, 98
Tierney, George, 97
Times, 15, 168–9, 202, 203, 216, 219, 242, 244, 296, 298
Tindal, Charles, 269, 70
Tooke, Thomas, 345n16
Tory party (Birmingham),

26, 73, 87, 90, 127–8, 130–1, 164–5, 259, 271–2, 293, 300
Tory party (Commons): and Birmingham, 102–3, 209; economy, 53, 73, 76, 79–80, 104, 107–8, 121–2; and reform, 88, 95, 103–4, 195–6
Triennial parliaments, 103, 269

Ultra-Tories, 135, 158, 165, 178, 192
Unitarians, 26, 139, 159
United Irishmen, 206, 212
United States, 34, 37–8, 40–1, 45, 262
Universal suffrage, 158, 172, 180, 189, 245, 273, 278, 280

Valentia, Lord, 312n15
Vansittart, Nicholas (Lord Bexley, 1823), 53, 59, 80, 104–5
Vauxhall Gardens, 28
Victoria, 270, 285–6
Villiers, George, 290
Villiers, George (Birmingham), 42
Vincent, John, 279

Wade, Arthur Savage, 229, 344n3
Wakefield, Daniel, 260, 275, 295
Wakefield, Edward Gibbon, 260–1, 294
Wales, 195, 278, 297

Walker, Joseph, 146
Wallace, Colonel, 219, 224, 271
Walsall, 215, 230–1, 237, 241, 271
Ward, John William, 314n4
Warwick, 93–4, 196, 259
Warwickshire election (1820), 92–4
Warwickshire Peace Commission, 249
Wason, Rigby, 251
"Waverers," 213, 216
Wednesbury, 141, 215, 269
Wellington, 1st duke of: attempt to form government (1832), 217, 219–20, 221–2; (1834), 253–4; Attwood's opinion, 47, 98, 164; Catholic emancipation, 158; economy, 145; fear of Union, 206–7; and Reform Bill, 187, 195, 200, 223–4; resignation (1830), 187
West Bromwich, 269
Western, Charles, 82, 96, 105, 107, 153, 166, 184, 238–41, 248, 345n28
Westminster Review, 15
Wharncliffe, 1st Lord, 204, 207–8, 213
Wharton, Thomas, 78
Whig party (Birmingham): local politics, 73, 78, 129–31, 136, 160, 170, 191–2, 256–8, 300; and

reform, 139, 191; and Union, 159–60, 164–5, 191–2, 216–17, 272
Whig Party (Commons): and Attwood, 101–2, 178, 197, 201–2, 224–5, 254, 257, 259; and political reform, 13, 102, 103, 177, 188, 193, 195, 196–8, 199–200, 209–11, 216–17, 222, 223; reformed Parliament, 238, 249, 253, 254; and Union, 15, 102, 175, 208, 224, 242–3, 247
Whitmore, William, 135
Wicksell, Knut, 60
Wilberforce, William, 42, 49
Willenhall, 215
William IV, 187, 188, 198, 200, 209, 213, 217, 220, 223, 270
Wire-drawers, 25, 136
Wolesley, Sir Charles, 77
Wolverhampton, 215
Wolverhampton Grammar School, 22–3, 27
Women's Political Union, 276
Wooler, Thomas, 77
Worcester & Gloucester Union Canal, 115
Wynn, Charles Watkin Williams, 145

Yorkshire political unions, 192
Young, Arthur, 71, 88